Atlas of Crime

Atlas of Crime
Mapping the Criminal Landscape

Linda S. Turnbull
Elaine Hallisey Hendrix
Borden D. Dent

Oryx Press
2000

The rare Arabian Oryx is believed to have inspired the myth of the unicorn. This desert antelope became virtually extinct in the early 1960s. At that time, several groups of international conservationists arranged to have nine animals sent to the Phoenix Zoo to be the nucleus of a captive breeding herd. Today, the Oryx population is over 1,000, and over 500 have been returned to the Middle East.

© 2000 by The Oryx Press
4041 North Central at Indian School Road
Phoenix, Arizona 85012-3397
www.oryxpress.com

Published simultaneously in Canada
Printed and bound in the United States of America

∞ The paper used in this publication meets the minimum requirements of
American National Standard for Information Science—Permanence
of Paper for Printed Library Materials, ANSI Z39.48, 1984.

Library of Congress Cataloging-in-Publication Data

Atlas of crime: mapping the criminal landscape/[edited by] Linda S.
Turnbull, Elaine Hallisey Hendrix, and Borden D. Dent.
    p. cm.
Includes bibliographical references and index.
    ISBN 1-57356-241-6 (alk. paper)
    1. Crime—United States—History—20th century. 2. Crime
analysis—United States. 3. Applied human geography—United States.
I. Turnbull, Linda S. II. Hendrix, Elaine Hallisey. III. Dent, Borden D.
    HV6783.A85   2000
    364.973'09'04—dc21   00-009772
                                                          CIP

In Memory of Simon
1980-1999

In remembrance of our esteemed and inspiring mentor,
colleague, and friend . . . Borden D. Dent

CONTENTS

LIST OF FIGURES AND TABLES

List of Figures and Tables

List of Figures and Tables

CONTRIBUTORS

William V. Ackerman is associate professor in the Department of Geography, The Ohio State University. His research interests include crime, small city revitalization, and rural-urban land use conflict. In addition to his academic duties, Dr. Ackerman enjoys spending time in Wyoming.

Kathleen C. Basile received her Ph.D. in sociology in 1998 from Georgia State University. She is currently a research associate at the Applied Research Center, also at Georgia State. Her major research interest is violence against women.

Jacqueline Boles is professor of sociology at Georgia State University. She has published extensively on male, female, and transvestite prostitution. With a grant from the Centers for Disease Control and Prevention, she conducted research with a colleague on HIV seroprevalence among sex workers and their customers.

Damon D. Camp is an associate professor of criminal justice at Georgia State University in Atlanta, Georgia, where he has taught since 1982, serving six years as the department chair. He has conducted research and provided specialized training in a number of areas, including domestic terrorism.

David Canter, Ph.D., FAPA, FBPsS Cpsychol, is professor of psychology in the Department of Psychology at The University of Liverpool, where he directs the Centre for Investigative Psychology. He has published widely on many aspects of criminal behavior and police investigative processes. His book *Criminal Shadows* won awards in both Great Britain and the United States.

Chanchalat Chanhatasilpa is a doctorate candidate in the Department of Criminology at the University of Maryland. He also received his bachelor's and master's degrees from the University of Maryland. His research interests include race and crime, sentencing, and spatial patterns of crime and its correlates.

W. Jerry Chisum has 38 years experience in crime laboratories in California. He has taught crime scene investiga-

tion for more than 23 years in several states. Best known for his work on crime reconstruction, he has endeavored to maintain criminalistics as a part of the investigative process. He retired from public service in 1998 but continues to teach and consult.

George J. Demko is a professor of geography at Dartmouth College in New Hampshire. He is the author or editor of 18 books and over 90 articles on social science problems in foreign countries. For many years, he served as a geographer for the State Department in Washington, D.C., where he provided information and advice on issues of international importance to U.S. foreign policy.

Borden D. Dent had a distinguished career as professor of geography for 30 years at Georgia State University in Atlanta. He served as chair of the Department of Anthropology and Geography in the years before his retirement. He graduated in geography with specializations in cartography from Towson State University, the University of California at Berkeley, and Clark University. Professor Dent was the author of several professional papers on cartography and geography, and active in the designing and publication of special purpose maps. He was an authority on thematic mapping, recently publishing the 5th edition of his textbook *Cartography: Thematic Map Design.*

Denise A. Donnelly, Ph.D., is an assistant professor of sociology and women's studies at Georgia State University in Atlanta. She received her Ph.D. from the University of Florida in 1990, and completed a two-year National Institutes of Mental Health Postdoctoral Fellowship in family violence training at the Family Research Lab, University of New Hampshire. Her research interests include services to battered women, culturally competent approaches to ending violence, women in sado-masochistic relationships, and sexless marriages.

Ute J. Dymon is an associate professor of geography at Kent State University. She co-authored, with the commissioner of the Massachusetts Department of Fisheries, Wildlife and

Environmental Law Enforcement, the *Atlas of Massachusetts River Systems: Environmental Designs for the Future*. In 1991, she was appointed a cartographer with the United Nations in New York. She now pursues a research interest in the use of Geographic Information Systems (GIS) during natural disasters.

Leslie Edwards is a Ph.D. candidate in geography at the University of Georgia and an avid reader of detective novels. She received her B.A. in English literature from the University of Virginia, and studied cartography and cognitive mapping at Georgia State University.

Jill Kathleen Fleury is a program assistant for the National Institute of Justice's Crime Mapping Research Center. Her research interests include individual level theories of offending, issues in research design, and the application of criminological theory to crime mapping investigations. Currently, she is pursuing her doctoral degree in criminology at the University of Maryland at College Park.

Patricia Gilmartin is professor of geography at the University of South Carolina in Columbia. She received her Ph.D. from the University of Kansas and, prior to moving to South Carolina, taught in the Geography Department at the University of Victoria, British Columbia. She teaches various graduate and undergraduate courses in cartography, as well as a graduate course entitled "Women Explorers and Travelers." Dr. Gilmartin's research interests in cartography center on cognitive issues, such as map-reading and way-finding processes.

Keith Harries is professor of geography and environmental systems at the University of Maryland Baltimore County. He is author or coauthor of a dozen books, most on criminal justice topics. His recent publications include *The Geography of Execution: The Capital Punishment Quagmire in America* (with Derral Cheatwood) and *Mapping Crime: Principle and Practice*, published by the National Institute of Justice. His current research involves GIS applications in criminal justice.

Elaine Hallisey Hendrix has worked in several cartography- and GIS-related positions since 1983. She is the GIS research coordinator in the Department of Anthropology and Geography at Georgia State University. She teaches GIS courses and provides GIS support for faculty projects as well as for projects outside the department. Ms. Hendrix designed a cartography student workbook and wrote a chapter on Geographic Information Systems for the latest edition of Borden Dent's *Cartography: Thematic Map Design*. She is interested in the construction of GIS databases from spatial data on the Internet and issues relating to spatial data processing.

Samantha Hodge is a research fellow within the Centre for Investigative Psychology at the University of Liverpool. She recently completed her Ph.D., which examined the spatial behavior of serial murderers. She is currently carrying out a large-scale research project investigating young people and distance from crime.

John Jarvis serves in a training and research position in the Behavioral Science Unit of the Federal Bureau of Investigation. He holds a Ph.D. in sociology from the University of Virginia and conducts studies involving crime trends and analysis, law enforcement, and social control.

Eric S. Jefferis is a social science analyst with the Crime Mapping Research Center, National Institute of Justice. His research interests include the dynamics of police-citizen interactions, media influence on citizens' perceptions of police organizations, and the spatial and temporal analysis of crime patterns. His recent publications include "An Examination of the Productivity and Perceived Effectiveness of Drug Task Forces," and "The Use of Standard Deviational Ellipses for Program Evaluation." He is currently pursuing a Ph.D. from the University of Cincinnati, Division of Criminal Justice.

Robert J. Kaminski is a social science analyst with the Office of Research and Evaluation, National Institute of Justice, and a Ph.D. candidate in the School of Criminal Justice, the University at Albany. He has published research articles on topics related to police work. His current research includes such specific topics as the spatial analyses of police use of force and nonfatal assaults on police in three cities, a time series analysis of felonious killings of police officers, and an analysis of police officer satisfaction with defense and control tactics training.

Nancy G. La Vigne is the founder and director of the Crime Mapping Research Center at the National Institute of Justice, U.S. Department of Justice, in Washington, D.C. Her research areas include the geographic analysis of crime, situational crime prevention, and community policing. She is also the Department of Justice delegate to the Federal Geographic Data Committee and an active member of the Department of Justice's GIS Working Group. Dr. La Vigne is the author of over a dozen publications in journals, edited volumes, and technical reports in the areas of crime prevention, policing, and spatial analysis.

Jose Javier Lopez is assistant professor in the Geography Department at Minnesota State University, Mankato. In 1997, he received The Benjamin Moulton Award from Indiana State University for outstanding scholastic and research achievements. Besides teaching courses on quantitative techniques, economic geography, and Latin America, Dr. Lopez conducts research in the geography of crime and violence in the Caribbean. Originally from the Commonwealth of Puerto Rico, he is an avid Caribbean music fan.

Joanne McDaniel is the research director of the Center for the Prevention of School Violence. Ms. McDaniel has been studying the problem of school violence and prevention strategies since 1993. She has made presentations on this topic to law enforcement officials, educators, and community members across the country. Ms. McDaniel is an adjunct faculty member in the Department of Political Science and Public Administration at North Carolina State University in Raleigh. She is also a doctoral candidate at the University of North Carolina, Chapel Hill.

Christopher G. Missen, Ph.D., is a visiting research fellow with the University of Liverpool's Centre for Investigative Psychology and is the head of Forensic Psychology at APU in Cambridge, UK. He is an expert in the field of serial murder, having spent 25 years studying and gathering data on the topic. In addition to his research on serial killers, he is an ex-pop musician and former member of a "motorhead" band.

Pamela Riley, Ed.D., has been the executive director of the Center for the Prevention of School Violence since its establishment in late 1993. Dr. Riley has experience as a high school principal and was responsible for implementing creative curriculum and management strategies. She has worked in North Carolina's Department of Public Instruction (DPI) as an education consultant and instructional specialist on citizenship education. Because of her expertise, Dr. Riley has been interviewed by local and national media, including *USA Today, Newsweek*, Time, Fox, and CBS on the subject of school violence.

Joseph Szakas currently teaches computer science with the University of Maryland, University College. He was a programmer analyst with the University of Michigan, while he worked at the National Institute of Justice's Crime Mapping Research Center. He received his B.S. in computer science from the University of Michigan-Dearborn, his M.S. in computer science from Western Michigan University, and his M.S. and Ph.D. in geodetic science (computer cartography) from The Ohio State University.

George E. Tita graduated from Carnegie Mellon University, Heinz School of Public Policy with a Ph.D. in public policy and management. He won the Carnegie Mellon William W. Cooper Dissertation Award, which is presented annually to the outstanding policy or management dissertation. Dr. Tita is affiliated with the University of California at Irvine in the Department of Criminology & Law & Society. He is currently working as a policy analyst for the Criminal Justice Unit at the RAND Corporation and is mapping gang territories and crime in Los Angeles in an effort to inform the Los Angeles Police Department of gang intervention strategies.

Linda S. Turnbull is a Ph.D. candidate in sociology at Georgia State University in Atlanta, with a specialization in criminal and deviant behavior. She has a B.A. in geography from the University of South Carolina and an M.A. in geography from Georgia State University. She teaches and researches criminal spatial behavior in the Department of Anthropology and Geography at Georgia State and has worked in community service for over 20 years. Her current research is on the topics of child maltreatment and animal cruelty.

Susan M. Walcott is an assistant professor of geography in the Department of Anthropology and Geography at Georgia State University in Atlanta. A specialist in urban economic geography and regional development, she teaches courses in urban geography, location analysis, and the geography of East Asia. A particular interest is the health industry. She has published articles on diverse topics, from "The Indianapolis 'Fortune 500': Eli Lilly and Regional Renaissance" to "Tea Cultivation in South Carolina."

Doug Williamson, the author and co-author of numerous articles, is a doctoral candidate at the City University of New York (CUNY). He is also a research associate for the Center for Applied Studies of the Environment at CUNY. His current research interests are the use of GIS in law enforcement, spatial statistics, and cartographic visualization. He has worked on a number of projects using GIS and spatial statistics, most recently developing a mapping application for the New York City Police Department.

Nancy L. Winter, an independent scholar, was awarded her Ph.D. in natural and technological hazards from Clark University, Worcester, Massachusetts. She has been invited twice by the International Cartographic Association (ICA) to present her research in Barcelona, Spain, and Stockholm, Sweden. Dr. Winter's risk and hazards research encompasses the development of geographic information systems for crisis mapping in the aftermath of disasters, for post-disaster applications to speed economic recovery, and for the cartographic presentation of environmental issues.

Gordon R. Wynn is a senior consultant for BellSouth. He is also an adjunct instructor for the Federal Bureau of Investigation and the Department of the Treasury. His specialty is computer crime and he has presented papers on "Cyberculture and Differential Association" to the American Sociological Association in Toronto and on "The Net Effect on Juvenile Delinquency" to the National Criminal Justice Association in Washington, D.C.

PREFACE

Inspired by the work of geographer Keith Harries, I decided to pursue an academic life of crime. When developing a class in criminal spatial behavior in early 1995, I searched diligently for an atlas that dealt with crime, but found only a few crime maps in atlases on other general topics. The students were enthusiastic about the geographical aspects of crime and through the readings became aware of how space affects the decisions criminals make. One of their assignments was to map the criminal's brain based on those readings. Figure 1, below, is the composite map that resulted from the students' efforts. They were interested in the motivations of criminals as represented by such categories as "Easy Money," "Notoriety," and "Thrill." The inclusion of South America, known for its Colombian drug cartels, and Louisiana, identified as the most dangerous state based on statistical data, gave a geographic element to the criminal's brain. Examples of environmental factors associated with crime were "Quick Exit Route Locator," "Hot Temps," "Full Moon," and "Abandoned Houses."

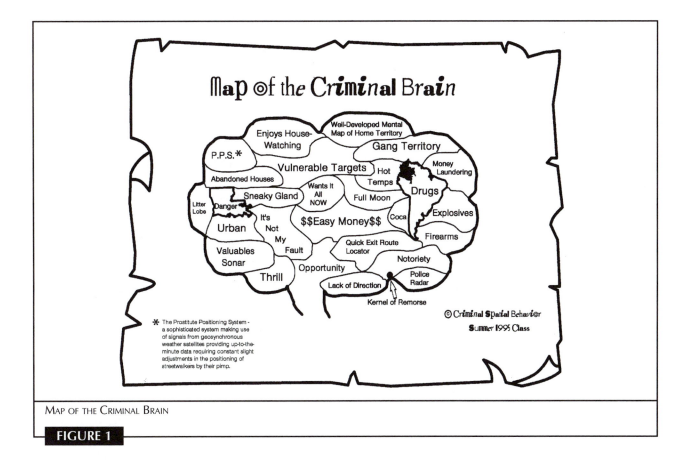

Map of the Criminal Brain

FIGURE 1

The class also studied statistical tables by state, city, and county, but the spatial dimension was lost visually. Questions arose in the classroom: Which region has the highest murder rate? Where do drug dealers get their drugs? Where do gangs hang out? Which city has the most incidents of burglary? Which state has the highest incidence of child abuse? Which country has the most terrorism? A number of cartography students became interested in mapping crime in this and in other classes. Eventually, crime maps began appearing in the department with noticeable frequency. At that point, it became apparent that we needed an atlas of crime.

The atlas envisioned was to be a unique collection of maps and essays for a general audience: the interested public, academic researchers, and students. This atlas would also demonstrate through innovative cartographic techniques how geography could be applied to the study of crime. The scope of the work was intended to be the "where" of criminal activity rather than the "who," since many existing volumes contain demographic information. The atlas would primarily include a national perspective on the geography of crime, with added glimpses of local, historical, and international distributions.

The contents for the atlas evolved over time, constantly changing and improving as the project progressed. Fortunately, colleagues and other professionals made suggestions that helped in determining the direction of the atlas. The characteristics of each crime topic and the varying availability of both quantitative and qualitative data determined the nature of the individual essays. This project's specific goal was to produce a work that embodied imaginative ways of examining the criminal landscape. It was not simply to be pages of maps, although some maps were presented for the purposes of eliciting further interest. It was to function as a book of methods: How to view crime in space and time. The proposed work would use graphics in gray-scale to make the atlas usable in the classroom. In addition, the work was designed to not only increase the reader's knowledge, but also to help him or her understand and extrapolate geographic patterns of criminal activity that are obscured in tabular presentations.

The *Atlas of Crime: Mapping the Criminal Landscape* comprises eight chapters, each containing several essays by experts and scholars in a particular crime specialty. Chapter 1, "Geographical History of Crime," offers an essay on the history of crime mapping and showcases, in its introduction, a cartographic presentation of violent crime in the United States from the historical perspective. Chapter 2, "Crimes of Personal Violence," includes essays on homicide, assault, rape, and robbery. Chapter 3, "Crimes Against Property," offers essays on burglary, motor vehicle theft, environmental crimes, and computer crimes. Chapter 4,

"Family Violence," has essays on intimate abuse, child maltreatment, elder abuse, and animal cruelty. Chapter 5, "Organized and Entrepreneurial Crimes," presents essays on gang territories, drug trafficking, prostitution, and maritime piracy. Chapter 6, "'Film at 11' Crimes," focuses on sensational topics in the news media, such as serial killers, terrorism, hate crimes, and school violence. Chapter 7, "Mental Mapping," comprises essays with a psychological aspect, including criminals' mental maps, cognitive maps of fear, and maps in detective fiction. Chapter 8, "Criminal Justice," covers law enforcement, community policing, crime scene sketches, police and geographic information systems, and capital punishment.

One of the remarkable aspects of geography is that its technique can be applied to other disciplines. In addition to geography, this volume includes contributors from five other disciplines: criminology, psychology, sociology, education, and criminal justice. This multidisciplinary approach allows us to offer diverse views of criminal behavior while connecting them with a common spatial component.

Although this volume is designed to focus on national distributions of crime, it is also important to show the range of possibilities in the geographic presentation of criminal behavior. The intent is to give the reader creative ideas for approaching the study of crime through illustrations on various scales.

Geographers view the landscape from three scales: micro, meso, and macro. In this work, the micro-scale (e.g., room, neighborhood, city area) is represented in such essays as "Auto Theft and Detecting Chop Shop Locations" in Chapter 3; "Crime Scene Sketch" and "Police Department Use of Geographic Information Systems for Crime Analysis" found in Chapter 8; as well as the introduction to Chapter 2, "Crimes of Personal Violence." The meso-scale (e.g., province or county level) is found in such essays as "Assault" in Chapter 2 and "Intimate Violence" in Chapter 4. The macro-scale, as defined by the national view, occurs in nearly every chapter of the *Atlas* and the international view appears in such essays as "Prostitution" and "Modern Maritime Piracy" in Chapter 5 as well as in the introduction to Chapter 6, "'Film at 11' Crimes."

The purpose of the *Atlas of Crime* is to present distributions of crime rather than label any particular place with a negative image. From the micro-scale to the macro-scale, the *Atlas* delves into the spatial world of crime, both real and imagined. Like an old house delighting its explorer with nooks and crannies, the *Atlas of Crime* will enlighten its readers with knowledge of the most criminal of places, wherever they may be.

L.S. Turnbull
Atlanta 1999

ACKNOWLEDGMENTS

In a project of this magnitude, there are always countless individuals who should be acknowledged for their participation in making such an endeavor possible. First, we would like to thank our families who supported us throughout:

- Linda thanks John Turnbull, who often performed duties above and beyond with an air of English superiority.
- Elaine wishes to acknowledge the patience and good humor of Emily, Alison, Rachel, Rebecca, and Jerald.
- Borden would like to thank his wonderful family—Jeanne, Jeff, Andrew, Jenny, Lauren, and Anna.

We would also like to express our gratitude to Georgia State University and the Department of Anthropology and Geography for giving us a place to practice our craft. We are indebted to the Department of Anthropology and Geography staff without whose help this project would have been impossible. Special thanks go to Patricia Grant, Diane Belisario, Laura Miller, and Scott Kissman. Laura served as our "eyes" in a reading of the manuscript—thanks!

We would like to thank our colleague, Richard Pillsbury, who offered his valuable advice on how to successfully complete an atlas. Having done this himself several times, he always had a brilliant solution to any problem.

We are especially grateful to Shelly-Ann Williams in the Department of Anthropology and Geography for her expert research skills. Her hard work ensured that the project had a successful beginning.

We appreciate the expert assistance of Steve Bullard, who created some of the maps in the chapter introductions of the atlas, and Jeff McMichael and Betsy Herrman who provided helpful suggestions in the cartographic production process. Thanks also to Michael Laitta for his superb photography.

We gratefully acknowledge The Oryx Press for their faith in the *Atlas of Crime*. Our editor at Oryx Press, Donna Sanzone, deserves a standing ovation for her commitment to our project and her careful guidance to ensure the work was top quality. Our gratitude goes to John Wagner, senior editor, in whose skillful hands the book was perfected. Also at Oryx, Anne Thompson, Martha Wilke, Barbara Flaxman, Linda Vespa, Sean Tape, Angela duMont, and Linda Gorman were all incredibly helpful to us throughout the various stages of the creation of the atlas.

Finally, our heartfelt thanks go to each contributor. Your expertise and diligent efforts made this *Atlas of Crime* a reality for all of us!

Cartography in the *Atlas of Crime*

Elaine Hallisey Hendrix

The creation of the maps and graphics in this book included a process involving planning, data gathering and processing, and design and production. Although some of the graphics were reproduced from previously published works, such as the maps in "Maps in Detective Fiction" by Leslie Edwards, most of the illustrations are original to this volume. In some essays, the authors provided their own figures. The intriguing graphics provided by David Canter and Samantha Hodge in "Criminals' Mental Maps" are examples, as are William Jerry Chisum's starkly functional crime scene maps in "Crime Scene Sketch." However, production of most of the original maps and graphics took place in the Department of Anthropology and Geography at Georgia State University.

Use of the Internet was instrumental in the creation process for two reasons. First, it facilitated communication with almost all the geographically distant contributors regarding their maps. In addition to text communication, draft maps and graphics, in image format, were posted on Web sites set up for the individual contributors. This device was especially useful because the authors could view a much higher quality display than a facsimile and respond with comments and suggestions much more quickly than through regular mail. Second, the Internet enabled efficient and timely data research and processing. Most federal agencies in the United States that distribute data, such as the Bureau of the Census and the FBI, as well as numerous other agencies, organizations, and businesses, make their data sets available online. Often, the data available for downloading over the Internet are more current than printed data. Furthermore, because the data are already in digital format, data entry was unnecessary, which reduced both production time and the potential for error.

Although the data were already in digital format, they usually required conversion from one digital format to another, or some other processing (primarily in Microsoft's Excel), to make them usable in various mapping and geographic information systems software packages. For example, a data set used to create several of Denise Donnelly's maps on elder abuse and intimate violence was a large hierarchical text file, as opposed to the typical spreadsheet, which is unusable in any of the mapping software packages used to create the maps. To make this file accessible, the following steps were performed: (1) opened the file in SAS, a statistical analysis software package, (2) ran an SAS command file provided by the file distributor, (3) exported the required variables in .DBF file format, then (4) opened the .DBF file in my mapping software.

Other factors considered in working with these data sets were the availability of data, data bias, and the level of precision of each data set. In some cases, the desired data were just not available or accessible. For instance, no agencies gather nationwide statistics on elder abuse. In Donnelly's essay on elder abuse, the data set mentioned in the previous paragraph includes statistics on homicide by age and by relationship of the victim to the perpetrator. Although not optimal, these variables were used to map patterns of elder abuse in the United States. In other instances, data were collected for most of the study area, but some enumeration units did not report data. In Turnbull's map of substantiated child abuse and neglect, for example, the states of Mississippi, West Virginia, and Maryland did not report data. The editors decided that if data for more than 10 percent of the enumeration units were unavailable, a map would not be produced. The essay on computer crime by John Jarvis and Gordon Wynn was limited by the unavailability of detailed arrest data in the United States. Although the FBI gathers these data, they are inaccessible to the public at this time.

Data bias is another factor that must be addressed. Crimes often go unreported to police, resulting in statistics that for many types of crimes, such as rape, are lower than reality. In addition, much discussion has been focused on the reporting practices of some agencies. While officials would like to portray their jurisdictions in a positive light, recent disputes have arisen over the handling of police crime statistics in many cities, including Atlanta, New Orleans, New York, Philadelphia, and Boca Raton, Florida (*Atlanta*

Journal-Constitution 1999: C-1). These cities, among others, have been accused of underreporting certain crimes.

The statistics for Damon Camp's map of reported hate crimes for 1997 were obtained from the FBI *Uniform Crime Reports*. The data are provided to the FBI by city, county, and state law enforcement agencies. Three states, Alabama, Arkansas, and Mississippi, show no hate crimes for all of 1997, a wide disparity with surrounding states. Data from the Southern Poverty Law Center, however, indicate that as of 1998 these three states had relatively large numbers of hate groups, as shown in Camp's map of hate groups. Alabama, in fact, has 26 known hate groups operating within its borders, making it one of the top five states with regards to the number of active hate groups. Although serving as the headquarters for a variety of hate groups does not necessarily mean that hate crime is rampant in a particular state, it would seem to indicate an acceptance by some of the local population of the ideas espoused by these groups and therefore an increased likelihood of hate crime. Map readers should keep these potential biases in mind when viewing any map.

Another type of potential data bias may occur when rates are calculated. Unless otherwise stated, the crime rates for state level data were calculated as the total number of crimes in the enumeration unit per 100,000 persons residing in the enumeration unit. This works fairly well when working with data at the state level because all states have a population greater than 100,000. When working with counties, however, problems arise even when the denominator is lowered because some counties have small populations. On the map depicting the rate of police officers killed feloniously in the line of duty (per 10,000 persons in this case), in the essay "A Spatial Analysis of American Police Killed in the Line of Duty," a few of the counties with small populations display misleadingly large rates. The authors address this issue in their discussion. In Keith Harries's essay on homicide, Figure 2-4 illustrates homicide rates by county. In 1992, one murder occurred in Daniels County, Montana, yet this county falls within the highest homicide category with a rate of 8.7 per 10,000 persons. The reason is that in 1992 Daniels County had a small population of only 1,146 persons.

If, when using rates, the potential exists for some misleading information because of small populations, why not display all maps at the state level? Or why not use crime totals instead of rates? The answer to the first question is that, in general, the smaller the enumeration unit, the higher the level of spatial precision. In simpler terms, maps at the county level are more detailed than maps at the state level. At the county level, certain patterns and relationships are apparent that are "averaged out" of maps at the state level.

George Tita's essay, "Mapping the *Set Space* of Urban Street Gangs," addresses this issue of precision using the geographic boundaries of the increasingly smaller areas of neighborhoods, census tracts, and census block groups. The map displaying set space at the census block group level is more geographically precise, and therefore more accurate,

than the map displaying set space at the neighborhood level. Most cartographers aim for the highest level of detail when producing maps. Indeed, a particular type of map, the choropleth map (discussed in more depth below) is more "truthful" when a smaller enumeration unit is used because it is assumed that the value in the enumeration unit is uniform throughout the unit. Although the attempt has been made here to achieve this goal, it was not always met due to the data limitations described.

Although mapping at the state level is not as precise as mapping at the county level, state maps still produce some interesting patterns. Susan Walcott's essay on burglary includes a map of the burglary rate, at the state level, for the years 1989 and 1997. A striking pattern of burglary rates is immediately apparent; southern and western states have a much higher burglary rate than states in the Midwest and Northeast.

As to the second question—why not use crime totals instead of rates—some types of thematic maps may map raw data, but for other types of maps, the data must be derived, or normalized, using rates, densities, proportions, or percentages. For example, Kathleen Basile's map of rapes in cities of 100,000 or more is a proportional symbol map in which circles are drawn proportional in size to the total number of rapes committed. The data have been aggregated at points—cities in this case. Proportional symbols work well when the cartographer wishes to map raw values. They are also useful when total values are small, such as in Camp's series of maps on the various hate groups in the United States.

Walcott's burglary map is an example of a choropleth map in which enumeration units, states in this case, are shaded according to burglary rates. Generally, the darker the shade, the higher the rate. The areas of the enumeration units, which can vary greatly, are a factor to consider in this type of mapping. In a hypothetical example, a state small in area records a smaller total number of burglaries than a larger state. However, if a rate per 100,000 persons is calculated for each of the two states, the rates are equal. If total values are mapped using the choropleth technique inappropriately, the larger state is darker and, of course, larger than the smaller state, giving the impression of a high distribution of burglaries over a large area. In reality, the distribution for the two states is equal and should have been mapped using rates. In using choropleth maps, another consideration is the method of data classification. For most maps in the *Atlas*, the data were classed using equal intervals (e.g., 0 to 9, 10 to 19, 20 to 39, etc.). In some instances, a method called Jenks optimization, or the natural breaks method, was chosen. Based on the distribution of values for the enumeration units, Jenks optimization aims to promote similarity within each class while achieving heterogeneity among the various classes.

For each map, all these issues—availability of data, data bias, and the level of precision—affect decisions on the type of map to produce, as well as whether to use raw values or rates. A number of different thematic map types have been employed in the *Atlas*. The two most frequently used map types, proportional symbol and choropleth, have been discussed previously. Also included are cartograms and dot density maps. In Linda Turnbull's essay on child abuse, a value-by-area cartogram, created by Borden Dent, displays child deaths by abuse and neglect. The size of each state is drawn proportional to the number of child victims resulting in an eye-catching illustration of the data distribution. Unlike most of the computer-generated maps in the *Atlas*, the cartograms have been hand-drawn then converted to digital form, allowing for a unique interpretation of the mapped variable.

In Keith Harries's essay on capital punishment, dot density maps display the distribution of executions for various time periods in U.S. history. In this series of maps, each dot, placed in the county of conviction for a fairly high level of precision, represents four executions. County boundaries have been removed to reduce cartographic clutter, and state boundaries added for reader reference. These maps communicate well the variation in spatial density.

On a side note, the data set used to produce these maps, the Espy File, is a fascinating and exhaustive compilation of information on executions in the U.S. from 1608 to 1991.

The file, referenced in the figure captions, includes such variables as the name, race, sex, age, and occupation of the offender; the date and method of execution; and the county of conviction. This data set is potentially useful to researchers in many different areas of study.

As stated previously, the original maps were, for the most part, computer-generated. Some of the software programs used in data compilation and processing, Excel and SAS, have been mentioned. For creation of the maps themselves, several software packages were used. Both ESRI's ArcView, a desktop GIS that offers Jenks optimization, and Golden Software's MapViewer, a mapping package, were used for the choropleth maps. For the proportional symbol maps, MapViewer, which offers an effective symbol scaling routine, was the best choice. ArcView was used for dot density mapping. After draft maps were completed, final graphics editing was accomplished using Micrografx Designer.

Reference

Atlanta Journal-Constitution. 1999. "Crime Stats: Questions Linger After Atlanta Audit." January 28.

CHAPTER 1

Geographic History of Crime

This chapter provides a historical backdrop to the activity of crime mapping by first taking a brief look at the distribution of violent crime in the United States for the past 57 years and then by looking at a brief summary of the history of crime-mapping techniques. Because the common theme in this book is *mapping,* it is appropriate that the reader first look at how cartography has contributed to the geographic study of crime.

Crime generally is defined by society and its culture as the breaking of common rules and laws of government. Different societies have different laws and definitions of what constitutes criminal behavior. Anyone found in violation of these rules is therefore defined as a criminal. Although some activities are not universally recognized as crimes, other commissions are considered crimes in most places in the world. Treason in time of war and homicide are examples. Ultimately, a crime is considered a "public wrong."

Likewise, laws defining crime among the states of this country vary widely. For example, motor vehicle traffic violations, gambling, and prostitution are crimes defined differently from state to state and over time. However, a higher degree of uniformity appears to exist among the most serious offenses. Another interesting point is that all societies tolerate a certain amount of crime. In the United States, "organized crime" proliferated after World War I. A certain degree of this kind of crime is tolerated by society because many citizens benefit from it by way of recreational activities.

Since the 1930s, national crime data for the United States have been collected by the Federal Bureau of Investigation (FBI) from law enforcement agencies around the country. These crimes are reported in the following categories: *violent crimes* include murder, forcible rape, robbery, and aggravated assault, and *property crimes* include burglary, larceny (theft), motor vehicle theft, and arson (in some cases). Since 1975, the rate of crime per 100,000 persons, for *all* crimes, has decreased by approximately 7 percent (*see* Table 1-A). The focus of the following discussion of regional variation will center around violent crimes.

TABLE 1-A

UNITED STATES OVERALL CRIME RATES, 1975-1997

Year	Rate/100,000 persons
1975	5,299
1980	5,950
1985	5,207
1990	5,820
1994	5,374
1995	5,278
1996	5,087
1997	4,923

Source: Federal Bureau of Investigation, *Uniform Crime Reports: Crime in the United States,* various years.

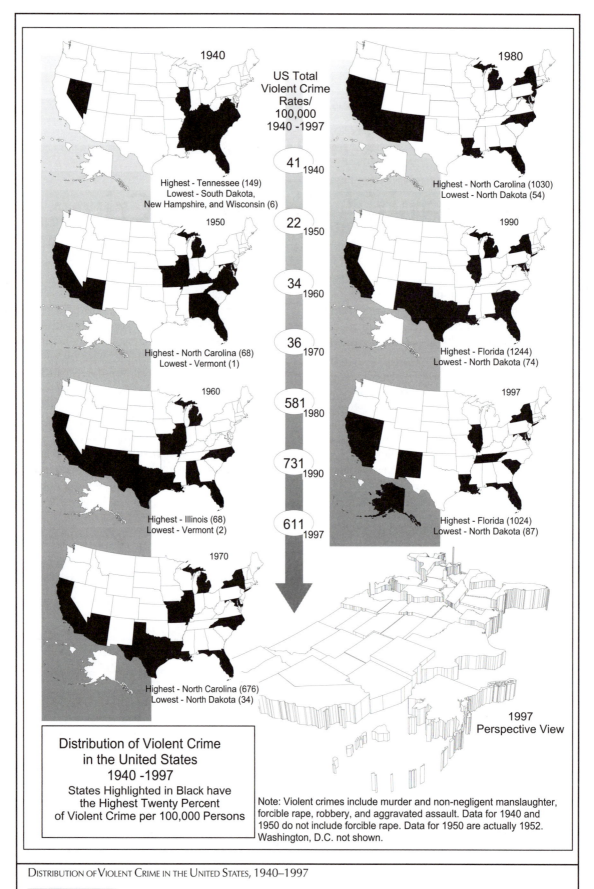

US Total Violent Crime Rates/ 100,000 1940 -1997

1940
Highest - Tennessee (149)
Lowest - South Dakota, New Hampshire, and Wisconsin (6)

41 1940

22 1950

1950
Highest - North Carolina (68)
Lowest - Vermont (1)

34 1960

36 1970

1960
Highest - Illinois (68)
Lowest - Vermont (2)

581 1980

731 1990

1970
Highest - North Carolina (676)
Lowest - North Dakota (34)

611 1997

1980
Highest - North Carolina (1030)
Lowest - North Dakota (54)

1990
Highest - Florida (1244)
Lowest - North Dakota (74)

1997
Highest - Florida (1024)
Lowest - North Dakota (87)

1997 Perspective View

Distribution of Violent Crime in the United States 1940 -1997
States Highlighted in Black have the Highest Twenty Percent of Violent Crime per 100,000 Persons

Note: Violent crimes include murder and non-negligent manslaughter, forcible rape, robbery, and aggravated assault. Data for 1940 and 1950 do not include forcible rape. Data for 1950 are actually 1952. Washington, D.C. not shown.

DISTRIBUTION OF VIOLENT CRIME IN THE UNITED STATES, 1940–1997

FIGURE 1-1

Source: Federal Bureau of Investigation, *The Uniform Crime Reports: Crime in the United States*, 1998.

A careful examination of Figure 1-1 reveals a number of recent changes to the regional distribution of violent crimes in the United States. It is important to note that the crimes mapped in Figure 1-1 are only those considered *violent* by the Federal Bureau of Investigation (the agency that collects these data from independent police forces around the country). The most noticeable change is the break-up of the "solid South" (plus Illinois) in the years between 1940 and 1997. Several states in the South still had high crime rates in 1997, but many other southern states (Virginia, Kentucky, North Carolina, Georgia, Alabama, and Mississippi) had disappeared from the category by that date.

Another remarkable aspect of the change in the distribution of violent crimes is the geographic *non-clustering* or *spread* that has occurred in the top category. In 1940, the only western state in the high category was Nevada. By 1990, all the middle and western states along the border with Mexico, except for Arizona, were included, as was Louisiana on the southern Gulf coast. In the Northeast, New York and Maryland became entrenched in the high category (except for 1960). Florida has remained in the high category for the whole period. North Dakota dominated the lowest category for nearly all the 57 years portrayed in the figure.

Data for the presentation in Figure 1-1 are by reported crimes per 100,000 persons. This method of reporting is the best way to illustrate *crime density*, especially in those geographic areas experiencing a considerable overall population increase (such as the United States since 1940). Two states, North Carolina and Florida, practically dominated the top crime rates between 1940 and 1997, while two others, Tennessee and Illinois, briefly took the top spot (1940 and 1960, respectively).

The United States total crime rates for violent crimes are also provided in the figure. These data reflect the average violent crime rates for all the states. It is important to note that the crime rates as published by the FBI suffer from several shortcomings that affect their accuracy. Not all police agencies report their crimes, and, until recently, there were no standards for reporting. Finally, there is often no control over the accuracy and reliability of the states' reports. The data source is the *Uniform Crime Reports: Crime in the United States* (1998). The general trend of overall violent crime rates remained much the same until 1970, when violent crimes took a major leap upwards, and then dropped between 1990 and 1997. However, as cautioned, the reader should consider the characteristics of the data before making summary judgments.

Using a sophisticated cartography computer program that allows an innovative view of these data, Figure 1-1 also provides a perspective view of the distribution of crime in the United States for 1997. This view offers a different look at the same data presented in the 1997 thematic choropleth (shaded) map just above it.

In the following essay, "Brief History of Crime Mapping," Borden D. Dent highlights some of the most important techniques of this form of mapping. Crime mapping techniques follow closely the overall history of the development of all thematic mapping. In general, thematic mapping (i.e., the mapping of specific numerical or non-numerical data) has had only a brief span of time in cartographic history. Data mapping appeared in the late eighteenth century at the end of the so-called Age of Enlightenment, especially in England and continental Europe. Data mapping grew in great spurts after countries began to conduct national censuses, and as the general interest in the quality of human existence increased. By 1860, people in several countries were involved in this kind of mapping, although thematic mapping in the United States lagged somewhat behind that of Europe.

In the United States, early crime mapping was centered around the mapping of juvenile delinquents, especially in the 1920s and 1930s. As time went on, and as more specific crime data appeared on the scene, just about any data were explored in map form. The following essay on crime mapping portrays this brief history and provides examples of the myriad of map types.

Brief History of Crime Mapping

Borden D. Dent

Mapping is an old activity dating back two millennia and beyond. Early maps were functional devices used to help way-find, or, as in the case of early Marshall islanders' maps, to locate waves and currents among the islands (Raize 1938). One of the earliest extant maps is a clay tablet found in the city of Ga-Sur, in northern Babylonia (Raize 1938). This map was translated as outlining the boundaries of a rich man's estate. Mesopotamian maps also included *cadastral maps*, or maps that identified land ownership (Robinson 1982). Fundamental locational features, such as rivers, mountains, and streams, dominated early mapping. The *encyclopedic* function of early maps predominated mapping activity until roughly the 1650s. Mapping the land with *contours of elevation*, a form of thematic map, came about this time, primarily for military purposes. Not until the late 1700s did people begin to map more abstract ideas and the results of national censuses.

Thematic maps, contrary to maps that show the location of general geographic features, have as their main purpose the showing of single themes.

> In contrast to the general map, the thematic map concentrates on showing the geographical occurrence and variation of a single phenomenon, or at most a very few. Instead of having as its primary function the display of the relative locations of a variety of different features, the pure thematic map focuses on the differences from place to place of one class of feature, that class being the subject or "theme" of the map. The number of possible themes is nearly unlimited and ranges over the whole gamut of man's interest in the present and past physical, social, and economic world, from geology to religion, and from population to disease. (Robinson 1982: 16)

Thematic maps did not appear until the late 1600s, and then only sporadically. Early ones included Edmond Halley's 1686 map of the trade winds and monsoons.

> One of the most significant contributors to thematic mapping was the English astronomer Edmond Halley (1656-1742), best known for his prediction of the periodic return of the comet that bears his name. We have mentioned the biblical and historical maps on Ortelius's *Theatrum*; we know that Oronce Fine, the well-known French cartographer, made biblical maps (now lost) in the mid-sixteenth century; and other examples could be cited. But these are very different from the thematic maps of Halley, who illustrated a number of his own scientific theories by cartographic means. (Thrower 1996: 95)

One of the most famous of the early thematic maps was done in 1775 by Benjamin Franklin and his cousin, Timothy Folger, who mapped a sea chart of the limits of the Gulf Stream in the Atlantic Ocean (Thrower 1996). Frere de Montizon's map of the population of France in 1830 was one of the first maps to use the so-called dot method (discussed more fully below) (Robinson 1982). The famous John Snow map of cholera in London was published in 1854 (Tufte 1983). The maps of Henry Drury Harness (1804-1883) must also be mentioned; he expanded the work of others by developing the *dasymetric* and true *proportional symbol* map forms (discussed below) (Thrower 1996).

Thematic maps became more or less commonplace by the 1860s and 1870s. In Europe, where thematic mapping had its beginnings, several statistical conferences held in the 1860s featured committees that dealt with mapping and the *graphical* representation of statistics, a trend that gave further impetus to thematic mapping (Funkhouser 1937).

In the United States, which lagged behind Europe in the development of thematic mapping, such maps did not get much official treatment until 1872, when publication of the *Decennial Census of the United States* made available data from the Ninth Census of the United States (1870). For the Ninth Census, several maps were commissioned for inclusion in the bound publications. Topics included the "production power" of wheat, corn, cotton, hay, tobacco, and dairy products for the agricultural portion of the census. Population statistics maps included population density, distribution of "colored" population, general foreign population, and the distributions of German, Irish, English and Welsh, Swedish and Norwegian, Chinese, and British Americans. Also included were two maps of illiteracy and wealth. The vital statistics volume of the census also contained a variety of maps, including maps of several diseases. The vital statistics volume had three environmental maps—temperature, rainfall, and elevation.

Thematic maps used for population and health were mainly of the choropleth type, while maps for physical subjects were isometric. Both types were printed in color. These types of thematic maps will be discussed more fully below, but it is instructive to know that these forms were used early in the history of special subject mapping.

Atlases devoted to thematic maps had a sporadic start, often coming in the form of instructional aids. Although the first such atlas was apparently done by Ritter in 1806, atlases of thematic maps were more common by the mid-1850s, when mineral production, temperature, precipitation, population, and similar subjects were frequently mapped (Robinson 1982).

Principal Kinds of Quantitative Thematic Maps

Although geographers like to map a variety of phenomena, both physical and cultural (human-made), maps can generally be divided into several overlapping classes. Maps that simply *locate* geographical features clearly dominated early cartography and mirrored the general history of "filling in the world map" as humans gained more and wider geographical awareness. More sophisticated mapping developed after the Age of Enlightenment in the eighteenth century, when cartographers and geographers began to map research findings and ideas and the results of numerical surveys (i.e., censuses).

In general terms, a thematic map may be either qualitative or quantitative. Qualitative maps show the locations of different *kinds* of things, while quantitative maps illustrate and document the *amount* of something (e.g., percent of population over 65, number or frequency of tornadoes). Because geographers and cartographers like to relate features on the earth's surface, it is natural for them to look at both kinds of maps. Because they required more abstraction and intellectual thought, and more sophisticated data, the techniques for mapping quantitative features came later in the history of thematic mapping. Through the years, several kinds of quantitative thematic maps have become more or less standard in the mapping arena. These include the simple dot map, choropleth, dasymetric map, proportional symbol map, isarithmic map, flow map, and, to a much lesser degree, the area cartogram (Dent 1996). The cartographic basis and general techniques for each map type are illustrated in Figure 1-2.

Perhaps the simplest in conceptual terms is the *dot map*, where (usually) a dot is placed on the map to show the location of a feature. In the one-to-one version, one dot represents one of the features being mapped. In the one-to-many version, the dot may represent multiples of the feature (e.g., one dot represents 10,000 people, or 5,000 acres). The dots are placed on the map carefully in accordance with the distribution of the phenomena. The map reader gains visual numeracy, or relative density, from these maps.

The *choropleth map* uses political or statistical boundaries for mapping. The quantity in the geographical division is represented by the color or shade of the area symbol placed in the enumeration unit. The cartographer makes several assumptions when using this form of map. First, the cartographer assumes that the quantity being mapped is uniform in the enumeration area. Secondly, he or she assumes that densities, rates, or ratios are more important than absolute values. Because enumeration units vary in size (in most choropleth mapping), symbolizing absolute values with shaded area symbols often leads to misinterpretation. With this kind of map, it is also important to remember that the boundaries separating the enumeration units do not have numerical values.

The third kind of quantitative thematic map is the *dasymetric map,* which looks similar in appearance to the choropleth, but is unique in construction. Enumeration units (such as those found in censuses, e.g., minor civil divisions, counties, and states) are not used. In the dasymetric type, areas on the map that contain similar data values and characteristics have similar area symbols applied to them. In this way, overall distributions are shown. As with the choropleth map, the boundaries separating areas do not have numerical values.

The *proportional symbol map* is yet another type of quantitative thematic map. Here a symbol is selected to represent the variable being mapped, and its size is made proportional to the values of the phenomena illustrated over the map. This type of map is used to map quantities at point locations (e.g., cities on a map of a very small scale), or can be used to show quantities of areas with the symbol placed in the center of the area. The proportional symbol map is popular and has found its way into many mapping computer software programs. Although squares, triangles, and other suitable symbol types have been used, the circle is probably the most popular.

Isoline maps are also a popular type of quantitative thematic map. Some common ones are those showing temperature, rainfall, or elevation above sea level. With this form of mapping, the cartographer connects points of equal value with a line, called an *isarithm,* or simply an *isoline.* The lines thus produced are thought to define a surface and enclose a volume of the phenomenon being mapped. The important distinction between this form of map, generally called an *isopleth map,* and the choropleth map described above is that the isoline map may use data that are continuous in nature, and not necessarily enumeration data. This form of map may be computerized, and is found less frequently in general publications.

Flow maps show connectivity between places, usually by lines that have their widths drawn proportional to the movement of ideas or goods between places. Flow maps were one of the earliest types of quantitative maps produced (Robinson 1982). They were found in many commercial geography textbooks of the early twentieth century (Parks 1987; Dent 1996). Flow maps, if done well, with provocative data, can be instructive in showing geographical associations and connectivity.

Of the major forms of quantitative thematic maps, the *area cartogram* is used the least often. It usually appears in collections of maps and atlases (such as in Rand McNally's *Goode's World Atlas*), and in special publications. The area cartogram is based on enumeration data, with the sizes of the enumeration units drawn proportional to the values being mapped, rather than having area patterns placed in the units to represent the data as one would with choropleth mapping. This form of map provides a provocative view of the data distribution, often attracting attention and eliciting interesting comments from readers. It has been proven to be pedagogically effective. One principal drawback of the cartogram is that the reader must be familiar with the geographic shapes and sizes of the enumeration units before area sizing and reshaping are done. As a result, many cartograms use states, provinces, or countries, rather than smaller geographical divisions, whose shapes are not easily recognized.

Most of the thematic maps just discussed had their beginnings in the early 1800s.

Geographic History of Crime

The significant, formative years in the development of portrayal techniques in thematic cartography were the first six decades of the nineteenth century. During that period most of the methods in use today were invented, tried out, modified, and finally settled upon. This is not to say that nothing innovative has occurred since then. Considerable sophistication in conceptual approach and in processing data had definitely been achieved. Some new methods of portrayal have been instituted, some successful, such as linkage displays where complex sets of movements are shown by connections of origins and destinations, and some not so successful, such as the attractive but misleading proportional spheres. Nevertheless, generally speaking, the great majority of the techniques used in thematic cartography today were devised and put to use before 1860. The list is long: proportional point symbols, the line of equal value (isoline), the choropleth and dasymetric methods, sectored circles or pie graphs, variable shading, the dot method, class intervals, and flow lines. Some of the first uses of the methods were buried in out-of-the-way places and had to be reinvented, some developed with controversy, and some came into being fully developed on the first try, so to speak. (Robinson 1982: 190)

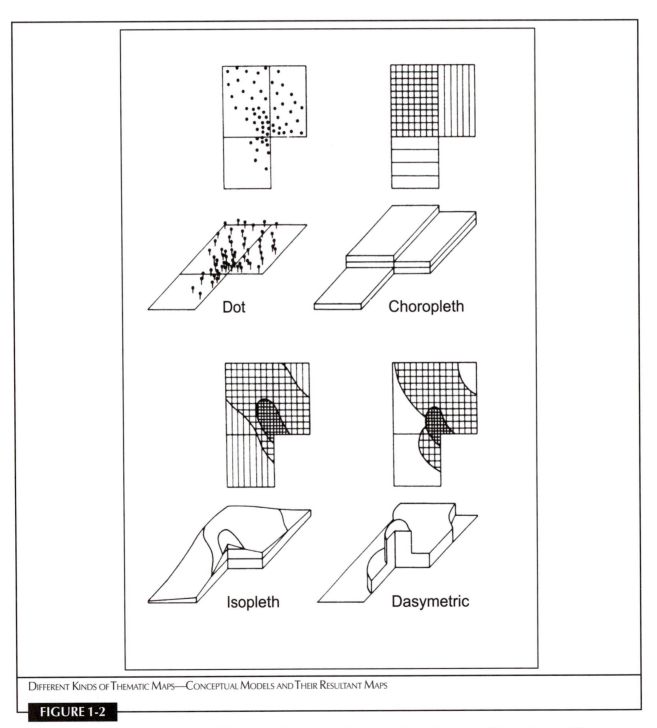

DIFFERENT KINDS OF THEMATIC MAPS—CONCEPTUAL MODELS AND THEIR RESULTANT MAPS

FIGURE 1-2

Source: Copied with permission from Norman J.W. Thrower. 1996. *Maps and Civilization*. Chicago: University of Chicago Press: p. 153.

Early Thematic Maps of Crime

The first period of the scientific study of crime has been called the "cartographic" or "geographic" school because the predominant form of inquiry was cartographic (Phillips 1972). The period is said to have flourished from about 1830 to 1880.

> The cartographic school began in France and spread rapidly to England. From its inception, the members of this school attempted to use newly available social data gathered by their governments in order to determine the incidence of crime, its variation, and its relationship to social and physical conditions. (Philips 1972: 87)

One of the earliest attempts of mapping crime occurred in France in the nineteenth century, where Adriano Balbi (an Italian) and André Michel Guerry mapped, by choropleth technique, crimes against property, crimes against the person, and level of (education) instruction. These maps were lithographed and colored by crayon shading (Robinson 1982). Soon after, Adolphe Quetelet (a Belgian), also working in France, produced maps showing crimes against property and against people (Robinson 1982). Quetelet's efforts were not choropleth maps, but maps that showed smooth transitions of shading from areas of high crime rates to low. For their times, these maps were innovative. In 1833, Guerry created still other maps of crime (Robinson 1982).

These early French endeavors were soon followed by other maps illustrating crime, notably in England and Ireland. In 1849, Joseph Fletcher published maps for England and Wales (Fletcher 1849) that depicted crimes of gross commitments of males, more serious commitments of crimes against persons and malicious offenses, commitments for offenses against property, and commitments for assaults (Figure 1-3). Fletcher was one of the first cartographers to employ the choropleth method. The mapped data were divided into six classes that were given in percent of the total above and below the mean. Data tables were also provided for each map.

The maps of Fletcher were followed by the crime maps of Henry Mayhew, the originator of *Punch* magazine (Robinson 1982). Mayhew's maps were an interesting form of choropleth map. They portrayed the following topics: the intensity of the criminality (in each county of England and Wales), the number of persons committed for rape, persons committed for carnally abusing girls, persons committed for assaults, persons with intent to "ravish and carnally" abuse, persons committed for bigamy, persons committed for abduction, and the criminality of females. In each case, the maps showed the rate per a certain number of the population. The maps rendered the English and Welsh counties in black or white, depending on whether their data were above (black) or below (white) the average for the country (Mayhew 1861). County averages were also printed within county boundaries.

For the rest of the nineteenth century, crime mapping mostly focused on the representation of census data gathered at regular census intervals.

Crime Mapping Matures

The so-called "ecological school" of crime appeared around the mid-twentieth century with the work of Clifford Shaw and Henry McKay (discussed below), which was fundamentally concerned with the relationship of crime to "such variables as urbanization, literacy, occupational differentiation, and poverty" (Phillips 1972: 87). However, from the late nineteenth century to the introduction of the ecological school in the mid-twentieth, crime and criminals were the subject of "topological criminology," in which crime was thought to be the result of deficiencies brought on at birth, such as physical defects and various psychopathologies. No particular cartographic products are representative of this topological period.

With regard to the ecological school, sociologists were among the first social scientists to map crime, especially if one considers juvenile delinquency as a crime. One of the most detailed maps was done by S.P. Breckenridge and E. Abbott in 1912, in their *The Delinquent Child and the Home*. Their mapping was an exhaustive one-to-one dot mapping form that showed the location of the homes of delinquent children in Chicago during the years 1899 to 1903. Each dot represented one home (Figure 1-4).

Other works continued to keep the mapping of crime an active pursuit. In a 1923 study of crime in Columbus, Ohio, R. D. McKenzie mapped, by the one-to-one dot method, the locations of the city's juvenile delinquents.

> As might be expected the majority of the dependency cases are segregated in the low economic areas surrounding the central business district. The colored cases form conspicuous groups near the railroad tracks and the river, also in the eastern part of the city near Franklin Park. The most striking feature concerning the geographical distribution of juvenile delinquency is the rather even dispersion of cases throughout the entire city.... There is, apparently, but slight correlation between the segregation of dependency and that of delinquency. (McKenzie 1923: 165)

McKenzie apparently used his eye to evaluate geographical correlation and dispersion. Today cartographers have more quantitative methods from which to draw such conclusions.

In a study just two years after McKenzie's, Cyril Burt, also writing on the subject of delinquency, mapped the distribution of delinquency in London, England (Burt 1925). He mapped delinquency as a ratio of the total reported cases to the total number of children for each electoral area in the city. This classic choropleth map has five classes. Burt's maps showed the areas with higher incidence closer to the downtown part of the city of London.

Although he did no mapping per se, R. Clyde White examined the relationship among felonies to environmental factors in Indianapolis, Indiana, in 1932. He divided the city into concentric zones, with each succeeding zone one mile further from the central city, and tabulated the incidence of crime in each zone. His contribution in the present context is that he charted the incidence in each zone, and showed the classic *distance decay curve* often used by geographers (White

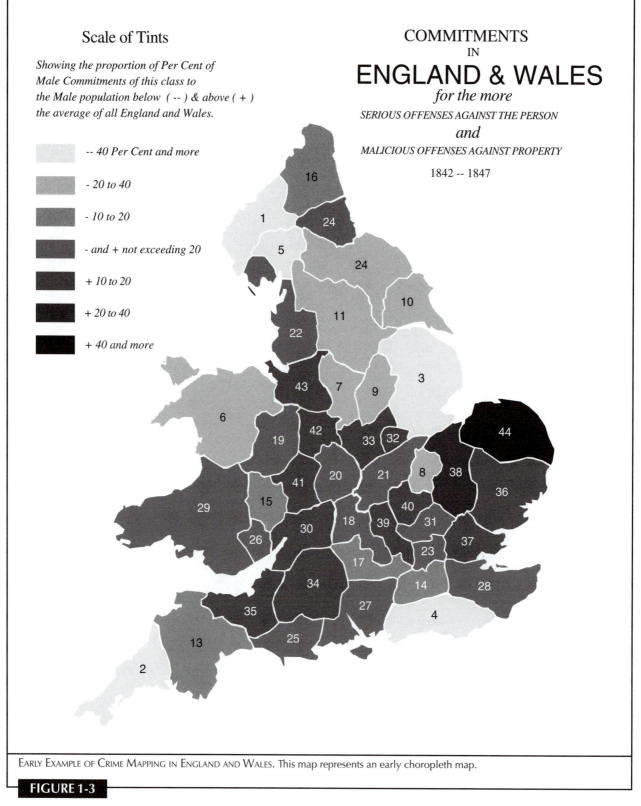

Scale of Tints

*Showing the proportion of Per Cent of
Male Commitments of this class to
the Male population below (--) & above (+)
the average of all England and Wales.*

-- 40 Per Cent and more

- 20 to 40

- 10 to 20

- and + not exceeding 20

+ 10 to 20

+ 20 to 40

+ 40 and more

COMMITMENTS
IN
ENGLAND & WALES
for the more

SERIOUS OFFENSES AGAINST THE PERSON
and
MALICIOUS OFFENSES AGAINST PROPERTY

1842 -- 1847

EARLY EXAMPLE OF CRIME MAPPING IN ENGLAND AND WALES. This map represents an early choropleth map.

FIGURE 1-3

Source: Redrawn from Joseph Fletcher. 1849. Moral and Educational Statistics of England and Wales. *Journal of the Statistical Society of London* 12: pp. 151-335.

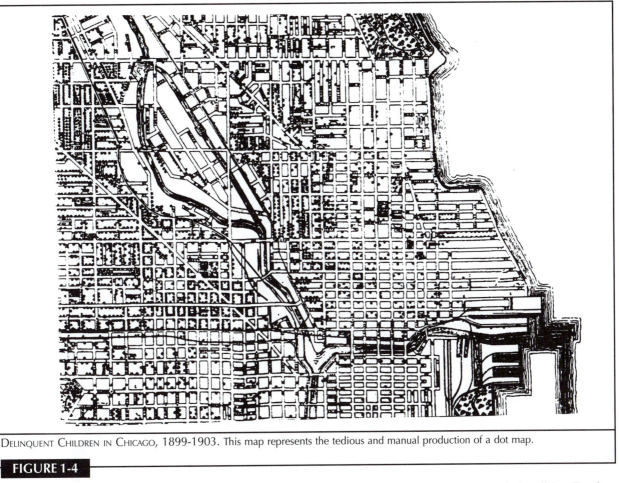

DELINQUENT CHILDREN IN CHICAGO, 1899-1903. This map represents the tedious and manual production of a dot map.

FIGURE 1-4

Source: Copied with permission from S.P. Beckenridge and E. Abbott. 1912. *The Delinquent Child and the Home.* New York: Russell Sage Foundation: p. 23.

1932). In this case, the incidence of felonies dropped off with distance away from the central business district, rapidly at first, then more gradually.

Another example of delinquency mapping can be found in Shaw and McKay's *Juvenile Delinquency and Urban Areas* (1942). Shaw and McKay created a choropleth map of the rate of delinquency among 2,953 male delinquents in the city of Chicago during the years 1927-1933 (Figure 1-5). Besides being shaded in the conventional choropleth mapping manner, this interesting map shows the actual rates of delinquency in each enumeration district. These authors attributed the spatial distribution of delinquency to other spatial variables, such as families on relief, poor homes, proportion of Negro and foreign born families, infant-mortality rates, mental disorders, and tuberculosis. As indicated by Figure 1-5, areas of high delinquency were concentrated in the inner parts of Chicago, abutting the central business district on the west and south. This distribution roughly followed the pattern suggested by E.W. Burgess (1925).

Sociologists continued to map delinquency in Mexico as well as in the United States. In 1946, for example, an examination of the distribution of delinquents in Mexico City found the distributional patterns to be similar to those in U.S. cities—higher rates near the central city and lower rates in areas

surrounding the downtown area (Hayner 1946). The mapping technique, once again, was the choropleth method.

Delinquency, however, was not all that was mapped. In his 1963 book, *Crimes of Violence,* F. H. McClintock included several maps of London that depicted the distribution of violence, including sexual offenses, violence in public houses and cafes, and violence in the streets.

> The distribution maps show that crimes of violence occur mainly in the inner divisions of the Metropolitan Office District and that large areas almost entirely free from this type of crime are the outer suburbs toward the Green Belt. Apart from the Piccadilly and the Soho areas–where a number of fights in clubs and cafes and streets occur–most of the crimes of violence take place in poor neighborhoods among people living in overcrowded tenement houses or under slum conditions. . . . Sexual offenses and attacks on police, on the other hand, are widely scattered, taking place in all types of neighborhoods. (McClintock 1963: 40)

McClintock's neatly executed maps included one-to-one dot maps of where violent crimes occurred, and choropleth maps of total numbers of crimes (technically an incorrect way of choropleth mapping, which should use rates rather than absolute numbers) (Figure 1-6).

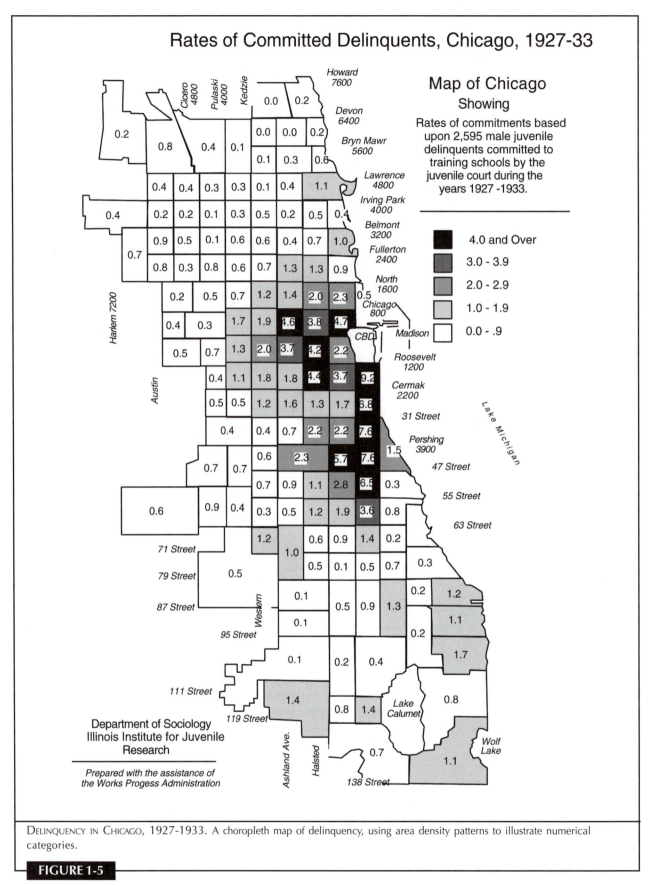

Rates of Committed Delinquents, Chicago, 1927-33

Map of Chicago
Showing

Rates of commitments based upon 2,595 male juvenile delinquents committed to training schools by the juvenile court during the years 1927-1933.

■ (black)	4.0 and Over
▨ (dark gray)	3.0 - 3.9
▨ (gray)	2.0 - 2.9
▨ (light gray)	1.0 - 1.9
□ (white)	0.0 - .9

Department of Sociology
Illinois Institute for Juvenile
Research

Prepared with the assistance of the Works Progess Administration

DELINQUENCY IN CHICAGO, 1927-1933. A choropleth map of delinquency, using area density patterns to illustrate numerical categories.

FIGURE 1-5

Source: Redrawn with permission from Clifford Shaw and Henry McKay. 1942. *Juvenile Delinquency and Urban Areas.* Chicago: University of Chicago Press: p. 70.

In 1954, Bernard Lauder provided a similar map for the city of Baltimore, Maryland, in his book *Towards an Understanding of Juvenile Delinquency*. Lauder mapped the rate of delinquency per 1,000 children aged 7-17. Again, the spatial distribution showed a clustering in the inner city, adjacent to the central business district, and decreasing from there to the outer edges of the city. Delinquency was also high near industrial areas.

Sociologists have also employed dot maps to chart crime and delinquency (Morris 1957). From such maps, the reader gains an understanding of the spatial distribution of the crime by recognizing the clusters of dots, or the "numerousness" of the dots over the map. When these maps provide adequate base map information (clues to location), then the distribution of the variable is generally obvious. These and other kinds of quantitative maps can suggest hypotheses for devising solutions to problems.

Other forms of crime mapping began to appear by 1970. For instance, instead of the one-to-one dot mapping so frequently used in delinquency mapping, some researchers were using a variant of this method, in which a dot symbolized more than one offense. In *Crime, Police, and Race Relations* (1970), John Lambert used two differently sized dots, one for a single occurrence of motorcycle or motor vehicle theft, and another size for two offenses. Although this method was unique, it did not convincingly show the geographical clustering of the crimes (Figure 1-7).

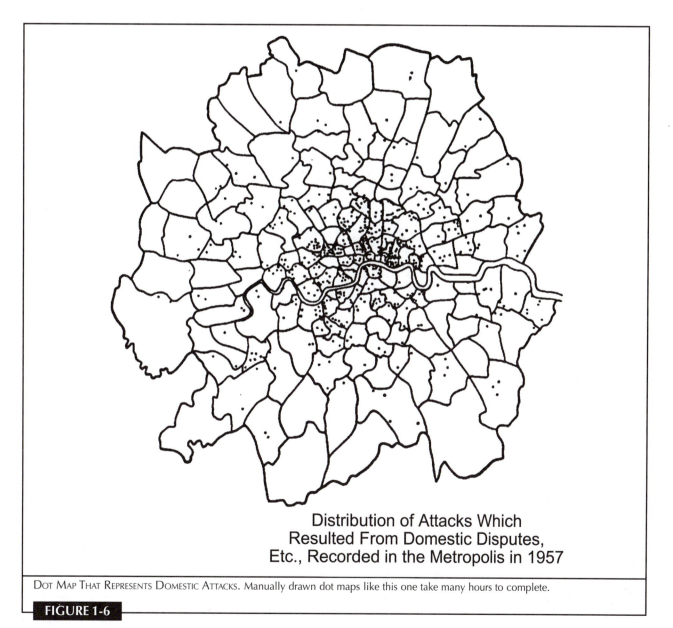

Distribution of Attacks Which Resulted From Domestic Disputes, Etc., Recorded in the Metropolis in 1957

Dot Map That Represents Domestic Attacks. Manually drawn dot maps like this one take many hours to complete.

FIGURE 1-6

Source: Copied with permission from F.H. McClintock. 1963. *Crimes of Violence*. London: Macmillan: p. 204.

Geographers Map Crime

By the 1970s, geographers were exploring other means of symboling crime activity. One such method was to connect the residence of an offender with the place of the crime with a line symbolizing the linkage (cartographers often call these "desire" lines). The resultant map, in this case, for the city of Miami, shows that a heavy incidence of desire lines overlap in the central part of the city (Capone and Nichols 1975: 205). The difficulty with this technique is that it suggests a strong density of crime where the lines overlap, which is not correct. Another form of desire line map is discussed below under "Gangs."

For the most part, geographers have used many of the same mapping techniques used by sociologists and others. Dot map and choropleth methods have predominated. The de-sire-line technique, linking offended residence and place of crime, was apparently first used by geographers. The desire line mapping technique was modified somewhat by Gerald Pyle (1974) and his associates when they mapped a version of the quantitative flow line showing the different number of linkages between census tracts and place of crime and the numbers of suspects entering the tract to perpetrate the crime. Pyle also used SYMAP choropleth techniques (discussed below in "Recent Crime Mapping").

In *The Geography of Urban Crime* (1982), David T. Herbert took on the task of bringing together much of the work that had been done on crime, and attempted to show how geographers might deal with this as a topical area, especially how they might contribute with their unique ability at spatial analysis. In the example described here, several map-

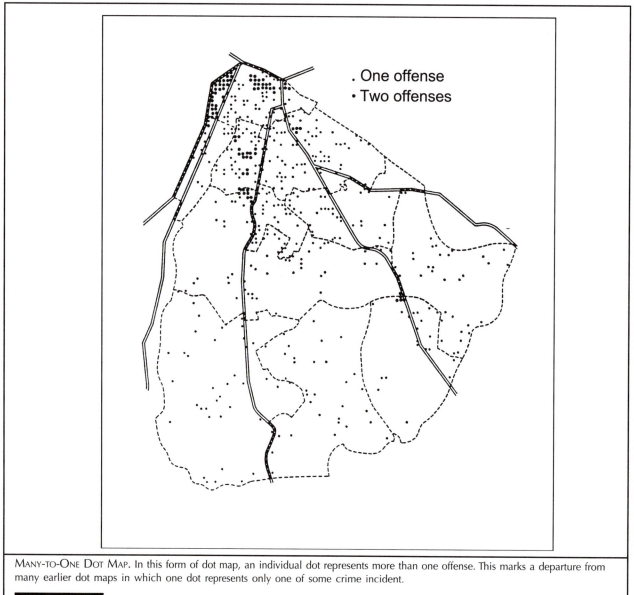

MANY-TO-ONE DOT MAP. In this form of dot map, an individual dot represents more than one offense. This marks a departure from many earlier dot maps in which one dot represents only one of some crime incident.

FIGURE 1-7

Source: Copied with permission from John R. Lambert. 1970. *Crime, Place, and Race Relations: A Study in Birmingham.* New York: Oxford University Press: p. 112.

ping techniques that had been done by other authors were included. One of the more interesting maps by Herbert is an earlier one, in which proportional circle symbolization depicted areas in Cardiff, Wales, where people do not wish to live, called "Areas of Low Residential Attractiveness." This map helped define problem areas within cities.

Geographer Susan J. Smith likewise brought to bear many of the findings by geographers and others in her book, *Crime, Space and Society* (1986). Although her work was skillfully done, Smith offered few mapping techniques and did not get beyond the simple choropleth and dot methods.

In *Social Problems and the City* (1979), editors David Herbert and David Smith included a paper on "Urban Crime: A Geographical Perspective," in which they mapped crime in two familiar ways, and one new one. They provided dot and choropleth-type maps, and they included a dot map on which clusters of offenders and linkages between clusters are shown. The clusters were identified by using statistical methods. Both the clustering and statistical methods were new applications.

The cartographic works of Phillip D. Phillips provided a new application. He created several crime maps at the United States scale showing, first, metropolitan area populations us- ing proportional squares, and then, an area symbol classed by the amount of the crime applied within each square (Phillips 1972). Figure 1-8 reproduces his aggravated assault map for the United States. These maps were drawn by computer plot- ter.

Perhaps the most prolific geographer researching and writing on crime in the United States is Professor Keith Har- ries, now at the University of Maryland, Baltimore County campus, and a contributor to this *Atlas*. He has mapped crime using a variety of techniques. In one of his earlier works (1971), Harries used the SYMAP program to map a variety of crimes throughout the United States, notably murder, rape, and rob- bery (Figure 1-9). These maps, although choropleth, actually resemble isoplethic maps because of the nature of character printers. In a paper written nearly 20 years later (1996b), Har- ries produced more choropleth maps of homicides.

Recent Crime Mapping

The earliest form of thematic mapping by computer was with a program called SYMAP, mentioned briefly above, distrib- uted by the Harvard University Laboratory for Computer Graphics and Spatial Analysis. One of the first applications of

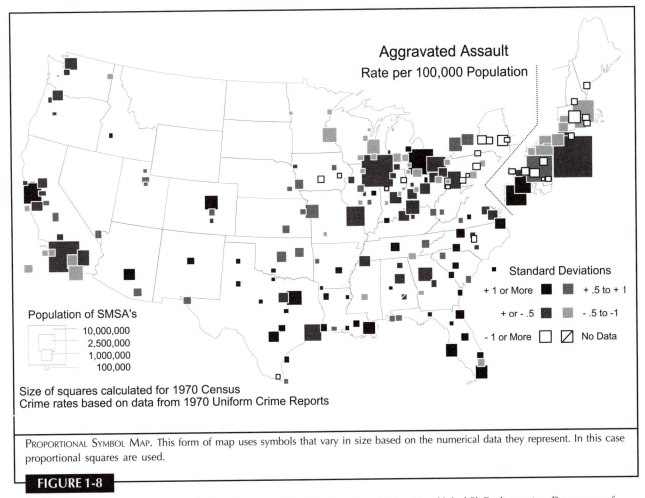

Aggravated Assault
Rate per 100,000 Population

Standard Deviations
+ 1 or More   + .5 to + 1
+ or - .5   - .5 to -1
- 1 or More   No Data

Population of SMSA's
10,000,000
2,500,000
1,000,000
100,000

Size of squares calculated for 1970 Census
Crime rates based on data from 1970 Uniform Crime Reports

PROPORTIONAL SYMBOL MAP. This form of map uses symbols that vary in size based on the numerical data they represent. In this case proportional squares are used.

FIGURE 1-8

Source: Redrawn with permission from Phillip David Phillips. 1973. *The Geography of Crime.* Unpublished Ph.D. dissertation, Department of Geography, University of Minnesota: p. 116.

this program for crime mapping was done by the Department of Geology and Geography at the University of Alabama (Shannon 1976; Sumrall 1978). These geographers mapped murder and rape, among other crimes, using isarithmic and choroplethic techniques. SYMAP's display output was by character printing (the only kind of printed output at that time), which yielded rather crude-looking maps, with little mapping detail. Nonetheless, it was the beginning of what is now the standard for mapping.

Different automated methods of crime mapping were introduced by the late 1970s. One such system provided graduated symbol maps.

> The first type of map may be illustrated by a graduate-symbol map where crime events within each statistical unit are shown by a figurative symbol in which the symbol size is proportional to the frequency of the crime in the unit. (Brassel and Utano 1979: 22)

This form of map symbolization was not new to cartography in the late 1970s, but was rather new to the arena of automated mapping, and for applications in crime mapping. Gerald Pyle, a geographer, used this same form of mapping and symbolization in 1976, in his "Spatial and Temporal Aspects of Crime in Cleveland, Ohio," although his maps were not from an automated or computer system.

Recent crime mapping can be roughly dated to the introduction of computer graphics and computer mapping in the mid to late 1970s. Following the early introduction of SYMAP, which used character-based printing, pen plotters were introduced to replace the human draftsperson. More importantly, with the ease of drafting that this technology brought about, it was possible to economically reproduce "statistical surfaces"—three-dimensional representations of volumetric data, such as were found with traditional maps showing such distributions as land elevation, temperature, and rainfall. This method also allowed the mapping of socio-economic data, such as crime. An early application of this method was done by geographers at Kent State University in Ohio (Corsi and Harvey 1975).

According to researchers Robert Figlio, Simon Hakam, and George Rengert, "While some people readily grasp the nature of relationships between variables from statistical analyses, others find maps quite helpful in showing the nature of *spatial* [my italics] relationships" (1986: 33-34). To illustrate this point, they include in their work several statistical surface maps at a neighborhood level (Figure 1-10). They point out that these maps show vividly where the crime concentration is, although they do not show the extent of the ecological variables of the crimes.

In the 1960s, geographers began to explore in earnest the nature of human spatial behavior by looking not so much at descriptions of that behavior, but by attempting to look into the origins of behavior, such as the examination of *why*. In other words, why do people take certain routes in their travels,

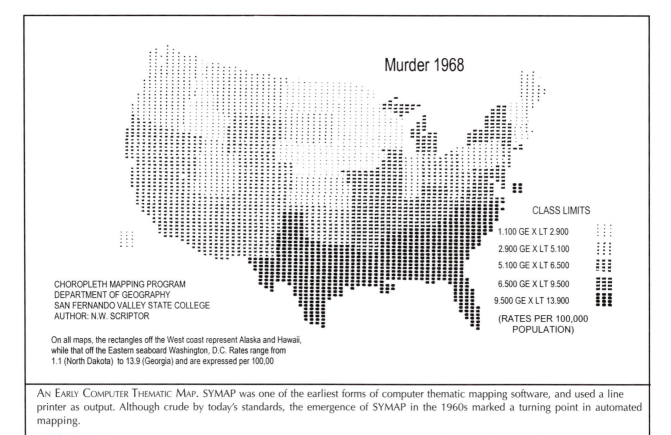

AN EARLY COMPUTER THEMATIC MAP. SYMAP was one of the earliest forms of computer thematic mapping software, and used a line printer as output. Although crude by today's standards, the emergence of SYMAP in the 1960s marked a turning point in automated mapping.

FIGURE 1-9

Source: Copied with permission from Keith D. Harries. 1971. *The Geography of Urban Crime. Journal of Geography* 70: pp. 204-10.

or why do they shop where they do? One of the strategies of that research was to assemble what are known as composite mental maps (cognitive maps held in the minds of many people).

> Information in the map is used to solve problems, form opinions, and direct actions. In the most general sense a cognitive map both expresses and determines what a person knows about the outside world. Stephen Kaplan has in fact defined cognitive mapping as a process by which an individual acquires and uses the knowledge needed to function adequately in a complex world. (Smith and Patterson 1980: 206)

A composite map is a kind of "average" cognitive map held by many people, and was and is used as a measure to determine views about the environment.

Researchers investigating crime began to explore the use of cognitive maps to help explain human spatial behavior. Not only were the mental maps of criminals explored, but also the mental maps of police officers. Because mental maps often form the basis for action, it was and is important to know the differences between these two groups. For example, Christopher Smith and Gene Patterson (1980) asked students on the University of Oklahoma campus to identify areas where they would be afraid to walk after midnight. Their responses were mapped, and the resultant image was called a "Cognitive Map of Fear." Their mapping is reproduced in Chapter 7 in the essay "Cognitive Maps and the Fear of Crime" by Patricia Gilmartin. I conducted a similar study among students at Georgia State University in Atlanta in the early 1980s, and the location most pronounced as a place to stay away from at midnight was in the immediate vicinity of the baseball stadium near downtown. A new statistical surface showing perceptions of crimes in Atlanta, Georgia, for 1998 is also provided here (Figure 1-11). The map of fear in Atlanta uses a computer-drawn statistical surface.

The map form used by both Smith and Patterson and myself, was the isopleth mapping technique, not a new method, but a new application of an old technique. Because a more detailed examination of mental mapping and crime is dealt with in Chapter 7 by Canter and Hodge's "Criminals' Mental Maps," nothing more will be said of it here.

The period of mapping crime (primarily the 1970s and 1980s) by using such devices as composite cognitive maps parallels the work of criminologists of the "situational school" during roughly this same time. The "situational school" takes the view that "the environment provides cues which mediate behavior and that crime is the outcome of the intersection of the perceptual worlds of offender and victim at a particular place and time. . . . The rise of situational crime prevention spawned a diversity of action projects concerned with housing, transport, city centers, and other public places." (Jones 1993: 2-3).

Gangs

Sociologists and others, including geographers, have also in the last two decades examined and mapped gangs and gang activities. Mapping this activity has not yielded any special cartographic symbolism. In *Dangerous Society* (1990), Carl Taylor (1990), provides a map showing the subcommunities

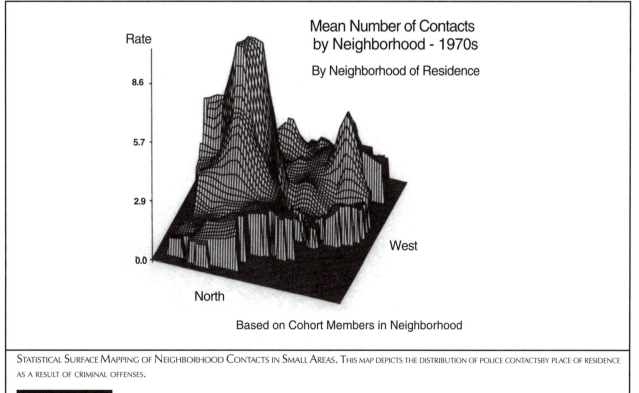

STATISTICAL SURFACE MAPPING OF NEIGHBORHOOD CONTACTS IN SMALL AREAS. THIS MAP DEPICTS THE DISTRIBUTION OF POLICE CONTACTS BY PLACE OF RESIDENCE AS A RESULT OF CRIMINAL OFFENSES.

FIGURE 1-10

Source: Copied with permission from Robert M. Figlio, Simon Hakim, and George F. Rengert, eds. 1986. *Metropolitan Crime Patterns.* Monsey, NY: Criminal Justice Press: p. 35.

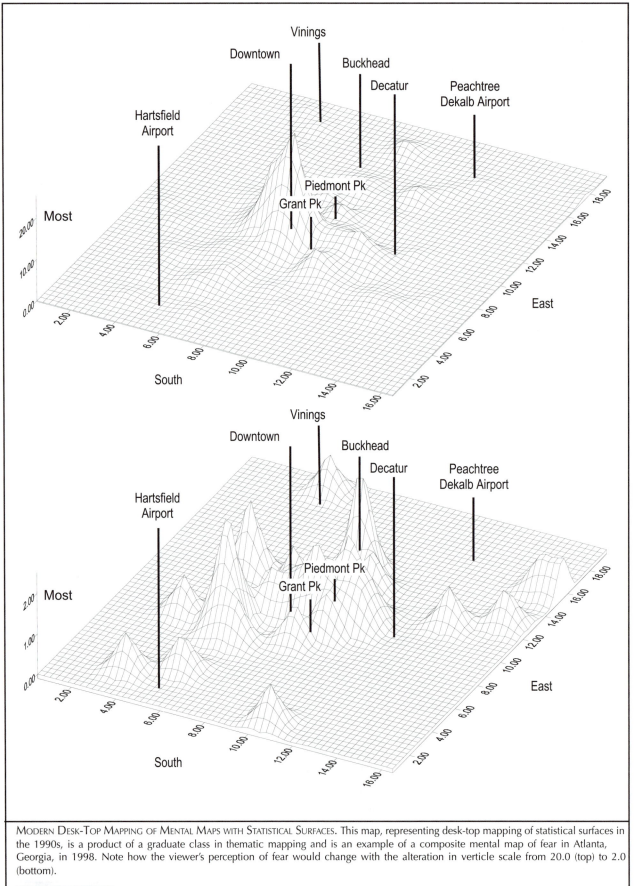

MODERN DESK-TOP MAPPING OF MENTAL MAPS WITH STATISTICAL SURFACES. This map, representing desk-top mapping of statistical surfaces in the 1990s, is a product of a graduate class in thematic mapping and is an example of a composite mental map of fear in Atlanta, Georgia, in 1998. Note how the viewer's perception of fear would change with the alteration in verticle scale from 20.0 (top) to 2.0 (bottom).

FIGURE 1-11

Source: Used with permission of Deborah Schwartz.

(gangs) of organized (corporate) and scavenger gangs in the city of Detroit (Figure 1-12). G. David Curry and Scott H. Decker mapped nationwide gang activity in 1998 using data from several studies and showing a progression of such activity from 1975 to 1994 in major metropolitan centers in the country. These maps are one-to-one dot distribution maps (Figure 1-13). The proliferation of problem sites in these maps is remarkable.

The desire line form of flow map has been used to map gang activity in urban areas. In a remarkable study using this technique, David Ley (1972) connected gang territories in Philadelphia by desire lines whose widths were proportional to the number of "incidents" between gangs (Figure 1-14). This method had not been used before for mapping crime, and is an excellent example of the desire line form of thematic map. Also, this map provides one of the first uses of the value-by-area (cartogram) form of map as a base on which the desire lines are drawn.

Explorations

Mapping crime has had nearly 160 years of development and maturation. Early mapping in France used rudimentary forms of choropleth maps to show crimes against property and people. Although crime mapping now may use computer-drawn illustrations, thanks to more thorough data collection and sophisticated computer software, many of the same techniques, such as dot mapping and choropleth mapping, are still being used. Although greater use is now made of statistical summa-

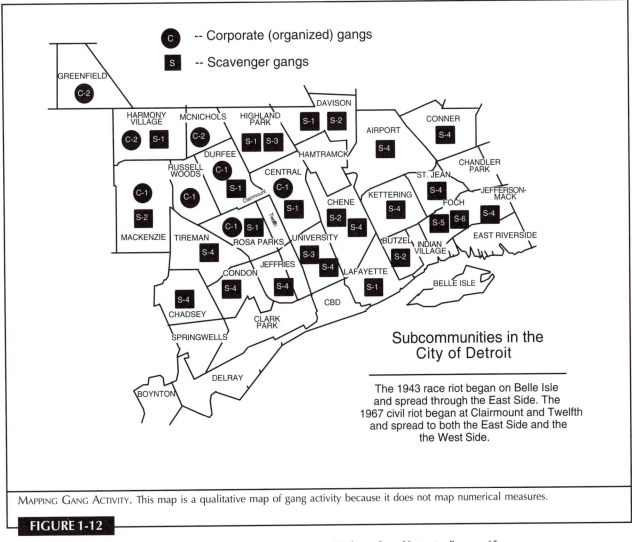

Mᴀᴘᴘɪɴɢ Gᴀɴɢ Aᴄᴛɪᴠɪᴛʏ. This map is a qualitative map of gang activity because it does not map numerical measures.

FIGURE 1-12

Source: Redrawn from Carl S. Taylor. 1990. *Dangerous Society.* East Lansing: Michigan State University Press: p. 15.

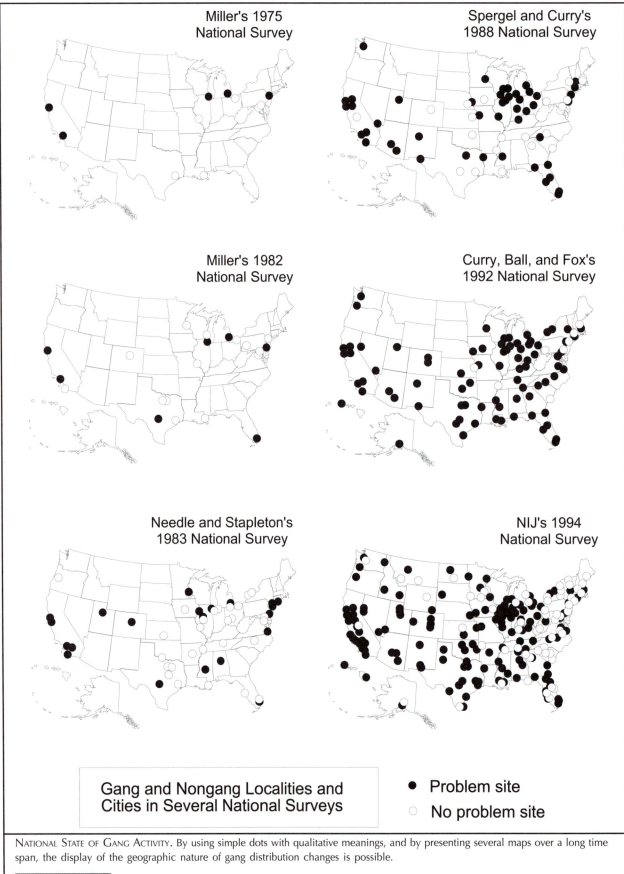

Miller's 1975
National Survey

Spergel and Curry's
1988 National Survey

Miller's 1982
National Survey

Curry, Ball, and Fox's
1992 National Survey

Needle and Stapleton's
1983 National Survey

NIJ's 1994
National Survey

Gang and Nongang Localities and
Cities in Several National Surveys

● Problem site
○ No problem site

NATIONAL STATE OF GANG ACTIVITY. By using simple dots with qualitative meanings, and by presenting several maps over a long time span, the display of the geographic nature of gang distribution changes is possible.

FIGURE 1-13

Source: Redrawn with permission from G. David Curry and Scott H. Decker. 1998. *Confronting Gangs.* Los Angeles: Roxbury: pp. 17-23.

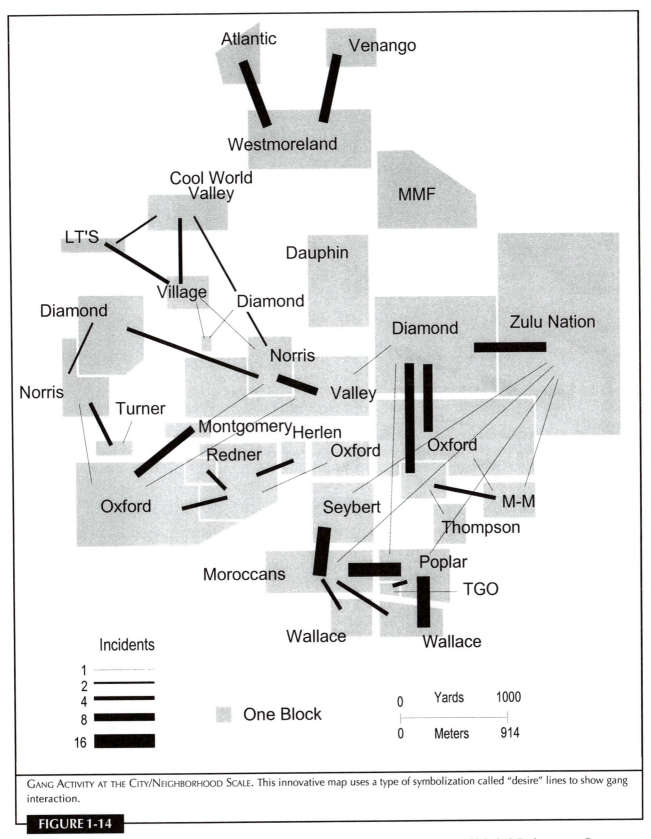

GANG ACTIVITY AT THE CITY/NEIGHBORHOOD SCALE. This innovative map uses a type of symbolization called "desire" lines to show gang interaction.

FIGURE 1-14

Source: Redrawn with permission from David F. Ley. 1972. *The Black Inner City as Frontier Outpost.* Unpublished Ph.D. dissertation, Department of Geography, Pennsylvania State University.

ries, mapping has changed little. The change in map techniques has mirrored faithfully all changes that have taken place in thematic mapping over the same period. Explorations and innovations are needed in this form of mapping, as in all forms of thematic mapping. This essay documents only some of the major developments, but will, perhaps, elicit enough interest in the reader to delve into the historical documents more closely, and to experiment with new forms of symbolization.

References

Baldwin, John, and A.E. Bottoms. 1976. *The Urban Criminal: A Study in Sheffield.* London: Tavistock Publications, Ltd.

Brassel, Kurt E., and Jack J. Utano. 1979. Linking Crime and Census Information Within a Crime Mapping System. *Public Data Use* 7:18-24

Breckenridge, S. P., and E. Abbot. 1912. *The Delinquent Child and the Home.* New York: Russell Sage Foundation (reprinted New York: Arno Press, 1970).

Burgess, E.W. 1925. The Growth of the City: An Introduction to a Research Project. In R.E. Parks, E.W. Burgess, and R.D. McKenzie. *The City.* Chicago: University of Chicago Press.

Burt, Cyril. 1925. *The Young Delinquent.* New York: Appleton-Century Co.

Capone, Donald L., and Woodrow W. Nichols, Jr. 1975. Crime and Distance: An Analysis of Offender Behavior in Space. *Proceedings, Association of American Geographers* 7: 45-49.

———. 1976. Urban Structure and Criminal Mobility. *American Behavioral Scientists* 20: 199-213.

Carter, Ronald Lee. 1974. *The Criminal's Image of the City.* Unpublished Ph.D. dissertation, Department of Geography, University of Oklahoma.

Corsi, T.M., and M.E. Harvey. 1975. The Socio-Economic Determinants of Crime in the City of Cleveland. *Ndift Voor Economischie en Sociale Geograffe* 66: 323-36.

Curry, G. David, and Scott H. Decker. 1998. *Confronting Gangs.* Los Angeles: Roxbury.

Dent, Borden D. 1996. *Cartography: Thematic Map Design.* 4th ed. Dubuque, IA: W.C. Brown.

———. 1998. *Cartography: Thematic Map Design.* 5th ed. Dubuque, IA: WCB/McGraw-Hill.

Figlio, Robert, Simon Hakim, and George F. Rengert, eds. 1986. *Metropolitan Crime Patterns.* Monsey, NY: Criminal Justice Press.

Fletcher, Joseph. 1849. Moral and Educational Statistics of England and Wales. *Journal of the Statistical Society of London* 10: 151-335. Reprinted in 1971 for William Dawson and Sons, Ltd. with permission of the Royal Statistical Society.

Funkhouser, Gary H. 1937. Historical Development of Graphical Representation of Statistical Data. *Orisis* 3: 269-404.

Golledge, Reginald G., and Robert J. Stimson. 1997. *Spatial Behavior: A Geographic Perspective.* New York: Guilford.

Harries, Keith D. 1971. The Geography of American Crime. *Journal of Geography* 70: 204-10.

———. 1980. *Crime and the Environment.* Springfield, IL: Charles C. Thomas, Publishers.

———. 1996a. *Serious Violence: Patterns of Homicide and Assault in America.* 2nd ed. Springfield, IL: Charles C. Thomas.

———. 1996b. The Southern Violence Construct: Evidence from the Survey of Youths in Custody. *Southeastern Geographer* 36: 128-39.

Harries, Keith, and Stanley D. Brunn. 1978. *The Geography of Laws and Justice.* New York: Praeger.

Hayner, Norman S. 1946. Criminogenic Zones in Mexico City. *American Sociological Review* 11: 428–438.

Herbert, David T. 1982. *The Geography of Urban Crime.* London: Longman.

Herbert, David T., and David M. Smith. 1979. *Social Problems and the City.* London: Oxford University Press.

Jones, Huwe, ed. 1993. *Crime and the Urban Environment: The Scottish Experience.* Aldershot, England: Avebury.

Knox, Paul. 1987. *Urban Social Geography.* 2nd ed. New York: John Wiley.

Lambert, John R. 1970. *Crime, Police, and Race Relations: A Study in Birmingham.* New York: Oxford University Press.

Lauder, Bernard. 1954. *Towards an Understanding of Juvenile Delinquency.* New York: Columbia University Press.

Ley, David F. 1972. *The Black Inner City as Frontier Outpost.* Unpublished Ph.D. dissertation, Department of Geography, Pennsylvania State University.

Lunden, Walter A. 1964. *Statistics on Delinquents and Delinquency.* Springfield, IL: Charles C. Thomas.

Mayhew, Henry. 1861. *London Labour and the London Poor.* Vol. IV. London: Griffin, Bohn, and Co.

Mays, John Barron, ed. 1972. *Juvenile Delinquency, the Family, and the Social Group.* London: Longman.

McClintock, F.H. 1963. *Crimes of Violence.* London: MacMillan and Co, Ltd.

McClintock, F.H., and N. Howard Arison. 1968. *Crime in England and Wales.* London: Heineman Educational Books, Ltd.

McKenzie, R.D. 1923. *The Neighborhood: A Study of the Local Life in the City of Columbus, Ohio.* Chicago: University of Chicago Press.

Morris, Terence. 1957. *The Criminal Area: A Study in Social Ecology.* London: Routledge and Kegan, Ltd.

Parks, Mary J. 1987. *American Flow Mapping: A Survey of Flow Maps Found in Twentieth Century Geography Textbooks, Including a Classification of the Various Flow Map Designs.* Unpublished Master's thesis, Department of Geography, Georgia State University.

Phillips, Phillip D. 1972. A Prologue to the Geography of Crime. *Proceedings of the Association of American Geographers* 4: 86-91.

Pocock, Douglas, and Ray Hudson. 1975. *The Geography of Crime.* Unpublished Ph.D. dissertation, Department of Geography, University of Minnesota.

———. 1978. *Images of the Urban Environment.* New York: Columbia University Press.

Pyle, Gerald F. 1974. *The Spatial Dynamics of Crime.* Research Paper Number 159. Chicago: Department of Geography, University of Chicago.

———. 1976. Spatial and Temporal Aspects of Crime in Cleveland, Ohio. *American Behavioral Scientist* 20: 175-98.

Raize, Erwin. 1938. *General Cartography.* New York: McGraw-Hill.

Rand McNally. 1990. *Goode's World Atlas.* 19th ed. Chicago: Rand McNally.

Robinson, Arthur H. 1982. *Early Thematic Mapping in the History of Cartography.* Chicago: University of Chicago Press.

Rose, Harold M., and Paula D. McClain. 1990. Albany: State University of New York Press.

Shannon, Mary Lee. 1976. *The Map Abstract of Criminal-Justice Information: Alabama.* University: University of Alabama Press.

Shaw, Clifford R., and Henry D. McKay. 1942. *Juvenile Delinquency and Urban Areas.* Chicago: University of Chicago Press.

Smith, Christopher J., and Gene E. Patterson. 1980. Cognitive Mapping and the Subjective Geography of Crime. In Daniel E. Georges-Abeyie and Keith D. Harries. *Crime: A Spatial Perspective.* New York: Columbia University Press.

Smith, Susan J. 1986. *Crime, Space, and Society.* Cambridge: Cambridge University Press.

Sumrall, Raymond O. 1976. *The Map Abstract of Criminal-Justice Information: Alabama.* University: University of Alabama Press.

———. 1978. *The Map Abstract of Trends in Calls for Police Service: Birmingham, Alabama, 1975-1976.* University: University of Alabama Press.

Tappan, Paul W. 1949. *Juvenile Delinquency.* New York: McGraw-Hill.

Taylor, Carl S. 1990. *Dangerous Society.* East Lansing: Michigan State University Press.

Thrower, Norman J.W. 1996. *Maps and Civilization.* Chicago: University of Chicago Press.

Tufte, Edward R. 1983. *The Visual Display of Quantitative Information.* Cheshire, CT: Graphics Press.

———. 1990. *Envisioning Information.* Cheshire, CT: Graphics Press.

United States Bureau of the Census. 1972. *Ninth Census of the United States.* Washington, DC: United States Department of Commerce.

Voss, Harwin L., and David M. Peterson, eds. 1971. *Ecology, Crime and Delinquency.* New York: Appleton-Century-Crofts.

White, R. Clyde. 1932. The Relation of Felonies to Environmental Factors in Indianapolis. *Social Forces* 10(4): 498-509.

CHAPTER 2

Crimes of Personal Violence

Most people are particularly concerned with crimes that cause harm or death to a person, even though in reality these crimes comprise a small proportion of all crimes committed. According to the *Uniform Crime Reports (UCR)* crime clock of the Federal Bureau of Investigation (FBI), a murder occurs every 29 minutes, a forcible rape every 5 minutes, a robbery every minute, and an aggravated assault every 31 seconds (Federal Bureau of Investigation 1997). This measure of frequency places violent crimes into a temporal framework that tells us we are more likely to be a victim of aggravated assault than of any other violence. Although this knowledge may seem strangely comforting, many crimes are connected to each other. For instance, an assault victim can also become a murder, rape, or robbery victim.

An estimated 1.6 million violent crimes were reported to law enforcement in 1997 (Federal Bureau of Investigation 1997). The good news is that violent crime has decreased to the lowest level since 1988. The highest violent crime rate (victims/100,000) was recorded in the South and the lowest was reported in the Midwest. According to 1997 FBI data, aggravated assault (63 percent) accounted for most violent crimes committed, followed by robbery (30 percent), forcible rape (6 percent), and murder (1 percent).

For *aggravated assault*, the 1997 data revealed the following:

- The rate was highest in the South and lowest in the Northeast.
- Reports decreased in all regions.
- The rate was highest in metropolitan areas.
- July was the peak month for aggravated assaults while February was the lowest.
- Of all aggravated assaults, 35 percent involved blunt objects and clubs; 26 percent involved personal weapons such as hands, fists, and feet; and 20 percent involved firearms.
- Aggravated assaults had a 58-percent clearance rate (number of solved crimes) by law enforcement.

For *robbery*, the 1997 data demonstrated the following:

- The rate was highest in the Northeast and lowest in the Midwest.
- Reports decreased in all regions.
- The rate was highest in cities with populations of one million or more.
- January was the peak month for robberies while February and April were lowest.
- Streets and highways were the most common setting for robbery.
- Robbery had a 26-percent clearance rate by law enforcement.

For *forcible rape*, the 1997 data showed the following:

- The rate was highest in the South and lowest in the Northeast.
- Reports decreased in all regions except the South, which remained constant.
- The rate was highest in metropolitan areas, despite a 10-year decline.
- July was the peak month for rape while December was the lowest.
- Forcible rape had over a 50-percent clearance rate by law enforcement.

For *murder*, the 1997 data indicated the following:

- The rate was highest in the South and lowest in the Northeast.
- Reports decreased in all regions.
- The rate was highest in metropolitan areas.
- July was the peak month while February was the lowest.
- The most frequent weapon used was a firearm.
- In 48 percent of murder cases, victims knew their assailant, while 14 percent of assailants were strangers and the remainder were unknown.
- Murder had a 66-percent clearance rate by law enforcement.

Official statistics reveal that the clearance rate for murder in 1997 was higher than for other violent crimes. Another interesting comparison is that July appears to be the month when most violent crimes are committed, except for robbery. Large metropolitan areas continue to have the highest rates even though those rates may have declined. Decreases in all types of violent crime occurred in all regions except for rape in the South. Also, the South is the region with the highest rates of all violent crime except robbery.

While the *Uniform Crime Reports (UCR)* by the Federal Bureau of Investigation (FBI) focuses on police reports and arrests, many crimes are never reported to police. Therefore, studies such as the *National Crime Victimization Survey (NCVS)* by the Bureau of Justice Statistics (BJS) attempt to capture the other side of crime by relying on surveys designed to measure the extent of crime reported and unreported. Because various statistical databases, such as these two mentioned, measure different aspects of criminal behavior, comparisons are not recommended. Also, geographic scale can affect interpretation. The Bureau of Justice Statistics (BJS) indicates that living in the West places a person at a higher rate of victimization for robbery, rape, and assault (U.S. Department of Justice 1997). However, data also confirm that those living in urban areas are at a higher risk of being victimized (U.S. Department of Justice 1998a). Therefore a person living in a rural community in the West may be at a lower risk than a person living in a large urban area in the Northeast.

An interesting finding is that crimes of violence take place most frequently on the street near home (19.3 percent), inside a school building or on school property (14.2 percent), or at or in one's home (14.0 percent) (U.S. Department of Justice 1998b). Figure 2-1 illustrates how prominent the home area is to each crime of rape, assault, and robbery. The darkest area depicts the one of highest risk. Most occurrences of rape occur inside the victim's home, although many take place more than five miles away. Most assaults take place more than five miles away from a victim's home, and most robberies occur within a radius of a one mile or less of home.

The following essays on crimes of personal violence are presented from the spatial perspective by experts in their fields. First, Keith Harries examines the spatial and temporal variations in homicide in the United States and explains why these variations occur. Second, Jose Javier Lopez discusses assault from three different areas: the United States, the state of Minnesota, and Puerto Rico. In her essay on rape, Kathleen Basile gives a brief historical background, provides details on the types of rape, and offers a spatial analysis based on statistical data. Doug Williamson's essay on robbery includes a description of the victims and perpetrators, focusing on arrests in the United States as well as on a case study from New York City.

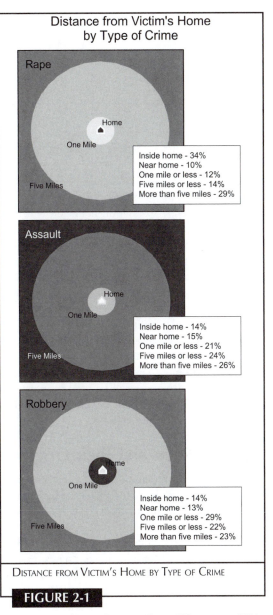

DISTANCE FROM VICTIM'S HOME BY TYPE OF CRIME

FIGURE 2-1

Source: Bureau of Justice Statistics, *Criminal Victimization, 1994.* NCJ-158022, 1996.

References

Federal Bureau of Investigation (FBI). 1997. *Uniform Crime Reports.* <http://www.fbi.gov>.

U.S. Department of Justice. 1997. Bureau of Justice Statistics. *Criminal Victimization 1996: Changes 1995-96 with Trends 1993-96.* Bulletin NCJ-165812. Washington, DC: U.S. Department of Justice.

———. 1998a. Bureau of Justice Statistics. *Criminal Victimization in the United States, 1995.* NCJ-171129. Washington, DC: U.S. Department of Justice.

———. 1998b. Bureau of Justice Statistics. *Perceptions of Neighborhood Crime, 1995.* Special Report NCJ-165811. Washington, DC: U.S. Department of Justice.

Homicide

Keith Harries

The terms *murder* and *homicide* tend to be used interchangeably in the literature, although there is some difference in meaning that should be clarified. *Homicide* is a generic term referring to the killing of a person. It may be accidental or intentional (and either justifiable, as in the case of self-defense, or not justifiable). Accidental homicide is usually referred to as *manslaughter*, as in vehicular manslaughter. *Murder* is generally more narrowly defined as the unlawful killing of a person with "malice aforethought." How this is interpreted legally from place to place depends on the laws of the 50 states and the federal government, as well as of the military, each of which has its own interpretation embodied in statutes. Legal variations determine, for example, the criteria for first degree or second degree murder, or the qualifications for the death penalty, if present. (*See also* my essay "Capital Punishment" in Chapter 8.) In this essay, the terms *homicide* and *murder* will be used interchangeably, but they will conceptually refer to murder, excluding justifiable homicides and manslaughters.

High U.S. Rates and Their Origin

Homicide is a particularly serious problem in the United States. Homicide rates, adjusted for population, are exceptionally high when compared to other developed nations, even when recent rate declines are taken into account. An in-depth comparison of victimization rates between the U.S. and England showed that for most major crimes, rates in England had overtaken those for the U.S. over the course of the last couple of decades. The conspicuous exception was the murder rate, with that of the U.S. in 1996 nearly six times that of England, a difference typical of that between the U.S. and the developed world (Langan and Farrington 1998). A fundamental question with respect to homicide in the U.S. is why do rates differ so radically from other roughly comparable nations? The answer to that question lies substantially in the social ecology of larger American cities. In 1997, cities in the over 250,000 size class had homicide rates on the order of 20 per 100,000 persons. This rate compared to about 12 per 100,000 persons for cities in the 100,000-249,000 class. Between 1977 and 1997, cities in the one million and over category had rates that were in every year sharply higher than the 500,000-999,000 and smaller size classes. The practical effect of this rate difference was that in a typical year, some 60 percent of all murders occurred in the larger cities, and the balance in smaller cities and suburban and rural counties.

A distinguishing feature of larger cities is the presence of substantial minority communities, which are often subject to profound social stresses in some ways typical of less developed countries, e.g., poverty, substandard public services, decaying infrastructure (including housing abandonment), lack of amenities, and high levels of drug and alcohol addiction and illicit gun transactions, accompanied by extraordinary levels of violent crime. If we were to zoom in on small areas of some larger cities, we would find homicide rates that in the recent past have exceeded 100 per 100,000 per year. This is equivalent to 10 murders in a year in a community of 10,000 persons, and this type of occurrence has been all but commonplace in various cities, including the nation's capital, Washington, D.C. (Figure 2-2).

One census tract in Washington had a homicide rate the equivalent of 126 per 100,000 per year for the 3.5-year period from January 1985 to June 1988, a time when the national rate was about 8.3 per 100,000. A set of 14 tracts in Washington, D.C., all had at least 10 homicides in the same period. These tracts were on average 94 percent African American and more than half the households were both low income and headed by females. Part of one tract, a street then called Drake Place, achieved national notoriety in 1988 when one housing project with a nominal population of about 4,000 had 8 murders, 92 reported assaults, 65 auto thefts, 154 drug arrests, and 27 robberies, all in the calendar year 1988 (Harries 1997).

Thus, a distinguishing characteristic of homicide in the United States is place-to-place variation that is so striking as to be almost incomprehensible. Not only is there variation, but that variation is accompanied by extremely steep gradients such that homicide rates, and the rates of other crimes, fall or rise sharply depending on one's direction of travel. One of the high homicide tracts in Washington referred to above was a mile from the White House. Another was a mile from Capitol Hill. These "spikes," or "hot spots" of homicide distinguish the U.S. from its developed peer nations and produce the elevated rates for larger cities and for the nation as a whole.

Another sharp difference between the U.S. and its peers rests in attitudes toward gun control. Many other developed countries (and many less developed nations) have a history of what Americans perceive to be strict controls, determining who can own what, how guns are to be stored, and who has access to them. The current position of American culture on the firearm issue does not, of course, directly cause murder or other violence, but may facilitate gun trafficking and the possession of guns by persons who eventually misuse them. Even on this question, we see geographic variation, with states differing in whether, and how, to deal with guns. One pattern that has been established is that illicit guns tend to flow, as one would expect, from states with less regulation to those with more. Thus Vir-

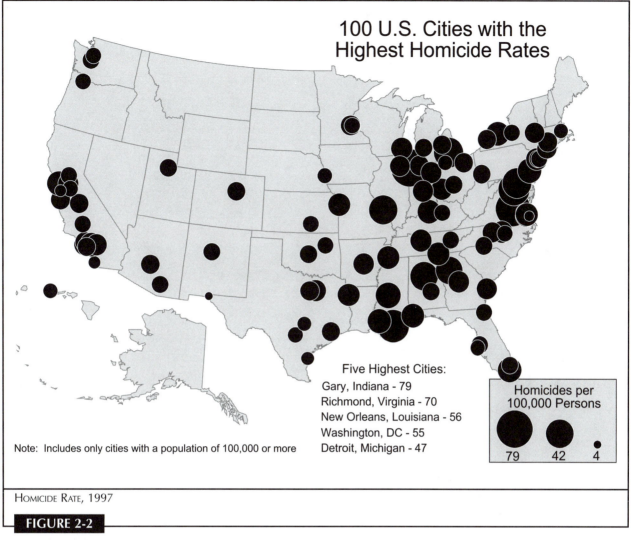

100 U.S. Cities with the Highest Homicide Rates

Five Highest Cities:

Gary, Indiana - 79
Richmond, Virginia - 70
New Orleans, Louisiana - 56
Washington, DC - 55
Detroit, Michigan - 47

Note: Includes only cities with a population of 100,000 or more

Homicides per 100,000 Persons

79   42   4

HOMICIDE RATE, 1997

FIGURE 2-2

Sources: FBI Uniform Crime Reports, 1997. Preliminary Annual Release and Statistical Abstract of the United States, 1998.

ginia is a supplier of illicit guns to neighboring Maryland and Washington, D.C.

Variation in Time and Space

Temporal variations in murder are no less interesting than the extraordinary geographic variations. When one combines temporal and spatial variation, questions arise as to why certain places may have higher or lower rates at certain times—or why their rates remain high or low over time. Far from the linear or exponential increase in murder rates over time that one might presuppose has accompanied alleged changing societal values in the U.S., there is in reality wide variation over time. Rates rose steadily from 1900 to a peak near 10 per 100,000 by the end of Prohibition in 1933. Rates then fell steeply to a low by the end of World War II in 1945, only to rise sharply when large numbers of young men returned from the military. By 1950, the national rate stood at about 5 per 100,000 persons, dipped to a post-1950 low of 4 in 1957, then rose to a twentieth-century peak of 10.2 in 1980 (Figure 2-3). Rates then fell through the mid-1980s only to rise again to a peak of 9.8 in 1991,

with a subsequent decline to 6.8 in 1997. Detailed analysis of these temporal variations is beyond the scope of this essay. However, demographic change, associated with the size of the population of youthful males, and cultural factors, such as the maturity of drug markets, the gun control environment, and the effectiveness of the criminal justice system and of trauma medicine, all play a role.

These factors all have geographic components affecting the pattern of homicides. Trauma medicine, for example, has the effect of depressing the homicide rate by turning events that would have been murders into aggravated assaults through timely medical intervention in the first hour following traumatic injury. Trauma centers have a distinctive geography, typically located in big cities, often in close proximity to underclass neighborhoods characterized by high murder rates. Thus, such centers have maximum effectiveness in blunting the murder rate. In Baltimore, Maryland, for example, two trauma centers (the University of Maryland Medical Center and the Johns Hopkins University Hospital) are located in or adjacent to the two principal persistent clusters of homicides.

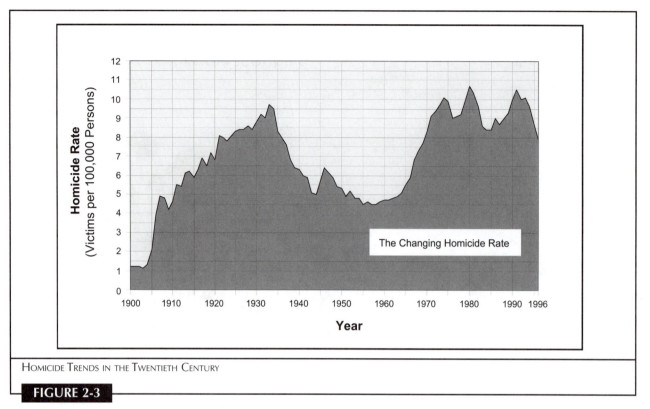

HOMICIDE TRENDS IN THE TWENTIETH CENTURY

FIGURE 2-3

Source: National Center for Health Statistics, *Vital Statistics*, Revised (11/22/98).

Regional Variation

Considerable interest has been generated over the last several decades as a result of research drawing renewed attention to elevated homicide rates in the American South. State-level geographies of murder rates by states for the quiquennia from 1940 through 1980 showed persistently high rates in a core of southern states: the Carolinas, Georgia, Florida, Alabama, Mississippi, and Louisiana (Harries 1997). This persistent southern concentration has been variously referred to as "the southern subculture of violence" (O'Connor and Lizotte 1979) and the "Southern Violence Construct (SVC)" (Hawley 1987). Interpretations have varied among cultural and economic causes, or combinations thereof. Although national statistics show that African Americans are seven times more likely than whites to be murder victims and eight times more likely to commit murder, racial interpretations of the homicide problem, whether in the South or elsewhere, have never withstood close examination. When geographic analyses of murder rates are controlled for economic factors, such as the poverty rate, the race variable loses significance. Indeed, middle class African-American communities typically enjoy low murder rates comparable to middle class white communities, as do integrated middle class neighborhoods.

Considerable controversy has centered on the role of culture in high southern homicide rates, and the argument remains largely unresolved. Proponents claim that the South is culturally different from the non-South, with different attitudes in matters such as the defense of personal honor, levels of firearm ownership, and values tied to the prevalence of fundamentalist Christianity. Opponents note that research using economic measures as independent variables has achieved high levels of explanation of regional homicide rate variations without resorting to measures of culture. One possibility is that both cultural and economic factors are important, but that cultural factors have been overlooked because they are more or less intangible and harder to measure compared to economic indicators that can be readily found in the decennial census and other statistical sources.

The recent geography of homicide rates (Figure 2-4) suggests some basis for assertions that rates are higher in the South. A swath of counties, particularly in the coastal Carolinas and into Georgia and Alabama, exhibit relatively high rates as do various counties in Arkansas, Texas, and other southern states. However, the pattern is by no means exclusively southern in its emphasis and this serves to remind that the intensity of the higher southern focus has faded somewhat in recent decades. Another complication is the difficulty presented in representing rates cartographically. While counties give the map a fine "grain" compared to states, larger counties tend to draw the eye, even though they may be insignificant in absolute terms. Conversely, some major sources of murders, such as Washington, D.C., or Baltimore, are too small to have a visual impact.

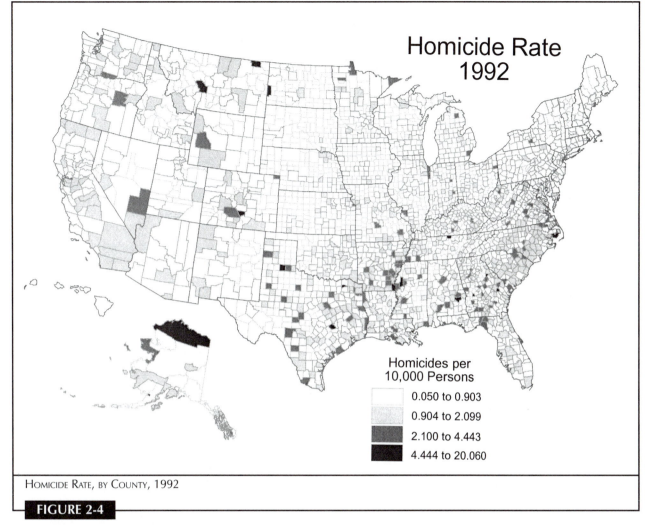

Homicide Rate 1992

Homicides per
10,000 Persons

☐ 0.050 to 0.903
▨ 0.904 to 2.099
▩ 2.100 to 4.443
■ 4.444 to 20.060

HOMICIDE RATE, BY COUNTY, 1992

FIGURE 2-4

Source: FBI Uniform Crime Reports, 1992.

Demographics and Geography

Place-to-place variations in demography provide an element of explanation for geographic variation. In terms of age, the 18-24 age group is dominant for both offenders and victims. Homicide is a male crime, with 68 percent of murders having a male victim and offender. Victimization rates for African-American males are some 10 times those of comparably aged white males, although rates have fallen in recent years. Offending rates are some 12 times higher, and have also fallen recently. Insofar as these demographics differ from place to place, homicide risk will also vary. Although the demographic dimension cannot tell the whole story, when combined with the economics of poverty, it is a strong predictor of a substance abuse and domestic abuse culture that in turn is a predictor of crime, including murder.

Guns and Geography

The Bureau of Justice Statistics has noted that "homicides are most often committed by guns, especially handguns" with a toll of some 10,000 persons in 1997 (Bureau of Jus-

tice Statistics 1999). Like other attributes of homicide, gun ownership and use has a spatial dimension. For example, gun ownership is more prevalent in the South than in other regions, and recent evidence shows that demographics and gun use are interrelated. A study of patients at Washington, D.C., General Hospital showed that the major risk of gunshot and stabbing injuries began at age 12 and continued to increase until age 18, when it fell off somewhat (Goldstein 1999).

Guns Used in Homicides

The use of guns in homicides varies regionally as shown in Figure 2-5 with some states, such as Colorado and New Mexico, in the 40–50 percent range, while others have levels as high as nearly 90 percent. While we might expect that this map would reflect general levels of gun ownership, this does not appear to be the case in that the southern tradition of high reported ownership levels is not particularly prominent. That the highest levels are observed in Wyoming, Arizona, and California serves to remind that direct comparisons between states are not always meaningful. Wyoming, with only about 20 homicides per year cannot be properly compared to California, with several thousand. More meaningful, perhaps, is examination of the impact of dysfunctional inner cities on this map, with their recent histories of elevated levels of violence rooted in drug market conflicts. Figure 2-5 reflects several factors: random variation based in some states on few cases (e.g., Wyoming), traditionally high levels of gun availability (the South), and the influence of embedded inner cities with patterns of illicit gun trafficking and ownership (e.g., California, Maryland, Illinois).

Guns and homicide became strongly intertwined after about 1985, when the cocaine/crack epidemic began to sweep through American cities, leading to fierce drug market territory conflicts. Changes in gun technology, with the wide availability of automatic weapons, meant devastating firepower on the streets. This availability had the effect of enabling shooting styles that were not feasible before, such as the drive-by, in which a burst of automatic or semiautomatic fire might hit the intended target, while minimizing risk for the perpetrators. Combined with new bullet technology, such as the hollow point that spreads internally on

impact, tearing up tissue, firearms became more lethal. Thus, the geography of drug markets became, to a considerable degree, a surrogate for the geography of homicide, with intense conflicts over high stakes. Given that there was an "origin-diffusion" effect in the spread of coke/crack, different places were affected at different times, with a lag as the epidemic took hold, perhaps fostered by the penetration of organized gangs, themselves an intensely territorial phenomena.

Boundary Effects

Geographic comparisons of crime rates in general, and in the present context, homicide rates in particular, are affected by the locations of political boundaries with respect to homicide hot spots. Typically, so-called inner cities have high rates owing to their disproportionate concentration of urban pathologies. However, inner cities are not created equal in the sense that some are "overbounded," most are "underbounded," and others, for want of a better term, "appropriately" bounded.

What does this mean? An underbounded city is one in which the urbanized area spreads far beyond the limits of

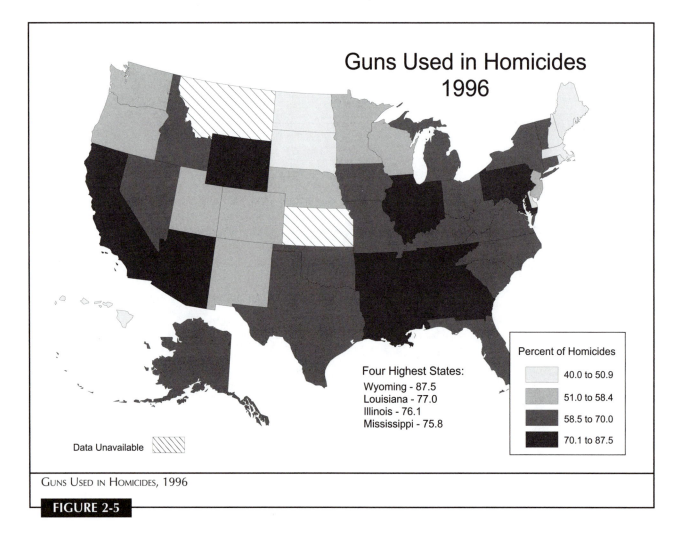

Guns Used in Homicides
1996

Four Highest States:
Wyoming - 87.5
Louisiana - 77.0
Illinois - 76.1
Mississippi - 75.8

Percent of Homicides

40.0 to 50.9
51.0 to 58.4
58.5 to 70.0
70.1 to 87.5

Data Unavailable

GUNS USED IN HOMICIDES, 1996

FIGURE 2-5

the "name" city of the metropolis. Most major cities are underbounded, with suburbs, many incorporated, spreading far from the center, spilling over the city limits. Chicago, San Francisco, Los Angeles, New Orleans, Atlanta, New York, and Washington, D.C., are obvious examples. The effect is to elevate the homicide rates of such cities above rates that would be expressed if the name city were to coincide in territorial extent with the urbanized, or actual built-up, area. This happens because calculated rates are a function of the relationship between numerator and denominator (homicides/population); if city crime rates were based on functional urban areas, the numerator (homicides) would be only slightly increased because suburban homicides were included. However, the denominator (population) would be substantially increased, thus deflating the rate. An example of one of the more unusual overbounded cities is Oklahoma City, with a homicide rate in a recent year of 14 per 100,000 compared to 46 for Atlanta, 44 for Baltimore, and 86 for New Orleans. One could conclude that Oklahoma City has no "inner city" pathology or underclass, but a more appropriate inference is that the suburbs of Oklahoma City statistically "wash out" the effects of the inner city owing to overbounding.

Conclusion

Homicide rates vary dramatically in time and space. One of the most striking geographic generalizations is that homicides tend to manifest as hot spots with remarkably high rates of occurrence in small areas, accompanied by steep gradients of decline with distance from those hot spots. Hot spots frequently persist over long time periods, expressing the enduring presence of an underclass and the substance abuse and other dysfunctionalities that typically accompany poverty. Another corollary consideration is the erosion of the urban tax base that might otherwise provide a social and economic safety net, given that depopulation characterizes most of the major urban centers with the highest homicide rates. Urban poverty is the central explanatory fact of the geography of American homicide. Regional variation is a secondary theme, as yet not fully understood. The question of capital punishment as a deterrent to homicide and other aspects of that issue is discussed in my essay on "Capital Punishment" in Chapter 8. Figure 8-47 in that essay combines the state-level homicide rate for 1997 with recent execution statistics as a supplement to that discussion.

References

Bureau of Justice Statistics. 1999. *Homicide Trends in the U.S.* <http://www.ojp.usdoj.gov/bjs/homicide/overview.htm>.

Goldstein, A. 1999. Violent Injury "Epidemic" Starts at Age 12: Risks of Serious Gunshot or Knife Wounds Increase through 17, D.C. Study Says. *Washington Post*, February 21, p. C5.

Harries, K.D. 1997. *Serious Violence: Patterns of Homicide and Assault in America.* 2nd ed. Springfield, IL: Charles C. Thomas.

Hawley, F.F. 1987. The Black Legend in Southern Studies: Violence, Ideology, and Academe. *North American Culture* 3: 29-52.

Langan, P.A., and D.P. Farrington. 1998. *Crime and Justice in the United States and in England and Wales, 1981-96.* Washington, DC: Bureau of Justice Statistics, U.S. Department of Justice.

O'Connor, J.F., and A. Lizotte 1979. The Southern "Subculture of Violence" Thesis and Patterns of Gun Ownership. *Social Problems* 25: 420-29.

Assault

Jose Javier Lopez

The criminal justice literature recognizes two major categories of assault: simple assault and aggravated assault. *Simple assault* inflicts minor or no physical injury on the victim (Adler et al. 1991). A felonious version of assault is the type denoted as *aggravated assault*. According to a recent Federal Bureau of Investigation (FBI) definition, "aggravated assault is an unlawful attack by one person upon another for the purpose of inflicting severe or aggravated bodily injury" (Federal Bureau of Investigation 1996: 31). This criminal action often includes the use of a weapon against the victim (Titus Reid 1988). Handguns are among the most commonly used weapons employed by the aggressor. This type of weapon was present in 32 percent of aggravated assaults involving strangers and 21 percent of the cases dealing with acquaintances (Harries 1997). In 1996, 34 percent of aggravated assaults were committed with blunt objects and other weapons; hands, fists, and feet (classed as personal weapons) accounted for 26 percent of assaults; firearms were used in 22 percent; and knives/cutting instruments totaled 18 percent (Federal Bureau of Investigation 1996).

With the addition of a firearm an aggravated assault can easily become a homicide. These two types of criminal behavior share similar characteristics. However, academics and professionals still debate the validity of related social factors in explaining the spatial and temporal dynamics of each of these crimes. For example, a significant portion of the criminal justice literature claims that the vast majority of assaults and homicides involve persons who are either known to or related to the victim(s). The 1994 *National Crime Victimization Survey*, however, found that 60.8 percent of aggravated assaults involved strangers (Bureau of Justice Statistics 1997: 29). Other common factors between assaults and homicide are similar geographic distributions and young, male offenders. Demographics for aggravated assault include 60 percent white, 38 percent black, and 82 percent male (Federal Bureau of Investigation 1996: 34). Likewise, other social behaviors and characteristics have been correlated to aggravated assault. Brawls due to the influence of alcohol and narcotics are a portion of the causal variables mentioned under assault and murder scenarios. For example, literature in criminology frequently presents investigations that point to a relationship between alcohol and violence. Alcohol can cause aggressive behavior due to the following factors (Adler et al. 1991: 327):

- Alcohol can reduce the restraints on aggression.

- Alcohol also escalates aggression by reducing people's awareness of what will happen to them if they act on their urges.

Alcoholism is prevalent in some of the most industrialized nations of the world. According to Park (1971), this problem has its historical origins in manufacturing nations, followed by developing regions, with industrialization strategies altering tradition-oriented communal attitudes. Industrialization causes the emergence of alienated labor with scattered moments of inactivity accompanied by hedonistic use of alcohol. In addition, the industrialist and capitalist character that emerges in a manufacturing region encourages the consumption of alcohol due to "money-making reasons" and as a way of "socializing." "Money-making reasons" refers to when alcoholic beverage producers aggressively market their products to newly affluent persons where industrialization has occurred. Heath (1995: 345) concurs with Park's observations by pointing out that "industrialization separates the workplace from the home and creates a new distinction between work and leisure." Alcohol abuse has definitely taken its toll in terms of family and community stability because its abuse often results in aggressive behavior.

Statistics reveal that 7 out of every 10 arrests for violent crime are aggravated assaults (Federal Bureau of Investigation 1996). Although assaults are the most commonly reported crimes to police, they are believed to be underreported (Adler et al. 1991; Macionis 1989). Family members or friends involved in an assault incident often prefer not to inform the police about the aggression, such as in domestic violence cases. In addition to the volume of cases, circumstances surrounding these incidents often remain unclear thereby making it more difficult for law enforcement agents to gather information on assault cases than on homicides.

Spatial and Temporal Dynamics of Assault

Criminologists and government agencies dealing with crime assert that assault and homicide are more common in urban areas. For instance, the FBI reports that in 1996 the assault rate in metropolitan areas was 424 per 100,000 inhabitants; cities outside these large metropolitan areas had a rate of 350; rural counties experienced a rate of 177. However, we need to remember that many criminals remain unknown to police in remote areas, something that may be the result of less surveillance in rural communities than in inner cities. A police car intensively patrolling the inner city is not a rare scene in urban areas. Nevertheless, the picture regarding assault is changing even though the areas reporting the highest rates of assault continue to be mainly urban, poor, and populated by minority groups. Ackerman (1998: 372) points to the "mounting evidence that crime is a growing problem for smaller communities." His analysis of crime in these places reviews findings by other researchers who observed that small cities (fewer than 100,000 inhabitants) witnessed a significant increase in property and violent offenses between 1977 and 1988, outpacing large metropolitan areas with populations over 500,000.

An industrial nation can suffer additional stress as it responds to post-industrial economic development. Sometimes the impact is negative for those affected by this transformation process (Rose and Deskins 1980). Various investigations illustrate this condition by showing that the arrival of a high-tech and capital-intensive industry coincided with a massive wave of social problems in several manufacturing regions. These factors—increasing unemployment rates, growing social inequality, and poverty—have been identified as problems that have affected the crime rate in parts of the American "Rustbelt" region and in Puerto Rico during the last decades. During the 1960s, most investment in Puerto Rico was oriented toward industries that employed a relatively low number of workers in high-tech and capital-intensive operations (Fortuno-Candelas 1993; Santiago-Valles 1994). The arrival of these industries did not necessarily provide benefits and prosperity to the host communities. These manufacturing activities are capital intensive and their chances of providing significant local employment are slim. The Midwest experienced a similar fate in some of its heavy industries. For example, during the 1990s, various American car manufacturing plants ceased operations or moved to the southern part of the country. Most of these plants were unable to operate with the same level of efficiency as their Japanese counterparts. Between the 1950s and 1970s, the island of Puerto Rico experienced a short-lived industrialization boom era compared in some way with the industrial revolution experienced by the Great Lakes states and the Midwest before World War II. Another similarity between Puerto Rico and some Midwestern states, such as Minnesota, is that the metropolitan area that hosts the capital also is the economic and industrial center of the state or territory. For example, the Minneapolis-St. Paul metropolitan region and San Juan, the capital of Puerto Rico, are politico-economic cores. Some of these industrial centers are changing in terms of the new industries arriving to these areas. During this same period, several Japanese car companies established factories in the Midwest, but did not employ as many people as the old American carmakers. The same situation is occurring with other types of industries in this region, and is even occurring in agriculture with highly mechanized commercial grain agribusinesses. Because many individuals lack the opportunity to find a job, unem-

ployment becomes a disruptive force and a source of social disorganization.

Maps showing the change in the occurrence of assault are pointing to areas that many of us perceive as free of violence. Some areas suffering an increase in the occurrence of assault are located in the Great Plains, the Midwest, and New England. For instance, the Minnesota counties that experienced dramatic increases in the number of assaults between 1992 and 1995 are outside the Twin Cities metropolitan area (Figure 2-6). Some of these counties have a rural socioeconomic character.

The presentation of various maps dealing with the changes in the occurrence of assault in the United States, the state of Minnesota, and the American territory of Puerto Rico is useful for the examination of this offense's geographic aspects. The maps present three areal units which are significantly different in terms of scale, population, socioeconomic complexity, and political-administrative importance. However, comparisons result in interesting similarities in the spatial occurrence of assault. For example, although Minnesota and Puerto Rico are diverse in terms of economics and demographics, location and size, they share the characteristic of increasing and decreasing rates of assault. Some of the areas experiencing an increase in assault are not necessarily the most heavily populated nor those with a long history of violence. The distribution of assault in Minnesota, for example, clearly shows that this offense is not simply an urban problem. Geographers ask such questions as: "Are rural areas experiencing an increase in the occurrence of assault?" and "How much of an increase or decrease in urban geopolitical units has occurred?" Observed patterns in the presented maps may offer answers.

One interesting observation about assault is that occurrences exhibit distinct peaking in summer, on weekends, and in evening and night hours when more interaction and socialization occur between individuals. Over a five-year period (1992-1996), the FBI (1996) has documented a seasonal trend of aggravated assault with July consistently the highest month.

Assault Distribution in the United States

It is possible to find regional differences in terms of assault rates. Harries (1973: 6) conducted a study about the spatial aspects of violence and metropolitan population in the early 1970s; he found that the "regional focus" of assault is in the southern United States. The map of assault rates for 1997 (Figure 2-7) demonstrates that this pattern still exists. The top four areas in assault rates (Washington, D.C., South Carolina, Florida, and New Mexico) are located in the southern portion of the country. However, if changes in the occurrence of assault are considered for three periods within the 1990s, some states outside of both the southern U.S. and the industrial Northeast exhibit increases in this crime (Figure 2-8). For example, Iowa experienced an

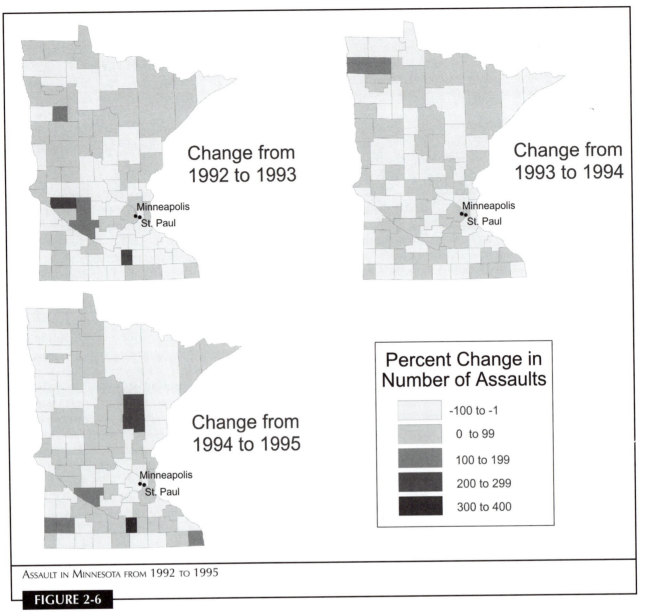

Change from
1992 to 1993

Minneapolis
St. Paul

Change from
1993 to 1994

Minneapolis
St. Paul

Change from
1994 to 1995

Minneapolis
St. Paul

**Percent Change in
Number of Assaults**

-100 to -1

0 to 99

100 to 199

200 to 299

300 to 400

ASSAULT IN MINNESOTA FROM 1992 TO 1995

FIGURE 2-6

Source: Minnesota Bureau of Apprehension.

increase during the first and third periods and South Dakota during the first and second periods. On the other hand, Alabama experienced a decline during these three periods even though it is in the South. Alabama is also not among the top four areas in assault rate on the 1997 map. Despite current evidence that Alabama appears to be an oasis in the region of violence, it has not always had this reputation. During the 1960s, Harries (1974) analyzed crime in the United States, and on one of his maps depicting the regional distribution Alabama appears among the states with the highest rate of assault. Florida was in the same category on the map that employed 1968 data. Harries's 1968 map and the 1997 map presented in Figure 2-7 have other similarities. For example, the Upper Midwest and the northeastern corner of the United States are the regions with the lowest rates of assault. Ironically, the maps illustrating the change in number of assaults show some states in these re-

gions reporting an increase of this crime. Another illustration is Delaware, which is not a state many people link with violence; however, in the first and third periods, increases in assault occurrence were present in the state.

Although these places are not traditionally associated with violence, smaller urban areas are reporting increases in the numbers of assaults. For example, Ackerman (1998) emphasized that smaller cities in the country are experiencing increasing rates of crime and that the largest increase in violent crime in Ohio occurred in small cities with a population between 50,000 and 99,999. This illustration contradicts the general perception that large metropolitan areas are more likely to experience a dramatic increase in the occurrence of violence.

Many Americans idealize small cities and reject living in large metropolitan centers. Nevertheless, the reality in the Midwest is that small cities have difficulty competing against the economic advantages that large urban areas possess. According to Ackerman (1998), small cities in the American manufacturing belt have problems inviting new productive activities, and some members of their population lack skills for employment in the service sector of the economy. For this reason, pockets of poverty and economic deprivation can be found in various communities across the Midwest. Some of these small cities hosted heavy industries that enjoyed significant importance during World War II. Their downtown areas are muted witnesses of the prosperity that once marked the landscape. Tall bank buildings erected before the 1940s are present in some cities that today have populations of less than 50,000. Today, however, some of these structures are currently vacant or severely neglected. On the other hand, nothing with more than 10 stories has been built in these small cities since World War II. Construction of business buildings has been unpretentious during the last decades. This contrast between edifices, erected before the 1940s, with more than a dozen levels, and the more recent modest structures demonstrates the economic transition and transformation of small urban areas in the Midwest.

Danville (Illinois), Terre Haute (Indiana), Lima (Ohio), and many other cities in this region possess central business districts that display these types of dichotomies suggesting a more prosperous past. Adjacent to the cities' declining areas are neighborhoods affected by poverty and neglect. High rates of aggravated assault are related to low family income (Harries 1997). In the case of rural towns linked with the agricultural sector of the economy, similar situations exist. For example, the suitcase farm, which is common in the Great Plains, is a type of operation that is owned and operated by individuals who do not live on the farm. In addition, most of the workers are migratory. According to Jordan and Domosh (1998: 103), this type of operation is rapidly replacing the traditional American family farm. Furthermore, the large commercialization of agricultural operations is responsible for the decline of job opportunities in the countryside. A visit to the center of some of these towns in farming regions reveals a picture similar to the central business district of small Midwestern cities.

Assault Distribution in Minnesota

Minnesota has experienced some of the socioeconomic transitions that the most populated states of the Midwest have witnessed during the last decades in terms of industry and

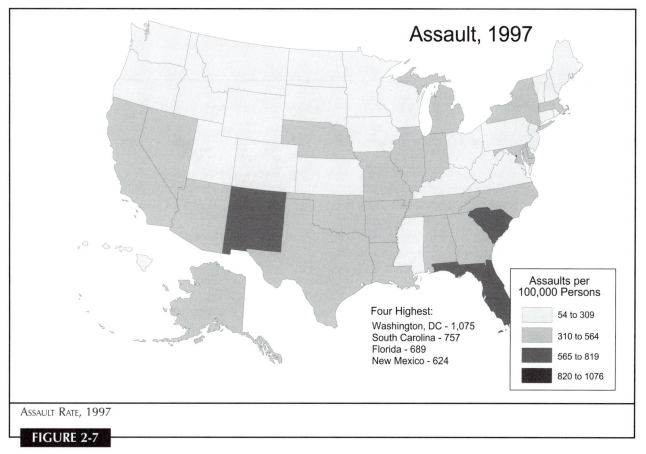

ASSAULT RATE, 1997

FIGURE 2-7

Source: FBI Uniform Crime Reports, 1997 Preliminary Annual Release.

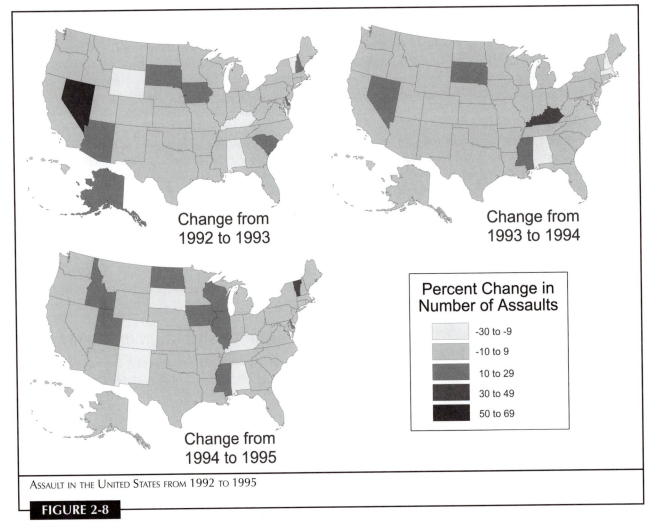

Change from 1992 to 1993

Change from 1993 to 1994

Change from 1994 to 1995

Percent Change in Number of Assaults

-30 to -9
-10 to 9
10 to 29
30 to 49
50 to 69

ASSAULT IN THE UNITED STATES FROM 1992 TO 1995

FIGURE 2-8

Source: U.S. Department of Justice.

agriculture. The maps indicating the percent change in the number of assaults in Minnesota (Figure 2-6) show counties outside the Twin Cities metropolitan area experiencing a significant increase in the occurrence of assault. For example, during the last period, 1994-95, Aitkin County reported a significant increase in the number of assaults. This north-central county is among the group of state subdivisions experiencing high unemployment in relation to other counties and high assault rates during the early 1990s. In addition, the median income is low in comparison to the rest of the state.

On the other hand, during the first period, 1992-93, and third period, 1994-95, Waseca County in the south-central part of the state presented the most significant increase of assaults in this part of Minnesota. This is not a county that people in Minnesota associate with poverty or violence, and the unemployment rate is low. Various counties in the west-central portion of the state experienced percentages of increase between 100 and 199 during the first and third periods. In addition, two counties in the northwestern part of Minnesota reported a similar increase during the first and second periods. Medium or large cities are non-existent in this region. Agriculture dominates the

economy of these areas. On the other hand, the east-central portion of the state, dominated by the Twin Cities metropolitan area, has never shown a high percentage of change in the number of assaults during the three periods presented on the maps.

Assault Distribution in Puerto Rico

The Commonwealth of Puerto Rico (Figure 2-9) has some similarities with Minnesota in terms of the areas experiencing increases in the number of assaults. The few municipalities that have experienced significant increases (more than 80 percent) are located outside the San Juan metropolitan area. One municipality, Yauco, in the southwestern portion of the island (1992-93) and another town on the southeast coast (1994-95) that have sustained problems in the agrarian sector suffered the highest increase in the number of assaults in the first and third periods, respectively. The outlying municipality of Culebra, located on a small island to the east of Puerto Rico, also reflects a similar situation during the last period in terms of isolation and a lack of strong economic activities. The municipality exhibiting the second highest percentage of change in the first period

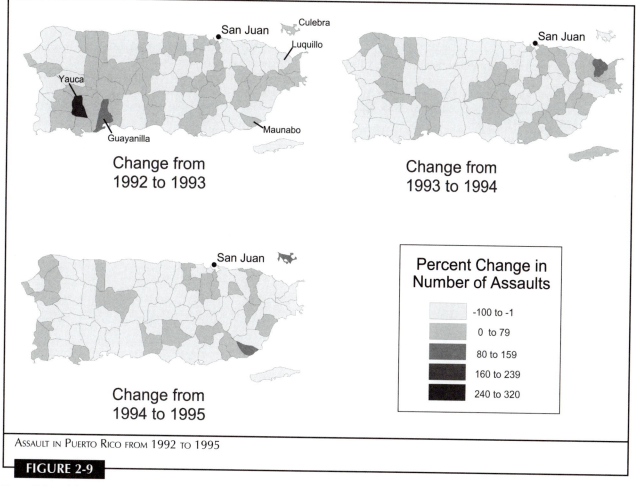

Change from
1992 to 1993

Change from
1993 to 1994

Change from
1994 to 1995

**Percent Change in
Number of Assaults**

-100 to -1

0 to 79

80 to 159

160 to 239

240 to 320

ASSAULT IN PUERTO RICO FROM 1992 TO 1995

FIGURE 2-9

Source: Police of the Commonwealth of Puerto Rico.

is Guayanilla, a harbor town that experienced the death of the heavy industrial sector of its economy during the 1970s. During the second period (1993-94), the area with the highest rate of increase is Laquillo, a municipality experiencing problems with its tourist industry and the closing of various manufacturing activities. Although Puerto Rico is part of the Caribbean and distant from the American Midwest, we can detect some similarities with some states of the Central Lowlands experiencing violence in sparsely populated areas distant from large urban centers.

Conclusion

The purpose of this essay is to show distributions of assault and the changes that have occurred over the study period. Assault is not a unique problem of metropolitan regions. The maps presented here demonstrate that rural areas are not immune to this type of crime. In some cases, this type of violence can be considered a growing problem for sparsely populated regions. Three types of political entities are compared, and although they differ in terms of size, population, and geography, some similarities exist. Minnesota and Puerto Rico are different in terms of culture, economy, and political status. However, they share the reality of growing

assault occurrence in zones far from the administrative and urban centers. Both territories have reported some of the most horrendous cases of violence in traditional rural areas or in communities losing prosperity. This phenomenon also is occurring regionally in other north-central states, which are reporting higher rates of increase in the number of assaults.

References

Ackerman, William. 1998. Socioeconomic Correlates of Increasing Crime Rates in Smaller Communities. *The Professional Geographer* 50(3): 372-87.

Adler, F., G. Mueller, and P. Laufer. 1991. *Criminology*. New York: McGraw-Hill.

Bureau of Justice Statistics. 1987. *Criminal Victimization in the United States, 1994*. U.S. Department of Justice: 29–30.

Federal Bureau of Investigation (FBI). 1992-95. *Uniform Crime Reports*. Washington, DC: U.S. Department of Justice, Government Printing Office.

———. 1996. *Uniform Crime Reports*. Washington, DC: U.S. Department of Justice, Government Printing Office.

Fortuno-Candelas, C. 1993. *El Auge de la Criminalidad en Puerto Rico*. San Juan: Bandera Roja.

Harries, Keith D. 1973. Spatial Aspects of Violence and Metropolitan Population. *The Professional Geographer* 25(1): 1-6.

———. 1974. *The Geography of Crime and Justice.* New York: McGraw-Hill.

———. 1980. *Crime and the Environment.* Springfield, IL: Charles C. Thomas.

———. 1989. Homicide and Assault: A Comparative Analysis of Attributes in Dallas Neighborhoods, 1981-1985. *The Professional Geographer* 41(1): 29-38.

———. 1997. *Serious Violence: Patterns of Homicide.* Springfield, IL: Charles C. Thomas.

Heath, Dwight B. 1995. *International Handbook on Alcohol and Culture.* Westport: CT: Greenwood.

Jordan, Terry, and Domosh, Mona. 1998. *The Human Mosaic.* New York: Longman.

Macionis, John J. 1989. *Sociology.* Englewood Cliffs, NJ: Prentice Hall.

Park, Peter. 1971. *Industrialization and Alcoholism: A Structural Explanation.* Society for the Study of Social Problems.

Policia del Estado Libre Asociado de Puerto Rico. 1992. *Informe Sobre Criminalidad: 1992.* San Juan, PR: Negociado de Servicios Tecnicos.

———. 1993. *Informe Sobre Criminalidad: 1993.* San Juan, PR: Negociado de Servicios Tecnicos.

———. 1994. *Informe Sobre Criminalidad: 1994.* San Juan, PR: Negociado de Servicios Tecnicos.

———. 1995. *Informe Sobre Criminalidad: 1995.* San Juan, PR: Negociado de Servicios Tecnicos.

Rose, Harold, and Donald Deskins. 1980. Felony Murders: The Case of Detroit. *Urban Geography* 1(1): 1-21.

Santiago-Valles, Kelvin. 1994. The Unruly City and the Mental Landscape of Colonized Identities: Internally Contested Nationality in Puerto Rico, 1945-1985. *Social Text* 38 (Spring): 149-63.

Titus Reid, Sue. 1988. *Crime and Criminology.* Fort Worth, TX: Holt, Rinehart and Winston.

Rape in the United States

Kathleen C. Basile

The popular societal image of a rape is that it occurs in a deserted location, the perpetrator and victim are strangers (Hall 1995), and use is made of force and weapons (Estrich 1987). While this is society's perception, it is only one kind of rape, and it is not the most prevalent kind. Research has found that rape is most commonly committed by someone known to the victim, and often committed without force or violence (Finkelhor and Yllo 1985; Russell 1990; Bergen 1996; Basile 1998).

In the last few decades, rape has been identified as a social problem in need of attention. The United States is estimated to have the highest incidence rate of forcible rape of any industrialized country (Allison and Wrightsman 1993). Furthermore, the rates of rape have increased over the last few decades (Baron and Straus 1989). However, one difficulty in understanding the extent of the problem is that rape is highly underreported. Research has indicated that rape on the whole is one of the most under-reported crimes in the United States (Allison and Wrightsman 1993). Rape by an intimate, which is estimated to be the most common type of rape, is also the most likely to go unreported.

The purpose of this essay is to use maps to graphically display the most recent statistics on rape in the United States. The data presented here are intended to give the reader an idea of how reported rape rates are dispersed across the country, as well as an indication of regional differences on rates of reported rapes. In addition, this essay brings attention to the least studied and discussed type of rape—wife rape.

Definition of the Problem

Rape can be defined in many ways, and legal definitions are not consistent. Historically, rape has been defined as "sexual intercourse by a male with a female, *other than his wife*, without the consent of the woman and effected by force, duress, intimidation, or deception as to the nature of the act" (Herman 1984: 21-22). More recently, rape has been acknowledged as a crime perpetrated on strangers as well as intimates, such as wives, girlfriends, or acquaintances. Although it is not as common, rape can also be perpetrated on men. For the purposes of this essay, rape is defined as any sexual contact (vaginal, anal, or oral penetration) against consent through force or threat of force, or when the victim was incapacitated with alcohol or other drugs (Koss, Gidycz, and Wisniewski 1987).

A Brief History of Rape

Rape has existed throughout history. Some researchers have linked the historical subjugation of women by men and women's dependence on men to women's fear of rape (Brownmiller 1975). Throughout most of history, rape of women was perceived as a crime committed against the men who "owned" them (i.e., fathers, husbands) (McColgan 1996). Until recently, history has largely denied the existence of rape, considering it to be a personal problem of unlucky women (Estrich 1987). A common American stereotype was that rapists are mentally deranged and typically black men who are strangers to their victims (Odem and Clay-Warner 1998). Not until recent decades has public attention focused on the possibility of rape being committed by non-strangers, non-mentally defective individuals, and non-blacks, such as in the recent highly publicized acquaintance rape case of William Kennedy Smith (Allison and Wrightsman 1993).

Rape Myths

Much research has documented several false ideas, or myths, about the circumstances surrounding rape, and the motivations of both victims and perpetrators (Sullivan and Mosher 1990; Hall 1995; Ward 1995). These myths can apply to all kinds of rape, from stranger rape to wife rape, because the myths stem from stereotypes that define the societally "appropriate" relationship between women and men. The following are some of the most prevalent rape myths:

- Women lead men on and therefore deserve to be raped (the "she was asking for it" mentality).
- All women want to be raped.
  No woman can be raped against her will.
- If you are going to be raped, you might as well enjoy it. (Brownmiller 1975: 311)

Other researchers have discovered the following additional myths:

- Rape is a crime of sexual passion.
- Women often make false accusations of rape.
- Most rapists are strangers to their women victims. (Ward 1995)

As P. Searles and R.J. Berger point out, these myths are "biases that have been reproduced in the legal system, making it difficult for women to achieve justice and hold men responsible for the harms they have perpetuated" (1995: 1).

Why Is Rape Underreported?

There are several reasons why rape is one of the most under reported crimes in this country. One major reason, due in part to the myths discussed above, is that victims do not think they will be believed (Odem and Clay-Warner 1998). Unfortunately, this is often the case; studies have found little support from the legal system for women who allege rape (McColgan 1996). Related to this is the belief of many rape victims that they were to blame for the rape. Stranger rape survivors (Herman 1984), acquaintance rape survivors (Warshaw 1988), and wife rape survivors (Mathias 1986) have been found to think that they could have done something differently to avoid the rape. These feelings minimize the experience and often prevent women from reporting the crime. Desire to avoid the heavy social stigma and embarrassment associated with being raped is another reason why women are less likely to report this crime (Odem and Clay-Warner 1998).

Rates of Reported Rape for 1997

The *Uniform Crime Reports* are a common source of data used by social scientists. Data on rates of reported rapes for the year of 1997 are offered in Table 2-A, rank-ordered by the 50 states and the District of Columbia. The rates offered in Table 2-A only include rapes against women and girls because they are disproportionately the victims of this crime. As shown in the table, Alaska had 140 reported female victims of rape per 100,000 women, the highest rape rate in the U.S. in 1997. Other states with high rates in 1997 were Delaware (126 per 100,000) and Nevada (122 per 100,000). West Virginia was the state with the lowest rape rate, with 38 per 100,000 women reporting.

Figure 2-10 gives a graphical display of the incidence of reported rape across the United States. As suggested by this mapping, the states with the highest reported rapes, between 115 and 140 per 100,000 women (indicated by the darkest shading) are located in either the western or southeastern regions of the country. The second largest category of rates, between 89 and 114 per 100,000 women, seems to be fairly evenly dispersed throughout the country, with representation in all regions except the Northeast.

Table 2-B allows for a regional comparison of rates of reported rape. The states were categorized into the following four main regions using Census Bureau classifications: Northeast, North Central, South, and West. As shown in the table, significant differences occur among the average rates of reported rape in the four regions. The West had the highest rates, followed by the South and the North Central region. The Northeast had the lowest average rape rate for 1997. Statistical tests reveal that the Northeast had a significantly lower average rape rate in 1997 than the South and the West.

TABLE 2-A

REPORTED RAPE RATES PER 100,000 WOMEN, RANK-ORDERED BY STATE, 1997

State	1997 Rate
Alaska	140
Delaware	126
Nevada	122
Tennessee	110
Minnesota	102
Washington	102
Michigan	101
Florida	100
New Mexico	99
South Dakota	95
South Carolina	95
Utah	94
Oklahoma	89
Colorado	85
Arkansas	84
Kansas	83
Texas	81
Louisiana	80
Oregon	79
Ohio	79
District of Columbia	77
Mississippi	75
Illinois	72
Rhode Island	71
Maryland	69
New Hampshire	66
Kentucky	65
Arizona	65
Indiana	64
Hawaii	64
California	63
Alabama	62
North Carolina	61
Georgia	60
Idaho	58
Wyoming	57
Missouri	55
Virginia	53
Pennsylvania	53
Vermont	52
Massachusetts	52
North Dakota	49
Nebraska	48
Connecticut	44
New York	43
New Jersey	42
Maine	40
Wisconsin	40
Iowa	39
Montana	39
West Virginia	38

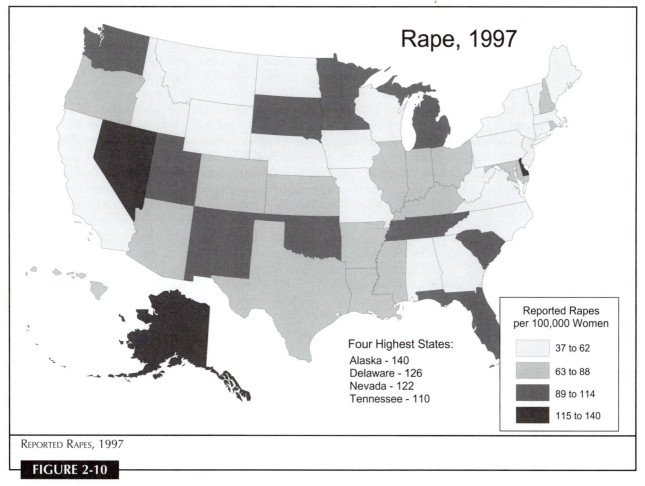

Rape, 1997

Four Highest States:

Alaska - 140
Delaware - 126
Nevada - 122
Tennessee - 110

Reported Rapes
per 100,000 Women

	37 to 62
	63 to 88
	89 to 114
	115 to 140

REPORTED RAPES, 1997

FIGURE 2-10

Source: FBI Uniform Crime Reports, 1997 Preliminary Annual Release.

TABLE 2-B

REPORTED RATES OF RAPE PER 100,000 WOMEN, REGIONAL AVERAGES, 1997

Region	Number of States	1997 Average Rate
Northeast	9	51
North Central	12	70
South	17	78
West	13	82
TOTAL	**51**	**72**

Reported rape rates differ for large U.S. cities. Figure 2-11 displays the 100 cities in the U.S. with the highest numbers of reported rapes in 1997. With the exception of New York City, which had the highest number of reported rapes of any city in the country (2,157), findings for cities are relatively consistent with the state data in Figure 2-10. The highest number of reported rapes remain in the West (Los Angeles) and the South (Memphis and Houston). Detroit also had a high number of reported rapes in 1997. It is likely that the number of reported rapes is highest in large cities, such as New York, Los Angeles, and Detroit, in part because there is a better concentration of resources in urban areas to deal with this crime, such as hospitals and rape crisis centers. A higher accessibility of services might be leading to a higher likelihood to report this crime.

Types of Rape

Although the statistics mapped in this essay do not differentiate distinct types of rape, it is important to discuss the different types, particularly to bring attention to the non-stereotypical ones—those committed by a non-stranger. Rape has three major types—stranger, date or acquaintance, and wife rape. Although rape by a stranger is estimated to be less common than intimate rape, it is believed to be the most commonly reported type of rape. N.M. Shields and C.R. Hanneke (1992) point out how rape by a stranger leads to a more serious sense of violation of physical privacy and fear of pregnancy than rape by an intimate. Recent years have seen an increased awareness of the prevalence of date and acquaintance rape. Along with this recognition has come the added difficulty of proving these kinds of rape, particularly because they are more likely to occur indoors and out of the view of potential witnesses (McColgan 1996), and there is typically public skepticism when a prior relationship existed between perpetrator and victim. For this and other reasons, date and acquaintance rapes are less likely to be reported—they are harder to prove and less likely to be believed by the justice system.

Wife rape is believed by some to be the most common type of sexual assault (Bergen 1996; Russell 1990; Finkelhor and Yllo 1985). Up until 1977, however, it was legally impossible in all states for a wife to be raped by her husband (Whatley 1993). Only in recent decades has the wife rape exemption, based on the English common law notion that women had given themselves up in marriage to their husbands and thus could not be raped, been removed from the laws on rape. Because the literature focuses less on wife rape, this essay closes by examining the status of all U.S. states regarding the laws on wife rape, using the most current information for each state.

Laws that consider rape of a spouse are not universal across the United States. For the purposes of this essay, two major categories will be reviewed with regard to laws on wife rape: (1) no exemptions from prosecution and (2) some exemptions from prosecution. At present, no state has complete exemption from prosecution. *In all states in the United States, one can be prosecuted for rape of a wife in one or more sections of the sex crime statutes for that state* (National Clearinghouse on Marital and Date Rape 1996). At present, wife rape is a crime in all 50 states. Most current data reveal that 17 states, in addition to the District of Columbia and federal lands in all states, have no exemptions on the books against prosecution for wife rape. No exemption means there is nothing written in the laws that can exempt a person from prosecution for raping a spouse. States with no exemptions can prosecute a husband accused of raping his wife in the same way as they prosecute a person accused of raping a stranger. This means that married women in these 17 states have the same protection against rape as other victims of rape (National Clearinghouse on Marital and Date Rape 1996).

The remaining 33 states have some exemptions from wife rape prosecution in certain sections of their sex crime statutes. This category is more complex. To have "some exemptions" means that these states have spousal exemp-

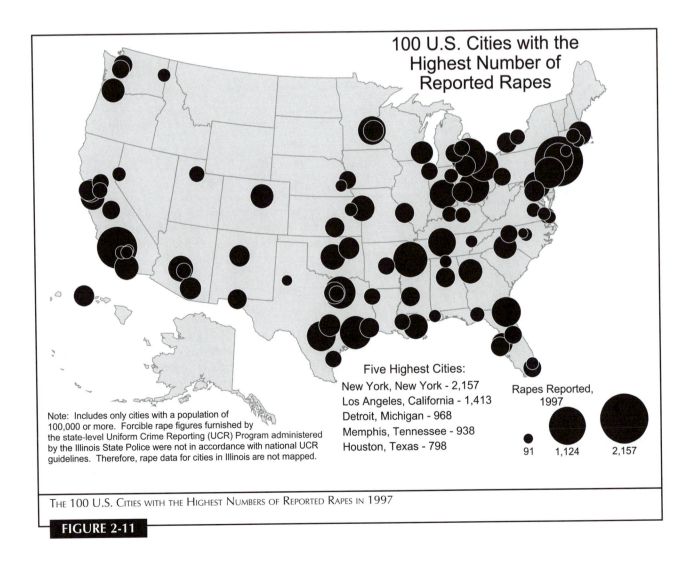

100 U.S. Cities with the Highest Number of Reported Rapes

Five Highest Cities:
New York, New York - 2,157
Los Angeles, California - 1,413
Detroit, Michigan - 968
Memphis, Tennessee - 938
Houston, Texas - 798

Rapes Reported, 1997

91   1,124   2,157

Note: Includes only cities with a population of 100,000 or more. Forcible rape figures furnished by the state-level Uniform Crime Reporting (UCR) Program administered by the Illinois State Police were not in accordance with national UCR guidelines. Therefore, rape data for cities in Illinois are not mapped.

THE 100 U.S. CITIES WITH THE HIGHEST NUMBERS OF REPORTED RAPES IN 1997

FIGURE 2-11

tions in certain sections of their statutes, but not for all sections. For example, some states have spousal exemptions in cases where the husband does not have to use force because his wife is vulnerable (i.e., physically or mentally impaired) and legally unable to give consent (National Clearinghouse on Marital and Date Rape 1996). The data used in this section are primarily based on statutes from the 1995 and 1996 legislative sessions. However, some states were reviewed for updates as recently as the summer of 1998.

Figure 2-12 presents a map of the United States, shading the 33 states that currently have some exemptions in certain sex crime statutes, in contrast to the 17 states shown in white that currently have no exemptions from prosecuting a husband for rape. The visual display is an effort to determine if there is a regional trend in this country with regard to the laws addressing wife rape. As shown in the figure, no clear regional trends emerge with regard to these laws; both the "no exemption" states and the "some exemption" states are about equally represented across the country.

Conclusion

The purpose of this essay is to display the most recent statistics on rape in the United States through the use of maps.

The findings on rape rates presented in Figures 2-10 and 2-11 do not take into account the types of rape committed, nor do they account for the numerous rapes that go unreported. As indicated above, rape of an intimate is estimated to be the most common type of rape, although the type least likely to be reported. Thus, it is difficult to determine the actual occurrence of this crime. However, the data presented here give the reader an idea of how reported rape rates are dispersed across the country, as well as an indication of regional differences on rates of reported rapes. The possible reasons for these variations include public and official attitudes regarding rape as well as accessibility of services to rape victims. These factors can all play a role in both the reporting of rape and the processing of rape cases. In addition, this essay has brought attention to the least discussed type of rape—wife rape. An examination of the legal status of wife rape across the United States indicated no determinable regional differences in the exemption status of the states. As is apparent for the numerous crimes discussed in this volume, mapping statistics regarding rape is a useful way to assess the degree of the problem for the country as a whole. In addition, viewing the legal status of wife rape across the American states allows the reader to see how the legal system of the country is addressing the problem.

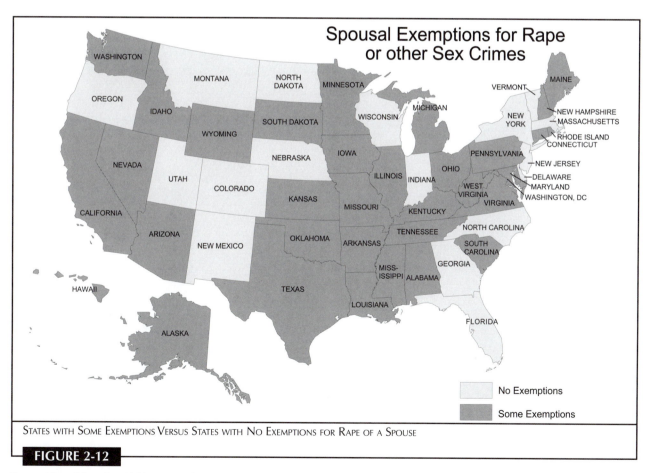

STATES WITH SOME EXEMPTIONS VERSUS STATES WITH NO EXEMPTIONS FOR RAPE OF A SPOUSE

FIGURE 2-12

Source: Adapted from the 1996 State Law Chart, National Clearinghouse on Marital and Date Rape.

References

Allison, J.A., and L.S. Wrightsman. 1993. *Rape: The Misunderstood Crime*. Newbury Park, CA: Sage Publications.

Baron, L., and M.A. Straus. 1989. *Four Theories of Rape in American Society: A State Level Analysis*. New Haven, CT: Yale University Press.

Basile, K.C. 1998. *From Unwanted Sex to Wife Rape: Examining Sexual Coercion in Marriage on a Continuum of Severity*. Unpublished doctoral dissertation, Georgia State University.

Bergen, R.K. 1996. *Wife Rape: Understanding the Responses of Survivors and Service Providers*. Thousand Oaks, CA: Sage Publications.

Brownmiller, S. 1975. *Against Our Will: Men, Women, and Rape*. New York: Fawcett Columbine.

Estrich, S. 1987. *Real Rape*. Cambridge, MA: Harvard University Press.

Finkelhor, D., and K. Yllo. 1985. *Licence to Rape: Sexual Abuse of Wives*. New York: The Free Press.

Hall, R. 1995. *Rape in America: A Reference Handbook*. Santa Barbara, CA: ABC-CLIO, Inc.

Herman, D. 1984. The Rape Culture. In J. Freeman, ed. *Women: A Feminist Perspective*. Palo Alto, CA: Mayfield Publishing Co., pp. 20-34.

Koss, M.P., C.A. Gidycz, and N. Wisniewski. 1987. The Scope of Rape: Incidence and Prevalence of Sexual Aggression and Victimization in a National Sample of Higher Education Students. *Journal of Consulting and Clinical Psychology* 55: 162-70.

Mathias, B. 1986. Lifting the Shade on Family Violence. *Family Therapy Networker* 10: 20-29.

McColgan, A. 1996. *The Case for Taking the Date Out of Rape*. London: HarperCollins Publishers.

National Clearinghouse on Marital and Date Rape. 1996. 1996 State Law Chart. Berkeley, CA: National Clearinghouse on Marital and Date Rape.

Odem, M.E., and J. Clay-Warner, eds. 1998. *Confronting Rape and Sexual Assault*. Wilmington, DE: Scholarly Resources Inc.

Russell, D.E.H. 1990. *Rape in Marriage*. Bloomington: Indiana University Press.

Searles, P., and R.J. Berger, eds. 1995. *Rape and Society: Readings on the Problem of Sexual Assault*. Boulder, CO: Westview Press.

Shields, N.M., and C.R. Hanneke. 1992. Comparing the Psychological Impact of Battering, Marital Rape and Stranger Rape." *Clinical Sociology Review* 10: 151-69.

Sullivan, J.P., and D.L. Mosher. 1990. "Acceptance of Guilded Imagery of Marital Rape as a Function of Macho Personality." *Violence and Victims* 5(4): 275-86.

Ward, C.A. 1995. *Attitudes Toward Rape: Feminist and Social Psychological Perspectives*. London: Sage.

Warshaw, R. 1988. *I Never Called It Rape*. New York: Harper and Row.

Whatley, Mark A. 1993. For Better or Worse: The Case of Marital Rape. *Violence and Victims* 8(1): 29-39.

Robbery

Doug Williamson

With the exception of murder and rape, robbery is considered one of the most insidious and frightening crimes. It is a problem in all areas of the United States and virtually no one is immune, although some groups are more susceptible than others. This essay gives a broad overview of some fundamental issues of robbery. It examines what robbery is, who perpetrates it, who it effects, where it takes place, how it is perpetrated, and what its effects are.

Most states base their definition of robbery on the Federal Bureau of Investigation's (FBI) *Uniform Crime Reports* (*UCR*). Robbery is defined as "the taking or attempting to take anything from the care, custody or control of a person or persons by force or threat of force or violence and/or by putting the victim in fear" (Federal Bureau of Investigation 1997: 28). New York State, like most other states, has a more detailed but similar definition. According to the New York State Penal Code (State of New York 1986: 96), "[r]obbery is forcible stealing. A person forcibly steals property and commits robbery when, in the course of committing a larceny, he/she uses or threatens the immediate use of physical force for the purpose of:

> 1. Preventing or overcoming resistance to the taking of the property or the retention thereof immediately thereafter the taking; or
>
> 2. Compelling the owner of such property or another person to deliver up the property or to engage in other conduct which aids in the commission of the larceny."

Thus, robbery involves theft (larceny) with the use or threat of force or violence against the victim. The FBI's *UCR* is an important source of statistical information about crime in the United States, including specific crimes such as robbery. The *UCR* is a city, county, and state law enforcement program that provides a nationwide view of crime, based on the submission of statistics by law enforcement agencies throughout the country (Federal Bureau of Investigation 1997). The *UCR* uses a crime index, which measures the changes in amounts and rates of crimes reported to law enforcement agencies. The index is based on the violent crimes of murder and non-negligent manslaughter, forcible rape, and robbery and assault, as well as on the property crimes of burglary, larceny-theft, motor vehicle theft, and arson. The *UCR* is based on *reported* crimes, and therefore underestimates the true state of crime in the United States. As an overall measure, it is extremely useful, but caution should be exercised when drawing specific conclusions from the figures.

Of particular relevance to this discourse are the figures for robbery. The number of robberies in 1997 was 497,950 at a rate of 186.1 per 100,000 people. This was a decrease of 1 percent for the number of offenses, and a 7.8-percent decrease in the rate over 1996 figures. The total number of robbery offenses in 1997 was the lowest since 1985. Robbery is often subdivided into commercial or personal classifications. A full discussion of commercial robbery is beyond the scope of this essay, which will pay particular attention to personal robberies mainly because they are of most concern to individuals.

Why Examine Robbery?

According to the FBI's crime clock, a robbery occurs in the United States every minute. Most authors agree that the effect of robbery on individuals and society as a whole is considerable and therefore worthy of in-depth examination. J. Conklin (1972: 4) asserts that robbery is "the best indicator of the type of crime most feared by the public" and suggests several reasons why robbery is such a cause for concern. More often than not, robbery is perpetrated by a stranger, in a highly threatening manner. Robbery involves violence that can result in serious injury, or even death for the victim. According to Conklin, who studied robbery in the 1960s and early 1970s, a period marked by a dramatic increase in the number of robberies, "It is probably the fear of robbery and unprovoked assault which keeps people off the streets, makes them avoid strangers and leads them to lock their doors" (1972: 4).

Another reason robbery is so serious is that it is defined as being two crimes—larceny and assault. Larceny, in itself a significant event, becomes a heinous crime when combined with the violence of assault. Conklin (1972) asserts that it is because robbery involves two threatening elements that it creates a more intense reaction from the public than either of the crimes individually. Robbery has several fundamental elements: It involves a perpetrator and a victim, must take place somewhere, and needs to be committed.

Perpetrators

The *UCR* records crime reported, but it also maintains information about arrests and those arrested. The perpetrators of reported robbery have a distinct demographic profile (*see* Figures 2-13 and 2-14). In 1997, 65 percent of all robbery arrestees were under 25 years of age, and 90 percent were males. Blacks accounted for 57 percent of the total robbery arrests, whites for 41 percent, and all other races for the remainder. To test this hypothesis, a correlation analysis was performed on two data sets, the density of robberies and the density of black males, ages 18-25. The source of the data was the New York City Police Department's COMPSTAT division and the United States Census Bureau. The study area was the area surrounding Central Park in northern Manhattan, New York (Figure 2-15). The result of a correlation analysis is a correlation coefficient or "spatial autocorrelation index" (Goodchild 1988). The correlation coefficient is a measure of how re-

lated values are in space. It ranges from –1 to 1, with values near 0 indicating no relationship, values near 1 indicating a strong relationship, and values near –1 indicating a strong negative relationship. The value is useful because it is a single value describing the spatial distribution of objects in space and it can be used to explore the cause of the spatial distribution of objects in space. The resulting map and correlation coefficient indicate a modest amount of correlation ® = 0.350) between robbery and the demographic data shown (Figure 2-16).

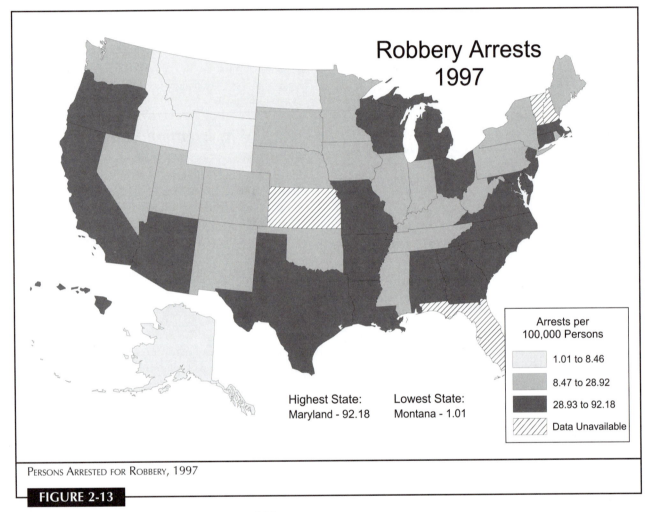

Robbery Arrests 1997

Highest State: Maryland - 92.18

Lowest State: Montana - 1.01

Arrests per 100,000 Persons

1.01 to 8.46
8.47 to 28.92
28.93 to 92.18
Data Unavailable

PERSONS ARRESTED FOR ROBBERY, 1997

FIGURE 2-13

Source: FBI Uniform Crime Reports, 1997 Preliminary Annual Release.

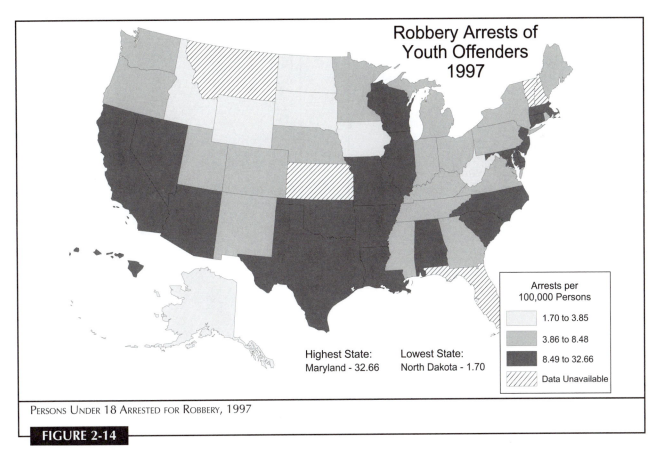

Robbery Arrests of
Youth Offenders
1997

Arrests per
100,000 Persons

	1.70 to 3.85
	3.86 to 8.48
	8.49 to 32.66
	Data Unavailable

Highest State:
Maryland - 32.66

Lowest State:
North Dakota - 1.70

PERSONS UNDER 18 ARRESTED FOR ROBBERY, 1997

FIGURE 2-14

Source: FBI Uniform Crime Reports, 1997 Preliminary Annual Release.

North Manhattan,
New York

North Manhattan

LOCATION OF THE STUDY AREA: NORTH MANHATTAN, NEW YORK

FIGURE 2-15

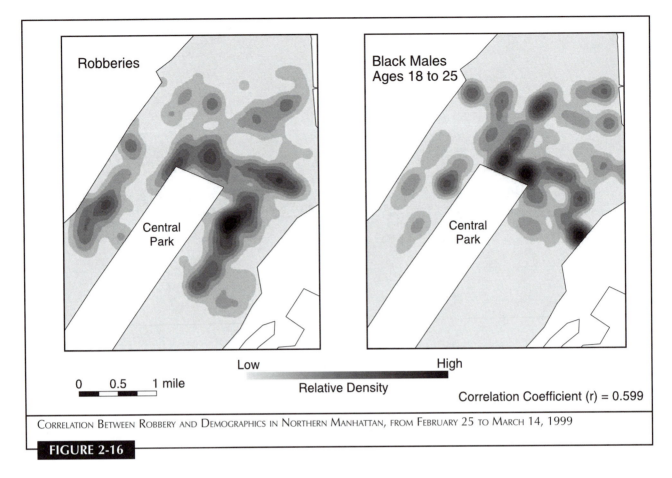

Low   High

Relative Density

0   0.5   1 mile

Correlation Coefficient (r) = 0.599

CORRELATION BETWEEN ROBBERY AND DEMOGRAPHICS IN NORTHERN MANHATTAN, FROM FEBRUARY 25 TO MARCH 14, 1999

FIGURE 2-16

The *UCR* figures above indicate that robbery is predominately a young man's crime, with race having some impact (Figures 2-13 and 2-14). Researchers have attempted to explain this phenomenon, most notably, Conklin (1972), Wright and Decker (1997), and Miller (1998), among others. In their research, R. Wright and S. Decker (1997: 6) attempt to describe robbery "through the eyes of those currently engaged in such crimes" via a field study with interviews.

According to Wright and Decker, the demographics of age, sex, race, and income are merely "casual agents" in the determination of perpetrators. Robbery, as defined earlier, is larceny with a violent element. This definition means that if there is no violence or threat of violence, the crime is a larceny. At the core of robbery then, is the quest for material or monetary reward. Most offenders often fall below the poverty line. Wright and Decker assert that robbery is a means to an end from which the motive is formed. J. Katz (1988: 4) notes that "the assailant must sense, there and then, a distinctive constraint or seductive appeal that [was not sensed] a little while before in a substantially similar place." In almost all cases, this constraint is economic, that is, the perpetrator, for one reason or another, feels a strong need for money. Perpetrators in Wright and Decker's survey gave several specific reasons for needing money or property. Among them were continuing their lifestyle of drinking, gambling, and using narcotics; protecting their

street reputation; and obtaining money for necessities such as bills and food.

Although money is the primary driving force, other factors, more psychological in nature, motivate people to commit robbery. The majority of offenders are young, black males, and as such have limited social and economic opportunities, but these young men do not necessarily become perpetrators. For example, Wright and Decker cite several offenders who, in addition to money, robbed for "control." They were acting out against their surroundings to gain control of their situation (*see also* Katz 1988). Several other factors included revenge, street justice, and thrill seeking.

The *UCR* statistics provided above indicate that robbery is perpetrated primarily by males. What the statistics obscure, however, is that although the numbers are small, women do commit robbery, and in rising numbers. While the total number of men arrested for robbery increased by 6.7 percent from 1988 to 1997, the number of women arrested jumped by 27.5 percent. Even more surprising is the age of female perpetrators. In 1988, the number of women under 18 years old arrested for robbery was 1,176. In 1997, that number increased to 2,297, an increase of 95.3 percent. J. Miller (1998) examined the issue of gender in robbery in an attempt to explain why women commit robbery. The results indicate women and men commit robbery for similar reasons; both use robbery primarily as a means of obtaining money or property (Miller 1998). Like Wright and Decker, Miller notes that many perpetrators seek a psychological or emotional thrill from robbery.

Most researchers agree that the demographic characteristics of the perpetrator are not necessarily determining factors of who commits robberies, but rather indicators of who is likely to be placed in a situation to commit robbery. The primary factor in most robberies is the need for "easy" money.

Victims

Crime statistics reveal that the majority of robbery perpetrators are low-income, young, black males, but what about the victims of robbery? Unfortunately, from a research standpoint, little data on the victims of robbery is available. The primary source of information on victims is the *National Crime Victimization Survey* (*NCVS*) published by the Department of Justice's Bureau of Justice Statistics. This survey, which began in 1973 with a revision in 1993, queries people 12 years and older. It asks whether a crime was reported or not; the type of crime(s) that occurred; the age, sex, and race of the victims; and the relationship with the perpetrator, among other things. The survey is a nationally representative sample that includes approximately 49,000 households with a total of about 101,000 persons.

According to the 1997 *NCVS*, males were more than twice as likely as females to be the victim of a robbery. The rate of robbery victimization for men was 6.1 per 1,000 compared to a rate of 2.6 per 1,000 for women. Similarly, blacks were almost twice as likely as whites to be robbed, with a rate of 7.4 per 1,000 compared to 3.8 per 1,000 for whites. All other races fell in the middle with a rate of 5 per 1,000. Age also appears to play a role in victimization. The age groups most likely to be robbed were 12-15, 16-19, and 20-24, with rates of 8.2, 10.2, and 7.4, respectively. Surprisingly, the lowest rates of victimization were found among the elderly (ages 50-54 and over 65), with a combined rate of 3.1. Thus, the data show that, like the perpetrators of robbery, the victims of robbery are more likely to be young, black males.

Other research supports the data presented above. For example, Wright and Decker (1997) found a large proportion, 60 percent of the perpetrators, that said they preyed on individuals who were themselves involved in illegal activity, particularly low-level drug activity. The primary reason for this was that these victims would be less likely to report the incident to the police. This is also supported by a correlation analysis similar to the one described above. In this case, the density of robberies was compared to the density of narcotics complaints. From Figure 2-16, and its associated correlation coefficient of roughly 0.6, it can be concluded that there is a high correlation between robberies and illicit drug activity.

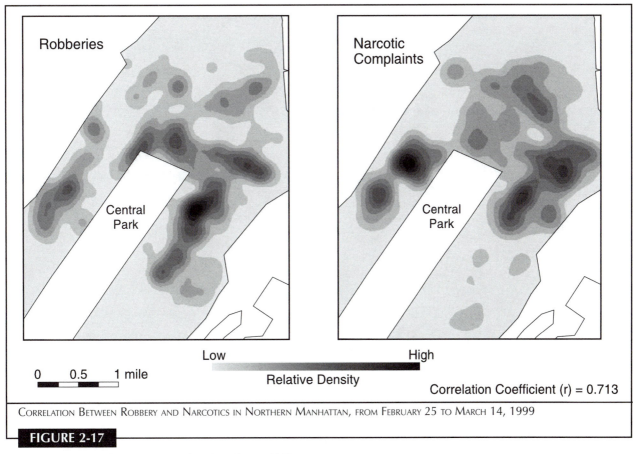

CORRELATION BETWEEN ROBBERY AND NARCOTICS IN NORTHERN MANHATTAN, FROM FEBRUARY 25 TO MARCH 14, 1999

FIGURE 2-17

Source: Federal Bureau of Investigation, *Uniform Crime Reports, 1997.*

However, when asked specifically about non-criminal victims and demographics, such as age, sex, and race, the responses were less supportive of the *NCVS* data. The primary motivation for robbery was economic. Perpetrators sought victims who appeared to have a lot of cash. Many perpetrators used race as a guide, but there was no consensus on whether blacks or whites were more likely to have cash (Wright and Decker 1997). Most stereotypes of robbery have an elderly woman as the victim, but this is not necessarily true. A few respondents in the Wright and Decker survey preferred elderly victims, for lack of resistance. Many, however, stated that these victims usually did not carry enough cash to make the risk worthwhile. The evidence presented here and in other places (*see* Cook 1990) does not necessarily substantiate the evidence from the *NCVS*.

Robbery Locations

Since the driving force behind robbery is money, one might suspect that most robberies would occur, "where the money [i]s" (Sutton 1976). This conclusion would suggest that most robberies occur in more affluent areas. However, this is not necessarily true. L. Pettiway (1982) found that a significant percentage (65.5 percent) of robbers who lived in economically deprived areas (what he terms a "ghetto")

committed their robberies in the same area. He also found that 90.6 percent of the perpetrators who do not reside in the "ghetto" do not go there to commit their crimes. Thus, robbery tends to be a "local" crime performed by perpetrators within their own neighborhoods. There may be some psychological barrier between entering and leaving one's neighborhood to commit robbery.

In their study in St. Louis, Wright and Decker (1997: 8) found that robbery was not evenly distributed across the city (*see also* Pettiway 1982 and Covington and Taylor 1989). They found that "in general, robbery rates increase as one moves from the predominately white south to the predominantly black north of the city, with the very highest rates in and around the most economically deprived black neighborhoods." They also described a strong link between robbery and other illicit activity, such as drug use and sales, which tended to flourish in certain neighborhoods (*see* Figure 2-17).

This idea is supported by a study of commercial robberies in Amsterdam by P. Van Koppen and R. Jansen (1998). They found that most robberies occurred near the offender's place of residence (*see also* Brantingham and Brantingham 1984, Capone and Nichols 1976, and Harries 1980). In general, the distance perpetrators travel depends on a number of factors, including drug use, mode of transportation,

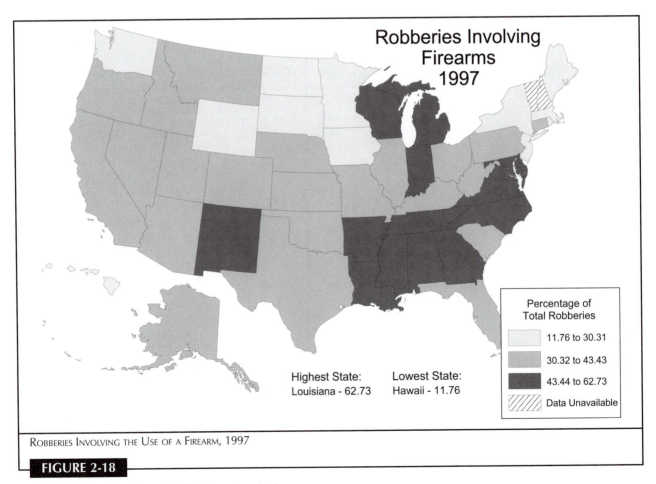

Robberies Involving
Firearms
1997

Highest State:
Louisiana - 62.73

Lowest State:
Hawaii - 11.76

Percentage of
Total Robberies

11.76 to 30.31
30.32 to 43.43
43.44 to 62.73
Data Unavailable

Robberies Involving the Use of a Firearm, 1997

FIGURE 2-18

Source: FBI Uniform Crime Reports, 1997 Preliminary Annual Release.

expected gain, and security measures. Typically, if robbers are under the influence of drugs, they will limit their activities to well-known locations. Similarly, if they have no means of transportation, they will be forced to operate locally. However, if they do have some mode of transportation, they have more potential targets at their disposal. Also, if the expected gain is high, perpetrators are willing to travel greater distances, and even take greater risks. One example of more risk is the presence of high security. If the potential gain is great, even though the distance is far, it may be worth the risk. Conversely, if the potential is slight and the distance far, the crime will not be committed at this location. Robbery is generally a crime of opportunity. When a potentially good opportunity arises, and when the need or perceived need for money exists, perpetrators will act.

The Crime

After a need for robbery has been "established," a victim chosen, and a site determined, the robbery itself is committed. Typically, robbery is classified into two groups—armed and unarmed or strong-arm. Wright and Decker (1997) describe a number of methods or techniques perpetrators

employ in committing the robbery, including attacking indoors versus outdoors, working individually or with others, and attacking head on or from behind. The most significant element, however, is the type of weapon used (Figures 2-18 and 2-19). This element is the most significant because it has an impact on the potential for injury, the ease of commission, and the level of punishment.

For the victim, the potential for injury is clearly most significant. According to the *NCVS*, 39.2 percent of robbery incidents did not involve a weapon, while 52.1 percent involved a weapon of some sort, of which a little less than half were firearms. Of the "successful" robberies, 59.6 percent involved a weapon while 33.1 percent did not. Of the "successful" robberies that did not result in injury, 67.5 percent involved weapons while 25.6 percent had no weapon present. These figures indicate that victims are more likely to give up their property when a weapon is used. Wright and Decker (1997), who found that most victims were more likely to "consent" when a weapon was present, support this conclusion. Typically, force was used only if the victim resisted.

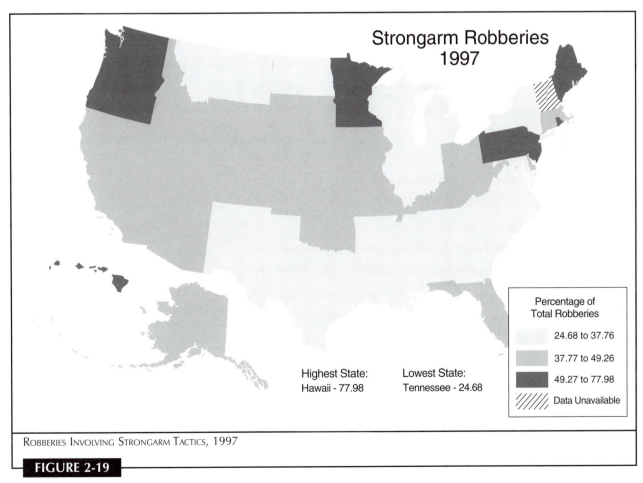

ROBBERIES INVOLVING STRONGARM TACTICS, 1997

FIGURE 2-19

Source: FBI Uniform Crime Reports, 1997 Preliminary Annual Release.

Effects

The effects of robbery are far reaching. Robbery has the potential for adversely affecting everyone involved as well as society as a whole. The effects are financial, physical, and psychological in nature. Clearly, the group most affected by robbery is the victims. The financial loss to victims is the most obvious effect. The *NCVS* collects information about economic loss to victims. In 1993, the estimated total loss as a result of robbery was $541 million. The mean loss for all robberies was $419. The economic loss can be examined further based on the demographics of victims. On average, males tended to lose more money than females, $475 compared with $396. Average losses for whites and blacks were relatively similar, $448 and $396, respectively; other races had average losses of $621.

More important than financial loss, however, are injuries that were incurred as a result of robbery. From the 1993 *NCVS*, 30.2 percent of females who were robbed sustained physical injury, while 27.8 percent of males were injured. Thirty percent of whites sustained physical injury, compared with 22.4 percent of blacks. The most startling figure from the *NCVS* is that when the offender was a stranger, 25.6 percent of the victims were injured. However, if the offender was someone the victim knew, the percentage of injured victims jumped to 41.8 percent.

Unfortunately, no measures or statistics exist for the psychological losses suffered by victims. However, victims of robbery describe the fear instilled during and after a robbery, the invasion of privacy, and the violation of one's personal safety. These psychological losses can have lasting effects. Because of this, society suffers as well. Neighborhoods are held captive and people live in fear of being another robbery statistic. Parents must keep a watchful eye on children. People are forced to remain indoors. "It is mostly fear of robbery that induces many citizens to stay home at night and to avoid the streets, thereby diminishing the sense of community and increasing the freedom which crimes may be committed on the streets" (Wilson and Boland 1976: 179).

Conclusion

Robbery is an extremely nefarious crime. It results in economic, physical, and psychological loss. Victims of robbery cover a broad spectrum in their demographic characteristics, as do the perpetrators. However, certain groups are more likely to be victims of robbery, just as certain segments of the population are likely to be perpetrators. Robbery is not evenly distributed throughout the country nor is it evenly distributed within cities. As with victims and perpetrators, certain areas are more likely to be prone to robbery than others. A robbery may take place in a number of ways, a factor that complicates the process of preventing robberies. However, if the likelihood of whom the offenders and victims are, and the most likely locations are identified, law enforcement agencies can develop strategies to prevent this heinous crime from occurring.

References

Brantingham, P., and P. Brantingham. 1984. *Patterns of Crime.* London: Macmillan.

Capone, D., and W. Nichols. 1976. Urban Structure and Criminal Mobility. *American Behavioral Scientist* 25: 199-213.

Conklin, J. 1972. *Robbery.* Philadelphia: J.B. Lippincott Company.

Cook, P. 1990. Robbery in the United States: Analysis of Recent Trends and Patterns. In N. Weiner, M. Zahn, and R. Sagi, eds. *Violence: Patterns, Causes, Public Policy.* New York: Harcourt, Brace and Jovanovich, pp. 85-98.

Covington, J., and R. Taylor. 1989. Gentrification and Crime: Robbery and Larceny Changes in Appreciating Baltimore Neighborhoods During the 1970s. *Urban Affairs Quarterly* 25(1): 142-72.

Federal Bureau of Investigation (FBI). 1997. *Crime in the United States, Uniform Crime Report, 1997.* Washington, DC: Federal Bureau of Investigation.

Goodchild, M. 1988. *Spatial Autocorrelation.* Concepts and Techniques in Modern Geography (CATMOG) No. 47. Norwich: GeoBooks.

Harries, K. 1980. *The Geography of Crime and Justice.* New York: McGraw Hill.

Katz, J. 1988. *Seductions of Crime: Moral and Sensual Attractions in Doing Evil.* New York: Basic Books.

Miller, J. 1998. Up It Up: Gender and the Accomplishment of Street Robbery. *Criminology* 36(1): 37-64.

Pettiway, L. 1982. Mobility of Robbery and Burglary Offender: Ghetto and Non-ghetto Spaces. *Urban Affairs Quarterly* 18(2): 255-70.

State of New York, Senate and Assembly. 1986. *Penal Law and Criminal Procedure Law of the State of New York.* Binghamton, NY: Gould Publications.

Sutton, W. 1976. *Where the Money Was.* New York: Viking Press.

U.S. Department of Justice, Bureau of Justice Statistics. 1996. *Criminal Victimization in the United States, 1993.* Washington DC: U.S. Department of Justice, Bureau of Justice Statistics.

Van Koppen, P., and R. Jansen. 1998. The Road to Robbery: Travel Patterns in Commercial Robberies. *British Journal of Criminology* 38(2): 230-46.

Wilson, J., and B. Boland. 1976. Crime. In W. Gorham and N. Glazer, eds. *The Urban Predicament.* Washington, DC: Urban Institute, pp. 179-230.

Wright, R., and S. Decker. 1997. *Armed Robbers in Action: Stickups and Street Culture.* Boston: Northeastern University Press.

CHAPTER 3

Crimes Against Property

Traditional property crimes covered in national crime statistics consist of burglary, larceny (theft), arson, and motor vehicle theft. Because the intent of this *Atlas* is to include crimes that are both interesting and non-traditional, the topics chosen for this chapter on property crimes are burglary, motor vehicle theft, environmental crimes, and computer crimes. Burglary and motor vehicle theft represent the mainstays of property crime while environmental and computer crimes are representative of the "new" crimes that provide a balance between the two categories.

Crimes against property comprise the majority of all serious crimes (Felson 1998). Although property crimes decreased in 1997, 11.5 million offenses were committed during that year (Federal Bureau of Investigation 1997). Because of their magnitude and the priorities of law enforcement, these crimes are not solved as often as violent crimes. A higher percentage of them are solved in the South than in any other region (Federal Bureau of Investigation 1997).

The cognitive image of burglary is that of a masked person, lurking in the shadows, waiting for a family to leave the house so that entry will be unimpeded. The reality is that household burglaries affect only about 4 percent of all U.S. households (Albanese 1999). However, where a residence is located may be a factor in whether it is targeted. One study revealed that houses too close to a road or too close together, and occupied houses, especially with barking dogs, are not good targets for burglars (Bennett 1989). Residences with low lighting, high botanical cover, porches, and a great distance from the street or between other residences are all attractive to the burglar. Unfortunately, these are also criteria many Americans use when choosing the perfect place to live. Readers will learn more about the spatial and temporal patterns of burglary in the U.S. in Susan Walcott's essay, which reviews the topic on several levels of locational analysis in addition to examining the factors surrounding this crime.

For those who have been stranded because their car has disappeared without a trace, here are some facts on motor vehicle theft.

- Every 23 seconds a car is stolen (Federal Bureau of Investigation 1997).
- In 1997, 1,394,238 motor vehicle thefts were reported in the U.S. (Federal Bureau of Investigation 1997).
- The Range Rover, Mitsubishi Montero, and Montero Sport are the vehicles most frequently targeted for theft losses (Highway Loss Data Institute 1999).
- Cars are stolen by joyriders, travelers, felons, shippers, and parts choppers (Felson 1998).
- The estimated value of all vehicles stolen in 1997 was over $7 billion (Federal Bureau of Investigation 1997).

The FBI reports that motor vehicle theft has a low clearance rate, so a car thief is not likely to be apprehended (1997). The West as a region has the highest arrest rate for auto theft in the U.S. According to the Highway Loss Data Institute, professional car thieves prefer to ship cars out of the country (1999), a fact that may account for the distribution of arrests in states with access to water routes. Thieves who steal a car to resell the parts drive it to a chop shop where it is disassembled. In their essay, "Auto Theft and Detecting Chop Shop Locations," Nancy LaVigne, Jill Fleury, and Joseph Szakas provide information on the direction and distance a stolen car might go after thieves drive it away.

Despite the permanence of environmental crime, it has only recently been given attention by other academic disciplines, such as criminology and law. Geographers, being global thinkers by nature, recognize the connection of each system on Earth—particularly winds and ocean currents. Knowing that the earth is one large island revolving in space gives rise to the realization that our planet has only one environment. What is dumped in an ocean or sky in a faraway place eventually migrates to *our* ocean or sky. In their essay, Nancy Winter and Ute Dymon explain the phenomenon of environmental crime—a complex topic composed of moral and criminal infractions with global implications. Although given little thought in today's busy world, environmental crime is life-threatening.

Computer crime was included in the *Atlas* because of the impact of computer technology on the future direction of crime. Computers are used to commit many different types of crimes, any of which would fit into several sections of this *Atlas*. However, it was included in property crimes because the crime committed most often by computer is theft (Albanese 1999). The following scenario is an indication of what can happen to an innocent victim of cybertheft:

> A 28-year-old California woman was the owner of a new $22,000 Jeep, five credit cards, an apartment, and a $3,000 loan. The problem was that she asked for none of it and never saw any of it. Another woman had impersonated her by obtaining personal information without the victim's knowledge. Generally, knowledge of an individual's Social Security number, employer, address, and driver's license number are enough to begin the fraud. It took months of phone calls, court appearances, and legal expenses for the victim to reclaim her identity and escape the bills in her name. (Albanese 1999: 488)

Computers can also be the object of crime rather than the means to crime. Software piracy and data alteration are growing areas of concern for law enforcement. The Computer Crime and Intellectual Property Section (CCIPS) provides the latest information on the Justice Department's Web site <http://www.cybercrime.com>. In their essay on computer crime, John Jarvis and Gordon Wynn discuss the difficulties in solving such crimes and how the spatial dimension may be applied to crime-solving in the next millennium.

References

Albanese, J.S. 1999. *Criminal Justice*. Boston: Allyn and Bacon.

Bennett, T. 1989. Burglars' Choice of Targets. In David J. Evans and David T. Herbert, eds. *The Geography of Crime*. London: Routledge, pp. 176-92.

Federal Bureau of Investigation (FBI). 1997. *Uniform Crime Reports*. <http://www.fbi.gov>.

Felson, Marcus. 1998. *Crime & Everyday Life*. 2nd ed. Thousand Oaks, CA: Pine Forge Press.

Highway Loss Data Institute. 1999. <http://www.carsafety.org/news_releases/pro52599.htm>.

Burglary

Susan M. Walcott

Burglary is essentially a crime against a place or property, rather than against a person (Scarr 1973). According to the United States Bureau of Justice Uniform Crime Reporting Program (Federal Bureau of Investigation 1998), burglary consists of "the unlawful entry of a structure to commit a felony or theft." This crime is further divided into the subclassifications of forcible entry, unlawful entry without the use of force, and attempted forcible entry. Canada has no separate classification for burglary, referring to all such offenses as "breaking and entering." Australia, the other source of national comparisons used in this report, employs the same terminology as does the United States. Burglary is a crime for which the penalties, risks, fear, expense, and frequency are all high. Perpetrators, however, are "rarely caught, prosecuted, or incarcerated" (Waller and Okihiro 1978: 1). Interest in understanding how burglary's spatial patterns can lead to possible prevention is also high. This essay deals with some of the known factors—the where, when, and why for both perpetrator and victim, and, especially, the numerous spatial features of this crime's locational patterns.

Spatial Patterns of Burglary in the United States

Cities with the highest rates of burglary present a pattern similar to that for cities with the highest murder rates, that is, they are concentrated in eastern and western coastal belts and in a Midwestern cluster (see Figure 2-2 in the "Homicide" essay by Keith Harries in Chapter 2). Of the top five cities with the highest rates of these crimes, two are in the Midwest (Gary, Indiana, and Rockford, Illinois) and three (Durham, North Carolina; Orlando, Florida; and Jackson, Mississippi) are in southern states. The geographic concentration of incidents is starkly apparent on a statewide basis, with a division of highest incidents in states south of the 37th parallel, from Arizona through North Carolina (Figure 3-1). The prevalence of long, warm summers in these areas, with a correspondingly higher number of days with open windows and outdoor activity, might be an explanatory factor. Lower population, combined with longer and colder winters, yielded smaller crime incidents in the Upper Plains and Mountain states in both 1989 and 1997. State statistics confirm that 1989 was a high point for burglaries, which then steadily diminished each year, reflecting the health of the national economy (U.S. Department of Justice 1998).

The seasonality of burglary can be illustrated by looking at burglary patterns in Marietta, Georgia—a middle-class suburb to the north of Atlanta (Figure 3-2). The po-

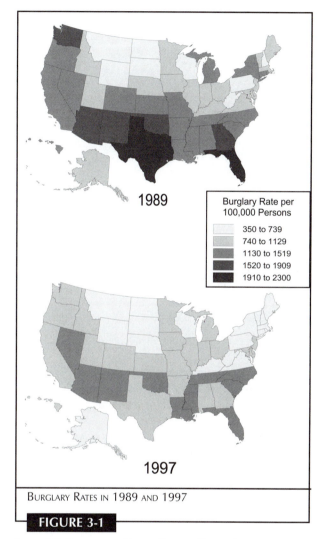

BURGLARY RATES IN 1989 AND 1997

FIGURE 3-1

Source: U.S. Department of Justice, Bureau of Justice Statistics, State Crime Data, 1960-96, from the FBI's *Uniform Crime Reports* and the *FBI Uniform Crime Report, 1997 Preliminary Annual Release.*

lice attribute peaks in the summer to more open windows and outdoor activity, as well as increased vacation absences (Figure 3-3). The December peak reflects a concentration of both goods and need at the holiday season. The locations of Marietta burglary incidents in 1997, the most recent year for full data records, correspond most closely with 1990 block group level census statistics for low median income (Figure 3-4) and high prevalence of rental units (Figure 3-5). As predicted in other studies, major highways provide an array of targets and good access for burglars, leading to a linear pattern of incidents. Location in an industrial park also increases the likelihood of burglary, as demonstrated by clusters on the Marietta map.

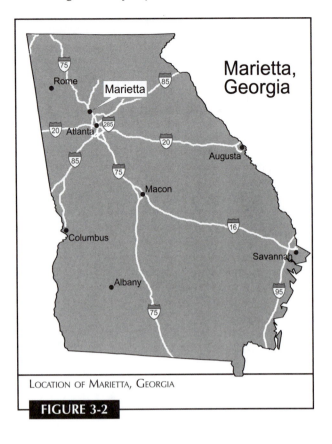

Marietta, Georgia

LOCATION OF MARIETTA, GEORGIA

FIGURE 3-2

Many reports note a gravity model-type effect, with the number of burglary incidents diminishing as distance increases from the center of town. Characteristics contributing the most to high crime rates in a Toronto study were density, a transient population, and proximity of public housing to areas being improved (Waller and Okihiro 1978). Areas of highest unemployment and transience are key burglary sites. Lowest rates are guarded entry areas, where security guards, dogs, or alarm systems present obstacles to entry. The presence of "eyes" in the form of homes with children or elderly residents also seems to provide deterrence. Burglars "play the odds" against detection, but designs specifically providing for "defensible space," such as easily surveyed wide halls, were of questionable value compared to restricted access (Mukherjee and Jorgensen 1985). Both occupancy status (including predictable regularity of absence times) and ease of observation of the residence are key factors triggering a burglar's assessment of the desirability of a particular target (Bennett 1989).

A report comparing Washington, D.C., and the adjacent suburban counties of Prince Georges (Maryland) and Fairfax (Virginia) noted that the highest rate of burglaries occurred in the central business district where rewards and availability of targets were the highest and occupancy of structures was the lowest. In the suburbs, rates at residential and non-residential properties are similar because of the prevalence of mixed-use land. Because central city land use tends to be divided between residential and business, burglary rates for each of these property types are different (Scarr 1973).

Suburban burglaries are characterized by planning rather than passion. Susceptible areas tend to fall within a range between profitability and detectability—not too poor to be unworthy of the risk involved, not too wealthy or visible for easy detection of an outsider (Rengert and Wasilchick 1985). Because it increases the perpetrator's familiarity and access, proximity to the burglar's home territory is also a plus, a fact that explains the vulnerability of areas undergoing gentrification. Where different income groups live in the same neighborhood, the more affluent present obvious targets (Johnson et al. 1997). An interesting study by Rengert and Wasilchick (1985) considered the geography of information—how burglars received information about the attributes of the places they considered plundering. Situational opportunities aside, sites falling along a home-work-leisure path were the most likely targets. Familiarity bred vulnerability for properties owned by the social class one step above the burglar's.

Location of burglarized property in relation to major roadways varied greatly from residential to business structures. Residences close to a highway are more susceptible, presumably due to ease of access and escape. Businesses close to busy roadways are less likely to be burglarized, presumably because increased traffic means more surveillance. Within business types, newer properties are more likely to be hit (53 percent). The increased burglary vulnerability of

Examinations of burglary sites have often tried to find a correlation between particular types of locations and the attributes of their human residents to predict the likelihood of victimization. A study of households in a northeastern, a Midwestern, and a southeastern sample city sought to combine individual factors of particular property protection with neighborhood social scale factors such as race, age, ownership, and income status (Smith and Jarjoura 1989). Victimization rates varied widely both from neighborhood to neighborhood and within neighborhoods, reflecting demographic as well as individual factors. Statistical analysis employed in the above study showed that while population density (apartments) affects victimization rates, it is not a significant factor on an individual basis. Income and racial heterogeneity were better predictors than single-person occupancy. Young, unmarried males experienced the highest rates of victimization. The researchers concluded that the best approach to predicting place vulnerability combines individual and community characteristics.

Burglaries of residential property usually occur by entry through a door. Whether front or back or a window entry depends on the type of structure and the visibility of location. A study focusing particularly on the vulnerability of student apartments found visibility, or "surveillability," the key factor affecting susceptibility of a structure to burglary (Robinson and Robinson 1997). Apartments located on a first floor corner, particularly when obscured by untrimmed foliage, provided a link between environmental characteristics and residential burglary.

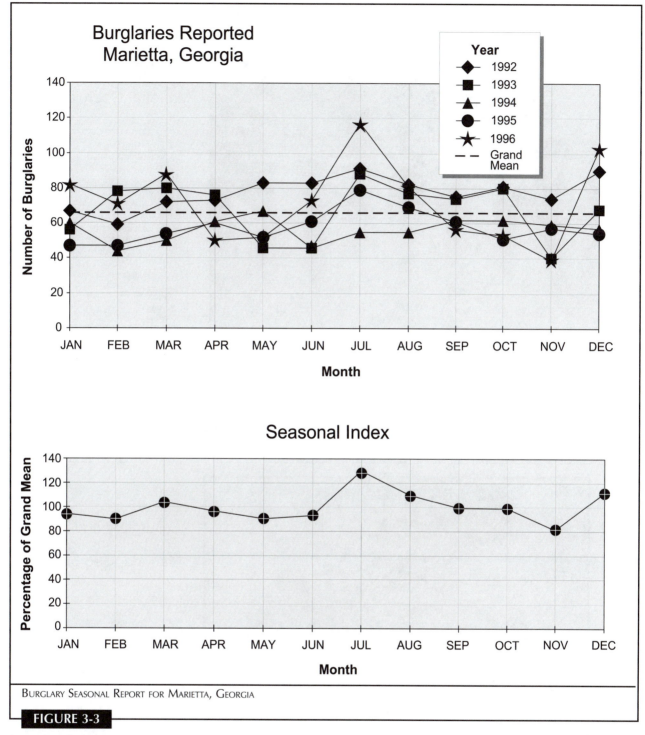

BURGLARY SEASONAL REPORT FOR MARIETTA, GEORGIA

FIGURE 3-3

Source: City of Marietta Police Department.

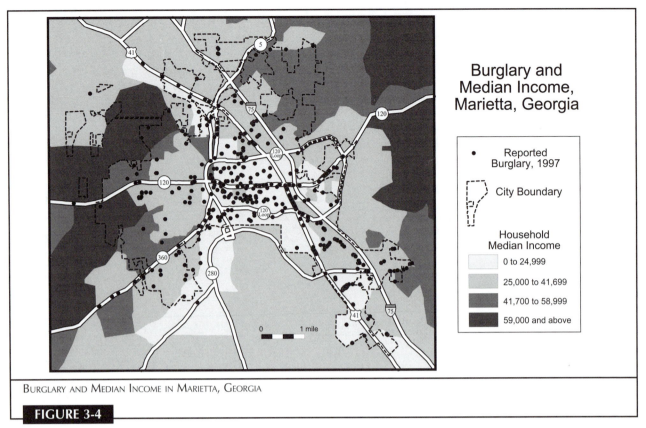

Burglary and
Median Income,
Marietta, Georgia

- Reported
  Burglary, 1997

City Boundary

Household
Median Income

0 to 24,999

25,000 to 41,699

41,700 to 58,999

59,000 and above

BURGLARY AND MEDIAN INCOME IN MARIETTA, GEORGIA

FIGURE 3-4

Sources: City of Marietta Police Department and U.S. Bureau of the Census, *Census of Population and Housing*, 1990.

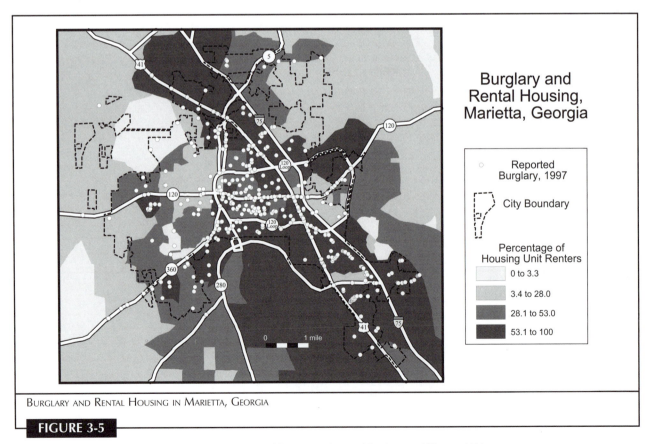

Burglary and
Rental Housing,
Marietta, Georgia

Reported
Burglary, 1997

City Boundary

Percentage of
Housing Unit Renters

0 to 3.3

3.4 to 28.0

28.1 to 53.0

53.1 to 100

BURGLARY AND RENTAL HOUSING IN MARIETTA, GEORGIA

FIGURE 3-5

Sources: City of Marietta Police Department and U.S. Bureau of the Census, *Census of Population and Housing*, 1990.

newer stores is due to the attractive goods and the lack of initial capital for installation of an adequate alarm system (Buck et al. 1993).

Businesses located in special zones just outside city centers seem most vulnerable to a variety of crimes. In the mid-1990s, burglary was by far the most common crime against businesses (Walker 1994). Repeat criminalization was rampant, with 63 percent of businesses likely to be hit more than once in the year of the original occurrence. The slowness of a business in protecting itself with sterner measures increased its chances of being hit again. Suspicion of "teenagers hanging around" was the perception factor that most fit the reality of risk.

On the national scale, states experiencing a change in burglary rates and the direction of this change in the years from 1989 to 1997 (generally peak high and low periods, respectively), are less easily explained. Southern states with the greatest drop in burglaries over this time period—Texas, Georgia, and Florida—all experienced large increases in immigration and economic improvement. Such increases were not the case in Mississippi and South Dakota, the states with the highest increase in burglary rates (Figure 3-6).

Timing of Burglaries

The precise time of commission of this crime is difficult to determine because victims are usually not present, perpetrators deny their presence, and evidence of time is often removed from the premises. Reported timing of occurrences varied from study to study. A Canadian study detected little variability in activity in prime locations from weekdays to weekends and throughout the day or night (Waller and Okihiro 1978), and a United States study noted changes between residential frequency during the day and non-residential property incidents at night (Scarr 1973). The latter study attributed the difference to peak times of non-occupancy. Federal Bureau of Investigation (FBI) figures recorded an increase in the 1970s of 120 percent in nighttime rates for residences, with daytime rates up by 337 percent during the same decade (Scarr 1973).

Timing patterns vary depending on the occupation pattern of residents. Predictable absence times of students from their off-campus apartments to attend classes and social events, for example, correlated with peak susceptibility periods (Robinson and Robinson 1997). Single-family residences in suburban settings followed a different pattern of

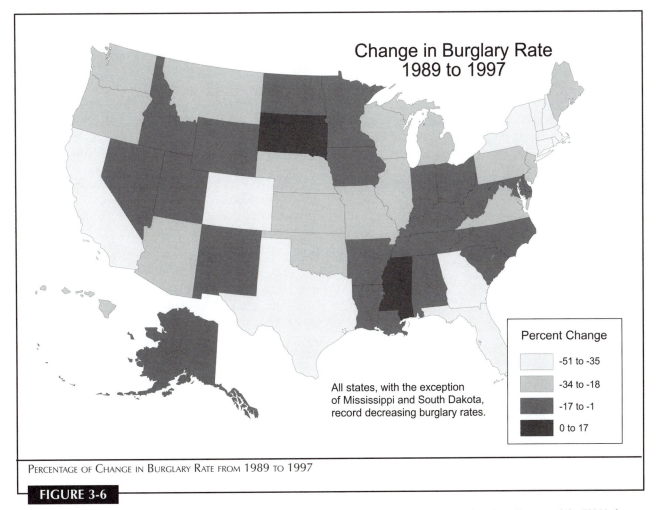

Change in Burglary Rate 1989 to 1997

All states, with the exception of Mississippi and South Dakota, record decreasing burglary rates.

Percent Change

- -51 to -35
- -34 to -18
- -17 to -1
- 0 to 17

PERCENTAGE OF CHANGE IN BURGLARY RATE FROM 1989 TO 1997

FIGURE 3-6

Source: U.S. Department of Justice, Bureau of Justice Statistics, State Crime Data, 1960-96, from the FBI's *Uniform Crime Reports* and the *FBI Uniform Crime Report, 1997 Preliminary Annual Release.*

susceptibility. Peak burglary periods between 9-11 A.M. and 1-3 P.M. correlated with women's likely absence patterns (Edmondson 1991).

Seasonality effects also vary widely. As early as 1917, one researcher suggested that thefts increased in winter because of employment difficulties (Falk 1952). One study of Toronto burglaries found that incidents appeared slightly higher in summer (Waller and Okihiro 1978), but other researchers (Conklin and Bittner 1973) observed little seasonal change. While overall rates seem stable from month to month regardless of section of the country (Scarr 1973), rates do vary greatly from area to area, depending on density, income, weather, marital status, and racial characteristics.

Criminal Conduct

FBI statistics reveal that apprehended burglars are overwhelmingly males under the age of 25 (Rengert and Wasilchick 1985; Federal Bureau of Investigation 1998). One Canadian study attributed the higher burglary rates in the United States to an historical difference in settlement patterns, with a "residual of respect" for the law adhering to Canadian residents compared to the more cavalier cowboy attitude they detected in U.S. residents. Because Australia, with a frontier and prisoner-pioneer past that is even more tumultuous than that of the United States, has a much lower rate of violent crimes than of property-related crimes such as burglary, one questions the applicability of this "historical type" explanation. In England, criminal analysis of susceptible sites begins by showing convicted burglars a video of a typical street, and having them analyze its vulnerability (Ekblom 1988). Breaking and entering offenders separate into novice and experienced groups, depending on mastery of the tools of the trade and network connections to a reliable "fence," an individual experienced in disposing of stolen property. The semi-skilled nature of the crime suits youthful perpetrators, who rely on opportunity more than planning. Methods are usually simple—break glass, force lock.

Burglary methods for determining targets can be divided into three behavior models (Edmondson 1991). The first is the primarily urban "smash-and-grab" used by drug addicts looking for quick money for their drug habit. Suburban burglars operating by automobile prefer the next two *modus operandi*. The "Marriage Model" holds that the longer the search, the lower the standards, e.g., the more time it takes to find a "perfect" house, the more the burglar relaxes his preferences. The "Homebuyer Model" is related, but starts with a short list of potential sites. No more than 30 minutes of looking is followed by approximately the same amount of time spent surveying a tentative target, followed by taking possession of the premises. Based on these patterns, Georgia instituted probation via time control. Burglary prime time restrictions may require a daytime job and an evening curfew. Given the opportunistic nature of the crime, high yield, age of perpetrator, and frequency of oc-

currence, the likelihood of recidivism is extremely high (Rengert and Wasilchick 1985).

Preventive Measures

Alarms, bars, locks, lights, dogs, and private security measures "harden" a location and lessen the chances of being victimized. A series of Australian studies urged that these measures be integrated with community-wide Neighborhood Watch organizations for improved deterrence. Signs identifying an area as a Neighborhood Watch site signaled similar deterrents. These efforts are often coupled with police-sponsored flashlight marches and door light awareness programs. The entire dwelling should be analyzed for vulnerability. Doors need strong locks and tight doorjambs within strong frames. Windows should be closed before leaving the premises (Ekblom 1988). Burglary can occur repeatedly at the same location if unsafe behavior continues. Alarms are a particularly good deterrent, reducing the likelihood of burglarization by a factor of four. Alarms are not a panacea, however, due to the length of time taken by police to respond and the value of goods that can be removed in that time span. An alarm sign by itself cuts the odds of burglary in half, although a British study found more respect for such signs in that country than in the United States (Wright et al. 1995). Deadbolt locks alone were far less effective deterrents. Locked but not otherwise secured properties represented 69 percent of burglarized structures (Buck et al. 1993).

Several urban police departments with Web sites stressed steps property owners could take to protect their sites (City of Austin 1998; Concord [CA] Police Department 1998). Fences begin the perimeter of defense, with visibility a key consideration. Deadlock bolts and jams for doors, closed and locked windows, secured skylights and fire escapes all encourage burglars to try elsewhere. Given the fixity of location and generality of neighborhood characteristics, individual premise protection is the only factor under the property owner's control.

Conclusions

Burglary is a crime of opportunity against unsecured property. Although violence against occupying owners in the name of burglary makes media coverage, such occurrences are far less likely than simple burglary. Location of property in relation to highways, shrubbery, and level above ground is important. Susceptibility varies with proximity to mixed income levels and type of property (business or residential or mixed use). Time of day and season also affect vulnerability levels, although the latter is disputed in various studies. However, the only data available to this researcher, when combined with mapped national statistics, agree with evidence that has the incidence of burglary peak during warm temperatures.

Studies agree on a few points. Burglars themselves are overwhelmingly young males. Differences present themselves when attempting to distinguish urban from suburban burglary settings, residential from business structures, time periods within a 24-hour span, and yearly and seasonal peaks. Prevention recommendations are similar, but studies disagree on their effectiveness, particularly from country to country. With burglary, increased knowledge leads to increased vigilance, but decreased peace of mind.

References

Bennett, T.H. 1989. Burglars' Choice of Targets. In D.J. Evans and D.T. Herbert, eds. *The Geography of Crime*. London: Routledge, pp. 176-92.

Buck, A., S. Hakim, and G. Rengert. 1993. Burglar Alarms and the Choice Behavior of Burglars: A Suburban Phenomenon. *Journal of Criminal Justice* 21: 497-507.

City of Austin. 11/26/98. BurglaryPreventionTips. <http://www.ci.austin.tx.us/police/burglary.htm>.

Concord (CA) Police Department. 11/26/98. Burglary Prevention. <http://www.ecis.com/noslo/burglary.html>.

Conklin, J.E., and E. Bittner. 1973. Burglary in a Suburb. *Criminology* 11: 206-32.

Edmondson, B. 1991. Time for Crime: The Habits of Burglars. *American Demographics* 13: 14-16.

Ekblom, P. 1988. Crime Prevention in England: Themes and Issues. In D. Challinger *Preventing Property Crime*. Canberra: Australian Institute of Criminology, pp. 11-30.

Falk, G. 1952. The Influence of Season on the Crime Rate. *Journal of Criminal Law, Criminology, and Police Science* 43: 199-213.

Federal Bureau of Investigation (FBI). 1998. *Uniform Crime Reports*. Bureau of Justice Statistics, Georgia Index Crimes <http://www.ojp.usdoj.gov>.

Johnson, S., K. Bowers, and A. Hirschfield. 1997. New Insights into the Spatial and Temporal Distribution of Repeat Victimization. *British Journal of Criminology* 37: 224-41.

Mukherjee, S.K., and L. Jorgensen, eds. 1985. *Burglary: A Social Reality*. Canberra: Australian Institute of Criminology.

Rengert, G., and J. Wasilchick. 1985. *Suburban Burglary: A Time and a Place for Everything*. Springfield, IL: Charles C. Thomas Publisher.

Robinson, M.B., and C.E. Robinson. 1997. Environmental Characteristics Associated with Residential Burglaries of Student Apartment Complexes. *Environment and Behavior* 29: 657-75.

Scarr, H. 1973. *Patterns of Burglary*. 2nd ed. Washington, DC: National Institute of Law Enforcement and Criminal Justice.

Smith, D.A., and G.R. Jarjoura. 1989. Household Characteristics, Neighborhood Composition and Victimization Risk. *Social Forces* 68: 621-40.

U.S. Department of Justice. 1998. Bureau of Justice Statistics, State Crime Data, 1960–96. Washington, D.C. <http://www.ojp.usdoj.gov>.

Walker, J. 1994. *The First Australian National Survey of Crimes Against Businesses*. Canberra: Australian Institute of Criminology.

Waller, I., and N. Okihiro. 1978. *Burglary: The Victim and the Public*. Toronto: University of Toronto Press.

Wright, R., R. Logie, and S. Decker. 1995. Criminal Expertise and Offender Decision Making: An Experimental Study of the Target Selection Process in Residential Burglary. *Journal of Research in Crime and Delinquency* 32: 39-53.

Auto Theft and Detecting Chop Shop Locations

Nancy G. La Vigne
Jill Kathleen Fleury
Joseph Szakas

Motor Vehicle Theft

Auto theft poses a significant crime problem in the United States, accounting for 10 percent of serious crimes in 1997 (Federal Bureau of Investigation 1999). The rate of auto theft has increased significantly over the last 40 years, although rates have declined from 1991 through 1997 (Federal Bureau of Investigation 1999). Nationally, auto theft rates vary by region, with distinct concentrations found along the West Coast and states bordering on Texas (Figure 3-7). Indeed, in the United States as a whole, just 10 states accounted for 46 percent of all auto thefts in 1997. Border states have historically been plagued by higher auto theft rates due to the relative ease in which stolen vehicles and parts can be exported (Clarke and Harris 1992).

Of those arrested for auto vehicle theft in 1997, 41 percent were individuals under the age of 18 (Federal Bureau of Investigation 1999). This statistic represents a downward trend in juvenile involvement in auto theft over time, suggesting that the crime has become more organized in nature and has shifted focus away from joyriding toward theft for the purpose of selling parts (Clarke and Harris 1992). These organized efforts involve offenders stealing specific car makes and models and driving these vehicles to chop shops, where they are dismantled and the parts are sold on the black market. It stands to reason that, from a law enforcement perspective, efforts associated with identifying chop shops and shutting them down would have a significant impact in reducing auto thefts.

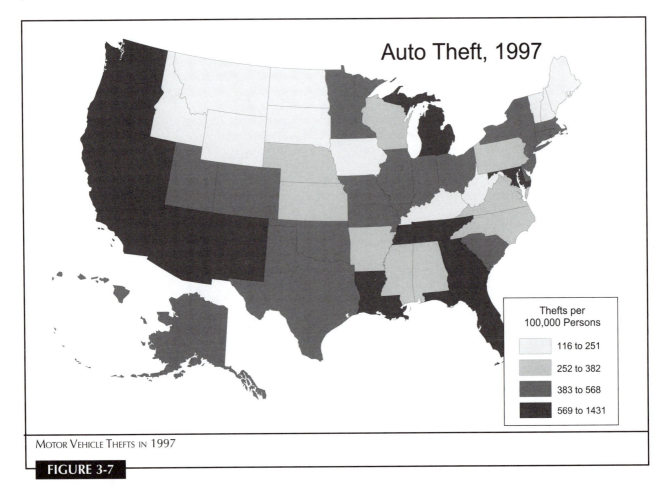

MOTOR VEHICLE THEFTS IN 1997

FIGURE 3-7

At the start of the twenty-first century, law enforcement agencies are moving toward a greater reliance on information technology to drive decision making at all levels of operation, from command and control policies to investigations and prevention efforts. Readily available data on crime patterns have allowed police to move beyond traditional techniques of criminal investigations toward methods that use information to identify spatial and temporal patterns of crime and criminal behavior (Sherman 1998). Prior research indicates that an understanding of the spatial components of crime is important for determining effective resource allocation, identifying patterns of crime within neighborhoods, improving community relationships, and evaluating crime fighting strategies. In addition to these purposes, the analysis of crime patterns plays a vital role in spatial search and investigation strategies (La Vigne and Wartell 1998).

Geographic Information Systems (GIS) allow law enforcement agencies to establish a platform for automated mapping and to undertake more advanced analysis of spatial components. For the investigation of auto thefts, GIS can illustrate the location of most thefts and the potential location of chop shops. The term "chop shop" is used here to describe places where stolen cars are taken for the purpose of stripping and reselling their parts. Often, these chop shops double as legitimate places of business (e.g., body shops), and identifying the likely location of such chop shops can be a valuable tool for law enforcement investigation efforts.

To develop a systematic chop shop search method using GIS, one must begin by establishing the potential patterns of criminal behavior associated with auto theft and chop shops by relying on a small but rich array of criminological literature. Using this core theoretical base, this essay will examine the spatial patterns of stolen cars from their point of origin to the chop shop. It is hypothesized that the relationship between the point of the offense and the chop shop will be grounded in the spatial components of the offender's journey to crime. Specifically, this essay examines both direction and distance of the offense to detect patterns that will lead to the identification of chop shop locations.

Patterns of Offending

We base our investigation of the spatial patterns of auto theft on two criminological theories of offending that draw from human ecology, economics, and criminology. By applying the distance-decay and rational choice theories to the patterns of auto thieves and their subsequent travel to chop shop locations, we can uncover a strategy that law enforcement agencies may consider in their investigations of these crimes.

Distance-Decay Modeling

The distance-decay theory suggests that if a person is searching for a target and several targets are in his or her proximity, then, all else being equal, the person will choose the closest target. Distance-decay modeling is based upon the reality that human movement is patterned, that it is a process by which individuals seek out and search for targets (Brantingham and Brantingham 1984). While all factors in offending can never be held equal, the pattern that emerges in this model has a strong spatial bias toward short trips to offending. Specifically, "within a crime classification, occurrences of crime should decline with increased distance. In comparison of several types of crime, the rate of decline with distance varies" (Brantingham and Brantingham 1984). This concept of distance decay can be applied to the act of auto theft.

Based on a rich literature of human spatial behavior, distance decay has been found to relate to many types of human interaction and decision-making processes. When applied to auto theft, the theory would indicate that criminals, like other rational persons, interact more with things and people that are close to their homes and other areas of routine activity, such as work, school, and recreation areas. Individuals are both more aware and have more experience with these areas and are therefore more comfortable searching within these domains.

The concept of distance decay has been found to be applicable to murder (Bullock 1955), property offenses (Baldwin and Bottoms 1976), robbery (Capone and Nichols 1976), and juvenile offending (Phillips 1980). This analysis extends the concept of distance decay to the idea that auto thieves search for cars in proximity to chop shops. Not only is it possible to determine that high concentrations of recovered vehicles may be proximal to chop shops, it may also be possible to determine what factors are favorable for choosing the area as a drop-off site. Examining both the direction and distance that the car was maneuvered from the point at which it was stolen to the point where it was discovered might allow the development of search strategies that maximize the benefits of these spatial clues.

Rational Choice

The rational choice perspective is consistent with the distance-decay premise, positing that individuals base their decisions upon micro-economic principles of cost-benefit analysis. Therefore, criminals choose their targets based on the extent to which they expect to maximize their rewards and minimize the risks and efforts associated with the crime (Clarke and Cornish 1985; Cornish and Clarke 1986). Crime is viewed as a deliberate behavior on the part of the offender to obtain things such as money or status. Obtaining these needs involves fundamental decisions and choices (Clarke 1997). The theory of rational choice focuses on the offender's decision-making process in which he or she evaluates the rewards of the effort in relation to the potential costs of the offense. Rational choice theorists have developed this theory of offending into models of rationality that incorporate limitations and constraints on potential behaviors, rather than assuming a purely rational calculation on the part of the offender (Clarke and Cornish 1985; Cornish and Clarke 1986).

Extending this theory to auto theft suggests that an offender's decisions to steal the car and to take it to a chop shop are also based on these evaluative processes. Because prior research on the influence of rational choice premises on auto theft alone have been supportive of its legitimacy (Light et al. 1993; McCullough et al. 1990; Spencer 1992), it is logical to extend this theory of rational choice to the analysis of car theft location and, specifically, to location of recovery. We would suggest that offenders act in a rational way to determine where they will steal the car in relationship to places where cars may be stripped of their parts.

Hypotheses

Using the above stated theories, we have developed hypotheses relating to the movement of stolen vehicles from location of theft to chop shop. We suggest that the location of chop shops from which the majority of vehicles are recovered will be closest in distance to the point from which the car was stolen. This hypothesis is based on the distance-

decay model whereby offenders will seek the closest possible point to offend, and based on rational choice, which would dictate that a proximal chop shop will reduce the risk of apprehension and increase the potentiality of a payoff for the car's parts. These chop shops are also likely to be located in a relational direction that is easily accessible to the point from which the car was stolen and in areas where the risk of detection is low. In exploring these hypotheses, we hope to develop a preliminary outline of offending that police departments may use in creating search strategies for chop shops within their own jurisdictions.

Methods

Sample

The data used in the subsequent analyses contained information on stolen automobiles over a seven-year period from 1991 to 1997. Data were obtained from the Baltimore County (Maryland) Police Department and comprised three primary spatial components: locations for where the car was stolen, where the car was recovered, and where chop shops were identified by the Baltimore County Police Department. Data on existing chop shop locations were derived from traditional police investigative techniques and are used as

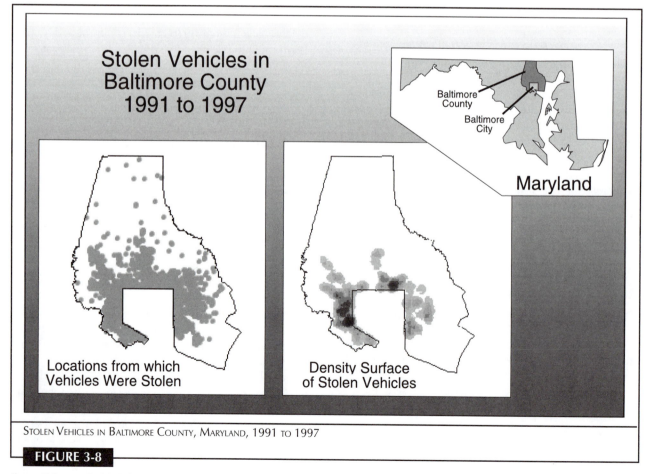

STOLEN VEHICLES IN BALTIMORE COUNTY, MARYLAND, 1991 TO 1997

FIGURE 3-8

Source: Baltimore County Police Department.

a final step in the following analysis to evaluate our method of predicting likely locations of chop shops. Because a stolen car may never be recovered, the data used in this analysis to explore the relationship between location of offense and location of recovery were composed of cases in which both a stolen and recovery location could be identified (n=4000).

Analysis

Variables that indicate where the car was stolen and its recovery are valuable in determining two potentially important spatial components: distance and direction. Through the use of these two measures, one can create a search strategy that takes advantage of these spatial cues. Further, using the remaining variable in this analysis—the location of chop shops already identified by police—we can evaluate the utility of this search strategy.

Using ArcView 3.1 along with the Arcview Spatial Analyst extension, both products developed by the Environmental Systems Research Institute, we created density surfaces by employing the simple grid method to determine

hot spots of auto thefts and recoveries. A density surface is created by draping a grid over the study area. The value for each component of the grid is then calculated from the number of points (i.e., the location of stolen automobiles) within a certain distance. When this grid surface is displayed on a map, heavier concentrations of stolen automobiles appear as darker areas. By examining the density map (Figure 3-8), we were able to identify and isolate the most active areas of auto theft. The two study areas, as shown in Figure 3-9, were used for the subsequent analyses of distance and direction from point of theft to the location of the chop shop and recovery.

The first study area (denoted as #1 in Figure 3-9) is located in the southwest area of Baltimore County, just west of the City of Baltimore. The second study area (denoted as #2 in Figure 3-9), is located in the southern portion of Baltimore County, just north of the City of Baltimore. After these study areas were established, the cases that occurred within these two locations for the remaining analyses were isolated for analysis purposes. Figure 3-10 hypothetically summarizes the strategies (discussed below) that were used to calculate direction and distance.

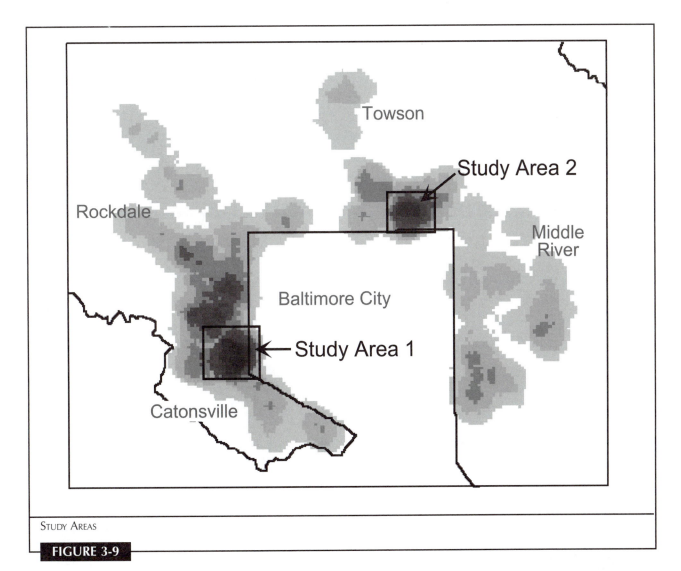

STUDY AREAS

FIGURE 3-9

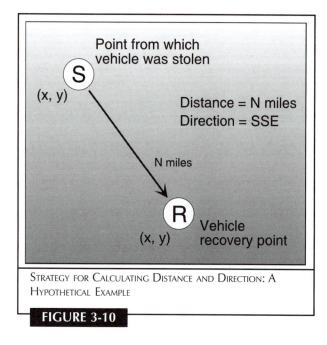

STRATEGY FOR CALCULATING DISTANCE AND DIRECTION: A
HYPOTHETICAL EXAMPLE

FIGURE 3-10

Results

Using case-by-case analysis of the latitude and longitude, calculations of the mean distance from theft to recovery were performed as well as the standard deviation for this distance. Results from this analysis for study area #1 (as shown in Figure 3-11) indicated that the average distance, from stolen to recovered, that offenders traveled with the vehicle was 3.4 miles. The standard deviation of this distance distribution was 2.8 miles. These findings suggest that the search strategy efforts for a stolen car should be concentrated within 1.9 to 4.7 miles of the center of study area #1 (*see* Figure 3-11a). In study area #2, we calculated an average distance, from stolen to recovered, of 3.9 miles, with a standard deviation of 3 miles. Using these findings for study area #2, we suggest that search strategy efforts be concentrated within 2.4 to 5.4 miles away from the center of the study area (*see* Figure 3-12a).

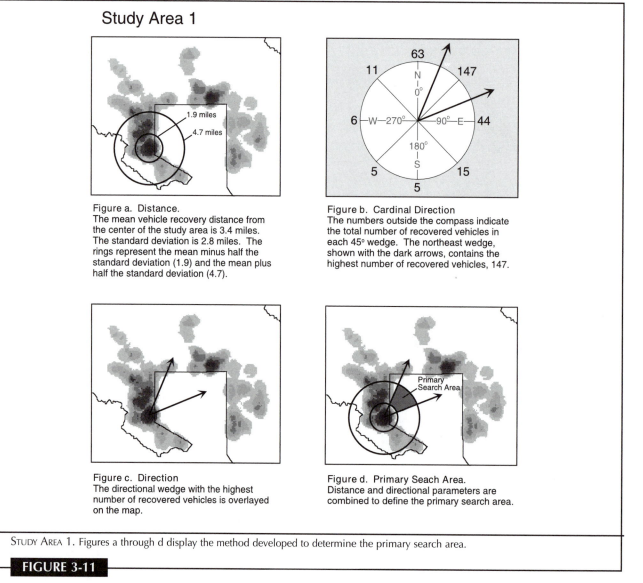

Study Area 1

Figure a. Distance.
The mean vehicle recovery distance from the center of the study area is 3.4 miles. The standard deviation is 2.8 miles. The rings represent the mean minus half the standard deviation (1.9) and the mean plus half the standard deviation (4.7).

Figure b. Cardinal Direction
The numbers outside the compass indicate the total number of recovered vehicles in each 45° wedge. The northeast wedge, shown with the dark arrows, contains the highest number of recovered vehicles, 147.

Figure c. Direction
The directional wedge with the highest number of recovered vehicles is overlayed on the map.

Figure d. Primary Seach Area.
Distance and directional parameters are combined to define the primary search area.

STUDY AREA 1. Figures a through d display the method developed to determine the primary search area.

FIGURE 3-11

Study Area 2

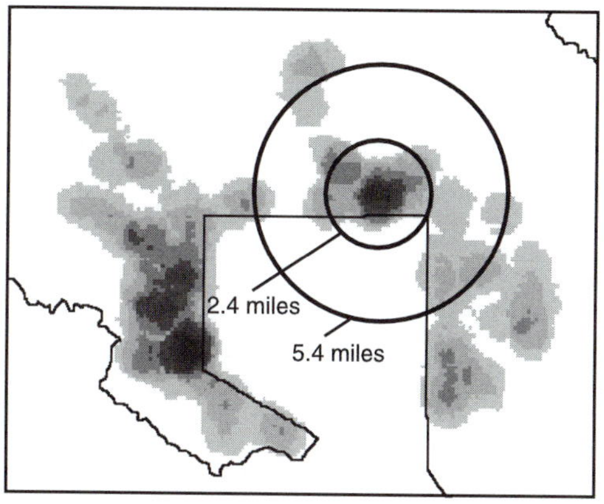

Figure a. Distance.
The mean vehicle recovery distance from the center of the study area is 3.9 miles. The standard deviation is 3.0 miles. The rings represent the mean minus half the standard deviation (2.4) and the mean plus half the standard deviation (5.4).

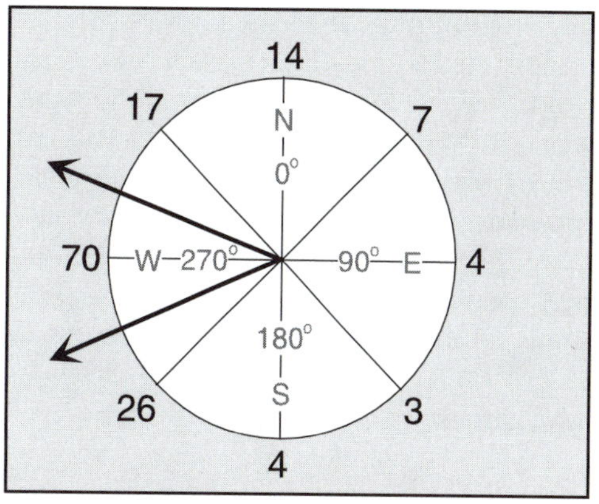

Figure b. Cardinal Direction
The numbers outside the compass indicate the total number of recovered vehicles in each 45° wedge. The west wedge, shown with the dark arrows, contains the highest number of recovered vehicles, 70.

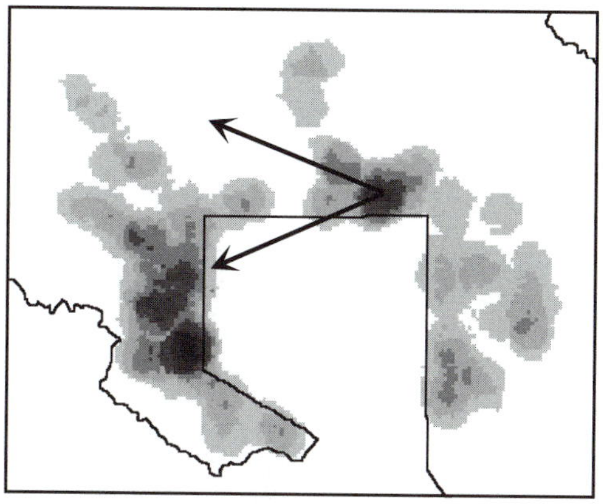

Figure c. Direction
The directional wedge with the highest number of recovered vehicles is overlayed on the map.

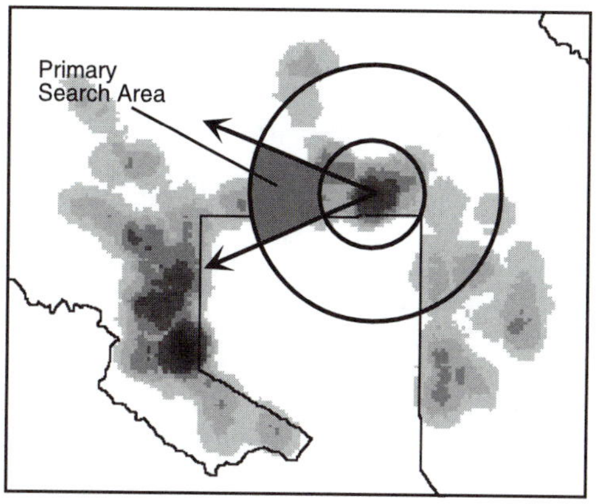

Figure d. Primary Seach Area.
Distance and directional parameters are combined to define the primary search area.

STUDY AREA 2. Figures a through d display the method developed to determine the primary search area.

FIGURE 3-12

To assess direction, we calculated, in degrees, the direction to the final recovery location from the point of theft. A zero-degree direction indicated a northerly movement, while 90-, 180-, and 270-degree directions indicated eastern, southern, and western movements, respectively. Each of these directional calculations were grouped into 45-degree intervals centered about each of the eight cardinal directions. Using the total number of cases within each of these intervals, the primary trend of directional movement was determined (Figures 3-11b and 3-12b). As can be seen in Figure 3-11c, one could speculate that in study area #1 most cars stolen in this area would be found in a northeast-erly direction. In study area #2, results indicate that most stolen cars in this area would be found in a westerly direction (Figure 3-12c).

Creating the Search Strategy

Combining these two trends of distance and direction allows the creation of a primary search area in which most chop shops should be located for each study area. In accordance with the postulates of both the distance-decay and routine activities theories, the location of chop shops should fall within the shortest distances defined by the above analyses.

The first step in defining the search strategy is to overlay the general or primary direction (45-degree wedge) on the map, centering the vertex of the angle directly in the middle (or centroid) of the study area. The second step is to delineate two circles around the centroid at two points: the mean distance plus ½ standard deviation to represent the maximum distance away from the search area; and the mean distance minus ½ standard deviation to represent the minimum distance away from the search area. The area within the wedge, lying between these two concentric distance zones, comprises the primary search area for chop shops (Figures 3-11d and 3-12d).

Evaluation of the Search Strategy

Evaluation of the above constructed search strategy is straightforward. As mentioned earlier, the Baltimore County Police Department provided a list of known chop shop locations. By examining the locations of these chop shops in relation to the primary search area of our predicted locations, we are able to evaluate the effectiveness of this distance and direction search method. Qualitatively, Figure 3-13 indicates that the primary selection for a search appears to be well founded for study area #1. This area of chop shop locations was clearly delineated according to both distance and direction to the locations of the auto thefts. Many of the chop shops identified by the Baltimore County Police Department were within the primary search area or close by. For study area #2, however, the results were not as promising. In this study area, no chop shops fall within the primary search area (Figure 3-14). Also, in study area #2 distance appears to play a greater role in determining the location of chop shops than does direction. Figure 3-15, however, reveals an even stronger pattern of distance over direction. By combining the search methods from the two study areas, a clear pattern of distance emerges along the outer bands of each circle.

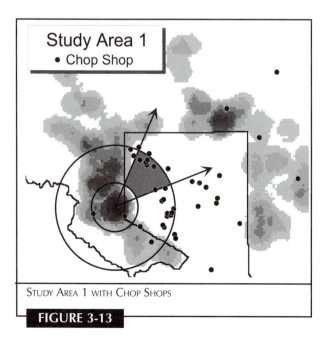

STUDY AREA 1 WITH CHOP SHOPS

FIGURE 3-13

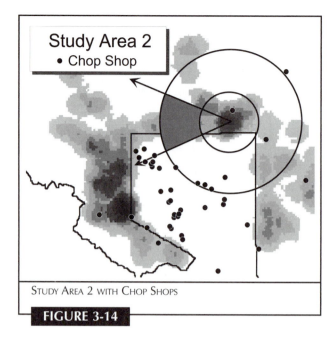

STUDY AREA 2 WITH CHOP SHOPS

FIGURE 3-14

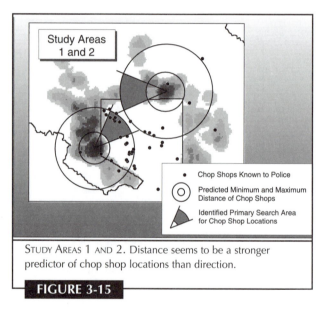

STUDY AREAS 1 AND 2. Distance seems to be a stronger predictor of chop shop locations than direction.

FIGURE 3-15

Discussion and Conclusions

The purpose of this essay was to explore how Geographic Information Systems can provide law enforcement agencies with additional information to support auto theft investigations. Specifically, distance and direction were examined as variables that define patterns dictated by distance-decay modeling and rational choice theory. It was suggested that car thieves would not travel long distances to steal cars in relation to locations of chop shops. A test determined the extent to which direction might play a role in predicting the locations of chop shops relative to where cars are stolen and recovered. The findings were partially supportive for the use by police officers of search strategies that employ these distance and direction variables. However, a number of limitations to our analysis may explain the limited power of this search strategy. First, the use of direction as a predictive variable does not adequately operationalize the concept of offenders limiting risks of apprehension, nor the effort associated with the crime. A better means of operationalizing this rational choice premise might be to examine direction in relation to land use. For example, it is possible that locations of chop shops are more prevalent in industrial areas, where fewer passersby are likely to notice activity late at night. Another means of more accurately delineating direction is along major thoroughfares, which serve as likely routes between locations of stolen and recovered cars. In this essay, we developed a search method that could be easily employed by local law enforcement agencies, and we therefore limited the amount and type of data and analytic power required to perform the search method. In doing so, we chose to use Euclidean distance rather than Manhattan distance. Manhattan distance indicates the orthogonal (right angle) distance measures along a street grid (e.g., the path traveled by a car requiring adherence to streets and thoroughfares while Euclidean distance indicates a straight line distance from one point to another, or "as the crow flies." Thus, it is likely that more meaningful results could be found by measuring distance along street networks and in relationship to land use.

Another limitation to the analysis employed in this essay is in the nature of the data set of known locations of auto thefts, recoveries, and chop shops. Because we were unable to isolate only those cars recovered with parts missing, we used all data for which a car was recovered, regardless of its condition. Naturally, these data will include a high percentage of cars stolen for joy riding that were received with parts intact. Because there is no reason to believe that joy riders would steal or deposit cars in proximity to chop shops, these additional data points may be masking an otherwise powerful search method. Finally, it is important to note that this method was tested against known chop shops identified through traditional investigative methods; there is no way of determining the location of chop shops not known to the police, and those locations may well have a spatial bias.

This research used spatial components inherent to the crime of auto thefts and outlined a process that may assist law enforcement agencies in performing their investigative functions. As mentioned above, future research would benefit from the inclusion of other factors that may influence the spatial patterns of auto thieves, such as land use data, the location of known body shops that may cover their illegitimate work with a legitimate facade, and the use of street

networks to help determine direction. Nonetheless, this current research highlights the merits of using GIS to identify patterns and to assist in auto theft investigations. Indeed, the use of distance alone to guide search methods for likely chop shop locations appears to be a powerful predictive variable. As the use of information technology grows in local law enforcement, more useful and powerful analytic tools in support of all types of law enforcement investigations are likely to be identified.

References

Baldwin, J., and A.E. Bottoms. 1976. *The Urban Criminal: A Study in Sheffield*. London: Tavistock.

Brantingham, P., and P. Brantingham. 1984. *Patterns in Crime*. New York: Macmillan.

Bullock, H.A. 1955. Urban Homicide in Theory and Fact. *Journal of Criminal Law, Criminology and Police Science* 45: 565-75.

Capone, C., and W.J. Nichols. 1976. Urban Structure and Criminal Mobility. *American Behavioral Scientist* 20: 199-213.

Clarke, R.V. 1997. *Situational Crime Prevention: Successful Case Studies*. Guilderland: NY: Harrow and Heston.

Clarke, R.V., and D.B. Cornish. 1985. Modeling Offenders' Decisions: A Framework for Police and Research. In Michael Tonry and Norval Morris, eds. *Crime and Justice: An Annual Review of Research*. vol. 6. Chicago: University of Chicago Press.

Clarke, R.V., and P.M. Harris. 1992. Auto Theft and Its Prevention. In M. Tonry, ed. *Crime and Justice: A Review of Research*, vol. 16. Chicago: University of Chicago Press.

Cornish, D.B., and R.V. Clarke. 1986. *The Reasoning Criminal: Rational Choice Perspectives on Offending*. New York: Springer-Verlag.

Federal Bureau of Investigation 1999. *Uniform Crime Reports: Crime in the United States*. Washington, DC: U.S. Department of Justice.

La Vigne, N.G., and J. Wartell. 1998. *Crime Mapping Case Studies: Successes in the Field*. Washington, DC: Police Executive Research Forum.

Light, R., C. Nee, and H. Inghan. 1993. *Car Theft: The Offender's Perspective*. Home Office Research Study, No. 130. London: H.M. Stationery Office.

McCullough, D., T. Schmidt, and B. Lockhart. 1990. *Car Theft in Northern Ireland*. Home Office Research Study, No. 132. London: H.M. Stationery Office.

Phillips, P. 1980. Characteristics and Typology of the Journey to Crime. In D. Georges-Abeyie and K. D. Harries, eds. *Crime: A Spatial Perspective*. New York: Columbia University Press.

Sherman, L.W. 1998. American Policing. In M. Tonry, ed. *Handbook of Crime and Punishment*. New York: Oxford University Press.

Spencer, E. 1992. *Car Crime and Young People on a Sunderland Housing Estate*. Crime Prevention Unit Paper 40. London: Home Office.

Environmental Crime

Nancy L. Winter
Ute J. Dymon

Environmental crime is a phenomenon of the twentieth century. Defining the term "environment" is critical to understanding the scope and complexion of such a crime. By mid-century in the United States, concern for the environment had grown because of blatant examples of misuse of the land and overwhelming examples of pollution. Awareness of concepts such as the "balance of nature" and the "web of life" developed, and the country's environmental consciousness rose to a level that supported mass public protest. Earth Day 1970 set the common conception of the environment as the natural "green" cycles of the Earth, focusing on the land, air, water, and biosphere, especially in relation to human health and quality of life. This common definition of the environment involving the land, air, water and biota became coupled with how human society exists in a built environment of technological complexity.

Conservationists organized to build public support for the maintenance of critical natural elements of life in the United States and to inform the public of environmental transgressions. Also important in engendering the concept of an environmental crime is the expanding insurance industry. Victims seeking to establish the existence of an environmental crime could seek recompense through lawsuits and insurance claims.

Types of Crimes

Crimes often are classed as *mala in se*, those thought to be immoral or intrinsically wrong, or naturally evil, such as murder, rape, arson, burglary, and larceny, or as *mala prohibita*, those not naturally evil, but prohibited by statute because they infringe the rights of others. Today, some environmentalists argue that environmental crimes are not only *mala prohibita*, but also *mala in se* because their cumulative negative effects on the natural and built environments make them both immoral and intrinsically evil in themselves. Technically, a crime is a punishable misdeed or violation committed against the public or even one member of the public and is prosecuted by the state, such as when the federal government takes poachers of endangered species to court. A wrong committed against an individual is a tort, and the victim may seek to remedy the wrong in court in a civil action, such as when cancer victims in Woburn, Massachusetts, sought recovery from certain chemical companies.

Environmental Legislation

Today, environmental crime in the U.S. centers around a series of laws passed since the first Earth Day. The 1970 National Environmental Protection Act (NEPA) was the umbrella law under which the lead federal agency in targeting offenders, the Environmental Protection Agency (EPA), was established along with a Council on Environmental Quality. Under NEPA, all federal agencies must assess the environmental consequences of proposed projects by filing impact statements describing the environmental effects of building such technological features as highways, bridges, airports, dams, and nuclear power plants (Golden et al. 1979). Extensive environmental regulation followed, including the Clean Air Acts of 1970 and 1990; the Water Pollution Control Act, as amended in 1972; the Safe Drinking Water Act in 1974; and the Resource Conservation and Recovery Act (RCRA) in 1976 (Golden et al. 1979). The 1980 Comprehensive Environmental Response, Compensation, and Liability Act (CERCLA), called the "Superfund Act," created a $1.6-billion fund to clean up hazardous waste sites. Other legislation covering toxic substances, noise, pesticides, ocean dumping, endangered species, and wilderness and wild and scenic rivers were enacted and supported not only enforcement, but also pollution research, standard setting, and monitoring. When antipollution standards are violated, empowered citizens can sue both government agencies and private industry. A prime focus of organizations such as the National Resources Defense Council and the Environmental Defense Fund is the filing of lawsuits over environmental issues.

U.S. Laws and Regulations

A labyrinth of environmental statutes and regulations develops as state and city governments pass protective laws. In the United States, court cases cover environmental crimes by individuals, corporations, institutions, and governments. The majority of cases involve civil actions, or tort cases, in which parties seek to redress a wrong. However, under such statutes as the Endangered Species Law and from actions such as illegal disposal of toxic wastes, actual criminal cases arise. In the U.S. today, many environmental situations are not legally crimes, but are considered "moral crimes" by society. The hierarchy of U.S. laws and regulations is diagramed in Figure 3-16. The majority of environmental liti-

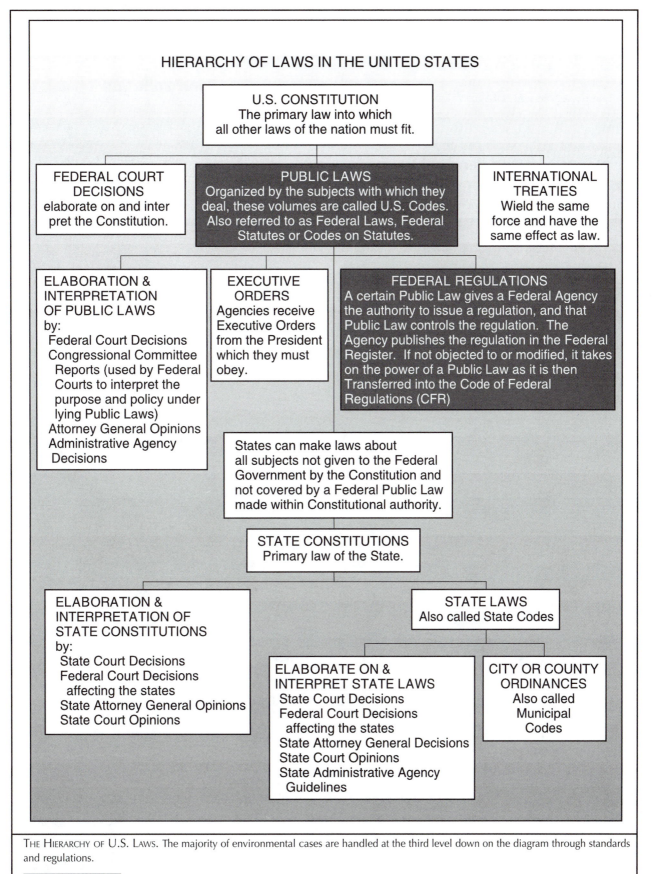

HIERARCHY OF LAWS IN THE UNITED STATES

U.S. CONSTITUTION
The primary law into which
all other laws of the nation must fit.

FEDERAL COURT DECISIONS
elaborate on and inter
pret the Constitution.

PUBLIC LAWS
Organized by the subjects with which they
deal, these volumes are called U.S. Codes.
Also referred to as Federal Laws, Federal
Statutes or Codes on Statutes.

INTERNATIONAL TREATIES
Wield the same
force and have the
same effect as law.

ELABORATION & INTERPRETATION OF PUBLIC LAWS
by:
Federal Court Decisions
Congressional Committee
Reports (used by Federal
Courts to interpret the
purpose and policy under
lying Public Laws)
Attorney General Opinions
Administrative Agency
Decisions

EXECUTIVE ORDERS
Agencies receive
Executive Orders
from the President
which they must
obey.

FEDERAL REGULATIONS
A certain Public Law gives a Federal Agency
the authority to issue a regulation, and that
Public Law controls the regulation. The
Agency publishes the regulation in the Federal
Register. If not objected to or modified, it takes
on the power of a Public Law as it is then
Transferred into the Code of Federal
Regulations (CFR)

States can make laws about
all subjects not given to the Federal
Government by the Constitution and
not covered by a Federal Public Law
made within Constitutional authority.

STATE CONSTITUTIONS
Primary law of the State.

ELABORATION & INTERPRETATION OF STATE CONSTITUTIONS
by:
State Court Decisions
Federal Court Decisions
  affecting the states
State Attorney General Opinions
State Court Opinions

STATE LAWS
Also called State Codes

ELABORATE ON & INTERPRET STATE LAWS
State Court Decisions
Federal Court Decisions
  affecting the states
State Attorney General Decisions
State Court Opinions
State Administrative Agency
  Guidelines

CITY OR COUNTY ORDINANCES
Also called
Municipal
Codes

THE HIERARCHY OF U.S. LAWS. The majority of environmental cases are handled at the third level down on the diagram through standards and regulations.

FIGURE 3-16

Source: Golden, Jack, Robert P. Ouellette, Sharon Saari, and Paul N. Cheremisinoff. 1979. *Environmental Impact Data Book.* Ann Arbor, MI: Ann Arbor Science Publishers, Inc., p. 242.

gation occurs three levels down on this legal framework principally in regards to federal regulations. Environmental regulations published in the *Federal Register* are traceable back to an authorizing statute, or public law (see level 2 of this figure) that requires standards to be developed, and based on these standards lawsuits can be filed or administrative actions can be taken by government agencies (Cutler 1999).

Nonpunishable Personal Crime

The spatial distributions of technological hazards often indicate the potential for environmental crime. However, the locations of hazardous substances that are ubiquitous and diffused in everyday life, such as asbestos, lead, and mercury, basically cannot be mapped. At the family or local level, many environmental offenses occur and go unpunished because the laws are not easily enforced. For instance, a car's catalytic converter is disconnected, or an endangered plant species is uprooted.

Point sources of pollution of land, air, and water provide the clues for determining liability in many environmental cases. At an exact location, outflow from a pipe or emission from a smokestack are the principal types of point sources. Culpability for non-point sources of pollution is

difficult to establish at any scale because pollutants are found spread out over such a wide area with no identifiable single source.

Land Pollution

Notable cases of land pollution have (1) forced promulgation of stricter regulations and outright bans on the use of certain chemicals, such as DDT, once sprayed on American farmlands; (2) compelled federal orders for abandonment of towns such as Love Canal, Niagara, New York, and Times Beach, Missouri; and (3) resulted in the identification of a National Priorities List (NPL) of "Superfund Sites" that require lengthy and expensive cleanup. Figure 3-17 presents the more than 1,200 NPL sites in the United States. A significant cluster is located in the Northeast. New Jersey has the highest number of sites at 110, followed by Pennsylvania and New York. In the Midwest, Michigan has the highest number of sites; in the West, California leads with 93 sites. Florida has more toxic sites than any other state in the South. North Dakota is the only state with no entries on the National Priorities List. Sites are considered "deleted" after remedial actions are taken. However, additional contaminated sites may be proposed.

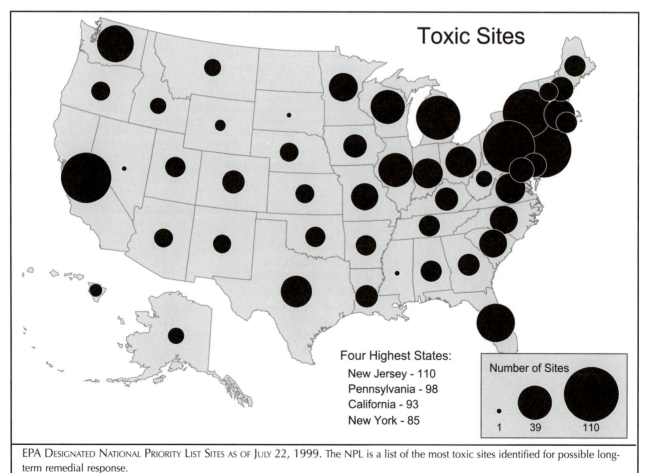

EPA Designated National Priority List Sites as of July 22, 1999. The NPL is a list of the most toxic sites identified for possible long-term remedial response.

FIGURE 3-17

Source: Environmental Protection Agency. Available online at <http://www.epa.gov/superfund/sites/reports.htm>.

Love Canal

Love Canal was the first case in which the federal and state governments forced evacuation of areas of a city to protect the health of residents from chemical contamination of the land. The State of New York and the federal government ordered Love Canal residents to evacuate their homes in 1978, and the area was declared a national emergency in 1980. Figures 3-18a and 3-18b are a composite aerial photo set. Figure 3-18a presents the rural Love Canal site in 1927. Figure 3-18b shows the structures, including 99th Street Elementary School and residential housing, built on the canal land after Hooker Chemical Company disposed of hazardous waste in the canal for decades. White patches on the land in Figure 3-18b are areas where toxic chemicals seeping to the surface allowed no vegetation to grow.

The Hooker Chemical Company and the City of Niagara Falls paid former residents $20,000,000 in settlement damages. In March 1998, Occidental Corporation settled claims from the final 900 families who sought damages for the years they lived at Love Canal. For 20 years, the State of New York sought federal funds to help pay for the Love Canal cleanup. In August 1998, the federal government agreed to pay a reimbursement of $6.1 million to New York, the amount spent by the state for Love Canal cleanup and finally awarded by the U.S. retroactively under CERCLA (or "Superfund").

Love Canal
Aerial Photos Before and After

a. Love Canal Area, 1927. Overview of the canal area in 1927. The canal is marked by the arrow. The northern branch of the Niagra River is visible at the bottom of the photograph. Open land surrounds the canal.

b. Love Canal Land Pollution. Infrared aerial photograph taken in the spring of 1978. The Canal has long been filled in. In the center of the photo is the 99th Elementary School. Two lines of homes border the landfill with the LaSalle Housing Development in the upper right. Leaching chemical contamination is assumed to show as white bare areas (circled) with no vegetation.

LOVE CANAL AREA IN 1927 AND 1978

FIGURE 3-18

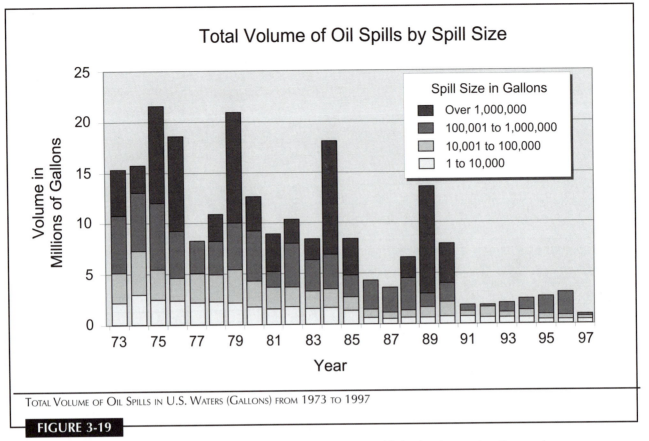

Total Volume of Oil Spills by Spill Size

Spill Size in Gallons
- ■ Over 1,000,000
- ■ 100,001 to 1,000,000
- ▨ 10,001 to 100,000
- □ 1 to 10,000

Volume in Millions of Gallons (y-axis: 0, 5, 10, 15, 20, 25)

Year (x-axis: 73, 75, 77, 79, 81, 83, 85, 87, 89, 91, 93, 95, 97)

TOTAL VOLUME OF OIL SPILLS IN U.S. WATERS (GALLONS) FROM 1973 TO 1997

FIGURE 3-19

Source: U.S. Coast Guard, *Polluting Incident Compendium* available at <http://www.uscg.mil/hq/g-m/nmc/response/stats/Summary.htm>.

Water Pollution

Water pollution, especially in the oceans, has led to expensive litigation. Coast Guard data reveal that from 1973 to 1997 the number of oil spills over 1,000 gallons in U.S. waters decreased. Figure 3-19 is a bar graph showing the total volume of oil spills by spill size (gallons) off U.S. shores from 1973 to 1997. One interpretation of this chart reveals that 67.5 percent of U.S. spills between 1973 and 1997 were greater than 100,000 gallons. Between 1991 and 1997 there were no spills greater than 1,000,000 gallons, indicating a positive trend. However, famous oil spills, such as the *Torrey Canyon* spill at the Scilly Isles off the south coast of Britain in 1967 and the 1989 *Exxon Valdez* spill in Prince William Sound, Alaska, produced litigation that required decades to resolve.

Until September 2001, Exxon Corporation will make annual payments to a Restoration Fund for the Alaskan cleanup. The 1967 *Torrey Canyon* spill combined with an oil well blowout off the California coast in the Santa Barbara Channel in 1968 led to passage in 1972 of the U.S. Federal Water Pollution Control Act and to international adoption of the International Convention for the Prevention of Pollution from Ships in 1973. Figure 3-20 is a map that compares the spatial extent of the *Exxon Valdez* shoreline oil contamination in Prince William Sound hypothetically with the eastern shore of the United States. If this had occurred on the East Coast, it would have spread from Maine to Georgia. This places the extent of the damage into an interesting geographic perspective. Yet, worldwide, the *Exxon Valdez* spill was only the 53rd largest in history.

Figure 3-21 is a world map of ocean oil spills from 1960 to 1997, each involving more than 10 million gallons of spilled oil. Most major oil spills have occurred in the Persian Gulf. Saddam Hussein's release of oil during the Gulf War is a contender for the largest worldwide oil spill to date. Other concentrations are off the coasts of Central America, South Africa, and Western Europe. The frequency of these spills and their enormous spatial extent on the globe refute those who believe the world ocean is too extensive to ever be seriously polluted.

The Mississippi River Initiative

The greatest river basin in the U.S., the drainage area of the 2,350-mile-long Mississippi, receives more diverse pollution than just oil. For most of the Mississippi's length, neither fishing nor swimming is advised. In the Gulf of Mexico, its contaminated waters may be causing an area as large as New Jersey, or 7,728 square miles, to be biologically dead (Grunwald 1998; Howe 1999). From September 1997

If the Exxon Valdez Oil Spill had Occurred on the East Coast

Exxon Valdez Spill—East Coast comparison. If the *Exxon Valdez* spill had been on the East Coast, beaches would have been oiled from Maine to Georgia. "In the Kenai Peninsula-Kodiak region, more than 1,000 miles of shoreline were found to be oiled."

FIGURE 3-20

Source: "What Happened on March 24, 1989?," available online at <http://www.oilspill /state.ak.us/col12.html>.

to September 1998, the EPA doubled its criminal enforcement staff along the river to try to stem the raw sewage, slaughterhouse waste, oil, heavy metals, cyanide, and other toxins continually added to its waters. Although this initiative targeted point sources of pollution, the EPA also supports efforts such as the Clean Water Action Plan established by President Bill Clinton to combat agricultural run-off, storm drain pollution, and other such non-point sources. A 20 percent cutback in the use of nitrogen fertilizers and pesticides on hog farms in Iowa and on fields in Illinois has been proposed (Howe 1999).

Begun in 1997, the multi-agency Mississippi River Initiative aims at reducing the point source industrial pollution pouring daily into the river. In its first year, 54 criminal convictions, nearly $30 million in fines, and a torrent of environmental penalties were generated. Besides these criminal cases, 18 civil cases against polluters in the Missis-

sippi basin were conducted, and the EPA handled 93 administrative cases. Included were violations such as illegal emissions, illegal dumping, wetlands destruction, sewage overflows, chemical discharges, oil spills, and falsifying of environmental reports. At fault were wastewater treatment plants, construction companies, auto dealerships, factories, a riverboat casino, and the City of New Orleans. To conclude its pollution case, New Orleans committed to building a new $200-million sewage treatment plant. For illegally dumping 55 barrels of hazardous waste, the owner of an automotive supply business in St. Louis must spend three years in a federal penitentiary. Shell Oil Company avoided criminal prosecution for alleged illegal emissions of sulfur dioxide, hydrogen sulfide, and benzene at an oil refinery in Roxana, Illinois, by agreeing to pay a $1.5-million fine, decrease the plant's emissions, and ameliorate environmental problems on the Mississippi by $10 million. The latter includes buying $500,000 worth of Mississippi River lands to be owned and preserved by the State of Illinois (Grunwald 1998).

Air Pollution

Regulations to combat both indoor and outdoor air pollution exist. Problems can arise from the tight insulation of modern structures which significantly reduce air flow for ventilation; brand new buildings have had to be abandoned because workers within them become ill in their environment. Potentially lethal air contamination results when asbestos materials are manipulated and "friable" (easily crumpled to pieces by the human hand) airborne particles of .5 microns or longer in size are released into the air. Taken into the lungs in just one brief exposure, asbestos particles can stay there causing a rare type of cancer called mesothelioma 20 to 40 years later (Brodeur 1980; Preger 1978). Laundry rooms in the homes of asbestos workers can also contain this danger if worker's clothes release particles into the air (Brodeur 1980). In the case of asbestos, first sold in 1866, standard setting took over 100 years until the danger of mesothelioma was revealed by a British cancer registry (Greenberg and Davies 1974). Without the historical and scientific data with which to develop a standard, prosecution for mishandling of asbestos was not possible. The leading U.S. asbestos company, Johns Manville, went bankrupt under the sheer weight of the number of lawsuits brought by workers exposed in World War II who 40 years later developed asbestosis or mesothelioma. Today, regulations prevent the public sale of products containing asbestos and require that old asbestos must be removed from a building using the most stringent, and relatively expensive, procedures.

Outdoor Air Pollution

The National Weather Service issues smog alerts for affected cities. Under the 1990 Clean Air Act, cities can be fined for failing to lower polluted air. One of the most vexing and contentious issues concerning air pollution in the

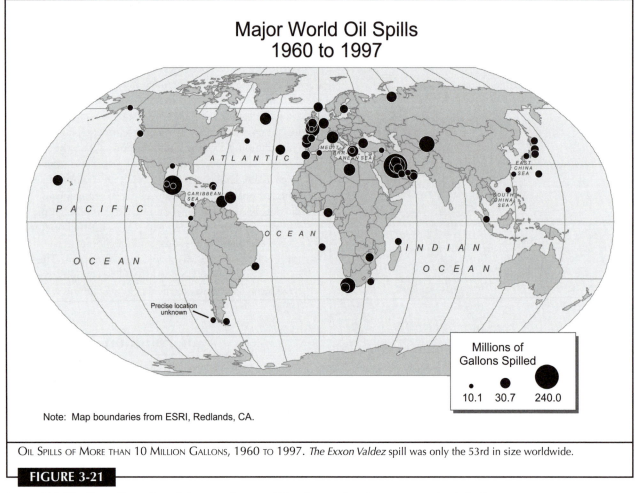

Major World Oil Spills
1960 to 1997

Millions of
Gallons Spilled

•　●　⬤
10.1　30.7　240.0

Note: Map boundaries from ESRI, Redlands, CA.

OIL SPILLS OF MORE THAN 10 MILLION GALLONS, 1960 TO 1997. *The Exxon Valdez* spill was only the 53rd in size worldwide.

FIGURE 3-21

Source: Oil Spill Intelligence Report, Cutter Information Corp., available online at <http://www.cutter.com/osir/biglist.htm>.

U.S. is the scientific appraisal of the causes and sources of acid rain. High smokestack industries are required to install scrubbers to clean their stack discharges before they are released. Fines are issued for lack of compliance. Perhaps the most lethal type of air pollution occurs when a nuclear facility releases a radioactive plume into the atmosphere. The polar projection of Figure 3-22 depicts the spread of Chernobyl's radioactive plume over the first 10 days after the uncontrollable fire and meltdown of the Soviet nuclear power plant. The radioactive cloud is spatially contained on April 27, 1986, within the Chernobyl area. However, its diffusion in various directions, mostly a westward flow, is obvious by May 6. The expansiveness of the cloud over time demonstrates the role of wind systems in environmental hazards. Several European countries attempted unsuccessfully to sue the Soviet Union for compensation following this environmental disaster.

OSHA and the Built Environment

Under provisions of the Occupational Safety and Health Act or OSHA (Public Law 91-596), the Department of Labor levies fines against employers who do not maintain certain standards of safety and health in the built environments of their workers. This broad spectrum of standards includes safety requirements for construction, demolition, electrical equipment, lighting, machine tools, ladders, elevators, boiler and pressure vessels, traffic, ventilation, accident prevention signs and tags, and many other areas. Unlike accidents, standards for the acceptable concentrations of toxic dusts and gases govern prevention of occupational diseases, which in many cases take 20 years or more to develop after exposure. Legislation in the U.S. redresses many occupational abuses, and under a system of insurance called workers' compensation, those who contract occupational diseases are aided.

In hundreds of industries, occupational hazards arise from worker exposure to metal dusts, chemicals, infective substances, and radiation. Pneumoconiosis, or dust-caused lung diseases, affect miners, granite workers, sandblasters, metal grinders, and others. Known commonly as black lung disease, the illnesses cause affected workers to have darkened lung tissue from the inhaled dust. Figure 3-23 shows the extent of coal fields in the U.S. The dominant region is in the South, from Tennessee southward along the Mississippi River, then west into Texas and east into Alabama.

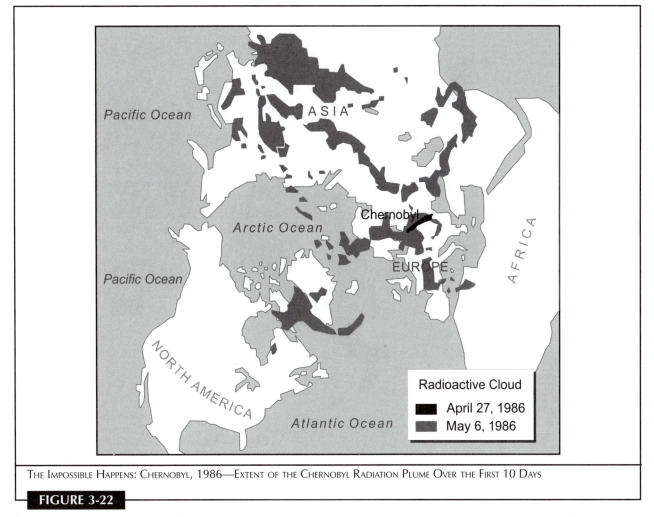

THE IMPOSSIBLE HAPPENS: CHERNOBYL, 1986—EXTENT OF THE CHERNOBYL RADIATION PLUME OVER THE FIRST 10 DAYS

FIGURE 3-22

Source: Redrawn with the permission of Lawrence Livermore National Laboratory from documents maintained by BRAMA, Inc., available at <http:// www.brama.com/ukraine/cbyl.html>.

Other main "coal belts" are found in the Montana-Dakotas, Iowa-Missouri, Illinois, and Pennsylvania-West Virginia areas. Employers of miners in these areas offer workers regular medical checkups to counter the onset of black lung disease. The Department of Labor's Mine Safety and Health Administration (MSHA) has a campaign to end black lung disease.

Endangered Species

A species of plant or animal is considered endangered if its ability to survive and reproduce has been imperiled by human activities. In accordance with the U.S. Endangered Species Act (1973), the United States government in 1992 classified 170 indigenous species as likely to become extinct or threatened, including the grizzly bear, the spotted owl, and the snail darter. At the locations of the latter two species, lumbering and construction, respectively, have in certain cases become illegal activities. Worldwide, 1,200 species also were classified as endangered. In the U.S., illegal hunting, trapping, and poisoning comprise most of the litigation under the 1973 law along with violations of the prohibition against any trading in endangered species and their products.

Land with Water: Wetlands

In the continental United States, it is estimated that less than 100 million acres of the original 215 million acres of wetlands existing 200 years ago have survived. The pace of wetlands loss accelerated in the 1970s and 1980s. Estimates released by the Office of Technology Assessment (OTA) reveal that more than half of the existing U.S. wetlands were destroyed in those two decades (U.S. Office of Technology Assessment 1984; Dahl et al. 1991).

Today, nearly one-third to one-half of the endangered species in the United States feed and spawn in wetlands. Loss of wetlands not only translates into fewer birds and less wildlife, but can also result in lost tourist dollars, reduced fisheries, and higher flood damage repair costs. Fines for illegal wetlands destruction are imposed by the EPA.

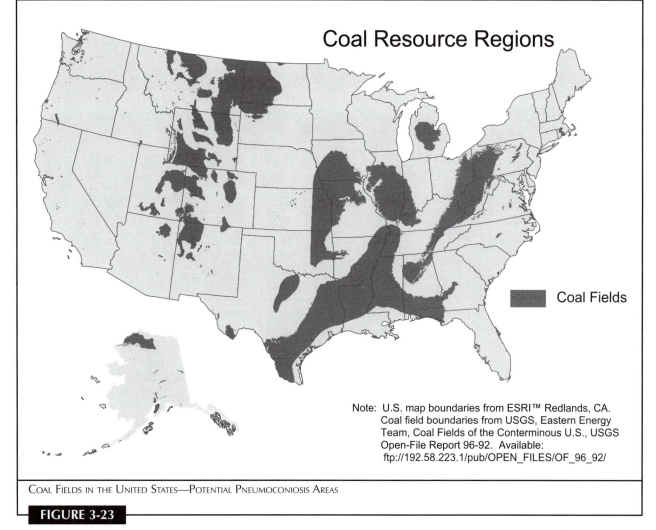

Coal Resource Regions

Note: U.S. map boundaries from ESRI™ Redlands, CA. Coal field boundaries from USGS, Eastern Energy Team, Coal Fields of the Conterminous U.S., USGS Open-File Report 96-92. Available: ftp://192.58.223.1/pub/OPEN_FILES/OF_96_92/

Coal Fields

COAL FIELDS IN THE UNITED STATES—POTENTIAL PNEUMOCONIOSIS AREAS

FIGURE 3-23

Source: United States Geological Survey.

Crimes Presumably Caused by Humanity

Scientific uncertainty and controversial views characterize many of the most perplexing, large-scale environmental situations. The scientific proofs necessary to convince humans to regulate their activities to combat acid rain, global warming, and ozone depletion are highly controversial because scientists differ in their interpretations of data. Despite this, in cases such as ozone depletion, control by international treaties and regulation is being attempted. Figure 3-24 reveals the increase in the size of the ozone hole over the South Pole through a measure of the marked decrease in the ozone readings over Halley Bay station in Antarctica for each October from 1956 to 1994. In the U.S., strict regulations prohibit the release of widely used chemicals called chlorofluorocarbons (CFCs) into the atmosphere where they destroy ozone. Under Title VI of the Clean Air Act, the EPA's Stratospheric Protection Division enforced this ban in fiscal year 1998 alone by referring 266 criminal cases to the Department of Justice and by levying $92.8 million in criminal fines. Offenses ranged from failure to remove CFCs from the air conditioners of cars before they were demolished to illegal smuggling of CFCs into the U.S. from Mexico. The smuggling of ozone-depleting chemicals was addressed nationally by a joint investigation of law enforcement agencies, including the Department of Justice, the Federal Bureau of Investigation (FBI), U.S. Customs, and the Internal Revenue Service (IRS) with an outcome of 80 convictions, hefty fines, and jail terms.

Because of their worldwide scale and ultimate effects on Earth's human population, such criminal actions are sometimes called "crimes against humanity," albeit the human species is the perpetrator of these crimes by its need for and acceptance of technology.

Environmental Crime Clues from a Causal Chain

Some of the most contentious environmental cases involve technological hazards in which the public is unwittingly

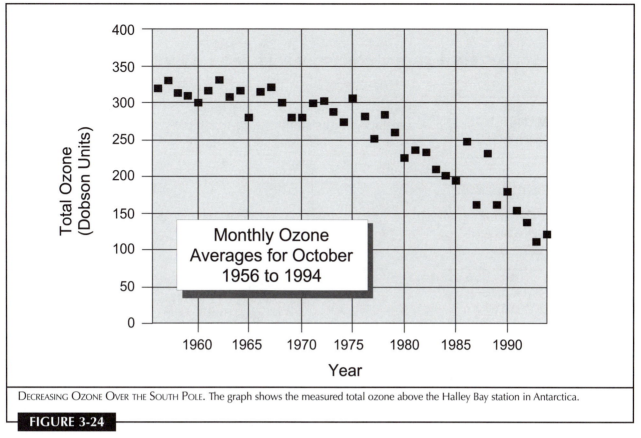

DECREASING OZONE OVER THE SOUTH POLE. The graph shows the measured total ozone above the Halley Bay station in Antarctica.

FIGURE 3-24

Source: Centre for Atmospheric Science, Cambridge University, available at <http://www.atm.ch.cam.ac.uk/tour/part2.html>.

affected by the negative consequences of the use of a technology. A valuable tool in the identification and management of a technological hazard is a causal chain (Kates et al. 1985). Often, through analysis, a causal chain reveals negative consequences that serve as clues to a "crime," litigation results from the effects of some technological hazard as tort cases are brought by the citizens affected. Each causal chain begins with some human need or want that is filled by the choice of a technology. Figure 3-25 depicts a causal structure showing the need for fire protection, the choice of the technological material asbestos (*see* Archer and Blackwood 1979 for the varieties of asbestos), and the resulting diseases. The intervening steps in the chain include initiating events, release of material, first-order outcomes, second-order outcomes, exposure, and consequences. Ultimately, the negative consequences in the case of asbestos were effects on human health. In the management of hazards, the higher up the chain that preventive actions or mitigation efforts take place, the fewer negative consequences. In the asbestos case, action had to be taken at the very top of the chain with a ban on use of the technology—asbestos.

"CLUSTER" Chains

Clues to an environmental crime are revealed by working through a causal chain in reverse order. Human health effects, asbestosis and mesothelioma, were clues that led to rejection of the use of asbestos as a technology. In Woburn, Massachusetts, a cancer cluster was the clue to chemical contamination of the town's water supply. A cancer cluster is a higher incidence of cancer cases in a geographically small area than would be the normal, expected rate of cancer in the general population.

A new type of clue, an autism cluster, is under investigation by two federal agencies—the National Center for Environmental Health at the Centers for Disease Control and Prevention and the Agency for Toxic Substances and Disease Registry (ATSDR). They seek to establish whether an unusually high number of cases (more than three times the national average) of autism among 3- to 10-year-olds in Brick Township, New Jersey, may be the negative consequence of some sort of environmental pollution problem there. Data are being collected on surface and ground water quality in Brick and any contamination from industrial sites, chemical spills, and waste dumping. Also highly suspect is the township's location just eight miles south of Toms River, where a cancer cluster among children and the possibility of contaminated water has led parents to hire a lawyer to pursue legal action.

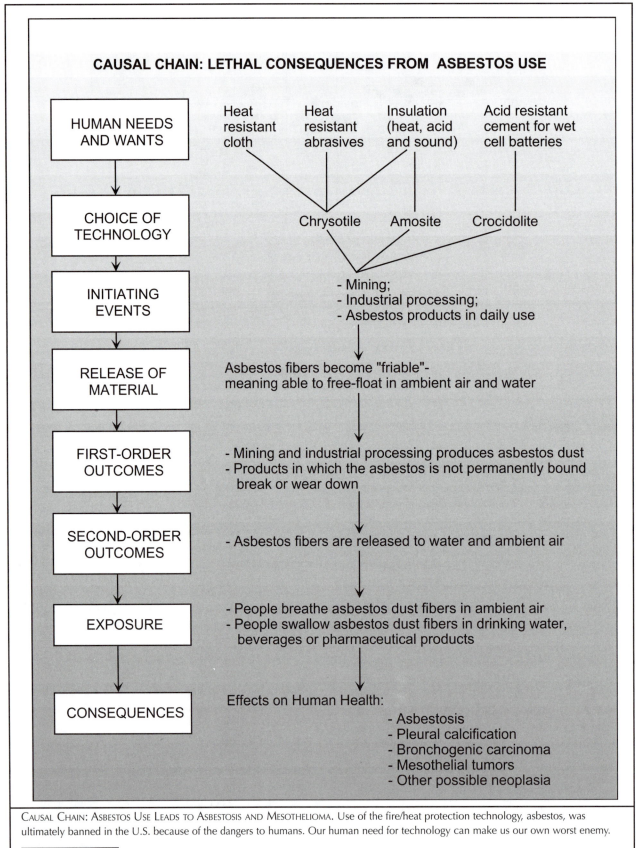

CAUSAL CHAIN: LETHAL CONSEQUENCES FROM ASBESTOS USE

CAUSAL CHAIN: ASBESTOS USE LEADS TO ASBESTOSIS AND MESOTHELIOMA. Use of the fire/heat protection technology, asbestos, was ultimately banned in the U.S. because of the dangers to humans. Our human need for technology can make us our own worst enemy.

FIGURE 3-25

Source: Nancy L. Winter, Ph.D.; concept of a causal chain from Kates, Robert W., Christoph Hohenemser, and Jeanne X. Kasperson, eds. 1985. *Perilous Progress : Managing the Hazards of Technology.* Boulder, CO: Westview Press.

Law Enforcement by the EPA

By 1998, the question arose as to whether enforcement of environmental laws in the U.S. was declining. The Environmental Law Institute convened a panel at the 1998 Annual Meeting of the American Bar Association to consider the state of environmental law enforcement. Differences in emphasis between various EPA regions were noted, and even stronger differences were seen between states with the most active enforcement compared with states with the least.

Statistics from the EPA Enforcement and Compliance Assurance Accomplishments Report for 1997 reveal that referrals to the Department of Justice for criminal enforcement reached the highest number in history, as did the number of defendants charged, and the number of months to which those convicted were sentenced, while, in finan-

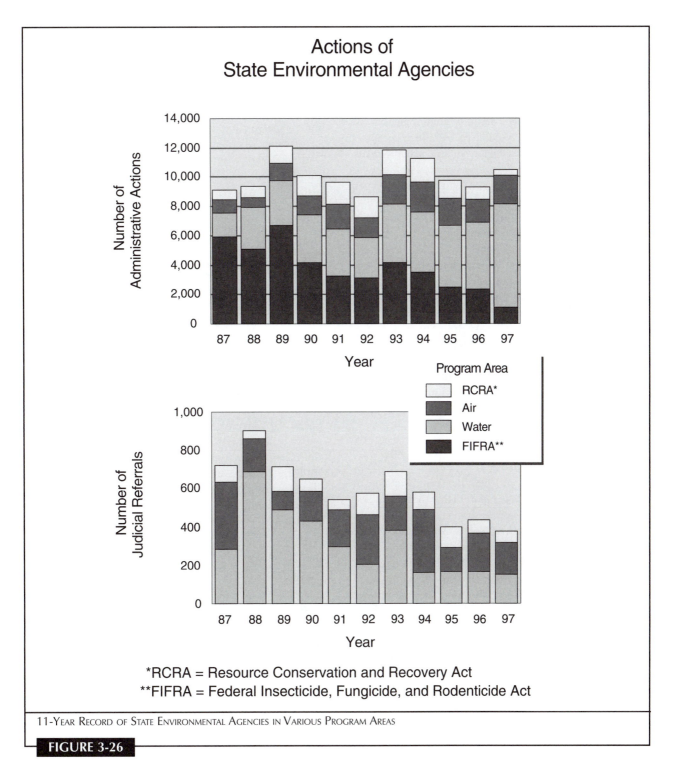

*RCRA = Resource Conservation and Recovery Act
**FIFRA = Federal Insecticide, Fungicide, and Rodenticide Act

11-Year Record of State Environmental Agencies in Various Program Areas

FIGURE 3-26

Source: U.S. EPA, *Enforcement and Compliance Assurance Accomplishments Report:* FY 1997.

cial terms, the criminal penalties rose sharply in 1996 and 1997. Civil enforcement showed more referrals to the Department of Justice in 1997 than in any other year except for 1994, and administrative actions by the EPA took an upward trend while, overall, administrative penalties increased (Yost 1998). Figure 3-26 shows the numbers of administrative actions and judicial referrals by state environmental agencies for the fiscal years 1987 through 1997 broken down by four program areas: (1) the Federal Insecticide, Fungicide, and Rodenticide Act (FIFRA), (2) Water, (3) Air, and (4) the Resource Conservation and Recovery Act (RCRA).

Win-Win Compliance

Compliance with environmental laws for the maintenance of a healthy and aesthetically desirable environment is the goal of enforcement efforts. Modern technology, such as computers for easily accessed data, infrared satellite imagery to detect subsurface leaks, and sensors in sewers around industrial plants, aids enforcement (Yost 1998). However, win-win negotiations with the business community that promote self-policing and negotiated compliance and market-driven remediation of contamination also can help achieve environmental improvement.

Nevertheless, an EPA enforcement official recently reported that there is a "surprisingly large universe" of companies who are completely ignoring environmental regulations and taking no steps toward compliance (Cutler 1999). This, despite the fact that a law such as Superfund spurs compliance in many other instances (Yost 1998). With this degree of noncompliance, the Strategic Environmental Enforcement Center in Denver now attempts to acquire facts about the environmental misdeeds not only of low-level employees but also of those with more authority in a given situation.

Approaches to Environmental Crime

At the international level, in 1998, the United Nations, in cooperation with INTERPOL, reported that the annual cost of environmental crime reaches as much as $20 billion. In the United States, new approaches to environmental crime are still being devised. Data compiled by the Transnational Records Access Clearinghouse (TRAC) indicate that during the Clinton administration, the U.S. Department of Justice tripled its prosecutions of environmental crimes. However, TRAC data show that this is much less than 1 percent of the Justice Department's overall prosecutions.

In 1998, Attorney General Janet Reno appointed 18 U.S. attorneys to serve on a federal advisory panel on environmental crimes. Formed in 1973, the Environmental Crimes Subcommittee of the Attorney General's Advisory Committee of United States Attorneys advises the U.S. attorney general. Also, three members of this subcommittee were named to the full advisory committee (Bureau of National Affairs 1999). At the state level, in 1998 in Mary-

land, federal, state, and local law enforcement agencies cooperated to establish a 24-hour hotline for citizens to report environmental crimes. Most promising is the recent approach to the decision-making that sets the environmental conditions in construction of new projects. Community-wide involvement of all stakeholders in the negotiating process facilitates beneficial decision-making.

However, environmental crime is still mainly shaped by the roles of both corporate and personal priorities, a lack of knowledge of certain species and the ecological balance, and the confounding issues of scientific uncertainty and trans-science in the standards setting process. The global, or largest, scale environmental questions are within the realm of trans-science, unable to be verified by the scientific process alone.

Looking back, many questions could be asked concerning business or private responsibility for the execution of environmental crimes. With no prohibitions against it and with limited understanding of species extinction, were the railroads that encouraged the random killing of bison by armed passengers shooting through their railroad coach windows committing environmental crime? Were the shooters? Technically speaking, no, but, with today's science and the judgment of history, we see its effects on the bison species. Environmental crime in every era is framed by the level of scientific knowledge available and the attitudes of humans on Earth.

Conclusions

The spatial view of environmental crime presented in this essay helps to focus on the importance of the global environment. Increased awareness of the issues surrounding these infractions and the nature of crimes against the environment are instrumental in directing policy-making for the future. By mapping various aspects of the phenomenon, patterns are revealed that benefit researchers who study the extent of environmental damage, epidemiologists who study the location and diffusion of disease, and agencies in charge of carrying out clean-up missions, among others. As stated earlier, these spatial distributions may indicate the potential for environmental crime.

References

Archer, S.R., and T. R. Blackwood. 1979. *Status Assessment of Toxic Chemicals: Asbestos.* Industrial Environment Research Laboratory, Office of Research and Development, EPA-600/2-79-210c. Dayton, OH: Monsanto Research Corporation. December. See Appendix I for varieties of asbestos.

Brodeur, Paul. 1980. *The Asbestos Hazard.* New York: New York Academy of Sciences.

Brown, Lester et al. 1989. *State of the World 1989: A Worldwatch Institute Report on Progress Toward a Sustainable Society.* New York: W.W. Norton and Company, pp. 77-96.

Bureau of National Affairs. 1999. Reno Names Federal Prosecutors to Advisory Group on Environmental Crime. *Daily Environment Report,* The Bureau of National Affairs, Inc. January 5.

Cutler, Joyce E. 1999. Large Number of Companies Noncompliant with Environmental Laws, EPA Official Says. *Environmental Reporter Current Developments* 29: 44, 2233.The Bureau of National Affairs, Inc. March 12.

Dahl, T.E., E.J. Graig, and W. E. Frayer. 1991. *Wetlands: Status and Trends in the Conterminous U.S. Mid-1970's to Mid-1980's.* Washington, DC: U.S. Department of the Interior, Fish and Wildlife Service.

Golden, Jack, Robert P. Ouellette, Sharon Saari, and Paul N. Cheremisinoff. 1979. *Environmental Impact Data Book.* Ann Arbor, MI: Ann Arbor Science.

Greenberg, M., and T.A. Lloyd Davies. 1974. Mesothelioma Register 1967-68. *British Journal of Industrial Medicine* 31: 91-104.

Grunwald, Michael. 1998. Shell Pays $1.5 Million for Polluting River; U.S. Effects Crackdown on Mississippi. *Washington Post,* September 10, A03.

Howe, Linda Moulton. 1999. Short Updates About Environmental Problems, EARTHFILES. <http://earthfiles.com/earth083.html>.

Kates, Robert W., Christoph Hohenemser, and Jeanne X. Kasperson. 1985. *Perilous Progress: Managing the Hazards of Technology.* Boulder, CO: Westview Press, pp. 67-89.

Preger, Leslie. 1978. *Asbestos-Related Disease.* New York: Grune and Stratton, p. 86.

U.S. Office of Technology Assessment. 1984. *Wetlands: Their Use and Regulation.*

Yost, Nicholas C. 1998. The State of Environmental Law Enforcement. (Speech presented at the American Bar Association's 1998 Annual Meeting.) *Environmental Law Reporter.* Environmental Law Institute, December.

Confronting Computer Crimes

John Jarvis
Gordon R. Wynn

The volume of crimes reported to the police in recent years has numbered approximately 13 million offenses (Federal Bureau of Investigation 1998). Each year, the Federal Bureau of Investigation (FBI) releases the numbers and types of serious crimes reported to law enforcement agencies, including such crimes as murder, rape, robbery, aggravated assault, burglary, auto theft, and larceny. However, a number of other criminal offenses are not directly reflected in these numbers. Among them are offenses generally considered crimes against society, including drug offenses, prostitution, and computer crimes.

To understand and combat the trends in these crimes, many law enforcement and criminal justice personnel have begun to use mapping technologies to chart where, when, and what types of crimes are occurring within their jurisdictions. Such maps are effective crime analysis tools and can be used for operational, intelligence, investigative, and administrative tasks in determining preventive and punitive strategies for policing. Mapping has been particularly useful in jurisdictions that have high volumes of crime occurring in relatively small geographic areas. These methods have been applied and found to be successful in various cities, including Atlanta, Philadelphia, San Diego, and Washington, D.C. (Sadler 1998).

While these methods have been found to be effective in confronting traditional street crimes, some other criminal behaviors have challenged such analytical strategies. Chief among these offenses is the increasing number of computer-related crimes. Before illustrating the challenges that these crimes pose for mapping technologies, a better understanding of the nature, scope, and frequency of computer-related crimes is required.

Computer Crime Offenses: Nature and Scope

The technology that has provided government, business, and private citizens with world-wide access and connectivity has changed forever many of the routine activities of daily life. However, concomitant with this new technology

has been its misuse by those inclined to subvert these computer applications toward criminal ends. Perhaps these activities have grown out of the penetration of personal computers and the Internet into our daily lives. Regardless of the etiology of computer crimes, they are occurring and there is much concern over the harm they may bring. However, it is appropriate to draw a distinction between crimes that are termed *computer-related* and those that are generally considered *computer crimes*. This distinction may appear minor or inconsequential, yet debate persists over the proper classification of crimes that involve a computer.

Typical offenses generally considered to be *computer crimes* include "telephone access number fraud, credit card fraud, drug trafficking, prostitution, and even pedophilia" (Hollinger 1990: xxii). These crimes should not be confused with *computer-related crimes*, which may involve the use of a computer, although the computer itself is not considered a tangible part of the behavior constituting the offense. Offenses of this nature include assaults involving computer hardware that is used as a weapon to directly cause physical injury, larceny-theft of computer parts, and other crimes where computers may be present but not part and parcel to the offense perpetrated. The focus in this essay is on those offenses considered to constitute computer crimes rather than the larger set of computer-related crimes. Computer crimes comprise some of the most "highly publicized incidents over the past ten years which have involved computers in fraud, embezzlement, terrorism, theft, larceny, extortion, malicious mischief, espionage, and sabotage" (Parker 1976). To fully understand the challenges that these crimes pose for mapping technologies, this essay will discuss the difficulties involved in identifying computer crimes, in investigating reported cases, in apprehending suspects, and in prosecuting these crimes.

Identification

One type of computer crime that has been in the news recently is that of hacker attacks of big-name Web sites such as Amazon.com and eBay. Figure 3-27 depicts the diffusion

Contributors' Note: We thank several interns, including Robin Diehl and Georgia Smith, for their assistance with this project. The views in this essay are those of the authors and do not represent the official position of the U.S. Department of Justice or the Federal Bureau of Investigation.

Editor's Note: In this rapidly changing technological revolution, computer crimes have become a new reality for investigators. The development of innovative tools, the new application of existing tools, and the collection of a larger geographic database will enable in future a more indepth analysis of the spatial aspects of cybercrimes. The diffusion paths of viruses, crime incidents within a company, city, state, or nation, and arrests and prosecutions are data from which computer crimes can be mapped. Through mapping, distributions can be identified as random or non-random, revealing places that are vulnerable to the cybercriminal and helping to direct attention to the reasons for their vulnerability.

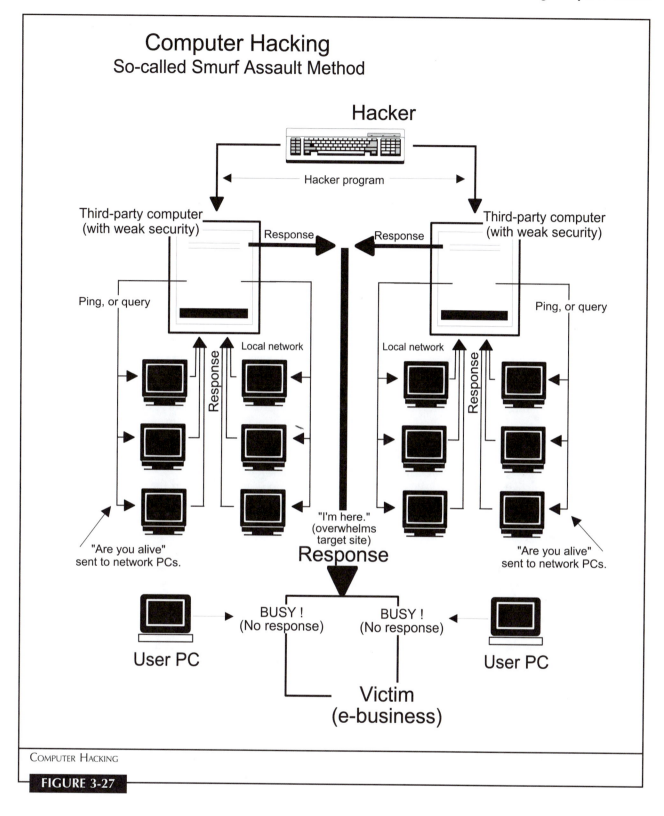

Computer Hacking
So-called Smurf Assault Method

Hacker

Hacker program

Third-party computer
(with weak security)

Response

Response

Third-party computer
(with weak security)

Ping, or query

Ping, or query

Local network

Response

Response

Local network

"Are you alive"
sent to network PCs.

"I'm here."
(overwhelms
target site)

Response

"Are you alive"
sent to network PCs.

User PC

BUSY !
(No response)

BUSY !
(No response)

User PC

Victim
(e-business)

COMPUTER HACKING

FIGURE 3-27

paths of a computer virus in a variation of an attack. The hacker first searches for potential targets (usually server or host computers maintained by a business or educational institution). Then, a "slave" software program is placed in the vulnerable computers by the hacker and awaits the attack command. After the hacker gives the signal, the slaves issue a "ping" or query to connected computers asking if they are alive (online). Replies are sent to a bogus return address that happens to be the real target of the attack. The target is overloaded with these replies, which can be in the hundreds or even thousands in number (Levy and Stone 2000).

Another virus attack was the "Love Bug," which sent disrupting love letter e-mails to computers around the globe. The diffusion path was traced and found to have originated in the Philippines. The first location to report problems was Hong Kong. From there, the virus spread westward to Sweden, then south to Denmark, and northwest to Britain. The final leg of its global path in cyberspace was across the Atlantic into the United States. As the day dawned, businesses and individuals found themselves faced with the most massive virus attack to date, costing billions of dollars (Kanel 2000).

Computer crimes are by their very nature difficult to detect. Part of this difficulty is a general lack of consensus on what constitutes a computer crime (Chen 1990). This lack of a consensus extends internationally, resulting in diverse definitions of computer crimes and equally diverse law enforcement (United Nations 1994). Recent media reports relative to viruses, worms, denial of service attacks, and computer trespass or vandalism have led to a proliferation of statutes defining such crimes, increased law enforcement efforts to train computer crime specialists, and sensitization of government, business, and private citizens to the risks and ramifications of such offenses. In addition, the frequencies of these offenses remain uncertain for several reasons. Perhaps the most significant of these uncertainties is the fact that few of these offenses occur on the street. A similarity to white collar crime exists in that criminal activities are conducted within private homes, public buildings, corporate businesses, or government offices. Where white collar crime emphasizes "position," computer crime emphasizes esoteric "knowledge." As such, these crimes are not openly visible to the casual observer and generally lack witnesses. As a result, a citizen report to the police of suspicious activity relative to computing is unlikely to occur. Often, the targets of computer crimes do not even know that they have had information or funds stolen. Only over a period of time will the frequency of attacks or severity of damage eventually alert the victim (Sterling 1992).

Complicating this problem is the fact that the victim is often not a person or property *per se* but an electronic medium—a bulletin board, Web page, server, or database. For these offenses to be detected, either a computer user or a system administrator must realize that something is not as it should be. In light of this fact, some computer criminals have adapted by either hiding their presence to appear as a legitimate user or are careful to avoid detection. Some are so confident in their ability to escape detection and apprehension that they regularly interrupt the services provided by these electronic systems (Sterling 1992).

Finally, problems in identifying computer crimes are further complicated when attacks are detected but not reported to authorities. Victim organizations may either prefer to address these computer security failures internally or do not wish to publicly acknowledge that such security problems exist. It is reasonable to assume that banking and financial institutions, along with other business and government entities, would not wish their constituents to become aware of the insecurity of their computer systems. Nonetheless, reluctance to report these incidents hampers any effort to accurately account for these incidents and denies official authorities the opportunity to fully investigate these crimes, determine the individuals responsible for such behavior, and prosecute the offending party.

While reliable data on the occurrences of these crimes are scant, one emerging data source is available for initiating some exploration and description of criminal offenses that involve the use of a computer. These data are the revised *Uniform Crime Reports*, termed the National Incident-Based Reporting System (NIBRS). This data collection effort was employed in 12 states in 1998 and is scheduled to be available nationwide in the coming years. A notation within these data indicates whether the criminal offense involved the use of a computer. While this does not distinguish between computer-related crime and computer crime as delineated above, these data do provide for some analyses of criminal offenses that come to the attention of police. From these data, the frequency and distribution of computer crimes can be determined for those jurisdictions reporting under NIBRS. Figure 3-28 shows these results for the 957 incidents reported in 1997.

While these data are not nationally representative of the computer crime experience, additional analyses of these criminal incidents and continued data collection from around the country may hold promise for future findings relative to the nature, scope, and extent of this criminal behavior. Not enough states report into the NIBRS to make any serious judgment as to the regional nature of these crimes. However, of those states reporting, Michigan and Colorado stand out among the others, with South Carolina a strong third. The remaining states showed little difference.

From a crime analysis perspective, problems with the identification and enumeration of computer crimes may significantly impact the validity and reliability of any analytical strategies that might be employed to combat this growing problem. Additionally, the nature of these offenses and the difficulties noted above clearly hamper most traditional efforts to display the locations and densities of these offenses geographically. At a minimum, these problems impose considerable limitations that further complicate analytical efforts and perhaps hinder many enforcement and preventive strategies that are available to confront these crimes. Nonetheless, attempting to examine the available information and seeking to identify some approaches for combating the problem of computer crimes may still prove fruitful.

Investigation

Crime mapping technologies have been found effective in assisting law enforcement in the investigation of crimes reported. In particular, mapping technologies have transformed the pin maps of old into the electronic Geographic Information Systems of the present and future. These capabilities allow law enforcement to determine hot spots of

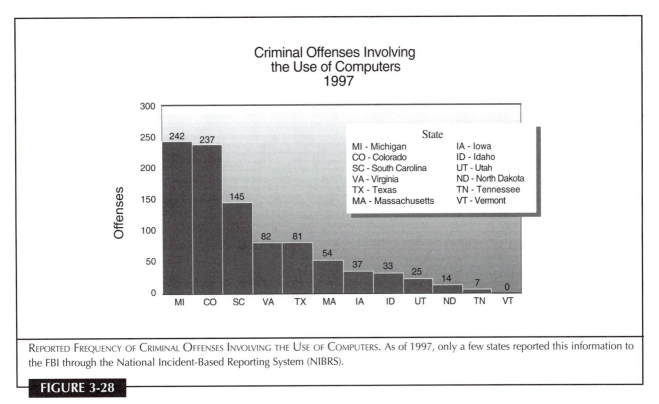

REPORTED FREQUENCY OF CRIMINAL OFFENSES INVOLVING THE USE OF COMPUTERS. As of 1997, only a few states reported this information to the FBI through the National Incident-Based Reporting System (NIBRS).

FIGURE 3-28

Source: 1997 FBI NIBRS.

criminal activity, analyze possible criminal targets, and produce crude projections of future criminal activity. As noted earlier, most of these applications in the past have focused on conventional street crimes that regularly come to the attention of police.

Computer crimes, in contrast, are not as regularly reported and the available information on victims, targets, and offenders involved in computer crimes suffers as a result. This situation poses a challenge to the interpretations and generalizations associated with any analysis of computer crime. However, crime mapping technologies still have some application to the investigation and analysis of these offenses. In particular, while computer crimes generally do not occur in the public view, these crimes continue to be conventional in at least some respects—the crime still requires the recognition of an identifiable offense, the availability of a victim, and the perpetration of the act by an individual offender, or offenders, all elements that are linked together (Cohen and Felson 1979). The challenge posed by computer crime is that the elements discussed above generally do not come together in the same physical space (e.g., street, building, residence), but rather are connected by an electronic space (i.e., the telephone, the Internet, an Intranet, various electronic bulletin boards, or other electronic connection), known as "virtual" or "cyberspace" (Gibson 1984). As a result, these crimes are much more difficult to identify, report, and investigate than conventional crimes.

Several other unique investigative challenges confront law enforcement when it comes to computer crimes. One challenge is the secondary nature in which these crimes become known to law enforcement. A computer system administrator who maintains a network of computers for an organization is often the first individual to detect and identify an anomaly in the system's operation. These anomalies are often attributed to operation maintenance problems and are not identified as criminal activity. Historically, these computer operators (commonly known as system administrators or sysadmins) would conduct a preliminary investigation that would disturb the "virtual" crime scene. These investigations by system administrators have not always hampered law enforcement efforts; these inspections usually only reveal the system problems created by the attack rather than the attack itself. However, in the past, when computer systems administrators suspected that a computer criminal had victimized their system, their initial countermeasures sometimes hampered the successful investigation and apprehension of the offender. For example, in years past, the first impulse of many individuals was to lock out the intruder. By doing so, the offender was alerted and an opportunity to monitor and eventually detect and pursue the offender was lost. Such action also often failed to prevent the intruder from accessing the target computer later when he or she had found other avenues of access. Standard operating procedures in many large American corporations require that all perceived computer crimes be reported first to executive management. The executives then decide whether it is in the company's best interest to file a complaint or to keep the intrusion an in-house matter.

Fortunately, in more recent times, system administrators have served as better detectives, educators, witnesses, and general training resources in assisting law enforcement in the pursuit of cybercriminals. Because law enforcement has traditionally lagged behind in this area of high technology, the informed system administrator has become a valuable resource to policing efforts (Adler et al. 1998).

Applications of Mapping Technologies

In an effort to further understand and confront these crimes, one tool of the crime analyst that may be of particular merit is the Geographic Information System (GIS). This tool is commonly and successfully employed to identify patterns and trends in conventional crimes that are confronted on a daily basis by law enforcement. However, the application of this tool to computer crimes is not straightforward. As can be seen in Figure 3-29 on the scope of Internet access, the use of GIS to describe this scope holds limited analytical value. Whereas most of the world is connected to the Internet, some places in Africa, the Middle East, and Asia have not attained this level of technology.

Computer crimes can be perpetrated from virtually anywhere in the world and do not require geographic proximity between the motivated offender and the potential target. This geographic distribution of potential computer violations serves to underscore the challenges that computer crime investigations must confront. Besides the fact that the offenders may be thousands of miles away at the time their crime is committed, investigators may also need to travel to various parts of the world before the offender can be identified and apprehended as in the recent case involving the "Love Bug" virus where investigators traced a suspect to the Philippines. Many law enforcement efforts may be hampered due to complicated jurisdictional issues that may arise in the course of investigating these offenses (United Nations 1994).

Valuable information for investigating these crimes may be obtained by examining the points from which computer crimes originate, that is, the Internet Service Providers (ISPs) that form the World Wide Web; they are the backbone over which these activities are most commonly perpetrated. Computer crimes can also emanate from educational, governmental, or military sites, but many of these

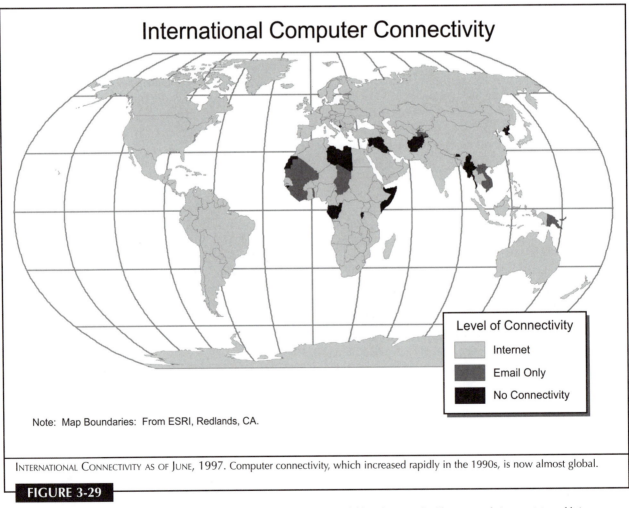

International Computer Connectivity

Level of Connectivity

Internet

Email Only

No Connectivity

Note: Map Boundaries: From ESRI, Redlands, CA.

INTERNATIONAL CONNECTIVITY AS OF JUNE, 1997. Computer connectivity, which increased rapidly in the 1990s, is now almost global.

FIGURE 3-29

Source: Copyright 1997 Lawrence H. Landweber and the Internet Society. Data available online at <ftp://ftp.cs.wisc.edu/connectivity_table/>.

institutions contract with major commercial ISPs for their services; where these organizations do not contract for services, they have unique domain names that identify their source. ISPs maintain records and serve as a source of evidence that will assist in the successful investigation and apprehension of the individuals responsible for these illegal behaviors. To this end, the identification and distribution of ISPs represents the web of connections that computer criminals may traverse in perpetrating their crime. While enumeration of every ISP is difficult, examining the distribution and location of domain names, equated to ISP addresses, may prove more useful. Figure 3-30 shows the truly Web-like character of only a single ISP. The United States has the highest number of active CONE domains of any country in the world. Canada ranks second with the United Kingdom third.

The actual number of Internet providers and their associated web of connections is many times greater than this graphic represents, yet the same point is conveyed. Useful information from an investigative and prevention stand-

point may be to identify and map the medium on which these criminals operate. In other words, map the virtual space (*see* <www.cyberspace.com> for further information and advances in this area of cybergeography). By doing so, several findings may become apparent. First, the network of operations that represent the Internet may be of analytical, investigative, and criminal preventive use. Second, by mapping such activities and identifying frequently used providers, regulations and policies for licensing and operation of Internet providers may emerge.

The application of GIS to computer crimes may be useful in confronting the challenges presented by outside intruders against the individual, business, or government. However, more significant challenges may be posed by the criminal activities of employees, students, contractors, visitors, acquaintances, or partners within business, education, government, or industry. Criminal acts perpetrated by individuals related to these targets, in any of these ways, would make the computer criminal an "insider." Individuals who commit computer crimes from within the organization may

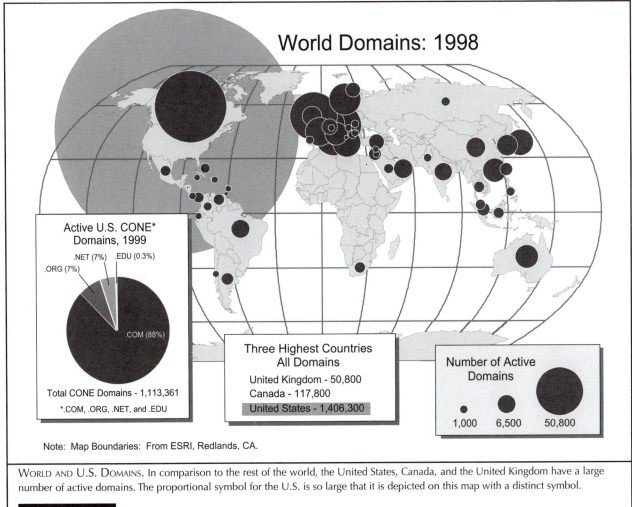

WORLD AND U.S. DOMAINS. In comparison to the rest of the world, the United States, Canada, and the United Kingdom have a large number of active domains. The proportional symbol for the U.S. is so large that it is depicted on this map with a distinct symbol.

FIGURE 3-30

Source: Internet.org available online at <http://www.internet.org>.

be even more difficult to identify and investigate because many of them would have legitimate access to the targeted computer system. The particular problem of the organizational insider who commits computer crime may only be marginally addressable at all by crime mapping technologies.

Whether the intruder is outside or inside, another problem that persists is that few system administrators apply mapping technologies to their computer system design and fewer still retain such information. Current crime mapping technologies offer help in resolving computer crime if used properly. The technology is available, but computer systems administrators must regularly employ and maintain these system maps for them to be useful.

Conclusion

While mapping technologies at the present time may be able to assist in the detection of the computer criminal who operates outside the intended target site, they are of little help when it comes to insiders. The activities of criminal insiders would more likely be controlled through programs of information security, personnel management, and hardware and software developments that serve as target hardening measures. To date, much of the effort in this area has been in dealing with these insider problems. The future understanding of these crimes will involve hardware, software, security, and a better understanding of the forces that motivate and orient the behavior of these criminals. Understanding the psychology, sociology, and criminology of computer criminals will assist in the prevention and investigation of these crimes. In the long run, businesses, educational institutions, governments, and industry will be able

to further advance the security and applications of the communications superhighway that has changed our physical and social world.

References

Adler, Freda, Gerhard O.W. Mueller, and William S. Laufer. 1998. *Criminology: Third Edition.* Boston: McGraw-Hill.

An Atlas of Cyberspaces. 1999. Available at <http://www.cybergeography.com>.

Chen, Christopher. 1990. Computer Crime and the Computer Fraud and Abuse Act of 1986. In Richard Hollinger, ed. *Crime, Deviance and the Computer.* Brookfield, VT: Dartmouth Publishing Company.

Cohen, Lawrence, and Marcus Felson. 1979. Social Change and Crime Rate Trends: A Routine Activity Approach. *American Sociological Review* 44: 588-608.

Federal Bureau of Investigation. 1998. *Crime in the United States, 1997.* Washington, DC: U.S. Government Printing Office.

Gibson, William. 1984. *The Neuromancer.* New York: Ace Books.

Hollinger, Richard C., ed. 1990. *Crime, Deviance and the Computer.* Brookfield, VT: Dartmouth Publishing Company.

Kanel, Michael E. 2000. Poison-pen Love Letter Circles the Globe, Sickening Computers. *The Atlanta Constitution.* Friday, May 5, p. A-1,21.

Levy, Steven, and Brad Stone. 2000. Hunting the Hackers. *Newsweek* (February 21): 38–44.

Parker, Donn. 1976. *Crime by Computer.* New York: Charles Scribner's Sons.

Sadler, Dan. 1998. *Exploring Crime Mapping.* National Institute of Justice, Crime Mapping Research Center.

Sterling, Bruce. 1992. *The Hacker Crackdown: Law and Disorder on the Electronic Frontier.* New York: Bantam Books.

United Nations. 1994. United Nations Manual on the Prevention and Control of Computer-Related Crime. *International Review of Criminal Policy*, Nos. 43 and 44.

CHAPTER 4

Family Violence

Chapter 4 of the *Atlas of Crime* covers the most hidden crimes—those found within the isolation of the home environment. Figure 4-1 illustrates violence against partners, children, the elderly, and animal companions in an ecological model of family violence. In terms of geographic patterns, it is reasonable to expect that where one form of maltreatment is found, so are other forms. National statistical geographic data (aside from homicide) do not exist for any form of family violence except child abuse and neglect. Despite these difficulties, this chapter contains four essays—on intimate violence, child abuse and neglect, elder abuse, and animal cruelty—that provide readers with some essence of the spatial component of each topic.

Traditional public attitudes in the U.S. have revolved around the notion that what goes on in the home is nobody's business. Therefore, it has been difficult to gain support for an intervention policy in the area of domestic violence. In the past 20 years, mostly due to efforts in the feminist movement, violence in the home has been brought into the spotlight.

> The level of feminist organization in a state is a significant determinant of the number of wife abuse services in that state. Moreover, the level of feminist organization is a more potent predictor of programs for battered women than is per capita income, political culture, individual feminist sentiment, or domestic violence legislation that allocates funds for services. (Kalmuss and Straus 1983: 372)

Nonlethal violence by an intimate includes rape, sexual assault, robbery, and aggravated and simple assault. According to a government report, there were approximately 840,000 nonlethal incidents of intimate violence and 2,000 murders by intimates in 1996 (Greenfield et al. 1998). This report also revealed the following geographic facts on intimate violence: (1) urban women are more likely to experience nonlethal violence by an intimate than women in a suburban or rural setting, and (2) most nonlethal incidents occur in the victim's home between the hours of 6 p.m. and midnight.

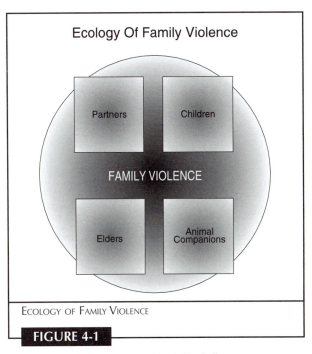

ECOLOGY OF FAMILY VIOLENCE

FIGURE 4-1

Source: Used with the permission of Linda Turnbull.

A study of intimate murder examined defendants in large urban counties (Langan and Dawson 1995). Husbands were more likely than wives to be found guilty and wives received shorter prison terms than husbands. In addition, wives were more likely to have been assaulted near or at the time of the murder.

In her essay "Intimate Violence," Denise Donnelly presents the spatial dimension of the murder of intimates across the U.S. Using the State of Georgia as a case study, she examines domestic violence shelters, domestic violence, and verbal violence in the spatial perspective.

The ecology of violence, as applied to child maltreatment, has been noted by both sociologists (Garbarino 1977) and psychologists (Bronfenbrenner 1979). Their philosophy is that explanations of behavior can be found in every level of a person's environment, from the microlevel of the family to the macrolevel of society (Bersani and Chen 1988). Sociologist James Garbarino posits that we are raising children in a socially toxic environment and names certain social toxins (e.g., poverty, high degree of geographic mobility, poor value systems, violence) as contributors to the dissolution of a healthy family. He urges society to be concerned with the drawing of each child's social map, which is constructed by the way the child learns to "get along in the world" (1995: 24). Childhood is a balance among play-

Animal Cruelty Investigations in Selected Cities in 1998*	
Biddeford, Maine	16
Spokane, Washington	75
Atlanta, Georgia	123
Marin, California	244
Sioux Falls, South Dakota	278
Lincoln, Nebraska	833
Pittsburgh, Pennsylvania	883
Salt Lake, Utah	1044
Fairport, New York	1235
Fort Wayne, Indiana	1306
Denver, Colorado	1360
Honolulu, Hawaii	1394
Tonawanda, New York	1891

*Data collected from Maine Animal Control Association, Spokane County (WA) Animal Control, Fulton County (GA) Animal Control, Marin (CA) Humane Society, Sioux Falls (SD) Animal Control, Lincoln (NE) Animal Control, Western Pennsylvania Humane Society, Salt Lake County (UT) Animal Control, Humane Society of Rochester and Monroe County (NY), Ft. Wayne, IN Animal Care and Control, Denver (CO) Dumb Friends League, SPCA-Erie County (NY), and Hawaiian Humane Society.

ing, working, and loving rather than conflict resolution through violence.

Linda Turnbull provides a spatial analysis of our "social maps" of maltreated children nationwide. Maps depicting reports of child abuse and neglect, child victims, incidents of neglect, physical abuse, and sexual abuse are highlighted in her essay "The Spatial Dimensions of Child Abuse and Neglect." In addition, child fatalities in the U.S. give the reader a sense of the horror surrounding this criminal behavior.

Elder abuse is a phenomenon relatively new to the research community. Although the actual incidence or prevalence is unknown, researchers have estimated that in 1996 there were between 820,000 and 1,860,000 abused elders in this country (National Center on Elder Abuse 1999). Information on elder abuse within the family is scarce. More often we hear about instances of elder maltreatment within the confines of a nursing home or hospital setting. However, abuse of the elderly most frequently occurs in the home by adult children (National Center on Elder Abuse 1999). Denise Donnelly describes the problems inherent in the study of elder abuse. Definitions for the types of elder mal-

treatment are presented and the spatial aspects of the murder of elders are examined.

The final essay in this chapter on family violence is concerned with the connection between violence against humans and animals. Most Americans have pets in the household (60 percent) and most regard their pets as family members (Gehrke 1997). Information gathered by surveys confirms that 79 percent of pet parents celebrate their pet's birthday, 33 percent talk to their pet by phone or answering machine when away, and 62 percent sign letters and cards with their pet's name included (LaCroix 1999). Pets provide unconditional love, trust, loyalty, and total acceptance—all benefits to our lives.

Linda Turnbull explores the ecological connection between violence against humans and animals in "Animal Cruelty: A Spatial Investigation." Like most family violence, animal cruelty has no national database. News reports give the impression that these crimes do not occur with any frequency. However, the list above, showing the incidence of animal cruelty for select locations, indicates that this behavior is not restricted to a few isolated incidents.

References

Bersani, C.A., and H. Chen. 1988. Sociological Perspectives in Family Violence. In Vincent B. Van Hasselt, Randall L. Morrison, Alan S. Bellack, and Michel Hersen, eds. *Handbook of Family Violence.* New York: Plenum Press, pp. 57-86.

Brofenbrenner, U. 1979. *The Ecology of Human Development.* Cambridge, MA: Harvard University Press.

Garbarino, J. 1995. *Raising Children in a Socially Toxic Environment.* San Francisco: Jossey–Bass, Inc.

———. 1977. The Human Ecology of Child Maltreatment: A Conceptual Model for Research. *Journal of Marriage and the Family* 39: 721-35.

Gehrke, B.C. 1997. Results of AVMA Survey of U.S. Pet-owning Households on Companion Animal Ownership. *Journal of the American Veterinary Medical Association* 211: 169.

Greenfield, L.A., M. R. Rand, D. Craven, P. Klaus, C. Perkins, C. Ringel, G. Wachol, C. Maston, and J.A. Fox. 1998. *Violence by Intimates: An Analysis of Data on Crimes by Current or Former Spouses, Boyfriends, and Girlfriends.* Washington, DC: U.S. Department of Justice.

Kalmuss, D.S., and M. Straus. 1983. Feminist, Political, and Economic Determinants of Wife Abuse Services. In D. Finkelhor, R.J. Gelles, G.T. Hotaling, and M.A. Straus, eds. *The Dark Side of Families: Current Family Violence Research.* Beverly Hills, CA: Sage Publications, pp. 363-76.

LaCroix, C.A. 1999. Another Weapon for Combating Family Violence: Prevention of Animal Abuse. In Frank R. Ascione and Phil Arkow, eds. *Child Abuse, Domestic Violence, and Animal Abuse.* West Lafayette, IN: Purdue University Press, pp. 62-82.

Langan, P.A., and J.M. Dawson. 1995. *Spouse Murder Defendants in Large Urban Counties.* Washington, DC: U.S. Department of Justice.

National Center on Elder Abuse (NCEA). 1999. *Domestic Elder Abuse Information Series.* <http:www.gwjapan.com/NCEA/basic/p1.html>.

Intimate Violence

Denise A. Donnelly

Unlike many other crimes covered in this volume, intimate abuse has not always been defined as a criminal activity. Only within the past 25 years have sexual and intimate violence come to be recognized as social problems affecting millions of Americans. Before the 1970s, violence inside the home or between intimates was viewed as a private family matter. Few laws protected victims of intimate violence, and the use of violence within the context of the family drew almost no social disapproval. Because of the publication of several influential books on woman battering, such as Del Martin's *Battered Wives* (1976) and Erin Prizzey's *Scream Quietly or the Neighbors Will Hear* (1977), and the efforts of grassroots women's organizations and activists, intimate abuse had been defined as a serious social, moral, and legal problem by the end of the 1970s (Schecter 1982).

Research abounds on the incidence and prevalence of intimate abuse, the causes and consequences of this type of violence, and the effectiveness of counseling and legal and social interventions. Two aspects less studied, however, are the geographic distribution of intimate abuse and the concentration of services designed for victims of domestic violence.

No databases contain state-by-state estimates of domestic violence or focus on the distribution of services to battered women (National Institute of Justice 1996). The only data currently available on the national level are state-by-state reports of intra-familial homicide. These data are mapped in Figure 4-2, which shows the geographic distribution of spousal murders for the entire United States. As becomes readily apparent, spousal murders are more likely to be committed in the South or Southeast, or in the southwestern states of Arizona, Texas, and Oklahoma. One explanation might be that factors such as regional income or religious differences are contributing to higher levels of violence (Straus 1994). Another possibility is that southern and southwestern states have a history of using force to

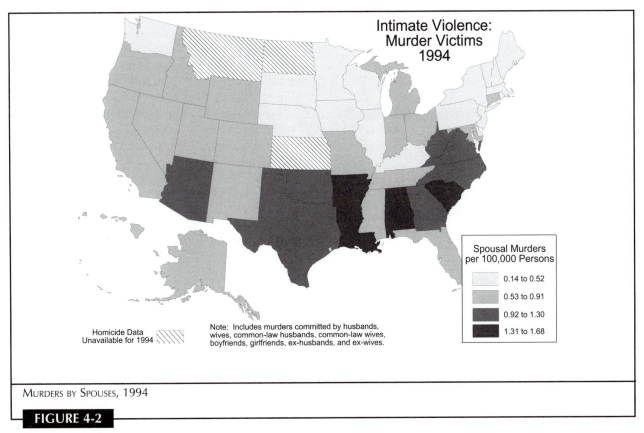

MURDERS BY SPOUSES, 1994

FIGURE 4-2

Sources: Fox, James Alan. UNIFORM CRIME REPORTS [UNITED STATES]: SUPPLEMENTARY HOMICIDE REPORTS, 1976-1994 [Computer File]. ICPSR version. Boston: Northeastern University, College of Criminal Justice [producer], 1996; Ann Arbor, MI: Inter-university Consortium for Political and Social Research [distributor], 1996; and U.S. Bureau of the Census, Census of Population and Housing, 1990.

solve problems, or that they are more approving of violence, exhibiting what Baron and Straus (1989) have deemed a "subculture of violence." Because we lack data on non-fatal spousal abuse on a state-by-state basis, there is no way to determine if other forms of intimate violence are also more prevalent in the South.

Given the gaps in data at the national level, the remainder of this essay focuses on the ways in which both intimate abuse and shelter programs are distributed in the State of Georgia. The decision to focus on one state, rather than conducting a nationwide analysis, was based on several factors. First, as mentioned earlier, there are no national data sets containing information about domestic violence for each of the states. Second, the examination of this issue on the county level allows for greater detail and depth of analysis. Finally, Georgia was chosen because of the racial and income diversity of the population, as well as for the range in size of its cities and towns. Georgia has 159 counties, most of them covering fairly limited geographic areas. Moreover, it encompasses Fulton County, which contains the city of Atlanta (the largest metropolitan area in the Southeast), surrounding counties that are comprised almost entirely of commuter bedroom suburbs, multiple counties with only mid-size and small towns, and a range of counties that are primarily rural agricultural areas.

Defining Intimate Abuse

Before beginning an examination of the distribution of intimate abuse in Georgia, it is necessary to define the term. Although women's advocates, researchers, and lawmakers each conceptualize family violence in different ways, it is defined in the Official Code of Georgia (19-13-1) as follows:

> One or more of the following acts between past or present spouses, persons who are parents of the same child, parents and children, stepparents and stepchildren, foster parents and foster children, or other persons living or formerly living in the same household:
>
> 1. Any felony; or
>
> 2. Commission of the offenses of battery, simple battery, simple assault, stalking, criminal damage to property, unlawful restraint or criminal trespass.

Since 1995, state law has required that all family violence incidents be marked as such by the investigating officer, and that the total number of incidents be reported by each county yearly to the Georgia Crime Information Center (GCIC), a part of the Georgia Bureau of Investigation. These incident reports include any family violence resulting in fatal injury, permanent disability, temporary disability, broken bones, gun/knife wounds, superficial injuries, property damage/theft, threats, abusive language, sexual abuse, and other abuse. Reports vary widely from county to county, however, at least in part due to differences in reporting.

For the purposes of this essay, three categories of intimate violence are defined. *Physical violence* includes all domestic violence incidents resulting in permanent or temporary disability, gun or knife wounds, broken bones, superficial injury, and any other abuse of a physical nature. *Property violence* includes all incidents resulting in property damage or theft, and *verbal violence* is defined as the number of domestic violence incidents resulting in threats or abusive language. This essay focuses only on physical, verbal, and economic intimate abuse because homicide and sexual violence are covered in other essays.

The maps presented here combine information on intimate abuse perpetrated by both sexes. The practice of grouping men and women together has been questioned by feminist researchers who have argued that because of male privilege, the violence perpetrated by men and women is qualitatively different (Dobash and Dobash 1979; Schecter 1982; Birns, Cascardi, and Meyer 1994). They argue that men and women tend to have different motivations for their use of violence and tend to be differentially affected by their partner's violence. Because the focus of this essay is the geographic distribution of domestic violence, rather than the gender dynamics of intimate abuse, the choice was made to use total rates as opposed to gender-specific reports.

Distribution of Intimate Abuse in Georgia

Figure 4-3 shows the distribution of physical abuse in Georgia. Rates of reported abuse appear to be higher in the Atlanta metropolitan area, the northern part of the state, and in the Albany and Savannah areas. The highest rates of physical abuse, however, are in Spalding, Ware, and Liberty Counties, all located south of the Atlanta metropolitan area.

The same general pattern holds true for rates of property violence, with the largest concentration of property damage occurring primarily in the area surrounding and north of Atlanta, and only sporadically in the southern part of the state (Figure 4-4). Houston and Chatham Counties are the two major exceptions to this pattern, with both reporting extremely high levels of property damage. Verbal violence and threats (Figure 4-5) are clustered primarily in the coastal counties surrounding Savannah, and to a certain degree in the northwestern counties from Columbus to Chattanooga.

As can be seen from Figures 4-3 to 4-5, eight counties did not provide domestic violence data to GCIC. Thus, it would appear that not all counties are complying with Georgia's reporting guidelines, and that some law enforcement agencies are failing to file the required reports on domestic violence. In fact, it is likely that the rates of intimate violence depicted in the maps above are influenced in part by local awareness of domestic violence, whether or not reporting procedures are followed, and the availability of personnel and resources for gathering data.

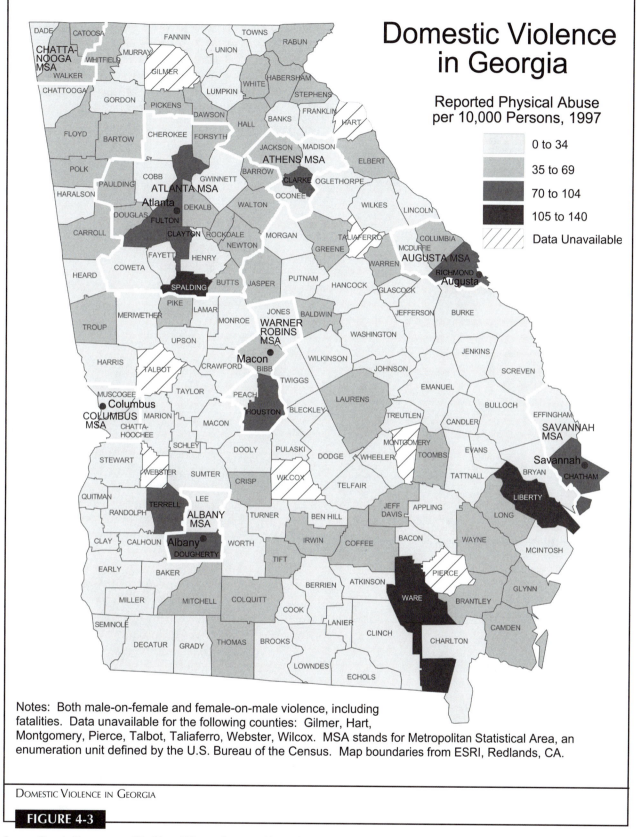

Domestic Violence in Georgia

Reported Physical Abuse per 10,000 Persons, 1997

- 0 to 34
- 35 to 69
- 70 to 104
- 105 to 140
- Data Unavailable

Notes: Both male-on-female and female-on-male violence, including fatalities. Data unavailable for the following counties: Gilmer, Hart, Montgomery, Pierce, Talbot, Taliaferro, Webster, Wilcox. MSA stands for Metropolitan Statistical Area, an enumeration unit defined by the U.S. Bureau of the Census. Map boundaries from ESRI, Redlands, CA.

DOMESTIC VIOLENCE IN GEORGIA

FIGURE 4-3

Sources: Georgia Department of Health and Human Services, 1997, and Georgia Crime Information Center, 1997.

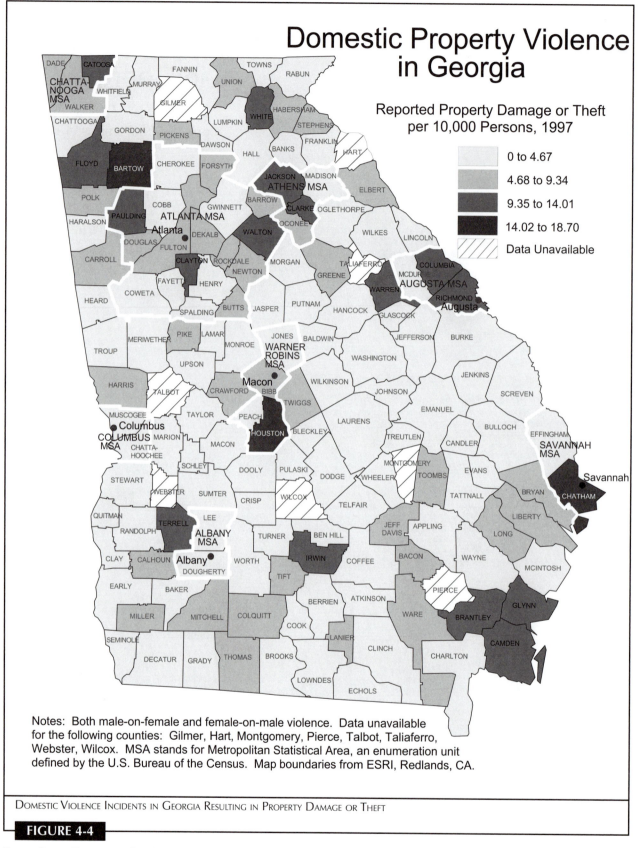

Domestic Property Violence in Georgia

Reported Property Damage or Theft per 10,000 Persons, 1997

- 0 to 4.67
- 4.68 to 9.34
- 9.35 to 14.01
- 14.02 to 18.70
- Data Unavailable

Notes: Both male-on-female and female-on-male violence. Data unavailable for the following counties: Gilmer, Hart, Montgomery, Pierce, Talbot, Taliaferro, Webster, Wilcox. MSA stands for Metropolitan Statistical Area, an enumeration unit defined by the U.S. Bureau of the Census. Map boundaries from ESRI, Redlands, CA.

DOMESTIC VIOLENCE INCIDENTS IN GEORGIA RESULTING IN PROPERTY DAMAGE OR THEFT

FIGURE 4-4

Sources: Georgia Department of Health and Human Services, 1997, and Georgia Crime Information Center, 1997.

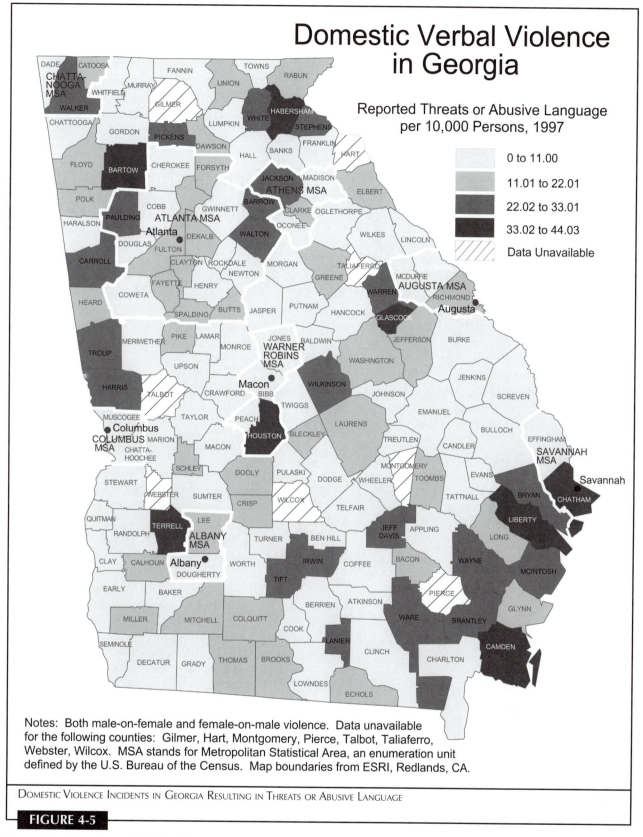

Domestic Verbal Violence in Georgia

Reported Threats or Abusive Language per 10,000 Persons, 1997

- 0 to 11.00
- 11.01 to 22.01
- 22.02 to 33.01
- 33.02 to 44.03
- Data Unavailable

Notes: Both male-on-female and female-on-male violence. Data unavailable for the following counties: Gilmer, Hart, Montgomery, Pierce, Talbot, Taliaferro, Webster, Wilcox. MSA stands for Metropolitan Statistical Area, an enumeration unit defined by the U.S. Bureau of the Census. Map boundaries from ESRI, Redlands, CA.

DOMESTIC VIOLENCE INCIDENTS IN GEORGIA RESULTING IN THREATS OR ABUSIVE LANGUAGE

FIGURE 4-5

Sources: Georgia Department of Health and Human Services, 1997, and Georgia Crime Information Center, 1997.

Distribution of Shelters for Battered Women in Georgia

As the map in Figure 4-6 vividly indicates, most of the shelters in Georgia are located in a band inside or north of the Atlanta metropolitan area. Shelters are sparsely located in the southern part of the state, tending to cluster around mid-size cities, such as Savannah, Valdosta, and Albany, and to appear in several coastal counties and those bordering Florida.

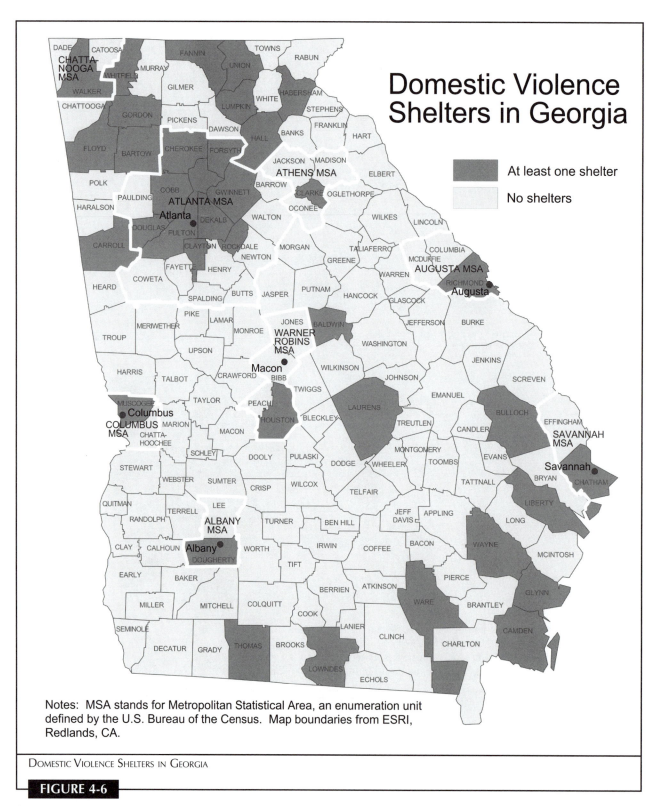

Notes: MSA stands for Metropolitan Statistical Area, an enumeration unit defined by the U.S. Bureau of the Census. Map boundaries from ESRI, Redlands, CA.

DOMESTIC VIOLENCE SHELTERS IN GEORGIA

FIGURE 4-6

Source: Georgia Department of Health and Human Services, 1997.

Distribution of Race and Income

In addition to location, other factors such as race/ethnicity and income distribution may be affecting rates of domestic violence. Georgia is a diverse state in terms of both race and income, but as Figures 4-7 and 4-8 show, these characteristics are not equally distributed over the state.

Sixty-nine percent of the total population in 1997 was white, and 31 percent was non-white. Although dividing the population into only two categories obscures finer details of the racial diversity of the state, it makes the county-by-county presentation of racial distribution much clearer. As can be seen from the map in Figure 4-7, the northern third of the state is predominately white, while the lower

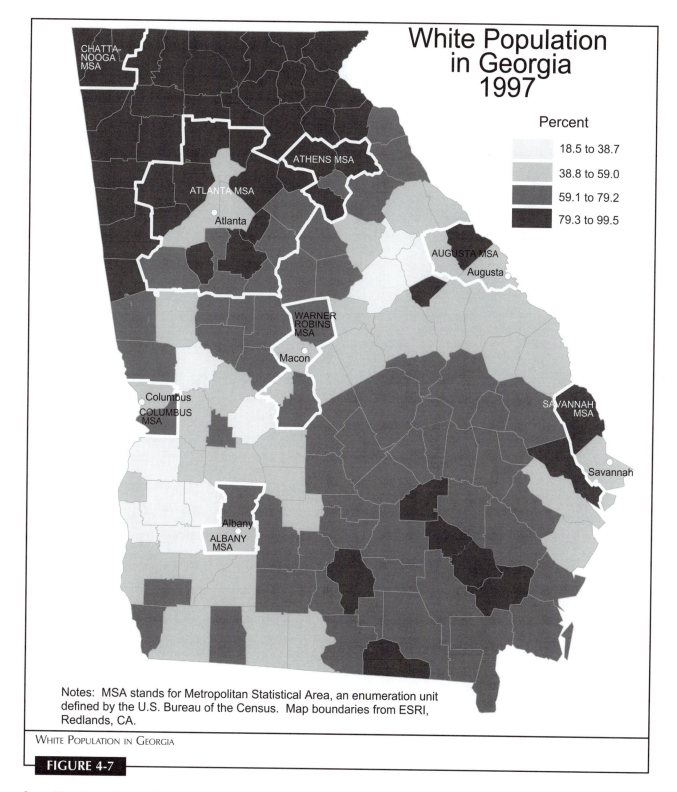

Notes: MSA stands for Metropolitan Statistical Area, an enumeration unit defined by the U.S. Bureau of the Census. Map boundaries from ESRI, Redlands, CA.

WHITE POPULATION IN GEORGIA

FIGURE 4-7

Source: United States Bureau of the Census at <http://www.census.gov>.

two-thirds contains a higher percentage of non-white groups. The major exceptions to this pattern are Fulton and DeKalb Counties where the City of Atlanta is located. These counties have a much higher percentage of non-whites than the areas surrounding them.

The income distribution of the state also shows striking differences between the north and south. As can be seen from Figure 4-8, the highest median incomes are con-

centrated in the northern half of the state, with most of the southern counties reporting median incomes of less than $30,000. The exceptions are the coastal counties of Effingham, Bryan, Glynn, Camden, and Chatham. Savannah is located in Chatham County. Other counties in the southern half of the state with high levels of income are Richmond County, where Augusta is located, and Lee County in the southwest corner of the state.

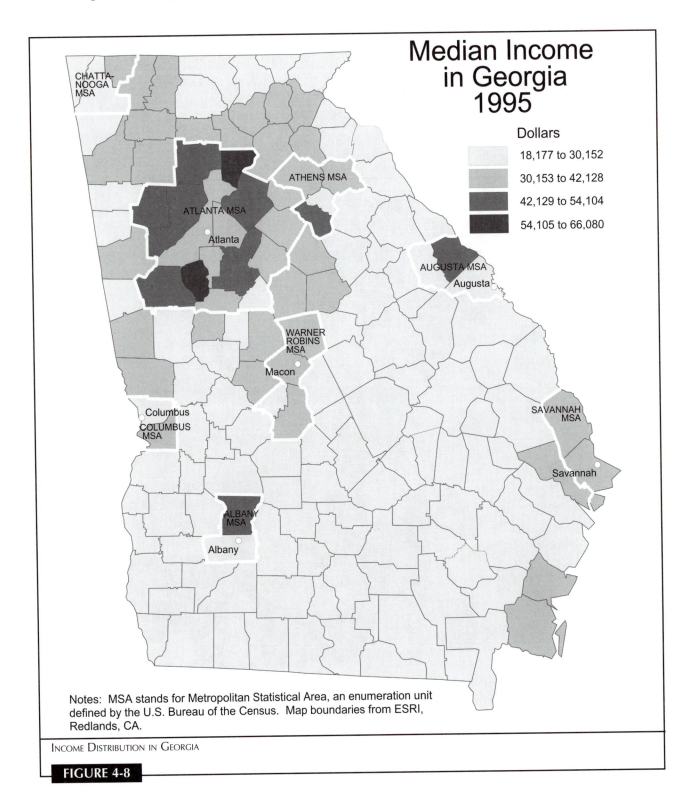

Median Income in Georgia 1995

Dollars

18,177 to 30,152
30,153 to 42,128
42,129 to 54,104
54,105 to 66,080

Notes: MSA stands for Metropolitan Statistical Area, an enumeration unit defined by the U.S. Bureau of the Census. Map boundaries from ESRI, Redlands, CA.

INCOME DISTRIBUTION IN GEORGIA

FIGURE 4-8

Discussion

It is no accident that both rates of reported violence and counties having shelter services are clustered around urban or tourist areas. These are precisely the parts of Georgia with the highest concentrations of resources, both in terms of persons and money. They tend to have persons who are educated about and interested in issues of abuse, and often have pre-existing political or activist networks. Volunteers are easier to recruit in these areas, and there are universities and colleges nearby to offer their expertise. Media, such as TV, radio, and advertising, are more densely concentrated in these locations as well.

To confirm what was becoming evident from examining the maps, statistical correlation coefficients were obtained between the presence of shelters and median incomes. Findings indicated that counties with higher median incomes are more likely to have shelter programs ($R=.47$, $p<.01$), thus tending to support the contention that shelters are clustered in areas with higher levels of income and other resources.

When comparing the distribution of shelters to the distribution of intimate violence, it becomes clear that counties with shelters also tend to have higher rates of reported violence. As expected, statistical correlations support the visual evidence from the maps. Counties with shelters had higher levels of reported physical violence ($R=.45$, $p<.01$), property damage ($R=.49$, $p<.01$), and verbal abuse ($R=.49$, $p<.01$).

Do these correlations mean that having a shelter *causes* rates of violence to increase or that areas with the most intimate violence tend to have the most shelters? Not necessarily. Both reports of violence and shelter presence depend not on actual distribution of abuse, but on access to resources, community awareness, and nearness to metropolitan areas. Counties with shelters are more likely to have battered women's advocates involved in various levels of social services and the legal system. These professionals advocate for better reporting and help keep law enforcement aware of the issue.

Research conducted on the individual level has shown that non-whites and low income families are more likely to be represented in police reports of intimate violence than white families and families with higher income levels (Hutchison, Hirschel, and Pesackis 1994). The data presented here do not support this finding, however. There were no statistically significant relationships between race and any of the types of violence, and counties with the highest reported rates of violence in Georgia actually had incomes higher than the state median. Specifically, income was weakly but positively associated with reports of physical violence ($R=.24$, $p<.01$), property damage ($R=.29$, $p<.01$), and verbal abuse ($R=.29$, $p<.01$).

Conclusions

The findings presented here confirm what past studies have shown. Reports of intimate violence actually increase with public awareness of the issue. As the public becomes more cognizant of intimate abuse, they are more likely to report it. Counties with higher levels of resources are more likely to be aware of domestic violence, support policies and programs to combat it, and have mechanisms for complying with state reporting guidelines. Thus, when counties are doing a good job of raising public awareness, it may appear that rates of violence are skyrocketing. What is happening, however, is that people are simply more aware of intimate violence and resources for combating it, and that both individuals and law enforcement officials are more likely to make reports.

References

Baron, L., and M. Straus. 1989. *Four Theories of Rape in American Society*. New Haven, CT: Yale University Press.

Birns, B., M. Cascardi, and S. Meyer. 1994. Sex-role Socialization: Developmental Influences on Wife Abuse. *American Journal of Orthopsychiatry* 64(1): 50-59.

Dobash, E., and R. Dobash. 1979. *Violence Against Wives: A Case Against the Patriarchy*. New York: Free Press.

Hutchison, I., J. Hirschel, and C. Pesackis. 1994. Family Violence and Police Utilization. *Violence and Victims* 9: 299-313.

Martin, D. 1976. *Battered Wives*. San Francisco: Glide Press.

National Institute of Justice. 1996. *Domestic and Sexual Violence Data Collection: A Report to Congress Under the Violence Against Women Act*. NCJ Publication 161405.

Prizzey, E. 1977. *Scream Quietly or the Neighbors Will Hear*. Hillside, NJ: Enslow Publishers.

Schecter, S. 1982. *Women and Male Violence: The Visions and Struggle of the Battered Women's Movement*. Boston: South End Press.

Straus, M. 1994. *Beating the Devil Out of Them*. Boston: Lexington Books.

The Spatial Dimensions of Child Abuse and Neglect

Linda S. Turnbull

According to the United States Department of Health and Human Services (1998), over two million reports of alleged child maltreatment occurred in the United States in 1996. Although mass media has brought the plight of suffering children to the public's attention, journalists prefer a sensational coverage of "horror stories" involving the death of a child (Johnson 1995). Consequently, the public's perception of child maltreatment may differ from reality. This social problem, nevertheless, astounds us all by its mere volume. In the latest national study, over three million children were suspected of being abused and neglected (U.S. Department of Health and Human Services 1998). The purpose of this essay is to answer the question: Where does this happen?

Historical Background

The origins of child abuse and neglect may be traced through the medical literature (Lynch 1985). Historically, unless injuries required the care of a physician, no one questioned parents' treatment of their children. The first documented medical cases of child maltreatment came to light around 900 A.D. in Rhaze's *Practica Puerorum* (Lynch 1985). Rhaze, a Persian pediatrician practicing in Baghdad, only casually mentions that a child may have been struck intentionally to explain the injuries he found.

Infanticide, killing of a newborn or infant with parental consent, was, and still is, widely practiced in many cultures, often as a means of population control (Conrad and Schneider 1992). The victimization of children was inherent in Greek culture, which supported infanticide out of fear that the defects of crippled children might pass to future generations. Plato accepted this attitude and Aristotle actually recommended a law prohibiting the rearing of crippled children. The mentally handicapped child was also at risk. The idea that such children were possessed by the devil existed in Europe and other places around the world. This idea also influenced the decision to drown female babies in seventeenth-century China (Radbill 1987).

Sexual abuse also has an early history in many cultures. In England, boys had no statutory protection from forced sodomy until 1548, and girls under 10 had no legal protection from forcible rape until 1576 (Tower 1999). Although some cultures tolerate incest (Wallace 1996), a taboo in American society deems this a criminal act. Our denial in admitting that something so horrific could be possible retards effective and forthright actions against it (Tower 1999).

A common problem in Western societies plagued with poverty was the abandonment of children, many of whom became involved in criminal pursuits as a survival strategy or fell under the control of unscrupulous adults (Costin et al. 1996). For example, child prostitution and pornography flourished in the late nineteenth century alongside the prim and proper norms of Victorian society (Tower 1999).

The children's rights movement, which began in the United States in the 1870s, brought the problem of child abuse and neglect to the center of the nation's social agenda. The impetus for this social movement was a legal case in the State of New York. A nine-year-old named Mary Ellen was abused by her adoptive parents (Conrad and Schneider 1992). Efforts to intervene had been unsuccessful because of a popular view of absolute parental rights. In desperation, church workers took the girl to the American Society for the Prevention of Cruelty to Animals. Her case, which was accepted and successfully litigated, ultimately resulted in social reforms and the formation of the Society for the Prevention of Cruelty to Children. Private organizations maintained an aggressive policy of removing children from the home. This coercive approach became unpopular and was replaced by a preventative approach, which initiated a shift in the focus of child protection from abuse to neglect. This new focus dominated social intervention well into the twentieth century (Costin et al. 1996).

Child welfare agencies were overwhelmed following the two world wars and the Great Depression, when many children were left with only one parent and in abject poverty. Beginning in the late 1940s, a slow but steady trend re-established public fervor for children's rights (Costin et al. 1996). An increase in medical papers addressing child injuries and their possible causes was instrumental in this reawakening. In 1946, pediatrician and radiologist John Caffey concluded that the evidence he had for the children under study suggested they had been injured more than once (Lynch 1985). A landmark paper presented to the American Academy of Pediatrics in 1961 by C. Henry Kempe identified the Battered-Child Syndrome and rallied the medical community to support the cause of child abuse by confirming its existence (Lynch 1985). This realization led to the creation of state agencies (Child Protective Services) for the purpose of investigating cases of child abuse and neglect (Conrad and Schneider 1992).

Societal Attitudes

Two conflicting views on child-rearing affect the statistical extent of child abuse and neglect. The traditional view says parents have total control over how their children are reared, while the more contemporary view states that parents who rear their children in a harmful manner should be held legally accountable. The degree of child abuse and neglect varies from society to society (Korbin 1987b). What is perfectly acceptable in one society may be seen as criminal in another. Individuals also have different perceptions of different situations. An additional element is the fact that there is a dynamic temporal process to this complex phenomenon. For example, 50 years ago most children in the United States experienced corporal punishment as regular discipline. Today, much of that same "discipline" is defined as physical abuse (Straus and Donnelly 1994). Therefore, changing definitions reflect society's changing attitudes towards the welfare of children (Giovannoni and Becerra 1979).

To understand the spatial nature of this phenomenon, this essay offers several maps based on data collected in the *Reports from the States to the National Child Abuse and Neglect Data System* published by the U.S. Department of Health and Human Services (1998). When viewing these maps, the reader must recognize that the definitions, laws, policing, reporting, and investigating procedures of child abuse and neglect have a geographical and temporal dimension (Turnbull 1994). In other words, how child abuse and neglect is viewed and handled varies from place to place and over time. The importance of mapping child abuse and neglect data is essentially the identification of problematic areas and the initiation of a theory process for the purposes of possible social intervention (Turnbull 1994).

Data Limitations

Several problems with child abuse and neglect data must be mentioned. The collection process and reporting procedures are not universally standard. Some agencies may count one case for each child in a household while others count individual cases in the same household as one case. Some count repeated calls on one child separately (duplications), whereas some count each call on the same child as one case. Some collect from only state child protective agencies, while some also include cases from private organizations. There is also the factor of participant response in a study. For example, not all participants will answer every question. These are specific factors in data source variations.

More general problems with data include definitions that have already been discussed. Some may count slapping a child as physical abuse while others may not (Straus and Donnelly 1994). People make value judgments that determine whether or not to report cases or, in the instance of caseworkers, count them as confirmed or not confirmed. When definitions are revised or expanded, the statistical

data change. Another consideration when viewing official statistics is that laws vary from state to state as do the interpretation and enforcement of those laws. All the maps should be viewed with these factors in mind.

Spatial Dimension of Child Abuse and Neglect

The reasons for child abuse and neglect identified in the academic literature are varied. They are dependent on many factors involving social, economic, and cultural processes. Some factors identifying families at risk are (1) a high degree of poverty and financial stress, (2) substance abuse, (3) social isolation, (4) a large number of children with one natural parent in the household, and (5) residence in areas with limited or non-existent services and facilities (Garbarino and Crouter 1978; Korbin 1987a; Vondra 1990; Merkel-Holgun and Sobel 1993). Ecological studies of child abuse and neglect confirm that most cases of neglect occur in low income families (Andrews 1985; Deccio et al. 1994). The *National Incidence Study of Child Abuse and Neglect* (NIS-3) found that children from families with an annual income less than $15,000 were 25 times more likely to be abused or neglected (U.S. Department of Health and Human Services 1996). As people climb the socioeconomic ladder, they generally take their attitudes and behavior patterns with them. In addition, financial devastation, substance abuse, and other stressors can happen to anyone. Therefore, the risk factors prevalent in these households can cause maltreatment to occur on any socioeconomic level.

Most reports of child maltreatment for 1996 came from professionals (52 percent) with those in education being the most frequent reporters. In every state, professionals are mandated by law to report all suspected cases of child maltreatment (Wallace 1996). In many states, the public is also required to report. Family members, including victims themselves, accounted for 18 percent of the cases; friends and neighbors reported 9 percent and 22 percent were from other sources, such as anonymous callers (U.S. Department of Health and Human Services 1998).

As shown in Figure 4-9, Washington, D.C., had the highest rate of reports of child maltreatment (109.7 per 1,000 children). With all states reporting, Idaho has a substantially higher rate than any other state (93.2). Each state has its own criteria for reports, as discussed earlier in the essay. It may be interesting to examine the dynamics of child maltreatment in Idaho as compared to Minnesota, for example, where there is a low incidence of reporting. Whether there is actually more child abuse and neglect to report in high-rate states as compared to low-rate states is unknown because many factors (e.g., definitions, perceptions, education, and awareness) affect these rates. Clusters of high report rates appear in the West and in the Midwest. A cluster of relatively high rates of reporting also occurs in the Lower Plains region. Certain questions should be asked by the map

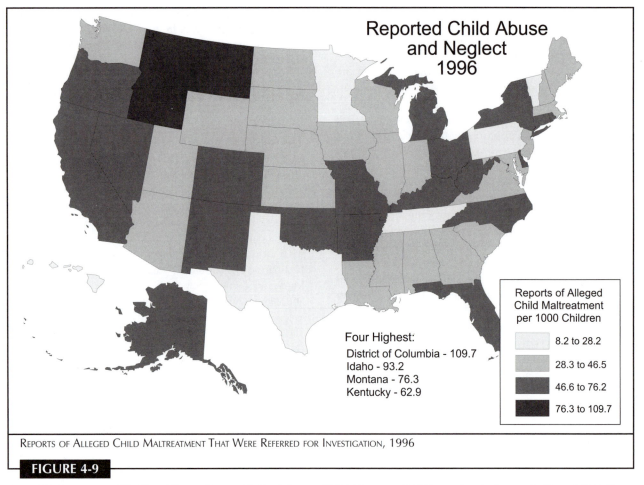

Reported Child Abuse and Neglect 1996

Four Highest:
District of Columbia - 109.7
Idaho - 93.2
Montana - 76.3
Kentucky - 62.9

Reports of Alleged Child Maltreatment per 1000 Children

8.2 to 28.2
28.3 to 46.5
46.6 to 76.2
76.3 to 109.7

REPORTS OF ALLEGED CHILD MALTREATMENT THAT WERE REFERRED FOR INVESTIGATION, 1996

FIGURE 4-9

Source: U.S. Department of Health and Human Services, Children's Bureau, *Child Maltreatment 1996: Reports from the States to the National Child Abuse and Neglect Data System*, Washington, DC: U.S. Government Printing Office, 1998.

reader when viewing these spatial patterns. In areas of high incidence: Do states with higher rates of reporting have more child abuse and neglect? Are those reporting more cognizant of the signs of child maltreatment in states with a high rate? Are high rates of reporting in certain areas a result of moral panic precipitated by media reports of local cases? In areas of low incidence: Are there indeed fewer incidents of child abuse and neglect to report? Are professionals and the public doing their duty in reporting? Are adequate educational, treatment, and investigative services available and accessible?

Nearly three million children were suspected as victims, but only an estimated one million were confirmed as being victims. Disparity between reports and confirmations may be an effect of variation between legal and public definitions of child maltreatment. In areas where professionals, such as medical personnel, reported most incidents, the difference between the two rates should be less. Conversely, large disparity is expected in areas where non-professionals (such as neighbors and others who are unfamiliar with legal definitions) report most cases. In Figure 4-10, child victims are presented in the spatial context. The nation's capital has the highest rate with 53.6 children out of 1,000 con-

firmed as being maltreated. Alaska (40.9), Kentucky (28.3), and Idaho (25.3) are states showing the highest rates of child victims. Regional variations occur, with the West and Southern Atlantic relatively high, and other less significant clusters located in the Midwest and New England.

Types of Child Maltreatment

In 1996, neglect comprised 52 percent of the total number of cases; physical abuse 24 percent; sexual abuse 12 percent; emotional maltreatment 6 percent; and medical neglect 3 percent (U.S. Department of Health and Human Services 1998). The remainder of the cases involved such cruelties as abandonment and congenital drug addiction. Mississippi, West Virginia, Maryland, Pennsylvania, and North Dakota do not have data available for types of maltreatment. In this essay, discussion is limited to neglect, physical abuse, sexual abuse, and child fatalities.

Although legal and research variations occur from place to place with regard to specifics, generally the terms used to define child maltreatment are similar. Children suffering from neglect are chronically deprived of the basic essentials, such as clean or adequate clothing, proper nutrition,

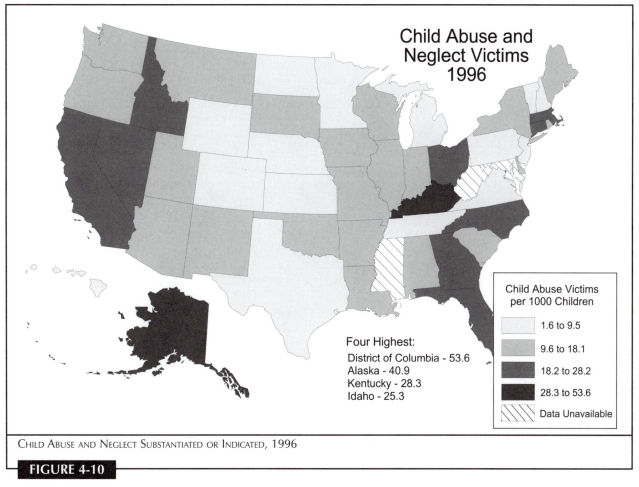

Child Abuse and
Neglect Victims
1996

Four Highest:
District of Columbia - 53.6
Alaska - 40.9
Kentucky - 28.3
Idaho - 25.3

Child Abuse Victims
per 1000 Children

1.6 to 9.5
9.6 to 18.1
18.2 to 28.2
28.3 to 53.6
Data Unavailable

CHILD ABUSE AND NEGLECT SUBSTANTIATED OR INDICATED, 1996

FIGURE 4-10

Source: U.S. Department of Health and Human Services, Children's Bureau, *Child Maltreatment 1996: Reports from the States to the National Child Abuse and Neglect Data System,* Washington, DC: U.S. Government Printing Office, 1998.

or medical care (Besharov 1990). Neglect also can stem from educational and emotional issues, such as not attending school or not receiving the affection needed from a parent (National Clearinghouse on Child Abuse and Neglect 1999a). There were 1,105,605 confirmed (substantiated and indicated) child victims of neglect in 1996 (U.S. Department of Health and Human Services 1998). Where are these victims? Figure 4-11 shows several states that have a relatively high incidence of child neglect: Alaska, Connecticut, Georgia, Kentucky, Massachusetts, New Mexico, North Carolina, and Oklahoma. Washington, D.C., a unique geopolitical unit, has the highest rate of child neglect, 42.3 victims per 1,000 children. Because neglect is often associated with poverty and minorities (Besharov 1990), it can be concluded with a reasonable amount of certainty that some of these states have a high number of families living below the poverty level in terms of household income. Another possible reason for the high incidence classification in states where poverty is not as widespread may be a higher rate of reporting by professionals and public citizens who are witnesses to the signs of neglect. Surprisingly, rates of neglect are low in some southern states. One theory that might explain this is that in areas of widespread poverty only the most severe cases are generally reported to social services.

Physical abuse of a child refers to a non-accidental injury caused by punching, kicking, burning, biting, shaking, or beating (American Humane Association 1998). In 1996, there were 229,332 known child victims of physical abuse, which is the second most prevalent form of maltreatment (U.S. Department of Health and Human Services 1998). A high number of victims are found in the states of Massachusetts, Alaska, Idaho, and Kentucky (Figure 4-12). Three areas of high incidence are located in the northern central, southern, and western sections of the country. Another cluster is located in New England. This map may reflect those attitudes concerning child discipline and the acceptability of children's rights, as opposed to parental rights. For example, Massachusetts has a high rate of physical abuse not necessarily because more children are physically abused there than other places, but rather that there may be less tolerance of behavior practices, such as corporal punishment, which can lead to physical abuse. On the other hand, North Carolina, as an example, has a low incidence. Physical abuse may be lower there than other places. Or, it may be that physical discipline for children is there an accepted practice not only legally, but also by parents, schools, and other social institutions in that state. These socio-cultural

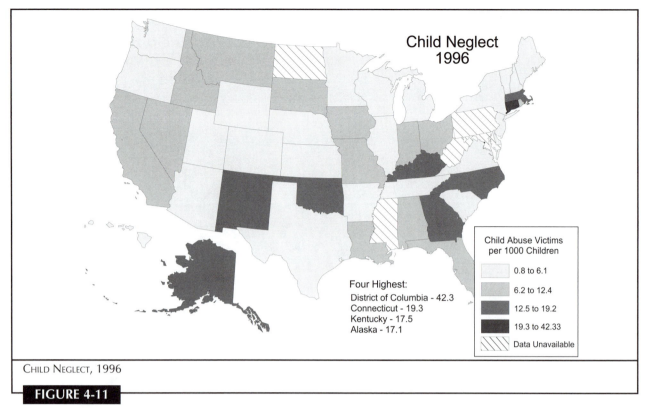

CHILD NEGLECT, 1996

FIGURE 4-11

Source: U.S. Department of Health and Human Services, Children's Bureau, *Child Maltreatment 1996: Reports from the States to the National Child Abuse and Neglect Data System*, Washington, DC: U.S. Government Printing Office, 1998.

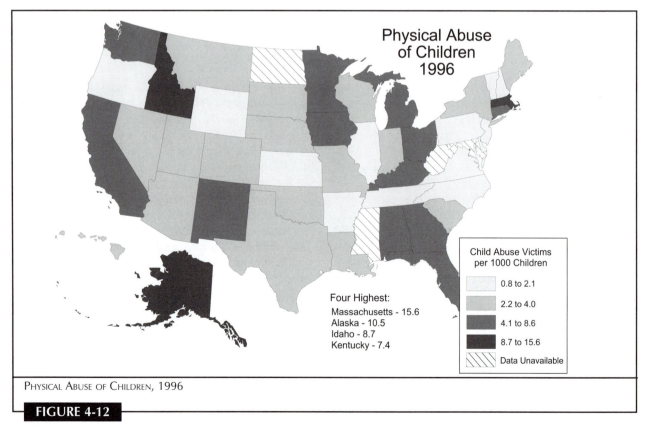

PHYSICAL ABUSE OF CHILDREN, 1996

FIGURE 4-12

Source: U.S. Department of Health and Human Services, Children's Bureau, *Child Maltreatment 1996: Reports from the States to the National Child Abuse and Neglect Data System*, Washington, DC: U.S. Government Printing Office, 1998.

factors are important in analyzing the relative context of the rates of child physical abuse.

Sexual abuse is a type of maltreatment rarely discussed by individuals because of its private and explosive nature. This behavior ranges from the fondling of a child to actual rape or sodomy of a child. It also includes the exploitation of children, as in the use of children in prostitution or pornography. This type of abuse is often not reported because of the psychological dynamics involved. Many children are bribed or threatened into being victimized, and, as a result, are reluctant to report their abuse because of shame or fear (Wolfe et al. 1988).

With a U.S. total of 119,397 known victims (U.S. Department of Health and Human Services 1998), the four states with the highest incidence of child sexual abuse are Wisconsin, Idaho, Alaska, and Vermont (Figure 4-13). The overall geographic pattern produces two clusters: a western region of child sexual abuse (California, Oregon, Washington, and Utah) and a region encompassing parts of the Midwest and the South (Wisconsin, Iowa, Missouri, Arkansas, Oklahoma, Indiana, Ohio, Kentucky, Tennessee,

Alabama, Georgia, and Florida). Whether these groupings reflect intra-familial (in the family) or extra-familial (outside the family) sexual abuse is unavailable in the statistical data. Some areas of high incidence indeed may be areas where more pedophiles and child molesters live or where more incest occurs. However, one also could theorize that residents of high incidence locations may be more supportive of victims and sensitive to the issues surrounding child sexual abuse. Due to the under-reporting of this crime, a low incidence rate does not naturally signify a low actual occurrence.

The most extreme form of maltreatment is the death of a child. Violence against children has gained the attention of epidemiologists at the Centers for Disease Control and Prevention (CDC). Their research on child deaths from violence has been published in academic journals since the early 1980s (Jason 1984; Jason and Andereck 1983). A recent study of industrialized countries by the CDC revealed that the United States had the highest rate of childhood homicide and suicide of any of the selected countries in 1997 (Rochell 1997). The explanatory theories ranged from working women and a high divorce rate to society's accep-

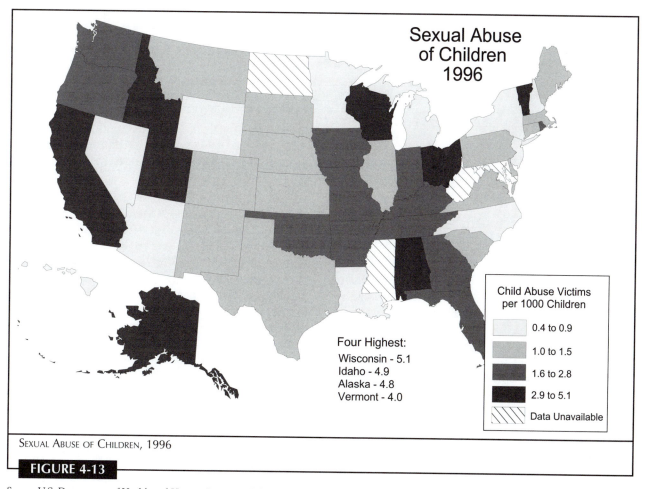

SEXUAL ABUSE OF CHILDREN, 1996

FIGURE 4-13

Source: U.S. Department of Health and Human Services, Children's Bureau, *Child Maltreatment 1996: Reports from the States to the National Child Abuse and Neglect Data System*, Washington, DC: U.S. Government Printing Office, 1998.

105

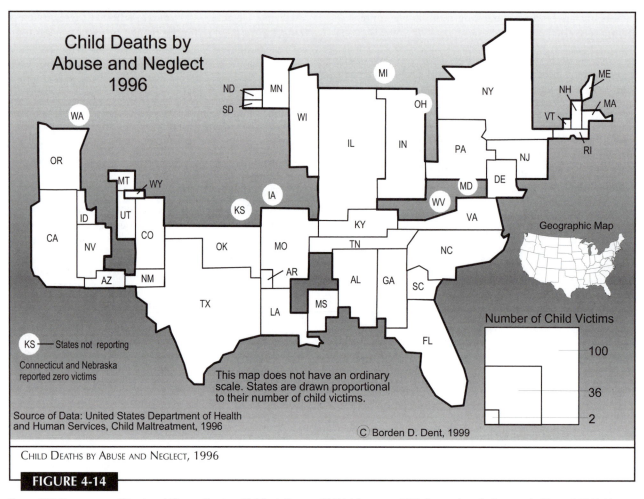

CHILD DEATHS BY ABUSE AND NEGLECT, 1996

FIGURE 4-14

Source: U.S. Department of Heath and Human Services, Children's Bureau, *Child Maltreatment 1996: Reports from the States to the National Child Abuse and Neglect Data System*, Washington, DC: U.S. Government Printing Office, 1998.

tance of violence. Other social ills thought to be reasons were poverty, lack of social programs, and handgun availability (Rochell 1997).

Many states have child death review teams comprising professionals from law enforcement, social services, and the legal and medical communities to examine the circumstances surrounding the death of a child. A child's death can be a result of severe neglect or abuse. Many of these children, who are generally under the age of three, die of such injuries as severe head trauma, Shaken Baby Syndrome, trauma to the abdomen or thorax, scalding, drowning, suffocation, or poisoning. Neglect deaths have unique characteristics, e.g., *chronic neglect* causing starvation or medical problems from malnutrition or *supervision neglect* such as drowning in a bathtub while the parent is absent (National Clearinghouse on Child Abuse and Neglect 1999b).

Although estimates by researchers vary as to the number of children who die each year from maltreatment, child protective services documented a total of 1,077 child deaths in the U.S. in 1996 (U.S. Department of Health and Human Services 1998). Of the reporting states, a high concentration of child deaths is found in the Midwest (Figure

4-14). Illinois, Indiana, and Wisconsin are prominent in that region. New York, Pennsylvania, New Jersey, and Delaware are highest in the Northeast. North Carolina, Florida, and Alabama lead the South. Missouri, Oklahoma, Louisiana, and Texas also form a cluster of relatively high incidence. In the West, California and Oregon have a high number of child deaths. Why are child death rates higher in some states than in others? In some places, environmental stressors, such as poverty, substance abuse, and isolation, may explain the distribution. Another factor may be that in states where review teams are diligent, cases are resolved and counted accurately, thereby raising the rate. In contrast, areas low in child fatalities may not have the investigative resources to determine the circumstances surrounding the death of each child.

Conclusions

Most of the geographic patterns found display both random and non-random distributions. The unavailability of data in some states makes exact patterns difficult to determine. Areas of clustering appear in several parts of the country, with the West and Midwest noticed repeatedly for high incidence. Whether this high rate is because of increased reporting or because risk factors are greater is unknown. In certain circumstances, the Southwest, Northeast, and South also can be labeled problematic. The region lowest in incidence rates appears to be the Great Plains.

Higher rates of maltreatment are expected in areas characterized by weak social networks leading to family isolation, an absence of adequate and appropriate services, inaccessibility to those services when available, and a high degree of poverty and other social and environmental stressors. However, high rates are not necessarily an indication that an area has more child maltreatment. Likewise, an area with a low rate may be a result of the low reporting rate rather than an indication of a safer environment.

Attitudes also affect spatial distributions, particularly in the reporting, investigating, and disposition of child maltreatment cases. For instance, these maps in part may be a reflection of children's rights versus parents' rights. Individual definitions as well as individual levels of social responsibility play a role in whether a child is brought to the attention of social services. The spatial perspective is valuable in that it aids in directing future research questions leading to appropriate placement of education, treatment, and prevention programs with a hope of reducing the number of child victims.

References

American Humane Association (AHA). 1998. Answers to Common Questions About Child Abuse and Neglect at <http://www.americanhumane.org>.

Andrews, Howard F. 1985. The Ecology of Risk and the Geography of Intervention: From Research to Practice for the Health and Well-being of Urban Children. *Annals of the Association of American Geographers* 75 (3): 370-82.

Besharov, Douglas J. 1990. *Recognizing Child Abuse.* New York: The Free Press.

Conrad, Peter, and Joseph W. Schneider. 1992. *Deviance and Medicalization.* Philadelphia: Temple University Press.

Costin, Lela B., Howard Jacob Karger, and David Stoesz. 1996. *The Politics of Child Abuse in America.* New York: Oxford University Press.

Deccio, Gary, William C. Horner, and Dee Wilson. 1994. High Risk Neighborhoods and High Risk Families: Replication Research Related to the Human Ecology of Child Maltreatment. *Journal of Social Service Research* 18 (3-4): 123-37.

Dhooper, Surjit Singh, David D. Royse, and L.C. Wolfe. 1991. A Statewide Study of the Public Attitudes Toward Child Abuse. *Child Abuse and Neglect* 15: 37-44.

Fontana, Vincent J., and Douglas J. Besharov, eds. 1996. *The Maltreated Child.* 5th ed. Springfield, IL: Charles C. Thomas.

Garbarino, James, and Ann Crouter. 1978. Defining the Community Context for Parent-Child Relations: The Correlates of Child Maltreatment. *Child Development* 49: 604-16.

Giovannoni, Jeanne M., and Rosina M. Becerra. 1979. *Defining Child Abuse.* New York: The Free Press.

Jason, Janine. 1984. Centers for Disease Control and the Epidemiology of Violence. *Child Abuse and Neglect* 8: 279-83.

Jason, Janine, and Mark Andereck. 1983. Fatal Child Abuse in Georgia: The Epidemiology of Severe Physical Child Abuse. *Child Abuse and Neglect* 7: 1-9.

Johnson, John M. 1995. Horror Stories and the Construction of Child Abuse. In Joel Best, ed. *Images of Issues: Typifying Contemporary Social Problems.* New York: A. De Gruyter.

Korbin, Jill E. 1987a. Child Maltreatment in Cross-Cultural Perspective: Vulnerable Children and Circumstances. In Richard J. Gelles and Jane B. Lancaster, eds. *Child Abuse and Neglect.* New York: Aldine de Gruyter, pp. 31-55.

———. 1987b. Child Abuse and Neglect: The Cultural Context. In Ray S. Helfer and Ruth S. Kemper, eds. *The Battered Child,* 4th ed. Chicago: The University of Chicago Press, pp. 23-42.

Lynch, Margaret A. 1985. Child Abuse before Kempe: An Historical Literature Review. *Child Abuse and Neglect* 9: 7-15.

Merkel-Holgun, Lisa A., with Audrey J. Sobel. 1993. *The Child Welfare Stat Book 1993.* Washington, DC: Child Welfare League of America, Inc.

National Clearinghouse on Child Abuse and Neglect. 1999a. *In Fact. . .Answers to Frequently Asked Questions on Child Abuse and Neglect* at <http://www.calib.com/nccanch/pubs/infact.htm>.

———. 1999b. *Frequently Asked Questions About Child Fatalities* at <http://www.calib.com/nccanch/pubs/fatality.htm>.

Radbill, Samuel X. 1987. Children in a World of Violence: A History of Child Abuse. In Ray S. Helfer and Ruth S. Kemper, eds. *The Battered Child,* 4th ed. Chicago: The University of Chicago Press, pp. 3-12.

Rochell, Anne. 1997. Children Slain in U.S. at 5 Times Rate of Other Countries. *The Atlanta Journal,* 7 February: 1(A).

Straus, Murray A., with Denise A. Donnelly. 1994. *Beating the Devil Out of Them.* New York: Lexington Books.

Tower, Cynthia Crosson. 1999. *Understanding Child Abuse and Neglect.* 4th ed. Boston: Allyn and Bacon.

Turnbull, Linda Susan. 1994. A Spatial Perspective on Child Victimization in Georgia, 1988-1990. An unpublished master's thesis, Georgia State University, Atlanta.

U.S. Department of Health and Human Services (DHHS), National Center on Child Abuse and Neglect. 1996. *Third National Incidence Study of Child Abuse and Neglect: Final Report* (NIS-3). Washington, DC: U.S. Government Printing Office.

———. 1998. *Child Maltreatment 1996: Reports from the States to the National Child Abuse and Neglect Data System.* Washington, DC: U.S. Government Printing Office.

Vondra, Joan I. 1990. The Community Context of Child Abuse and Neglect. *Marriage and the Family Review* 15 (1): 19-35.

Wallace, Harvey. 1996. *Family Violence.* Boston: Allyn and Bacon.

Wolfe, David. A., Vicky V. Wolfe, and Connie L. Best. 1988. Child Victims of Sexual Abuse. In Vincent B. Van Hasselt, Randall L. Morrison, Alan S. Bellack, and Michel Hersen, eds. *Handbook of Family Violence.* New York: Plenum Press, pp. 157–86.

Elder Abuse

Denise A. Donnelly

Of all the crimes of sexual and intimate violence, elder abuse was the last to be discovered by policy makers and researchers, and the last to be defined by the public as a social problem. Recognition of elder abuse began in the United Kingdom in the 1970s, with sensational media reports of "granny bashing" (American Medical Association 1992). Interest in the problem soon spread to the United States, where attention was first focused on institutional abuse, and later on abuse within families. Beginning in the mid-1970s, the U.S. Senate convened committees on aging that investigated reports of abuse and neglect in nursing homes, and later conducted hearings in which elders gave testimony about their own experiences with abuse in both institutional and non-institutional contexts. In 1990, the Elder Abuse Task Force was created by the U.S. Department of Health and Human Services, and in 1991, a National Institute on Elder Abuse was established (American Medical Association 1992). While all 50 states now have laws against elder abuse (Stiegel 1995), research in this area dates back only about 20 years (Utech 1994). Much is left to learn about the causes, dynamics, and outcomes of the maltreatment of the elderly.

Defining Elder Abuse

One of the most persistent areas of controversy within the study of intimate violence involves defining elder abuse. Definitional issues begin with determining the point at which a person becomes elderly. Most states consider persons over 65 to be elderly, but this is simply an arbitrary designation that was developed by the Social Security Administration in the 1930s to determine eligibility for "old age" programs (Atchley 1988). With the social and health advances made in the last 60 years, 65 may no longer be "old." While some persons in their 50s seem physically and emotionally old, others in their 70s are still vigorous and self-sufficient.

Elder abuse is also difficult to define because some older persons are frail and weak and need more protection than younger adults. Yet, they are still just that, adults, and must be treated as such. The agency and self-determination of older persons must be taken into account when creating laws and policies to deal with elder abuse. Some elders choose not to report their abuse, or they do not realize that they are being mistreated. The unique status of older adults means that laws covering younger adults or those protecting physically or mentally incapacitated adults of any age may not be sufficient for their needs. Yet, laws and policies modeled after those for children are often perceived as in-

sulting and demeaning by older persons because the laws do not take into account their autonomy and agency as adults.

An additional definitional issue centers around determining which behaviors are abusive. For example, is tying an elder to a potty chair so that he or she does not fall abusive? Is not visiting one's aging parents or attending to their needs neglectful? Is taking over the financial affairs of an aging parent against his or her will abusive? Under what circumstances? Is sexual activity between two nursing home residents sexual abuse or simply the exercise of the adult right to self-determination?

Another issue factor in defining elder abuse is the identity of the abuser. For example, if an elder person is abused by a spouse, is this elder abuse or spouse abuse? Is an elder who neglects his or her cleanliness or eats only mashed potatoes for a week simply an adult exercising his or her autonomy, or is this self-abuse? Finally, what is the difference between elder abuse committed by families, and elder abuse in institutional settings?

Further complicating the definitional issue is a lack of federal legislation on elder abuse. As mentioned earlier, each of the 50 states now has laws requiring mandatory reports of elder abuse, but these laws vary considerably from state to state (Stiegel 1995). Thus, no uniform reporting or data collection requirements exist on the national level. In about three-quarters of the states, adult protective services is responsible for investigating reports, but in the remaining states, state units on aging assume that responsibility (National Center on Elder Abuse 1999). Moreover, no national agency or central location compiles state-by-state information on elder abuse (National Center on Elder Abuse 1999). In this essay, rather than trying to define elder abuse, I present the types of elder abuse as identified by researchers and practitioners.

Types of Elder Abuse

The elderly can be abused in a variety of ways; some are similar to the abuse of other adults, some are similar to the abuse of children, and still others are unique to elderly persons. Some types of abuse are intentional, while others are unintentional. The most common type of elder abuse is neglect. *Elder neglect* is an act of omission, or the withholding of care or assistance that puts an elder at risk for physical or psychological harm. *Self-neglect* occurs when an older person becomes unable to care for his or her needs, or when the person makes choices that may have harmful consequences (Sellers, Folts, and Logan 1992). For example, elder persons may become too frail to clean their homes adequately or make regular trips to the grocery store. Some may choose not to eat, not to go to the doctor, or to have pets that they can no longer clean up after, thus creating potential health problems. Because they are adults, such situations create dilemmas for concerned relatives, friends, and neighbors. Should the elderly person be forced to accept help, enter a supervised facility, or go to the doctor? Or, as adults, should their rights to self-determination be respected? As Phillipson (1993) points out, there are no clear norms about who is responsible for elder care.

Elders may also be neglected by those responsible for caring for them. This type of neglect may be active (intentional) or passive (non-intentional), and is more common among the frail elderly who are unable to care for themselves. It includes not providing adequate health care, nutrition, hygiene, housing, or safety for an older person in one's care (American Medical Association 1992).

Physical abuse includes threatened or intentional acts of violence that result in physical pain or emotional suffering for the elder. The most common forms of physical abuse are hitting, slapping, pinching, pushing, and using more force than is necessary to accomplish a task (such as rough treatment in assisting an elder with hygiene, toileting, or moving about). The American Medical Association (1992) also includes force-feeding, incorrect positioning, and improper use of physical restraints or medications in the category of physical abuse.

Emotional abuse occurs when an elder person is berated, threatened, harassed, or caused to experience fear for his or her safety and well-being. Other forms of emotional abuse are isolating the elder person from friends or family, leaving him or her alone for long periods of time, or treating the person in a demeaning or condescending way. Some researchers also include the violation of human rights in this category.

Sexual abuse, the rarest form of elder abuse, involves forcing an elderly person to participate in any activity of a sexual nature, including fondling, attempted intercourse, talking "dirty," or making nude pictures or movies of an older person against his or her will. Sexual abuse can also include acts of a sexual nature committed in the presence of, but not physically involving the elder, such as exposing one's self or masturbating (Ramsey-Klawsnik 1991).

Economic maltreatment of the elderly includes both abuse and neglect. Abuse is taking money or possessions from elder persons, coercing or tricking them into signing away money, rights, or possessions, or denying them the right to a home. Neglect occurs when available funds are not used to care for the physical, emotional, and medical needs of the older person.

Abusers of the Elderly

Most elderly persons are abused by family members (Pillimer and Suitor 1992; Taler and Ansello 1985). Commonly, the abuser is the elder person's adult child, son- or daughter-in-

law, grandchild, or spouse (Tatara 1993). Less frequently, older persons are abused by others responsible for their care, such as other relatives, home health care providers, adult daycare attendants, and nursing home or residential staff. They may also be abused by visitors, strangers, or intruders.

For some families, abuse is an ongoing or inter-generational issue. Adult children may abuse parents who were abusive to them when they were growing up, and who may still be emotionally or physically abusive. Abusive spouses continue to abuse their mates in old age, and may simply be continuing patterns set much earlier in the marriage (Pillimer and Suitor 1992). Sometimes, abused spouses will become abusive to partners who have abused and berated them for years once the abusive spouse becomes physically or mentally incapacitated. In other cases, the elder being cared for becomes violent with the caretaker, and the caretaker returns the violence (Pillimer and Suitor 1992).

Often, dependency plays a major role in elder abuse. Elderly persons may be dependent on a caretaker for many or all of their needs (Fulmer, 1990). The elder may be physically incapacitated, or may suffer from dementia. Caretakers experience stress as they try to meet the needs of elderly spouses or parents who may be needy or demanding. They may also feel pulled between the needs of the frail elder, the needs of other family members, and their own personal needs. While none of these situations justifies abuse in any way, it does set the stage for elder abuse in some families.

Some adult children find it difficult to acknowledge the role reversal that occurs as parents age, and may resent the fact that the parent can no longer "take care of them." These dependent adult children may strike out at their parents in frustration, or feel that their mother or father somehow owes them continued housing, financial support, or other types of support (Pillimer 1985).

Rates of Abuse

Currently, no organization or entity maintains data on the incidence of non-fatal elder abuse on a state-by-state basis (National Center on Elder Abuse 1999). In 1994, 241,000 cases of elder abuse (excluding self-neglect) were reported in the U.S., but a breakdown of this figure by state is not available (National Center on Elder Abuse 1999). We do know, however, that states with larger concentrations of elderly are more likely to be faced with greater numbers of abused elders, and that those with the greatest percentages of elderly, relative to persons under 65, will experience the most strain on their resources as they deal with problems of elder maltreatment. Figure 4-15 presents the percentage of persons over 65 in each state in 1997.

As becomes readily apparent, except for Florida, the states with the highest percentages of persons over 65 tend to be in the Midwest and Northeast. This finding does not mean that older people move to these states upon retirement, rather that they are remaining in place while their children and grandchildren move to areas of greater economic opportunity. Thus, the states with the highest con-

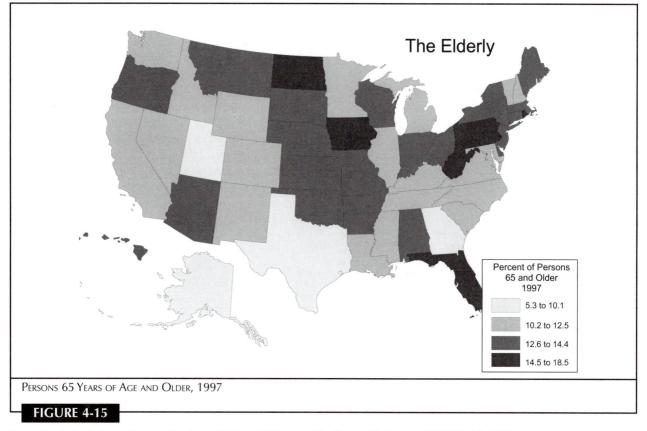

The Elderly

Percent of Persons
65 and Older
1997

5.3 to 10.1

10.2 to 12.5

12.6 to 14.4

14.5 to 18.5

PERSONS 65 YEARS OF AGE AND OLDER, 1997

FIGURE 4-15

Source: Population Estimates Program, Population Division, U.S. Bureau of the Census, Washington, DC 20233, July 1997.

centrations of elderly are in many cases also the ones with the least resources to expend on elder abuse.

Because incidence data on non-fatal elder abuse do not exist on a state-by-state basis, homicide data for each of the 50 states are discussed next. As Bachman (1993) notes, elderly persons are among the least likely persons to be murdered, and murders by family members are even rarer than murders by strangers. This fact should be kept in mind when examining Figure 4-16, which depicts the number of elders who were murdered by family members in each state in 1994. No relationship appears between the number of elderly killed by family members in a state, and the concentration of elderly in that state, probably because of the incredibly small number of elder homicides by family members each year. Elder homicide is more common on the West and East coasts, and in the South, than in the Midwest.

Most fatal violence against elderly family members is perpetrated on females (Figure 4-17). In seven states (Kentucky, Massachusetts, Minnesota, Nevada, Rhode Island, Utah, and Wyoming), only males were the victims of fatal violence, but these tended to be states where the total number of over 65 fatalities at a family member's hands did not exceed four. On the other hand, six states (Alaska, Colorado, Indiana, Maine, Missouri, and Tennessee) had only female fatalities, and the number of female fatalities nationwide was much greater than the number of male fatalities. Given that females outnumber males in ever increas-

ing ratios after age 65, this is not surprising. Because females live, on average, seven to eight years longer than men, most elderly are women; thus, elder abuse is predominately a female problem (Dunn 1995; Utech 1994).

Conclusion

As this essay illustrates, several issues complicate the collection of elder abuse data on a state-by-state basis. First, elder abuse is the most underreported form of family violence (Pillimer and Finkelhor, 1988). Older people often do not recognize their abuse, are reluctant to report it, or may not wish to press charges. Second, rates of abuse differ depending on whether reports are made by law enforcement, social service agencies, or the elders themselves. A third and related problem is that definitions of abuse vary from researcher to researcher, between states, and at the federal level. For example, *Uniform Crime Report* data, such as those used in this essay, typically do not conform to state or local definitions of elder abuse. Finally, adult protective service agencies in many states address the maltreatment of all mentally and physically impaired adults (over 18) without distinguishing between abuse of those under and over 65, thus their data may lack the specificity necessary to determine if elder abuse has occurred.

Improved systems of data collection on elder abuse are desperately needed, particularly for state level data. An in-

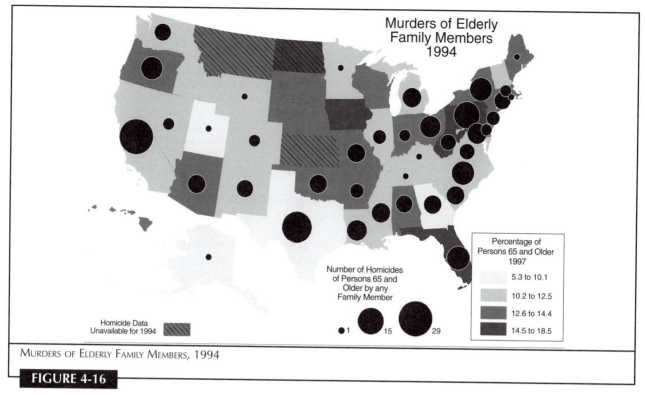

MURDERS OF ELDERLY FAMILY MEMBERS, 1994

FIGURE 4-16

Sources: Fox, James Alan. UNIFORM CRIME REPORTS [UNITED STATES]: SUPPLEMENTARY HOMICIDE REPORTS, 1976-1994 [Computer File]. ICPSR version. Boston: Northeastern University, College of Criminal Justice [producer], 1996; Ann Arbor, MI: Inter-university Consortium for Political and Social Research [distributor], 1996; and Population Estimates Program, Population Division, U.S. Bureau of the Census, Washington, DC 20233, July 1997.

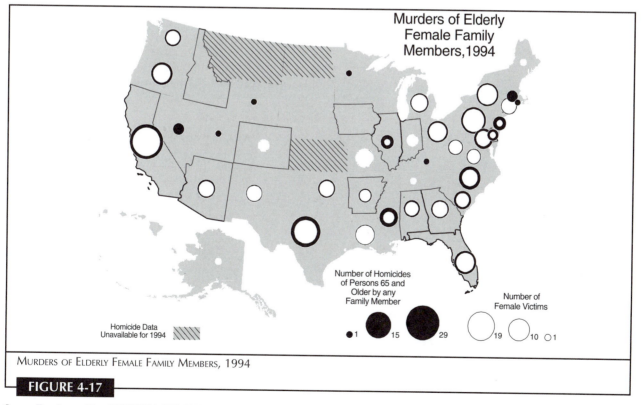

MURDERS OF ELDERLY FEMALE FAMILY MEMBERS, 1994

FIGURE 4-17

Source: Fox, James Alan. UNIFORM CRIME REPORTS [UNITED STATES]: SUPPLEMENTARY HOMICIDE REPORTS, 1976-1994 [Computer File]. ICPSR version. Boston: Northeastern University, College of Criminal Justice [producer], 1996; Ann Arbor, MI: Inter-university Consortium for Political and Social Research [distributor], 1996.

tegrated system of reporting at the national level would be useful in understanding the distribution of elder abuse in the U.S., in examining how the problem varies geographically, and in comparing state laws and interventions. Until accurate state level data exist, federal resources and services cannot effectively be directed towards solving this problem, and accurate comparisons between states cannot be undertaken.

References

American Medical Association. 1992. *Diagnostic and Treatment Guidelines on Elder Abuse and Neglect*. Chicago: American Medical Association.

Atchley, R. 1988. *Social Forces and Aging*. Belmont, CA: Wadsworth.

Bachman, R. 1993. The Double Edged Sword of Violent Victimization Against the Elderly: Patterns of Family and Stranger Perpetration. *Journal of Elder Abuse and Neglect* 5(4): 59-76.

Dunn, P. 1995. "Elder Abuse" as an Innovation to Australia: A Critical Overview. In J.I. Kosberg and J.L. Garcia, eds. *Elder Abuse: International and Cross-Cultural Perspectives*. Binghamton, NY: Haworth, 13-30.

Fulmer, T. 1990. The Debate Over Dependency as a Relevant Predisposing Factor in Elder Abuse and Neglect. *Journal of Elder Abuse and Neglect* 2: 51-58.

National Center on Elder Abuse. 1999. Elder Abuse Information Series. <http://www.interinc.com/NCEA/Statistics/>.

Phillipson, C. 1993. Abuse of Older People: Sociological Perspectives. In P. Decalmer and F. Glendenning, eds. *Mistreatment of Elderly People*. Newbury Park, CA: Sage, pp. 88-101.

Pillimer, K. 1985. The Dangers of Dependency: New Findings on Domestic Violence Against the Elderly. *Social Problems* 33(2): 146-58.

Pillimer, K., and D. Finkelhor. 1988. The Prevalence of Elder Abuse: A Random Sample Survey. *Gerontologist* 28: 51-57.

Pillimer, K., and J. Suitor. 1992. Violence and Violent Feelings: What Causes Them Among Family? *Journal of Gerontology: Social Sciences* 47(4): 165-72.

Ramsey-Klawsnik, H. 1991. Elder Sexual Abuse: Preliminary Findings. *Journal of Elder Abuse and Neglect* 3(3): 73-90.

Sellers, C., W. Folts, and K. Logan. 1992. Elder Mistreatment: A Multidimensional Problem. *Journal of Elder Abuse and Neglect* 4(4): 5-23.

Stiegel, L. 1995. *Recommended Guidelines for State Courts Handling Cases Involving Elder Abuse*. Washington, DC: American Bar Association.

Taler, G., and E. Ansello. 1985. Elder Abuse. *Association of Family Physicians* 32: 107-14.

Tatara, T. 1993. Understanding the Nature and Scope of Elder Abuse with the Use of State Aggregate Data. *Journal of Elder Abuse and Neglect* 5(4): 35-57.

Utech, M. 1994. *Violence, Abuse, and Neglect: The American Home*. Dix Hills, NY: General Hall.

Animal Cruelty: A Spatial Investigation

Linda S. Turnbull

Social scientists have demonstrated a cycle of violence that theoretically links animal cruelty to violence against humans. Anthropologist Margaret Mead commented that the killing or torturing of a living creature is a diagnostic sign that should be an alert to all child therapists (Mead 1964). Backgrounds of violent offenders often reveal the presence of animal cruelty. For instance, the 15-year-old Oregon high school shooter, Kipland Kinkel, tortured animals (Cloud 1999) and Wayne Wooten bombed the Tacoma, Washington, office of the NAACP one year after sadistically killing a cat (Fox 1999). There also is evidence that cruelty to animals is a predictor of future violent behavior. The purpose of this essay is to provide the reader with information demonstrating the link between violence against humans and animals and to introduce a spatial component to the problem of animal cruelty.

Historical Viewpoints

Arguments on the ethical treatment of animals appeared as early as the thirteenth century. Saint Thomas Aquinas posited that those who were cruel to animals also had the capacity for cruelty to humans (Regan and Singer 1976). Other philosophers, such as Immanuel Kant, wrote on the duties of humans towards animals, stating that if one does not feel sympathy towards them, then that individual's ability to feel the suffering of humans is also weakened (Regan and Singer 1976).

Another indicator that society was concerned with the abuse of animals leading to the abuse of humans is found in a publication written by William Hogarth in the eighteenth century. Entitled *Four Stages of Cruelty*, this essay communicates the fear of a progression of torture beginning as a child with an animal, then as a young man beating a horse, and finally causing the death of a woman (Lindsay 1979).

Contemporary philosopher Peter Singer begins his book, *Animal Liberation* (1975), by introducing a concept that had previously been suggested in parody. In the late 1700s, Cambridge philosopher Thomas Taylor penned *A Vindication of the Rights of Brutes* to mock the suffragette Mary Wollstonescraft's *Vindication of the Rights of Women*. He argued that if women were given rights, then granting them to dogs, cats, and horses would come next. Singer and other contemporaries, such as Tom Regan and Bernard Rollin, base their philosophies on the idea that animals also have rights. Of course, animals cannot be given the same rights as humans (e.g., the right to vote), but they can be extended the right to be treated with respect and compassion and the right of protection from harm under the law (Singer 1975).

Animal Cruelty Linked with Serial Killers

Psychological profilers have become adept at identifying common themes of aberrant, anti-social behavior (Ressler and Shachtman 1992). Animal cruelty has been found by FBI profilers to be one common theme in the backgrounds of many violent criminals. Aside from overt cruelty, there are cases in which violence against animals is symbolic. Instead of actually killing a live animal, the offender carves up stuffed animals or photographs of animals (Lockwood and Church 1996).

David Berkowitz, who terrorized New York City as the "Son of Sam," shot his neighbor's Labrador retriever. He claimed the dog was responsible for his killings (Lockwood and Hodge 1986). As a child, Ted Bundy witnessed his grandfather assault people and torment animals. Bundy was connected through circumstantial evidence to a graveyard

Contributor's Note: The Animal Legal Defense Fund (ALDF) (e-mail at info@aldf.org) is an organization in Petaluma, California, that assists in prosecutions across the country. They offer their services in a number of ways: finding expert witnesses, making recommendations in the disposition of cases and sentencing of the offender, and collecting a national database on cases that provides information from one jurisdiction to another. I thank Bradley Woodall of ALDF for his assistance in providing statistical information for the animal cruelty prosecution map.

I also thank Kim Roberts and Sally Fekety from the Humane Society of the United States in Washington, D.C., for their assistance in collecting information on the animal cruelty statutes and on the First Strike Campaign (e-mail at fstrike@ix.netcom.com), which aids communities in public awareness programs on the link between animal cruelty and human violence.

My gratitude also goes to Bill Garrett, executive director, and Evelyn Albertson, education director, of the Atlanta Humane Society, and to Shirley Jenkins, shelter manager of Fulton County Animal Control, for their assistance in gathering statistical information on animal cruelty in Fulton County, Georgia.

Appreciation also goes to John Mays from the National Animal Control Association for his help in collecting data on animal cruelty incidence.

of animal bones (Lockwood 1989). Albert DeSalvo, the self-confessed "Boston Strangler," was known to trap cats and dogs in orange crates into which he shot arrows (Lockwood and Hodge 1986). Jeffrey Dahmer, who was convicted of killing and cannibalizing humans, butchered animals while growing up in Milwaukee (Everitt 1993). All these individuals witnessed or participated in heinous acts towards animals. These are just a few of the incidents that could be cited to link the behavior of killers with cruelty to animals.

Animal Cruelty Linked with Family Violence

Serial killers are not the only ones who abuse animals. In their recent article, Jorgensen and Maloney comment that, "Like charity, pathology begins at home" (1999: 145). Research has carefully illustrated the connection between animal cruelty and family violence. Animal cruelty, child maltreatment, and domestic violence have been linked as overlapping domains (Ascione 1999). Although this phenomenon does cross gender lines, most of these offenders are male (Feldman 1997). Abusers victimize the vulnerable—usually women, children, and animals.

The objectification of women, children, and animals is a focus of provocative feminist research. Literature on abused women contains numerous accounts of men controlling and dominating their partners through threats of or actual harm to their pets (Adams 1994). A study in which women in a domestic violence shelter were interviewed found that 71 percent had pets who were threatened, hurt, or killed by their battering partner (Ascione 1998). Furthermore, a pet killing is a sign of a life-threatening situation for the woman (Burstow 1992). Many women who kill their husbands in self-defense feared they would suffer the same fate as the family pet (Browne 1987). In contrast, women who have been killed by their husbands may not have understood the significance of a previous act of animal cruelty.

Holding pets hostage is used not just to control women. Entire families have witnessed the brutal murder of the family pet by the father (Russell 1990). In addition, children who have been sexually molested are often warned to keep silent about the incident or something will happen to their loved pet (Vachss 1993). In a recent study of clients in a domestic abuse shelter, women had witnessed animal abuse in 76 percent of the cases and 54 percent of their children who had witnessed violence against animals imitated that behavior (Quinlisk 1999).

Research investigating family dynamics disclosed alarming facts with regard to the treatment of family pets. One study identified a large number of families investigated for animal abuse that also were known to social services for children at risk (Hutton 1983). Another study involving families reported to social services found a connection between the physical abuse of children and pets. The abusers of the pets were either abusive parents or the abused child (DeViney et al. 1983).

The elderly are often unable to handle their legal and financial affairs because of infirmities. This may put them at risk for victimization from guardians or caretakers (Schuleter 1999). Elders are often the most hidden members of our society, whereas animals are the most visible. Sometimes the investigation of one type of abuse will lead to the discovery of the other. For example, while investigating animal cruelty, an officer may find an abused or neglected elder in the same household.

Until recently, the link between animal and human violence was ignored by law enforcement, the judicial system, and other agencies. Family violence issues in general have taken the spotlight in the past 20 years. Close examination has revealed that "animal abuse is not just the result of some personality flaw in the abuser, but a symptom of a deeply disturbed family" (Lockwood and Hodge 1986: 5). Early research, established that children who abuse animals have personal backgrounds of severe parental neglect and physical and emotional abuse (Tapia 1971).

More recent research suggests that a simple explanation for this absence of compassion is inadequate. A complex myriad of abnormal interrelationships is pivotal to the child's decision to inflict cruelty. One study showed that a large number of abused and delinquent children sampled had felt a deep sense of loss over pets who were killed (Robin et al. 1983). Resulting anger can manifest itself through the causing of harm to subsequent pets they love to "prove" to themselves that the loss did not hurt. According to experts, it provides an emotional release for abused children (Hodge and Lockwood 1990). Cruelty to animals by children can also be attributed to other factors such as "expected behavior" (i.e., children who are told they are bad will live up to that expectation), the imitation of violent behavior known as "normal" in their family, a demonstration of power and authority to offset their own feelings of helplessness, and an attitude that life has little or no value (Lockwood and Hodge 1986).

Societal Response to the Animal Cruelty/Human Violence Link

Agencies are now recognizing that where one finds animal abuse one will also find child abuse and partner abuse. An ecology of maltreatment emanates from a family in distress. In response to this knowledge, agencies in a number of cities in the United States and Great Britain are exchanging case data between animal welfare workers and child welfare workers. In addition, various organizations are working together to cast their "protective net" over a wider area. For instance, in Ohio, the Toledo Humane Society trains its investigators to recognize the signs of child abuse. In Cincinnati, a widespread collaborative effort by the Domestic Violence-Animal Abuse Research Group brings together veterinarians, hospitals, prosecutors, women's shelters, and animal welfare agencies to combat violence (Fisher 1997).

In response to the human-animal link, the Broward County (Florida) Sheriff's Department handles all abuse cases involving animals, children, the handicapped, and the elderly. Purdue University Veterinary School in West Lafayette, Indiana, provides a foster care program for the pets of women in domestic violence shelters. In La Crosse, Wisconsin, social service workers are encouraged to also check on the family pet (Feldman 1997).

National humane organizations, such as The Humane Society of the United States, offer materials to assist communities across the country with local campaigns to educate the public on the link between animal cruelty and human violence. These are some ways in which grass-roots movements have responded to the research concluding that animal cruelty is a social problem with potentially dangerous consequences.

Geography of Animal Cruelty Laws

Along a continuum of family violence, strong evidence suggests that animals are the first stage along the path to hu-

man violence. Nevertheless, the criminal justice system still largely views animal abuse as a minor offense. The first animal abuse laws in the world date back to 1641 in the Massachusetts Bay Colony (Arkow 1999a). The first anti-cruelty statute in the United States was passed in Maine in 1821 (Favre and Tsang 1993). New York in 1829 was the origin of the first wave of animal anti-cruelty laws passed across the country. However, early laws protected only animals of value, such as cattle, and the penalties for a misdemeanor were so small as to be ineffective deterrents. The laws reflected the social attitudes of the time. For example, in Pennsylvania the punishment for beating a horse was a maximum of $200; punishment for abandoning a child under the age of seven was $100 maximum (Favre and Tsang 1993). Laws were based on a monetary value rather than an ability to suffer. In the 1860s, proponents of animal rights aggressively pursued the passage of legislation to protect animals, which ultimately opened the door to children's rights (see essay in Chapter 4 entitled "The Spatial Dimensions of Child Abuse and Neglect"). Humane organizations

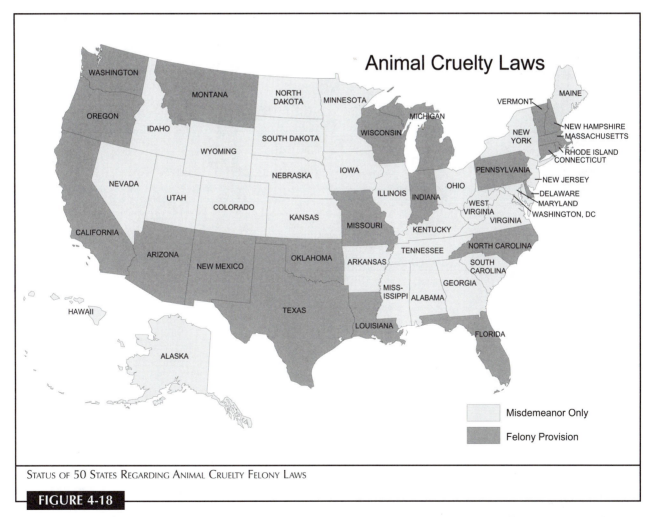

STATUS OF 50 STATES REGARDING ANIMAL CRUELTY FELONY LAWS

FIGURE 4-18

Source: Existing State Anti-Cruelty Felony Laws prepared by The Humane Society of the United States, Government Affairs Department, Washington, DC, December 1998.

in their earliest form were designed to protect not only animals, but also children, and some still do today (Arkow 1999a).

Because laws vary across space and time, direct comparisons of state laws are inadvisable. Even as these maps are being viewed, the real-time cartographic landscape has changed. However, the relative context assists the reader in gauging the status of animals across the nation at one point in time. In other words, a spatial view of animal cruelty statutes in the United States provides a measure of where this link of abuse is accepted and where it is not yet considered significant (Figure 4-18). There are 21 states with anti-cruelty felony laws: Arizona, California, Connecticut, Delaware, Florida, Indiana, Louisiana, Massachusetts, Michigan, Montana, New Hampshire, New Mexico, North Carolina, Pennsylvania, Oklahoma, Oregon, Rhode Island, Texas, Vermont, Washington, and Wisconsin. Spatial patterns show a clustering, or non-random distribution, in the Pacific West Coast area extending into the Southwest to Louisiana. Other less significant clusters appear in New England and the Great Lakes. Areas that have not adopted

a felony statute for animal cruelty are concentrated in the Plains and in the South.

Some states have strong misdemeanor laws whereas others have weak felony laws. A criticism of the felony statutes is that they are narrow in scope. For instance, New Mexico's felony law applies to the willful and malicious poisoning, killing, or injuring of livestock belonging to another. Companion animals such as dogs and cats are exempted as well as livestock belonging to the abuser. In contrast, Oregon's felony statute holds that to maliciously kill or intentionally or knowingly torture an animal results in penalties up to $100,000 and up to five years in prison. An offender in Louisiana could spend as long as 10 years in prison doing hard labor (Humane Society of the United States 1998).

Animal cruelty laws may also include provisions for other forms of punishment designed to rehabilitate the offender. Psychological counseling for animal abusers is found to have a separate legal provision in only seven states: California, Colorado, Michigan, Minnesota, Oregon, Washington, and Vermont. Again, the dominant cluster is located

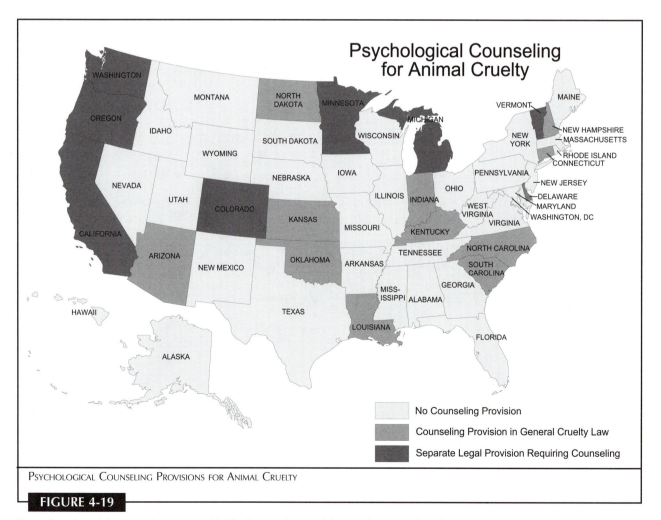

PSYCHOLOGICAL COUNSELING PROVISIONS FOR ANIMAL CRUELTY

FIGURE 4-19

Source: State Animal Protection Laws, prepared by The Humane Society of the United States, Office of Government Affairs, Washington, DC, November 1998.

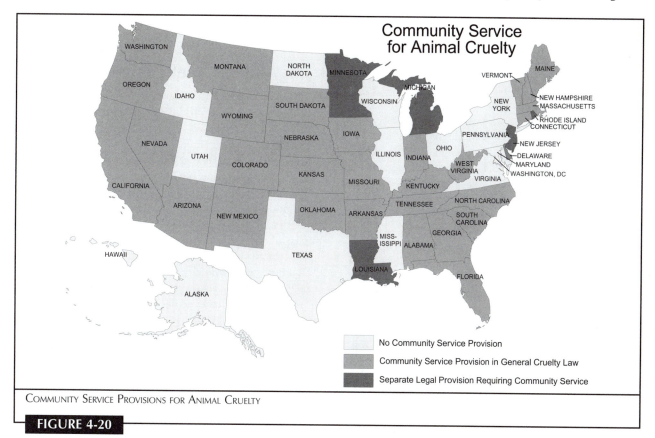

COMMUNITY SERVICE PROVISIONS FOR ANIMAL CRUELTY

FIGURE 4-20

Source: State Animal Protection Laws, prepared by The Humane Society of the United States, Office of Government Affairs, Washington, DC, November 1998.

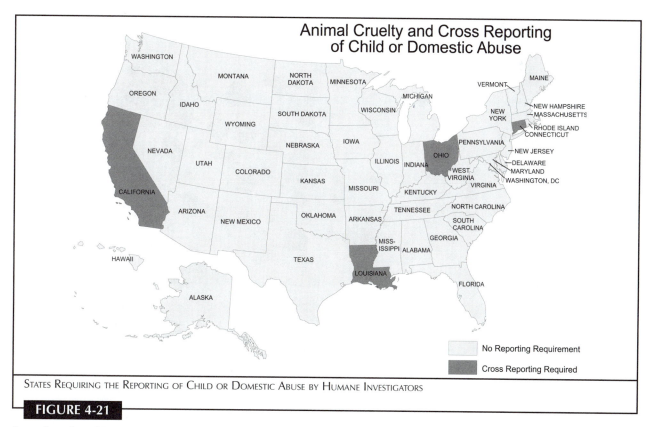

STATES REQUIRING THE REPORTING OF CHILD OR DOMESTIC ABUSE BY HUMANE INVESTIGATORS

FIGURE 4-21

Source: State Animal Protection Laws prepared by The Humane Society of the United States, Office of Government Affairs, Washington, DC, November 1998.

in the Pacific West Coast (Figure 4-19). Most states do not have a provision for counseling, which signifies that animal cruelty as a pathological behavior has not yet been recognized throughout the country.

Many states view animal cruelty as a crime for which community service is an appropriate punishment in certain cases (Figure 4-20). States without community service provisions are Alaska, Hawaii, Idaho, Illinois, Maryland, Mississippi, New York, North Dakota, Ohio, Pennsylvania, Texas, Utah, Virginia, and Wisconsin. Volunteer work is believed to be helpful in turning young, first-time offenders from an abusive path. Many successful intervention programs illustrate that children from violent surroundings can develop a sense of empathy (Rathmann 1999).

Lawmakers in several states have accepted the connection between human and animal violence. As a result, mandates for the cross-reporting of animal cruelty investigators to child and domestic abuse agencies have been included in their statutes (Figure 4-21). These states are located randomly across the country: California, Connecticut, Louisiana, and Ohio. Recently, Rhode Island established a commission for cross-reporting legislation (Arkow 1999b). The City of San Diego, California, requires child welfare agents to report suspected animal abuse within 24 hours; reciprocally, animal investigators report suspected child abuse (Cohen 1999). At the present time, no geographical databases are available on cross-reports.

Animal Cruelty Prosecutions

Attitudes regarding the importance of animal cruelty is a major factor in the criminal prosecution of such cases (Tischler 1999). Figure 4-22 shows the states with the highest number of prosecutions: California, Florida, New York, Pennsylvania, and Texas. Other areas of interest are the Pacific Northwest and the Midwest. Minimal legal activity on behalf of animals occurs in Montana and South Dakota, and none in North Dakota. According to experts, many cases involving teens as offenders are not prosecuted because of the community attitude that a stressful event triggered this act or it was just a childish prank (Tischler 1999). Therefore, animal cruelty is frequently trivialized by adults, including parents, teachers, coaches, and principals.

The types of cases prosecuted vary in degree of severity and include stabbing to death, bestiality, organized fights, starvation, burning, blowing up with fireworks, torture, poisoning, inadequate medical care, abandonment, animal collecting (having more animals than can be cared for properly), bludgeoning, mutilation, shooting, dragging behind a

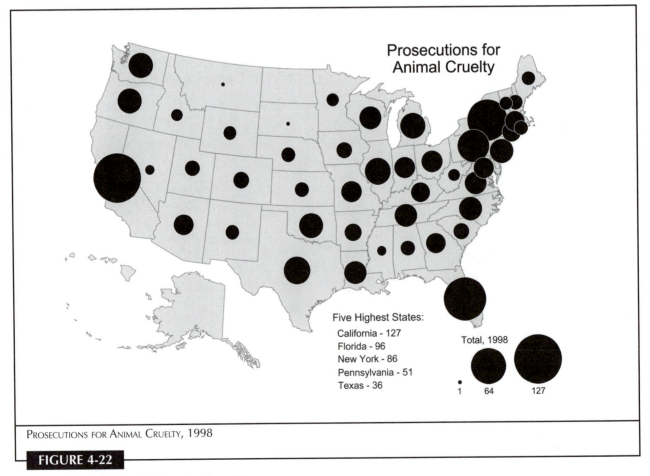

PROSECUTIONS FOR ANIMAL CRUELTY, 1998

FIGURE 4-22

Source: Animal Legal Defense Fund at <http://www.aldf.org>.

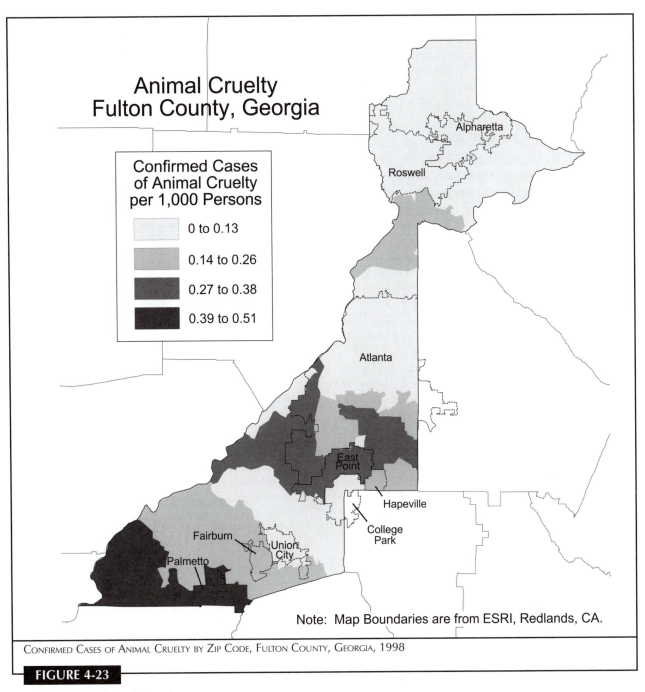

CONFIRMED CASES OF ANIMAL CRUELTY BY ZIP CODE, FULTON COUNTY, GEORGIA, 1998

FIGURE 4-23

Source: Fulton County Animal Control.

vehicle, and other forms of abusive and neglectful behavior.

Case Study in the Geography of Animal Cruelty

Unfortunately, no national statistics exist for animal cruelty. Therefore, its incidence and prevalence are unknown. One alternative is to research it on a smaller geographic scale. The spatial distribution of animal cruelty in Fulton County, Georgia, gives the reader an idea of how mapping cases can assist educators and investigators (Figure 4-23).

The map shows a non-random distribution, which means that cases are concentrated in specific areas. This distribution enables a geographer to theorize that factors present in those particular areas contribute to the abuse and neglect of animals. The southern section of the county has the highest incidence rate. This area is characterized by low income, poor housing conditions, and low educational levels. The second highest area is a working class section of the county with moderate housing, and educational levels less than other areas. Low incidence of animal cruelty appears, for the most part, to be concentrated in the northern section of the county. These areas have populations of

119

higher income and higher education. A previous study examining socioeconomic factors influencing dog abuse and neglect in Fulton County found that "people employed in areas where the work may not be consistent, or deemed 'blue-collar,' and earning a relatively low wage are more likely to abuse or neglect their dogs" (Turnbull 1990: 16).

Conclusion

Research linking the connection of violence against humans and animals presents information to those interested in the cycle of violence. Legal spatial patterns reveal a growing concern for the protection of animals, but some areas either have not been exposed to or have not accepted the research presented on the topic. Few states mandate psychological counseling for offenders or require the cross-reporting of cases between agencies despite the evidence connecting animal cruelty to family violence as well as to other forms of violent behavior.

Prosecutions for animal cruelty are found in large numbers primarily in the West and Northeast regions of the country. There may be more animal cruelty in these populous regions to account for this distribution. However, the attitudes surrounding this crime are also a major consideration when explaining the spatial patterns. The priority given to animal cruelty cases by law enforcement and the judicial system is also revealed in these patterns.

As seen with the Fulton County example, a geographical application on the micro-scale serves the purpose of directing the efforts of humane educators, investigators, and law enforcement officers. The question of where to place prevention and education programs and treatment services is answered through the identification of target areas.

Companion animals as a part of the model of violence, particularly family violence, are an important element in the study of human interactions. According to psychologist Frank Ascione, "A better understanding of the factors leading to abuse, of humans and of animals, may help transform landscapes of terror into safer havens" (1999: 59).

References

Adams, Carol J. 1994. Bringing Peace Home: A Feminist Philosophical Perspective on the Abuse of Women, Children, and Pet Animals. *Hypatia: A Journal of Feminist Philosophy* 9: 63-84.

Arkow, Phil. 1999a. The Evolution of Animal Welfare as a Human Welfare Concern. In Frank R. Ascione and Phil Arkow, eds. *Child Abuse, Domestic Violence, and Animal Abuse*. West Lafayette, IN: Purdue University Press, pp. 19-37.

————. 1999b. Statewide Commission Created for Cross-Reporting Legislation. In Frank R. Ascione and Phil Arkow, eds. *Child Abuse, Domestic Violence, and Animal Abuse*. West Lafayette, IN: Purdue University Press, pp. 338-42.

Ascione, Frank R. 1999. The Abuse of Animals and Human Interpersonal Violence: Making the Connection. In Frank R. Ascione and Phil Arkow, eds. *Child Abuse, Domestic Violence,*

and Animal Abuse. West Lafayette, IN: Purdue University Press, pp. 50-61.

————. 1998. Battered Women's Reports of Their Partners' and Their Children's Cruelty to Animals. *Journal of Emotional Abuse* 1: 119-33.

Browne, Angela. 1987. *When Battered Women Kill*. New York: Free Press.

Burstow, Bonnie. 1992. *Radical Feminist Therapy: Working in the Context of Violence*. Newbury Park, CA: Sage Publications.

Cloud, John. 1999. Just A Routine School Shooting. *Time*, May 31: 34–43.

Cohen, William S. 1999. A Congressional View of the Cycle of Violence. In Frank R. Ascione and Phil Arkow, eds. *Child Abuse, Domestic Violence, and Animal Abuse*. West Lafayette, IN: Purdue University Press, pp. 335-37.

DeViney, Elizabeth, Jeffrey Dickert, and Randall Lockwood. 1983. The Care of Pets within Child Abusing Families. *International Journal for the Study of Animal Problems* 4: 21-29.

Donovan, Josephine. 1990. Animal Rights and Feminist Theory. *Signs: Journal of Women in Culture and Society* 15 (2): 350-75.

Everitt, David. 1993. *Human Monsters: An Illustrated Encyclopedia of the World's Most Vicious Murderers*. Lincolnwood, IL: Contemporary Books.

Favre, David, and Vivien Tsang. 1993. The Development of Anti-Cruelty Laws During the 1800s. *Detroit College of Law Review* 1: 1-35.

Feldman, Linda. 1997. Cruelty to Pets—and People—As One Battle. *Christian Science Monitor*, September 10. Washington, DC.

Felthous, Alan. 1980. Aggression Against Cats, Dogs and People. *Child Psychiatry and Human Development* 10: 169-77.

Fisher, Ann. 1997. Animal Cruelty: A Sign of Other Abuse? *Dispatch*, November 17. Logan, Ohio. <http://www.cd.columbus.oh.us/news/newsfea2/nov/anim1117.html>.

Fox, Mitchell. 1999. Treating Serious Animal Abuse as a Serious Crime. In Frank R. Ascione and Phil Arkow, eds. *Child Abuse, Domestic Violence, and Animal Abuse*. West Lafayette, IN: Purdue University Press, pp. 306-15.

Hodge, Guy R., and Randall Lockwood. 1990. Cruelty to Animals. *Animals' Voice: Ontario SPCA* (Fall): 10-17.

Humane Society of the United States. 1998. The Role of the Community in Reducing Violence. *First Strike Campaign Information Packet*. Washington, DC.

Hutton, James S. 1983. Animal Abuse as a Diagnostic Approach in Social Work. In Aaron Katcher and Alan Beck, eds. *New Perspectives on Our Lives with Companion Animals*. Philadelphia: University of Philadelphia Press, pp. 444–47.

Jorgenson, Star, and Lisa Maloney. 1999. Animal Abuse and the Victims of Domestic Violence. In Frank R. Ascione and Phil Arkow, eds. *Child Abuse, Domestic Violence, and Animal Abuse*. West Lafayette, IN: Purdue University Press, pp. 143-58.

Lindsay, J. 1979. *Hogarth: His Art and His World*. New York: Taplinger Publishing Co.

Lockwood, Randall. 1989. Cruelty to Animals and Human Violence. *The Training Key #392*. Arlington, VA: International Association of Chiefs of Police, Inc.

Lockwood, Randall, and Ann Church. 1996. Deadly Serious: An FBI Perspective on Animal Cruelty. *The Humane Society News*, Fall: 1-4.

Lockwood, Randall, and Guy R. Hodge. 1986. The Tangled Web of Animal Abuse: The Links between Cruelty to Animals and Human Violence. *The Humane Society News*, Summer: 1-6.

Mead, Margaret. 1964. Cultural Factors in the Cause and Prevention of Pathological Homicide. *Bulletin in the Menninger Clinic* 28: 11-12.

Quinlisk, Jo Anne. 1999. Animal Abuse and Family Violence. In Frank R. Ascione and Phil Arkow, eds. *Child Abuse, Domestic Violence, and Animal Abuse.* West Lafayette, IN: Purdue University Press, pp. 168-75.

Rathmann, Carol. 1999. Forget Me Not Farm: Teaching Gentleness with Gardens and Animals to Children from Violent Homes and Communities. In Frank R. Ascione and Phil Arkow, eds. *Child Abuse, Domestic Violence, and Animal Abuse.* West Lafayette, IN: Purdue University Press, pp. 393-409.

Regan, Tom, and Peter Singer. 1976. *Animal Rights and Human Obligations.* Englewood Cliffs, NJ: Prentice-Hall.

Ressler, Robert H., and Tom Shachtman. 1992. *Whoever Fights Monsters.* New York: St. Martin's Press.

Robin, M., R.W. ten Bensel, J. Quigley, and R.K. Anderson. 1983. Childhood Pets and the Psychosocial Development of Adolescents. In A. Katcher and A. Beck, eds. *New Perspectives on Our Lives with Companion Animals.* Philadelphia: University of Pennsylvania Press, pp. 436–43.

Rollin, Bernard E. 1981. *Animal Rights and Human Morality.* Buffalo: Prometheus Books.

Rosen, Barbara. 1995. Watch for Pet Abuse—It Might Save Your Client's Life. *Shepard's ElderCare/Law Newsletter* 5, July: 1-9.

Russell, Diana E. H. 1990. *Rape in Marriage.* rev. and expanded ed. Bloomington: Indiana University Press.

Schuleter, Sherry. 1999. Animal Abuse and Law Enforcement. In Frank R. Ascione and Phil Arkow, eds. *Child Abuse, Domestic Violence, and Animal Abuse.* West Lafayette, IN: Purdue University Press, pp. 316-27.

Schweitzer, Albert. 1965. *The Teaching of Reverence for Life.* Translated by Richard and Clare Winston. New York: Rinehart and Winston.

Singer, Peter. 1975. *Animal Liberation.* New York: New York Review Press.

Tapia, Fernando. 1971. Children Who Are Cruel to Animals. *Child Psychiatry and Human Development* 2: 70-77.

ten Bensel, R.W. 1984. Historical Perspectives on Human Values for Animals and Vulnerable People. In R.K. Anderson, B. Hart, and L. Hart, eds. *The Pet Connection: Its Influence on Our Health and Quality of Life.* Minneapolis: (CENSHARE) University of Minnesota Center to Study Human-Animal Relationships and Environments, pp. 2–14.

Tischler, Joyce. 1999. Zero Tolerance for Cruelty: An Approach to Enhancing Enforcement of State Anticruelty Laws. In Frank R. Ascione and Phil Arkow, eds. *Child Abuse, Domestic Violence, and Animal Abuse,* West Lafayette IN: Purdue University Press, pp. 297-305.

Turnbull, Linda. 1990. *The Geography of Dog Abuse and Neglect in Fulton County, Georgia for 1989 and Influencing Socioeconomic Factors.* Unpublished paper, Georgia State University, Atlanta.

Vachss, Alice. 1993. *Sex Crimes.* New York: Random House.

CHAPTER 5

Organized and Entrepreneurial Crimes

The crimes covered in this chapter represent two subcultures: the organized criminals who are generally part of a large hierarchical structure such as the Italian Mafia, the Asian Tongs, or the Colombian Cartels, and the more casually structured entrepreneurial "street" criminals such as youth gangs or streetwalkers. Where these criminals operate is the focus of each essay in this chapter and could appropriately be labeled the "geography of hang-outs."

Crimescape features are physical characteristics of a criminal landscape. They provide the observer with a visual description of conditions that may exist for a certain type of criminal activity to occur. Each crime covered in this chapter has distinct crimescape features that assist readers in their geographical quests for gang territories, drug routes and markets, red light districts, and pirate ships.

Gang territories are often recognized by the graffiti found on walls, street signs, and the sides of buildings (Figure 5-1). Although graffiti may incorporate a form of art, it has a specific purpose and meaning to gang members. Graffiti not only delineates the spatial boundaries of a gang's territory, but also serves as a measure of a gang's strength, denotes areas in dispute with other gangs, functions as a directory of membership or indication of hierarchy within the gang, communicates insults and challenges, and advertises the type of gang activity (Shelden et al. 1997).

GRAFFITI ON THE SIDE OF A BUILDING

FIGURE 5-1

Source: Courtesy of Linda Turnbull.

George Tita, in his essay "Mapping the *Set Space* of Urban Street Gangs," explains the importance of territorial boundaries to gangs. He demonstrates that although what he refers to as *set space* may be perceived as an entire neighborhood, in reality it actually occupies a small part of a larger neighborhood.

One possible gang activity is drug sales and distribution. Drug market locations have been described in the literature. The crimescape features include broken windows, graffiti, debris, boarded-up houses, vacant lots, quick exit routes, and vantage watchpoints (Harries 1997). Figure 5-2 is an abandoned apartment building with boarded windows, secluded by heavy vegetation. It is elevated from the street level and situated a distance from the street with a long walkway. Drug dealers find this a desirable location because it gives them protection inside the apartment house while providing an advantageous spot to watch for unwanted intruders, such as police.

Many geographical aspects of drug trafficking are discussed in the essay "The Spatial Dimensions of Drug Trafficking" by Linda Turnbull. Where are drug crops grown? Where are they processed and where are they sold and distributed? These questions are answered for those who are curious about one of the most pressing problems in our social history.

Most people probably have not pondered the spatial dimensions of streetwalking. However, it is an area of study for some researchers. For example, geographer R. Riccio of San Diego State University observes that for streetwalkers to remain in business and avoid arrest, they must be cognizant of the "shifting environmental stimuli and react accordingly" (1992: 555). Prostitutes had their own spatial domain at one time, confined to red light districts. However, this is changing because of the renewal of urban cores and waterfronts. Today, streetwalkers are dispersed in the landscape along commercial strips. Some common crimescape features of streetwalking are corners, hotels and motels, bus stops, benches, phone booths, street lights, parking lots, gas stations, massage parlors, and adult bookstores (Riccio 1992).

Jacqueline Boles's essay, "Prostitution," carefully constructs the spatial world of the prostitute from global to street-level analysis. The inequalities of poverty and the lack of opportunities for women to earn a decent living wage contribute to their decision to become members of the world's "oldest profession." Although some argue that prostitution is not a crime, it deserves attention as long as arrests are being made.

A Charleston, South Carolina, walking tour on "Pirates, Prostitutes, and Pubs" electrifies the imagination with tales of local raids and hang-outs of the notorious pirate Major Stede Bonnet. He terrorized the Carolina coastline during the 1700s, the golden age of piracy in this area (Cordingly 1995). Our mental images glamorize the activities of such scoundrels, mostly due to the romantic portrayal of pirates in films and on television. Women may have

ABANDONED APARTMENT HOUSE

FIGURE 5-2

Source: Courtesy of Linda Turnbull.

swooned in the theaters, but did you know that there were also female pirates?

Two infamous women who sailed the high seas in the eighteenth century were Mary Read and Anne Bonny, who were both found guilty of piracy and sentenced to death (Cordingly 1995). An interesting work from Germany entitled *Women Pirates and the Politics of the Jolly Roger*, divides discussion into geographical areas (e.g., Chinese Sea, Mediterranean, Atlantic, Caribbean) and includes recipes actually prepared in the galleys from each area (Klausmann et al. 1997).

Readers may be surprised that piracy on the high seas has made a comeback. In his essay "Modern Maritime Piracy," George Demko takes us aboard, stopping at ports of criminal activity around the globe. He sets the record straight regarding the nature of piracy and discusses the actions taken by organizations to reduce the number of incidents of this insidious crime.

References

Cordingly, D. 1995. *Under the Black Flag*. New York: Random House.

Harries, K.D. 1997. *Serious Violence*. Springfield, IL: Charles C. Thomas.

Klausmann, U., M. Mainzerin, and G. Kuhn. 1997. *Women Pirates and the Politics of the Jolly Roger*. Translated by Tyler Austin and Nicholas Levis. Montreal, Canada: Black Rose Books.

Riccio, R. 1992. Street Crime Strategies: The Changing Schemata of Streetwalkers. *Environment and Behavior* 24 (4): 555-70.

Shelden, R.G., S.K. Tracy, and W.B. Brown. 1997. *Youth Gangs in American Society*. Belmont, CA: Wadsworth Publishing Co.

Mapping the *Set Space* of Urban Street Gangs

George E. Tita

Many years of gang research have revealed one constant: gangs "hang out" and need an identifiable physical space in which to do it. Surprisingly, this constant, almost defining feature of urban street gangs receives little attention in the gang literature. Despite a recent resurgence in the popularity of ecological studies of crime and neighborhoods, little empirical research specifically examines the community context of gangs. By determining if a gang's *set space*, i.e., the area where it hangs out, differs from areas without gangs, researchers can begin to understand the role that "place" (both in terms of the characteristics of the residents and the characteristics of the built environment) plays in the gang formation and maturation process. Furthermore, little is known about how the presence of a gang affects the local crime rate. Individual level studies find that gang membership greatly facilitates offending (Esbensen and Huizinga 1993; Thornberry et al. 1993), thus suggesting that gang presence will increase local crime rates. However, at least one qualitative study suggests that gangs may actually protect community members from certain types of crime (Sanchez-Jankowski 1991).

While the above topics are treated in detail elsewhere (Tita et al. 1998; Tita 1999), the current research focuses on the primary decision one faces when conducting a quantitative ecological study of crime—choosing the appropriate spatial unit of analysis. Although gangs are most often thought of as neighborhood phenomenon, this essay demonstrates that the set space of gangs occupies only a small part of the larger neighborhood.

Importance of Place in the Gang Literature

Independently of whether one is interested in how gangs form or the activities in which gangs participate, the lack of attention paid to the physical, social, and economic conditions of the locations where gangs hang out is unfortunate for several reasons. First, it is well documented that socializing or hanging out (also commonly referred to as "chilling") is a primary activity of all gangs. In his book *The American Street Gang* (1995), Malcolm Klein describes what life in a gang is like.

> [G]ang member life..., with the occasional exception of a boisterous meeting, a fight, an exciting rumor, is a very dull life. For the most part, gang members do very little—sleep,

get up late, hang around, brag a lot, eat again, drink, hang around some more. It's a boring life . . . .(p. 18)

Ronald Huff (1996) found that hanging out was the single most prevalent activity pursued by the gangs that he studied in his multi-city project.

Second, though the importance of physical space to the gang has been well documented, it has never been truly quantified. Frederick Thrasher (1927) was the first to hint at the importance of land-use and the locations where gangs hang out when he stated that one of the most important findings to emerge from his study was that "gangland" occured in the "interstitial" areas of Chicago. Thrasher did not find many gangs hanging out in areas that could easily be labeled as "commercial" or "residential." Instead, he found gangs where "better residential districts recede before the encroachment of business and industry" (Thrasher 1927: 23). However, he did not fully catalog the characteristics of these interstitial areas, and did not offer an adequate explanation of why gangs form and hang out in these particular areas of impoverished neighborhoods. Klein (1995) believes the most important role of "turf" is that it offers the gang something tangible to identify with and possess, similar to the function served by gang dress codes and hand signals. Klein labels such areas "*the life space* of the gang (p. 18)," but, like Thrasher, provides little insight into the characteristics of these places.

Third, by paying close attention to the spaces occupied by gangs, one soon realizes that gangs do not occupy the entirety of their "neighborhood," but rather they hang out in small, well defined localized areas within a community. While quantitative research on gangs continues to focus on the role of "neighborhood" or "community" in gang formation, qualitative research consistently demonstrates that gang activity actually takes place in much smaller areas within a neighborhood. The classic ethnographic works (Whyte 1943; Liebow 1967) along with more recent work (Moore 1991; Vigil 1988) demonstrate the highly restricted physical space that is home to the gang. As "Doc," the central informant from William Whyte's *Street Corner Society* (1943), points out,

> Fellows around here don't know what to do except within a radius of about three hundred yards. They come home from work, hang on the corner, get up to eat, come back on the corner, go up to a show, and then come back to hang on the corner . . . . Most of them stick to one corner. It's only rarely that a fellow will change his corner. (p 256)

It was no different for the gangs found in the barrios of East Los Angeles where "partying" was just another name for "hanging out." As one gang member described it, "[W]e went to the Lane [a dead end street] and just hung around there. It's like a lot of grass, palm trees. We used to sit around and just drink and listen to the radio and talk with the girls and stuff like that." Joan Moore described the Lane as a "rather barren, graffiti-smeared, but isolated part of the neighborhood" (1991: 50).

Moore's description of areas where gangs hang out suggests that the physical attributes of such areas matter. In the quotation above, the area in which the gang hangs out is described as being "isolated" from the rest of the neighborhood. Moore described other favorite hangouts of the gang as an "underdeveloped overgrown hilly spot" and the "front porch or backyard of a *permissive* [italics added] parent" (1991: 50). All the places she described possess features that suggest that a lack of social control is important in determining the location of gang activity, a finding that was later empirically substantiated (Tita et al. 1998).

Research Site and Methodology

This research maps the set space of urban street gangs in Pittsburgh, Pennsylvania, a classic "emerging gang city" (Curry and Spergel 1988) that only experienced an onset of youth gangs in the early 1990s. To circumvent the "what is a gang" debate, only violent "hardcore" youth gangs were included in the study. Borrowing liberally from the definition used by Joan Moore (1991) and John Hagedorn (1988: 5), "hardcore" (or simply "hard") violent gangs are defined as "groups of adolescent friends who are committed to the defense of a well defined territory and to one another in status-setting fights." In addition, "hard" gangs must be willing to participate in drive-bys either as initiator or retaliator.

Gangs and Sets

Most of the gangs in Pittsburgh call themselves either Bloods or Crips. However, the most important identifier is not so much the named "gang" one belongs to, but rather their affiliation with a smaller local "set." Sets most often take their name from the street on which they hang out, a tradition that dates back to the first American gangs studied (Thrasher 1927: 37). Because it is not uncommon for more than one set to claim a portion of an avenue or street as belonging to the set, the block number or street address is often added to the street name to distinguish where their set space lies. While a set is a subset of the larger named gang, there is little organizational relationship between a set and the gang. Crip sets, for example, are not all working to achieve the common goals of a nationwide, or even citywide, Crip organization. In fact, violent confrontations *between* sets with the same gang name are common.

Set Space

In the words of gang informants, set space is "where I hang or chill." If the gang member engages in the distribution of drugs, it is where he "hustles." As Gauge, a 16-year-old member of the West Side Bloods, related,

> When I wake up in the morning I immediately head up to the set to hang cause it ain't like you want anyone seeing that you still live with your mama. I hang there all day with my boys just chillin' and killin' time. If I need some money, I might do some hustling there too.

A gang may "claim" an entire neighborhood as its domain or "turf," but set space is the actual area within the neighborhood where gang members spend their time. Thus, just as sets are part of a larger gang, set space is a subset of gang turf or territory. A rival gang traveling through the non-set space areas of another gang's neighborhood may go undetected, or, even if detected, may go unmolested by the host gang. The act of trespassing through a rival's set space, however, is a clear provocation for a violent confrontation.

Identifying the Violent Gangs

To identify the set space of hardcore, violent gangs, the gangs themselves had to be identified, a task accomplished by collecting data from police homicide files, interacting with social workers, and, most importantly, listening to the impressions of actual gang members. Reading through the city's homicide case files provided an opportunity to document inter-gang rivalries from the gang affiliation of the victim or offender noted in these files. Any gang that had either victims or suspects involved in a gang-motivated homicide was included in the study. Because the definition of violent gangs only requires participation in a "drive-by" shooting, and not that the shooting results in a fatality, other sources of information were also used.

In addition to acting as conduits to the gang members, social workers introduced the notion of "sets." While police files often referred to gangs only in general terms (e.g., "Northside Crips" or "West End Bloods"), the social workers had a much better understanding of which sets of the Northside Crips were "hardcore" and which were imitating "wannabes." However, according to the gang members they worked with, social workers were, in general, too liberal in their definition of "violent" or "hardcore" gangs.

The final say as to whether a set was "hardcore" or not rested with the gang members. Some members were given maps containing the names and location of gangs. These initial maps were constructed using local police homicide data and with the help of social workers. Independently of one another, members of different "hard" sets were consistent in pointing out the locations of certain "wannabe" sets.

It is important to rely on more than one data source when conducting gang research. The information in the homicide files and from police detectives acted as an early filter, pointing in the right direction. But just as relying exclusively on the police to identify the "hard" gangs would not be prudent, only asking gang members to identify the most dangerous gangs is equally ill-advised. On several occasions, information from the police homicide files permitted a distinction between gang member bravado and reality. The three sources of information complemented one another through a series of checks and balances. As a result, this study includes all the violent gang sets located in Pittsburgh during the period 1991-1995.

Mapping Set Space

The first step in locating set space involved using a Geographic Information System (GIS) to construct street maps of the different neighborhoods where gangs were known to hang out. Approximately 50 gang members, plus an additional 10 non-gang members who lived in areas with gangs (all males), provided information for mapping the locations of set space. This was completed over several weeks and usually in small groups of six to eight informants. The participants did not consult with one another during the exercise.

Starting with their own neighborhood, informants were given a detailed street map and colored markers so that the individual could draw the boundaries of his set space. He was also asked to draw the set space of any other gangs in his neighborhood, and then, finally, any other set space that he was aware of from other parts of the city. The members of rival gangs were well aware of the exact location of each other's set space. Even if there was no history of conflict between two "hard" sets, they were always aware of one another at the neighborhood level, but much less adept at specifying exact location. Within the boundaries of their own neighborhoods, the maps produced by non-gang members and gang members were remarkably similar, suggesting that there is nothing secret about the areas in which the gangs hang out. This became even more apparent during later site visits to some of the set spaces. Most contain bold, brightly colored graffiti that announces the presence of the set or gang.

During the mapping exercise, the subjects were often eager to identify the street on which they usually resided, or where some other important event had occurred. In doing so, it became apparent that the areas where the gang members lived and the areas where they hung out were rarely the same. Thus, set space location does not appear to be simply a function of gang member residency. Though some gang members do live in close proximity to their set space, many came from other areas of the "hood." This point was emphasized while taking one gang member home after an interview and starting to drive in the general direction of his set. He quickly pointed out that he had long since moved out of that neighborhood. "Every morning when I wake up I grab a bus back to the set and hang with my boys." Even though he lived in a different neighborhood with its own "lame ass Creep" set (slang showing disrespect for a wannabe Crip set), he chose to remain a part of his original set.

Validation of set space came in various forms. In most cases, more than a single informant from each gang participated in the mapping exercise. Gang members from the same gang were not permitted to consult with one another while drawing the boundaries. The set space boundaries were then checked for discrepancies by comparing the maps. In the few cases in which there were minor discrepancies, social workers and a colleague working on another gang study were consulted. Many of the set spaces received personal visits so that they could be photographed further insuring that the boundaries indicated by the informants were accurate.

Results

Figure 5-3 provides an actual example of the borders of two neighboring, though rival, sets. The boundaries on the map include the single neighborhood, four census tracts, and nine census block groups. Even in the case of multiple set spaces within a single neighborhood, the activity space of the gang is extremely limited. The two set spaces span two of the four census tracts and three of the nine block groups.

The set space within public housing projects tended to differ significantly from the set space in more traditional urban neighborhoods. As Figure 5-4 demonstrates, set space within a housing project is less well defined and instead encompasses the entire street network. Of the eight major housing projects containing gangs, the set space in five of them was determined to be coterminous with local streets.

Three maps illustrate various possible geographic perspectives that one might employ in a quantitative ecological study of gangs. Using the neighborhood as the unit of observation (Figure 5-5), one is left with distinct regional groupings of neighborhoods with gangs. At the census tract level (Figure 5-6), the general spatial pattern holds, although reduced somewhat to include only sub-areas within the neighborhoods with set space. In Figure 5-5, it becomes clear that gangs do not hang out throughout an entire neighborhood or even complete census tracts. The area in the center of Figure 5-7 illustrates this well. The area within the circle that once appeared as a solid mass of "gangs" now emerges as two distinct areas. Interestingly, none of the gangs claim the main thoroughfare through the neighborhood as their set, but instead proudly identify with being from either the "east side" (depicted by the southeastern aggregate) or the "west side" (the northwestern aggregate) of the divide.

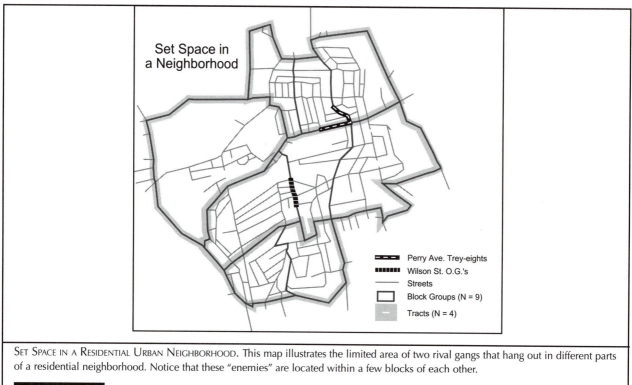

Set Space in a Neighborhood

Perry Ave. Trey-eights
Wilson St. O.G.'s
Streets
Block Groups (N = 9)
Tracts (N = 4)

SET SPACE IN A RESIDENTIAL URBAN NEIGHBORHOOD. This map illustrates the limited area of two rival gangs that hang out in different parts of a residential neighborhood. Notice that these "enemies" are located within a few blocks of each other.

FIGURE 5-3

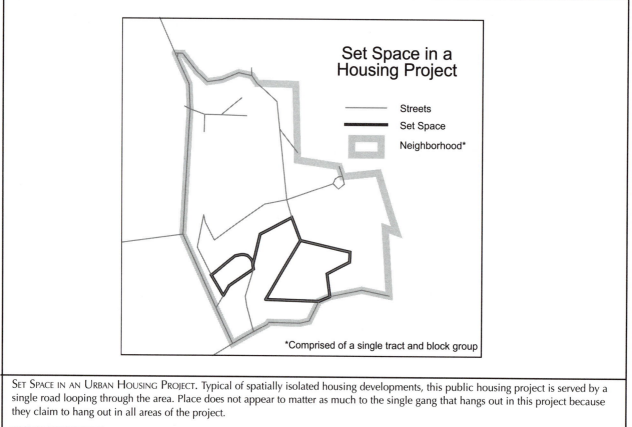

Set Space in a Housing Project

Streets
Set Space
Neighborhood*

*Comprised of a single tract and block group

SET SPACE IN AN URBAN HOUSING PROJECT. Typical of spatially isolated housing developments, this public housing project is served by a single road looping through the area. Place does not appear to matter as much to the single gang that hangs out in this project because they claim to hang out in all areas of the project.

FIGURE 5-4

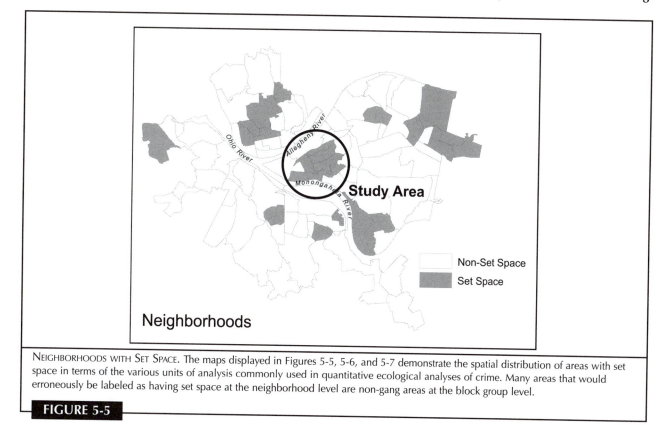

Neighborhoods

NEIGHBORHOODS WITH SET SPACE. The maps displayed in Figures 5-5, 5-6, and 5-7 demonstrate the spatial distribution of areas with set space in terms of the various units of analysis commonly used in quantitative ecological analyses of crime. Many areas that would erroneously be labeled as having set space at the neighborhood level are non-gang areas at the block group level.

FIGURE 5-5

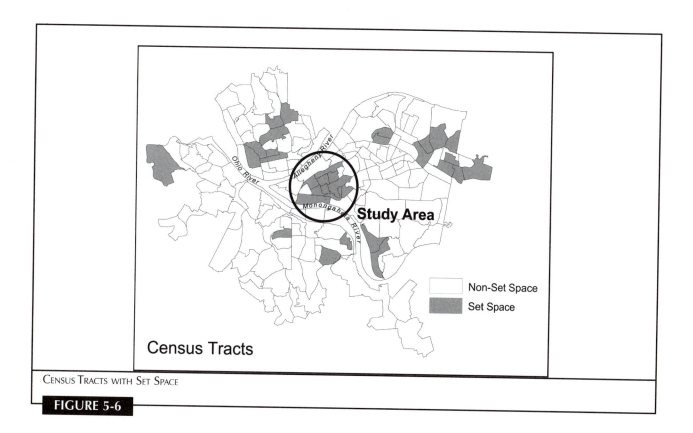

Census Tracts

CENSUS TRACTS WITH SET SPACE

FIGURE 5-6

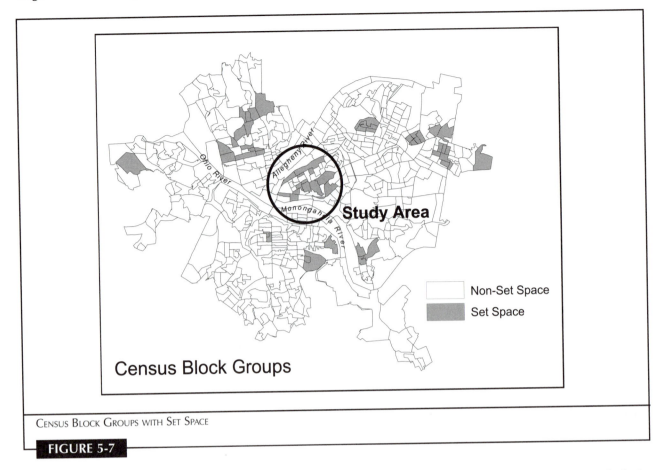

Census Block Groups with Set Space

FIGURE 5-7

Conclusion: Importance of Areal Unit

Whenever modeling the impact of physical space on social processes, it is important that the data are aggregated to the appropriate areal unit. Relying on gang member reports about the location of set space confirms what numerous qualitative studies have suggested—gangs hang out in only small areas of entire neighborhoods. Therefore, one must be careful not to mask important sub-neighborhood differences by treating gangs as a neighborhood-level phenomenon in quantitative analyses. Instead, one should employ a spatial unit of analysis that most closely approximates the geographic size of set space. Of course, practical considerations will also determine the final level of data aggregation chosen. For instance, set space often only encompasses a couple of street segments or block faces. Demographic and economic data that might help explain the location of the set space are unlikely to be available at this level. Thus, one must choose areal units that best approximate the true level of the phenomenon being studied (in this case, census block groups).

Demonstrating that set space is a sub-neighborhood phenomenon also has implications for community development and criminal justice responses to gangs. The mapping of gang set space is currently being used in the latest anti-gang strategy developed in Los Angeles. Known as "gang injunctions," these civil injunctions are akin to restraining orders because they remand certain individuals from congregating in particular areas. Areas in which the gang hangs out or deals drugs are put off-limits to the members of the gang. At the civil court proceedings, the gang members are given maps demarcating the areas that are off-limits to them.

In Pittsburgh, a local community activist found maps of set space to be useful in his efforts to combat the local media's labeling of particular neighborhoods as being "gang infested." Overstating the presence of gangs within a neighborhood can lead to "redlining" practices by service providers. Therefore, he used maps of set space to demonstrate to basic service providers (food delivery, cable/utility repair personnel) that the majority of streets in the "gang neighborhoods" were in fact free of gang hangouts. At the same time, he recognized that traversing certain areas required them to exercise caution.

Careful analysis of the types of places where gangs hang out may provide insight into the formation and maturation process of urban street gangs. The results of ecological studies of gangs can then be used to formulate economic and social policies that address the root causes of gangs rather than simply providing triage to the problems caused by gangs. Mapping of gang turf along with the social interactions between gangs was also undertaken in Boston as part of the problem-solving approach of the now-famous "Boston Gun Project" to reduce youth firearm violence. The mapping of gang territories proved to be valuable to the project because it helped to estimate both the geographic scale of the gang problem and the degree to which gang violence contributed to total violence (Kennedy et al. 1997).

References

Curry, David G., and Irving Spergel. 1988. Gang Homicide, Delinquency, and Community. *Criminology* 26: 381-405.

Esbensen, F.A, and David Huizinga. 1993. Gangs, Drugs, and Delinquency in a Survey of Urban Youth. *Criminology* 30: 565-89.

Hagedorn, John. 1988. *People and Folks: Gangs, Crime and the Underclass in a Rust Belt City.* Chicago: Lake View Press.

Huff, C. Ronald. 1996. The Criminal Behavior of Gang Members and Nongang at Risk Youth. In C. Ronald Huff, ed. *Gangs in America.* 2nd ed. Thousand Oaks, CA: Sage Publications.

Kennedy, David M., Anthony Braga, and Anne Piehl. 1997. Mapping Gangs and Gang Violence in Boston. In David Weisburd and Tom McEwen, eds. *Crime Mapping and Crime Prevention.* Monsey, NY: Criminal Justice Press.

Klein, Malcolm. 1995. *The American Street Gang: Its Nature, Prevalence and Control.* New York: Oxford University Press.

Liebow, Elliot. 1967. *Tally's Corner.* Boston: Little, Brown and Company.

Moore, Joan. 1991. *Going Down to the Barrio: Homeboys and Homegirls in Change.* Philadelphia: Temple University Press.

Sanchez-Jankowski, Martin. 1991. *Islands in the Street: Gangs and American Urban Society.* Berkeley: University of California Press.

Thornberry, Terrence, Marvin Krohn, Allan Lizotte, and D. Chard-Wierschem. 1993. The Role of Juvenile Gangs in Facilitating Delinquent Behavior. *Journal of Research in Crime and Delinquency* 30 (1): 55-87.

Thrasher, Frederick. 1927. *The Gang.* Chicago: University of Chicago Press.

Tita, George E. 1999. *An Ecological Study of Urban Street Gangs and Their Impact on Crime.* Unpublished dissertation, The Heinz School of Public Policy, Carnegie Mellon University, Pittsburgh.

Tita, George E., Jacqueline Cohen, and John Engberg. 1998. An Ecological Study of Violent Gangs: The Social Organization of "Set Space." National Consortium on Violence Research Working Paper. Pittsburgh: Carnegie Mellon University.

Vigil, James Diego. 1988. *Barrio Gangs: Street Life and Identity in Southern California.* Austin: University of Texas Press.

Whyte, William Foote. 1943. *Street Corner Society.* Chicago: University of Chicago Press.

The Spatial Dynamics of Drug Trafficking

Linda S. Turnbull

Drug abuse in the United States is considered to be a major problem in our society. Results from the 1997 National Household Survey on Drug Abuse (NHSDA) indicated that an estimated 13.9 million Americans were using illicit drugs. The use of alcohol, cigarettes, marijuana, heroin, and cocaine has increased among American youth aged 12 to 17. According to the study, marijuana is the most commonly used *illegal* drug by 80 percent of the users. In a study on how Americans view the nation's drug problem, adult respondents perceived crack cocaine as the greatest threat, while young adults felt that marijuana was the most prevalent drug problem (Gallup Organization 1996).

The NHSDA also revealed a link between drug use and criminal behavior (1997). Those who use drugs are not only more likely to commit crimes than non-users, but also commit crimes connected to the trafficking of illegal drugs. Figure 5-8 shows patterns of adult male criminals who tested positive for drugs at the time of arrest. There are large concentrations of high rates in the New York-Philadelphia-Washington, D.C., areas along the East Coast. Chicago and St. Louis in the Midwest, Ft. Lauderdale-Miami in the Southeast, and Portland-Seattle-Spokane areas in the Pacific Northwest are also centers of significantly high rates. Male arrestees most likely to test positive for drug use were those charged with drug sale and possession as well as those charged with robbery and burglary (U.S. Department of Justice 1994).

Becuse of this link of drugs to criminal behavior, public response has mirrored that of government. Most Americans feel that more money should be spent on preventing drugs from coming into the U.S. from foreign countries (Gallup Organization 1996). The spatial dimension of trafficking clarifies the origins and diffusion patterns that change over time depending on such factors as methods of transport, development of new drugs to meet consumer demands, and enforcement strategies. Cocaine, heroin, and marijuana are all controlled substances and subject to illegal production, processing, and distribution. Although other illicit drugs are found in the U.S., such as the chemically produced methamphetamines, this essay will focus only on those drugs produced agriculturally.

Historical Overview

Ironically, drugs now listed as illegal were viewed at one time as salubrious solutions for an improved life. The use of drugs for medicinal purposes did not originate in the United States, but diffused across the continents from many ancient cultures (Booth 1998). Drug addiction became troublesome in the U.S. and Europe in the nineteenth century when tonics and "cures" were marketed and sold by traveling peddlers.

Morphine, discovered in 1806, was considered to be the first of the wonder drugs. Morphine addiction was so widespread during the Civil War that it was called the "army disease" (U.S. Department of Justice 1992: 78). With the "sugar-free, dye-free, alcohol-free" medicines of today, it is hard to imagine that just last century morphine was a common ingredient in liquids used to calm children and babies. A popular elixir from Europe was Mrs. Winslow's Soothing Syrup, which contained one grain of morphine per fluid ounce (Booth 1998). For adults, the invention and availability of the hypodermic syringe in the mid-1800s increased the general use of narcotic substances (U.S. Department of Justice 1992). Morphine injections were used to treat inflammation of the eye, menstrual pain, and many other ailments (Booth 1998).

Heroin was originally thought to be non-addictive. By 1898, it was used as a treatment for morphine addiction as well as for respiratory illness. In the 1870s, public concern over the unrestricted use of opium dens resulted in the first recorded anti-drug law in the U.S., enacted in 1875 in San Francisco (U.S. Department of Justice 1992). Federal action followed in 1887 with the prohibition of opium imports into the U.S. by Chinese nationals.

The first wave of cocaine abuse occurred in the 1880s and lasted for 35 years (U.S. Department of Justice 1992). Coca was heralded as a health tonic and was endorsed by both the European and American medical communities. Among its benefits were its use as a remedy for asthma and toothache, and as a counteragent for opiate addiction. It was also known for giving an extra boost of energy at the end of a tiring day. On this recommendation, Coca-Cola contained coca leaves as a flavoring ingredient between the years 1884 and 1903 (Fuqua 1978).

History of Political Policy in the U.S.

The use and abuse of certain drugs have a cyclical pattern. Public and governmental attitudes towards their use varies over the course of our history. Drug policy in the first half of the twentieth century generated a series of anti-drug laws.

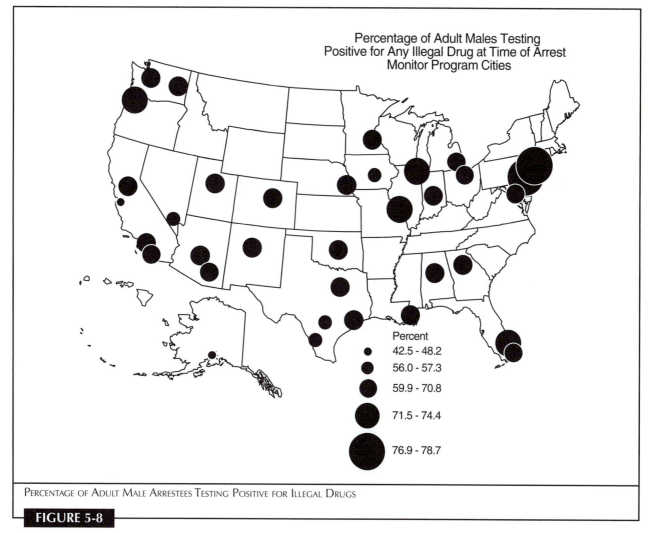

Percentage of Adult Males Testing
Positive for Any Illegal Drug at Time of Arrest
Monitor Program Cities

Percent

42.5 - 48.2

56.0 - 57.3

59.9 - 70.8

71.5 - 74.4

76.9 - 78.7

PERCENTAGE OF ADULT MALE ARRESTEES TESTING POSITIVE FOR ILLEGAL DRUGS

FIGURE 5-8

Source: Drug Enforcement Agency (DEA). Department of Justice, 1998 at <http://usdoj.gov/dea/stats/drugstats.htm>.

Several states initiated drug regulation around 1887 and soon thereafter all states had some form of drug control plan in place.

The Pure Food and Drug Act of 1906 required the listing of certain drugs on labels, but did not limit their use. The Harrison Act of 1914 taxed those who prescribed or distributed certain drugs. This measure caused a conflict between law enforcement and physicians. Although courts initially sided with physicians on the "decreasing dosage" treatment of addicts, the Supreme Court ruled in 1919 that it was illegal for a physician to provide addicts with prescriptions (U.S. Department of Justice 1992). This ruling left the nation with the problem of what to do with those addicted to drugs because they could no longer receive help from doctors. From 1919 to 1921, many cities opened clinics to provide this service, but all were closed by 1925. Public attitudes were that addiction was a threat to national security and sympathy was not wasted on addicts. However, hospitals specializing in treatment for imprisoned addicts were eventually allowed to open in Kentucky (1935) and Texas (1938) (Department of Justice 1992). Addicts in the general population were able to receive treatment until

1963, when the medicalization of narcotic addiction defined it as a mental illness.

The Federal Bureau of Narcotics (FBN), a division of the Treasury Department, was established in 1930. It was solely responsible for the enforcement of drug laws, excluding alcohol. Previously not considered a threat, marijuana was added to the FBN agenda with the passage of the Marijuana Tax Act of 1937 (U.S. Department of Justice 1992).

The second half of the twentieth century was marked by increased criminalization of drug use and intervention in the international trafficking of illegal drugs. A cultural shift in the 1960s introduced a more relaxed societal view of drug use with regard to marijuana, heroin, and amphetamines. Concern for rehabilitation rather than prosecution and the discovery of psychedelic drugs for recreational use, such as LSD, distinguishes this period of illegal drug history from the remainder of the century. In the 1980s, the government declared a war on drugs by enacting several key pieces of legislation: the 1984 Crime Control Act, the 1986 Anti-Drug Abuse Act, the 1988 Anti-Drug Abuse Act, and the Crime Control Act of 1990 (U.S. Department of Justice 1992).

Since 1973, drug enforcement has been the responsibility of the Drug Enforcement Administration (DEA) within the Department of Justice (Drug Enforcement Administration 1999). New laws increased penalties for drug offenses and trafficking. In addition, the laws provided funding that enabled law enforcement agencies to expand their efforts and aggressively devote their time to crop eradication, arrest and extradition of drug violators, and seizures of drugs and related assets.

Geography of Drug Crops

Crops used in drug production have been a part of everyday life in cultures around the world for centuries. Coca, for instance, is cultivated legally in areas of Peru, Bolivia, and Colombia for medicinal and personal use. Its uses include the relief of physical pain. In these countries, some people who live in poverty and lack adequate food chew the leaves to sustain the energy they need to work (Morales 1989; Rengert 1996). The manufacturing process of cocaine takes place in various locations (U.S. Department of Justice 1992). Initially, coca leaves are made into paste close to where they are grown. The paste is then processed into cocaine base primarily in Peru and Bolivia. Cocaine base is refined into hydrochloride (HCI), or powdered cocaine, mostly in Colombia. Crack cocaine, which is powdered cocaine dissolved in water, mixed with baking soda, and heated until rock crystals are formed, is produced after the cocaine base enters the U.S.

Leaves of the cannabis plant, which is grown mainly in Mexico for U.S. consumers, are dried to yield marijuana. Marijuana is commonly identified with the region in which it is grown, e.g., "Acapulco Gold" or "African Black." The names signal a dealer or buyer that this is a high potency, high quality product that increases sales (U.S. Department of Justice 1992).

Opium poppies are grown primarily in southern Asia and Mexico. The seeds from these flowers yield a straw or gum used in the manufacture of morphine base. This base is processed with the addition of chemicals to generate heroin. These processes usually occur within the crop-producing countries or nearby. Heroin dealers also use "marketing strategies" for their drug. Brand names such as "Death Wish" or "Kiss of Death" attract users who want to flirt with danger whereas "Evening's Delight" and "Magic" appeal to those seeking euphoric experiences (U.S. Department of Justice 1992).

The farther a product diffuses from its source, the more diluted and less pure it becomes with the addition of other ingredients to increase the volume of the product. Specific drugs have certain ports of entry in the United States. At these entry points, the drugs are divided into smaller amounts for retail sale.

Smuggling Methods

Smuggling transportation methods primarily range from concealment in maritime cargo vessels or small boats that blend into the local landscape, to aircraft, cars, and trucks (U.S. Department of Justice 1992). A popular method of drug disguise is "false labeling" the containers and concealing them among legal commodities such as cans of food. Technology has entered the drug trade on a large scale. Traffickers have the monetary resources to purchase the latest equipment to protect their business. An example is the waterproof box method. The drugs are placed inside the box which is dropped overboard at a specific marine site. The box is attached to weights that hold it on the seabed until it is retrieved days or weeks later. A signal is sent to release the weights and an attached buoy floats the drug box to the surface where it is recovered. This method works well for heroin, which is compact—a kilogram is about the size of an average book (Booth 1998).

According to smuggling lore, there are a variety of ways to cross borders concealing drugs. For instance, drug smuggling in the Middle East has involved the use of camels; in China, a woman hid opium inside a litter of dead kitten skins (Booth 1998). Individual carriers called *mules* have tried other unusual ways to sneak past customs officials. Illegal drugs have been detected between two layers of a postcard, dusted in the hair of an elderly man, and inside a "pregnant" woman. Smuggling by ingestion has been used since about 1945 (Booth 1998). "Swallowers" are adept at ingesting latex-wrapped pellets to avoid detection, although not always successfully (National Narcotics Intelligence Consumers Committee 1998).

Location is a major element in the success of smuggling. A good place is one that is too busy for police to search everyone. Hong Kong is an excellent example; the harbor is filled with a high volume of vessels and the airport is visited by millions of people (Booth 1998). The United States is another area attractive to drug smugglers. Our expansive coastlines dotted with small, isolated ports are conducive to secretive movements. Likewise, the desert areas in the Southwest make excellent airfields or parachute drop sites.

Cocaine Routes

Approximately, 0.7 percent of the population (1.5 million persons) are currently cocaine users (National Household Survey on Drug Abuse 1997). Most of the cocaine used in the U.S. is supplied by Colombia, which is located in the northwest corner of South America. Because of its geographic location, Colombia has access to both the Pacific Ocean and the Caribbean Sea—two excellent water routes to the U.S. Peru and Bolivia are also major producers of cocaine. A direct cocaine route links the three producers to transit points in Venezuela, Mexico, Panama, Ecuador, the Dominican Republic, and Costa Rica (Figure 5-9). The drugs are shipped or flown to wholesale trafficking points in Arizona, southern California, southern Florida, and Texas. Major retail markets are found in Boston, New York City, Newark, Philadelphia, and Richmond in the East; Chicago, Louisville, and St. Louis in the central U.S.; Orlando, Dallas, and Houston in the South; Los Angeles in the West;

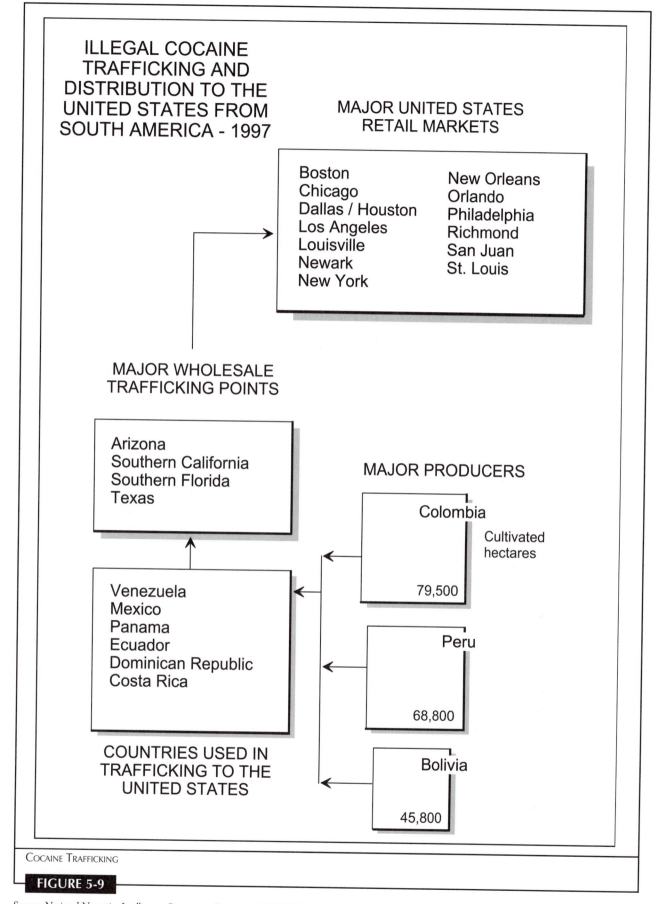

ILLEGAL COCAINE
TRAFFICKING AND
DISTRIBUTION TO THE
UNITED STATES FROM
SOUTH AMERICA - 1997

MAJOR UNITED STATES
RETAIL MARKETS

Boston
Chicago
Dallas / Houston
Los Angeles
Louisville
Newark
New York

New Orleans
Orlando
Philadelphia
Richmond
San Juan
St. Louis

MAJOR WHOLESALE
TRAFFICKING POINTS

Arizona
Southern California
Southern Florida
Texas

MAJOR PRODUCERS

Colombia

Cultivated
hectares

79,500

Venezuela
Mexico
Panama
Ecuador
Dominican Republic
Costa Rica

Peru

68,800

COUNTRIES USED IN
TRAFFICKING TO THE
UNITED STATES

Bolivia

45,800

COCAINE TRAFFICKING

FIGURE 5-9

Source: National Narcotics Intelligence Consumers Committee (NNICC) Report 1997. Drug Enforcement Administration, Washington D.C., 1998.

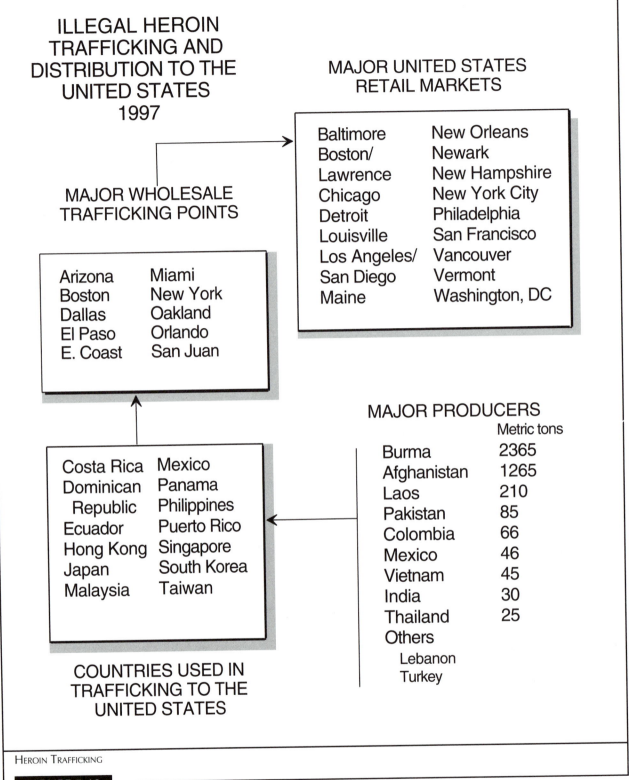

ILLEGAL HEROIN TRAFFICKING AND DISTRIBUTION TO THE UNITED STATES 1997

MAJOR UNITED STATES RETAIL MARKETS

Baltimore
Boston/
Lawrence
Chicago
Detroit
Louisville
Los Angeles/
San Diego
Maine

New Orleans
Newark
New Hampshire
New York City
Philadelphia
San Francisco
Vancouver
Vermont
Washington, DC

MAJOR WHOLESALE TRAFFICKING POINTS

Arizona
Boston
Dallas
El Paso
E. Coast

Miami
New York
Oakland
Orlando
San Juan

MAJOR PRODUCERS

	Metric tons
Burma	2365
Afghanistan	1265
Laos	210
Pakistan	85
Colombia	66
Mexico	46
Vietnam	45
India	30
Thailand	25
Others	
Lebanon	
Turkey	

Costa Rica
Dominican
  Republic
Ecuador
Hong Kong
Japan
Malaysia

Mexico
Panama
Philippines
Puerto Rico
Singapore
South Korea
Taiwan

COUNTRIES USED IN TRAFFICKING TO THE UNITED STATES

HEROIN TRAFFICKING

FIGURE 5-10

Source: National Narcotics Intelligence Consumers Committee (NNICC) Report 1997. Drug Enforcement Administration, Washington D.C., 1998.

and San Juan in the Caribbean. Puerto Rico is a main transit point and a rediscovered interest in Florida also makes cities such as Miami, Port Everglades, and Jacksonville prime cocaine ports (National Narcotics Intelligence Consumers Committee 1998).

The coastal configuration along the Gulf of Mexico provides secluded entries into the southern region. Commercial maritime vessels are also the preferred transport for traffickers into the West Coast. The California coast, with its numerous pleasure craft and secluded bays, inlets, and coves, is ideal for small vessels importing cocaine into the Pacific Coast region (National Narcotics Intelligence Consumers Committee 1998). Physical connectivity to Central America also gives traffickers land routes through Mexico.

Heroin Routes

The demand for heroin has increased steadily in the United States over the last decade. There were about 325,000 users of heroin in this country in 1997 (National Household Survey of Drug Abuse 1977). Most seizures of heroin (75 percent) are from South America, with 14 percent from Mexico and 11 percent from Asian sources (National Narcotics Intelligence Consumers Committee 1998).

During 1997, four source areas supplied the U.S.: Southeast Asia, South America, Mexico, and Southwest Asia/ Middle East (National Narcotics Intelligence Consumers Committee 1998). Heroin from South America (Colombia) is routed by air through either the Caribbean (Puerto Rico) into Miami and New York City, or through Central America into Mexico for markets in Dallas and New York. Mexican heroin, mainly the black tar variety that is usually injected, is delivered to buyers in the West. The Southeast Asian heroin from Burma and Thailand is smuggled through Hong Kong to points in Vancouver, Canada, and Los Angeles, while heroin from Southwest Asia is routed in the opposite direction through Central Asia and Europe to American cities.

The largest producers of heroin are Burma and Laos in Southeast Asia and Afghanistan in Southwest Asia (Figure 5-10). Other producers include Pakistan, Colombia, Mexico, Vietnam, India, Thailand and, to a lesser degree, Turkey and Lebanon. Heroin is shipped from the producers to staging sites in Costa Rica, the Dominican Republic, Ecuador, and Panama from South American sources, and to Hong Kong, Japan, Malaysia, the Philippines, Singapore, South Korea, and Taiwan from Asian and Middle Eastern sources. Wholesale trafficking points in the U.S. are Boston, New York City, Oakland, Orlando, San Juan, Miami, and other points in Arizona and on the East Coast (Figure 5-10). Examples of cities serving as retail markets are Baltimore, Detroit, New Orleans, San Francisco, and Washington, D.C. (Figure 5-10). Reports also confirm the expansion of the heroin market into Vermont, New Hampshire, and Maine.

Heroin from Mexico, the black tar and brown powdered varieties, is mostly routed across the U.S.-Mexican border. San Ysidro was the site of a significant seizure of 19.6 kilograms (National Narcotics Intelligence Consumers Committee 1998). Primary markets for Mexican heroin are Chicago, Denver, and St. Louis. Other cities involved in trafficking the black tar variety are Boston and Atlanta. Oakland, San Francisco, Los Angeles, and Stockton, California, are distribution points for the Black Guerilla Family (BGF), a gang specializing in Mexican heroin deals from prison using street dealers (National Narcotics Intelligence Consumers Committee 1998). Another heroin site is Plano, Texas, where 12 reported deaths occurred. An investigation revealed that black tar was distributed by a Mexican immigrant through Laredo into Plano.

Marijuana Routes

According to the National Household Survey on Drug Abuse (1997), 11.1 million Americans used marijuana in the past month. Three foreign suppliers provide marijuana to American consumers. Almost all foreign marijuana, no matter where the source, is brought into the U.S. via the southwestern border through Texas, California, New Mexico, and Arizona (National Narcotics Intelligence Consumers Committee 1998). Another less significant route is from Jamaica and the Bahamas into the southeastern U.S.

Although Colombia produces more metric tons of marijuana than any other country, Mexico is now the primary supplier to the U.S. Cities acting as wholesale points in m arijuana shipment include Tucson, Los Angeles, Las Cruces, San Francisco, Tampa, El Paso, and Houston (Figure 5-11). San Ysidro, California, holds the record for the highest number of seizures and the largest quantity seized of all southwestern border entry ports. Also, large seizures of marijuana marked for cities in the eastern U.S. occurred at several stash houses in McAllen, Texas, during 1997 (National Narcotics Intelligence Consumers Committee 1998). Retail markets include Boston, New York City, Dallas, Houston, Detroit, Newark, Norfolk, San Diego, and Cleveland.

Domestic cultivation and production of marijuana generally occurs in two ways: outdoors in remote areas, hidden by other vegetation, or indoors with a year-round, controlled environment. Significant outdoor cultivation was noted in California, Hawaii, Idaho, Kentucky, and Tennessee. Significant indoor cultivation was found in California, Florida, Kentucky, Oregon, and Washington. In California, the cultivation area known as the Emerald Triangle (Humboldt, Mendocino, and Trinity Counties) is located in the northern part of the state (National Narcotics Intelligence Consumers Committee 1998).

Local Distribution

Public perception is that the sale and distribution of illegal drugs are solely the work of large, organized cartels. However, opportunities also exist for smaller entrepreneurs brave enough to take the risks. The retail marketplace for the sale of illegal drugs is a "copping area" (U.S. Department of Justice 1992), usually an open area, such as a street corner,

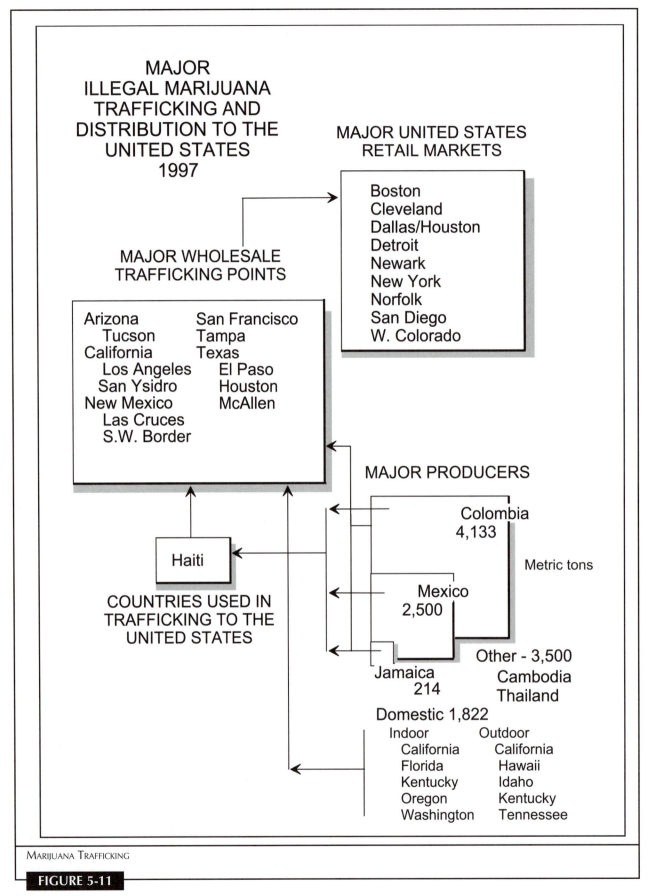

MAJOR
ILLEGAL MARIJUANA
TRAFFICKING AND
DISTRIBUTION TO THE
UNITED STATES
1997

MAJOR UNITED STATES
RETAIL MARKETS

Boston
Cleveland
Dallas/Houston
Detroit
Newark
New York
Norfolk
San Diego
W. Colorado

MAJOR WHOLESALE
TRAFFICKING POINTS

Arizona   San Francisco
  Tucson   Tampa
California   Texas
  Los Angeles   El Paso
  San Ysidro   Houston
New Mexico   McAllen
  Las Cruces
  S.W. Border

MAJOR PRODUCERS

Colombia
4,133

Metric tons

Mexico
2,500

Haiti

COUNTRIES USED IN
TRAFFICKING TO THE
UNITED STATES

Other - 3,500
Cambodia
Thailand

Jamaica
214

Domestic 1,822

Indoor   Outdoor
  California   California
  Florida   Hawaii
  Kentucky   Idaho
  Oregon   Kentucky
  Washington   Tennessee

MARIJUANA TRAFFICKING

FIGURE 5-11

Source: National Narcotics Intelligence Consumers Committee (NNICC) Report 1997. Drug Enforcement Administration, Washington D.C., 1998.

in large urban centers. However, a truck stop or suburban home can also be the location of a drug deal. The site is purposely situated in places that are difficult for police surveillance and where drugs can easily be disposed of in case of an encounter with law enforcement. A simple exchange of money for drugs occurs between strangers or casual acquaintances, and numerous transactions can occur within a short period of time.

"Shooting galleries," where heroin addicts go to share and use their drugs (Murphy and Waldorf 1991), are commonly found in abandoned or dilapidated buildings not too far from the open-air marketplace. Likewise, "crack houses" are where crack users gather. Two types were identified in a Detroit study: (1) a party atmosphere and (2) a "hole-in-the-wall" only for quick sale and no consumption on the premises (Mieczkowski 1988).

Locations of retail markets for street dealers can affect the success of their business, just as in legitimate enterprises. The added factor for both the dealer and the customer is risk (Rengert 1996). Preferred sites for dealers may be near a major transportation corridor or a high school (Rengert and Chakravorty 1995). Desirable locations afford accessibility to clients while providing visibility and escapability for dealers watching for police. Places of low risk to dealers (e.g., abandoned houses) are high risk to clients who prefer locations where they feel safe (e.g., cars or their own neighborhoods). Customers are often willing to pay more for the product to ensure their safety (Kleiman 1991).

Eck (1994) identified four types of drug markets: (1) neighborhood, (2) open regional, (3) semi-open regional, and (4) closed regional. On a small scale, the neighborhood is used by friends and neighbors and is a place in which both client and dealer feel comfortable. The open regional market, a high-risk site, is characterized by markers, such as shopping centers, schools, or main transportation routes. Transactions in semi-open markets occur between those who are acquainted through a social network but do not reside in the same neighborhood. These market locations are determined by the client and change with the transaction. Closed regional markets involve a closed network of friends over a wide area, such as in wholesale markets.

Conclusion

According to a recent report by the United Nations (1997), drug trafficking is a $400-billion-per-year business, and almost 40 million people around the world smoke marijuana and hashish, 13 million use cocaine, and 8 million use heroin. Society is concerned with the connection of drug use and criminal behavior. The U.S. Department of Justice (1992) reports that those who use drugs are often involved in other criminal acts to support their addiction or as part of a deviant lifestyle.

The geographic patterns of drug trafficking reveals that much of the cocaine used in the U.S. comes from South American sources. Entering at wholesale points located from Florida to California, cocaine is distributed to cities in every region. Heroin is produced in many areas of the world,

including Asia, South America, and Central America. Wholesale points of entry are diffused along the East and West coasts as well as the South. Retail markets are located in most major cities, with a concentration along the eastern seaboard. Marijuana is distinct from the other two crop drugs in that it is also domestically grown in abundance. Mexico is the chief foreign supplier of marijuana with the major trafficking route being the southwestern border into the U.S.

This essay demonstrates the importance of location to the trafficking, distribution, and sale of illegal drugs. The spatial dimension reveals the expansiveness of this social problem in terms of identifying regions as suppliers and main smuggling routes used by traffickers. It also provides an understanding of the difficulties involved in the control of international drug trafficking.

References

Booth, M. 1998. *Opium: A History*. New York: St. Martin's Press.

Drug Enforcement Administration (DEA). 1999. DEA Fact Sheet. <http://www.usdoj.gov/dea/pubs/factsheet/fact0299.htm>.

Eck, J. 1994. Drug Markets and Drug Places: A Case-Control Study of the Spatial Structure of Illicit Drug Dealing. Ph.D. thesis, University of Maryland, College Park.

Fuqua, P. 1978. *Drug Abuse: Investigation and Control*. New York: McGraw-Hill.

Gallup Organization. 1996. *Consult with America: A Look at How Americans View the Country's Drug Problem*. Rockville, MD: Office of National Drug Control Policy.

Kleiman, M. 1991. Economic Models of Drug Markets. Paper presented to the American Society of Criminology, San Francisco.

Mieczkowski, T. 1988. Crack Distribution in Detroit. Paper presented at the American Society of Criminology, Chicago.

———. 1986. Geeking Up and Throwing Down: Heroin Street Life in Detroit. *Criminology* 24 (4): 645-66.

Morales, Edmundo. 1989. *Cocaine: White Gold Rush in Peru*. Tucson: University of Arizona Press.

Murphy, S., and D. Waldorf. 1991. Kickin' Down to the Street Doc: Shooting Galleries in the San Francisco Bay Area. *Contemporary Drug Problems* 18 (1): 9-29.

Nash, J.M. 1997. Addicted: Why Do People Get Hooked? Mounting Evidence Points to a Powerful Brain Chemical Called Dopamine. *Time* 149, May 5.

National Household Survey on Drug Abuse. 1997. *Preliminary Results from the 1997 Household Survey*. <http://www.health.org/pubs/97hhs/nhsda977.htm>.

National Narcotics Intelligence Consumers Committee (NNICC). 1998. *The NNICC Report 1997: The Supply of Illicit Drugs to the United States*. Washington, DC: National Narcotics Intelligence Consumers Committee.

Rengert, G.F. 1996. *The Geography of Illegal Drugs*. Boulder, CO: Westview Press.

Rengert, G.F., and S. Chakravorty. 1995. Illegal Drug Sales and Drug Free School Zones. Paper presented to The Association of American Geographers, Chicago.

United Nations. 1997. *World Drug Report*. New York: United Nations International Drug Control Program.

U.S. Department of Justice. 1992. *Drugs, Crime, and the Justice System*. Washington, DC: U.S. Government Printing Office.

———. 1994. (September) *Fact Sheet: Drug-Related Crime*. Washington, DC: Bureau of Justice Statistics, NCJ-149286.

Prostitution

Jacqueline Boles

An act of prostitution is generally defined as an exchange of sex for money or some other commodity (e.g., drugs, cigarettes, or food). Prostitution is a complex activity often involving a large number of people: prostitutes, customers, pimps/procurers, law enforcement officials, and bar and brothel owners. There is great variation among prostitutes. Sex workers of all genders, sexual orientations, races, and ages service equally various customers.

Quantifying the amount of prostitution in any jurisdiction is close to impossible. First, in most jurisdictions around the world, at least some type of sex work is illegal (e.g., child prostitution, sexual slavery, and, in many places, all prostitution). In the United States, only Nevada has legalized prostitution in a few, largely rural counties. Consequently, most sex workers operate out of public view. Second, great variation exists between jurisdictions on the extent to which sex workers are arrested and prosecuted. Further, a given political unit may heavily prosecute at one time but not at another. For example, when researchers Boles and Elifson (1994) first started interviewing male prostitutes, sex workers packed the street that was their main stroll. However, three years later and prior to a major convention, the police put up barricades across the street every night, thus preventing potential customers from cruising it.

The Japanese refer to prostitution as a "water world" in which sex workers "float" in and out; still, many prostitutes follow predictable migration routes from city to city (Kamel 1983). Thus, the number of prostitutes in any given locality is impossible to determine with any reliability. For these reasons, most official statistics are untrustworthy. However, these statistics may prove useful as general indicators of the extent of prostitution.

Various authors have mapped prostitution areas. In *The Nightless City* (1971), first published in 1899, J.E. De Becker mapped the Yoshiwara brothel district in Tokyo (Figure 5-12). Other scholars have documented the geographic distribution of prostitution in various cities: Paris (Parent-Duchatelet 1857), San Francisco (Shumsky and Springer 1979), the Storyville district in New Orleans (Anonymous 1910-11), Jalapa, Mexico (Barrera Caraza 1974), Dallas (Reynolds 1986), and San Diego (Kamel 1983). In his classic text on the geography of female prostitution, *The Immoral Landscape*, Richard Symanski (1981: 4) argued that "Prostitution as an adaptive system reflects a well-known ecological principle, namely that the stability of a system resides in the diversity of its component parts or adaptations." Prostitution is a remarkably adaptive institution. Sex workers and the others integral to the institution constantly develop new strategies to reach customers. The United States currently has few brothels; sex workers now use newspaper and magazine ads and, of course, the Internet. Prostitution has gone global.

This essay provides three geographic snapshots of prostitution: (1) the extent of prostitution globally, (2) prostitution arrests by region in the United States, and (3) a description of two geographic concentrations in one large city. These three perspectives are meant to illustrate how our understanding of prostitution is affected by the geographic unit employed in our analysis.

Global Prostitution

The distribution of sex workers around the world is related to a number of factors, chief of which are the laws and law enforcement practices determined by those in power and by the income of the citizens. Figure 5-13 illustrates that those countries with the highest rates of prostitution are generally poor, give low status to women, and have politicians that encourage prostitution for economic reasons. Sex work is generally not a person's first choice; most sex workers come from poor families. They either choose sex work or are sold into it because it is the most viable economic option. Political jurisdictions, whether cities, counties, or nations, develop and enact laws and enforcement policies relative to prostitution; organized prostitution is usually revenue enhancing. Historically, some European cities, like Hamburg and Amsterdam, have profited from prostitution. Revenue from brothels (actually trailers sitting in the desert) comprise a substantial portion of the budget of some Nevada counties. Cities that depend on tourists or the military generally tolerate, if not encourage, prostitution.

Prostitution, like other industries in the global economy, is competitive; therefore, political jurisdictions may offer different services to attract customers. Travelers, sex tourist firms, and even some government entities post Web sites advertising and promoting sexual activities around the globe. Before the inexperienced traveler goes to Bangkok or Manila, for example, he or she can visit a Web site detailing the best locations, with fees, for specific sexual services.

Generally, the United States is intolerant of child prostitution. Consequently, those interested in sex with children go to countries in Southeast Asia and South America that are more tolerant. Some American cities with large gay populations accept male prostitution (hustling). The sex tourist industry consists of a number of firms that offer tours of cities in which various kinds of sexual activity are

140

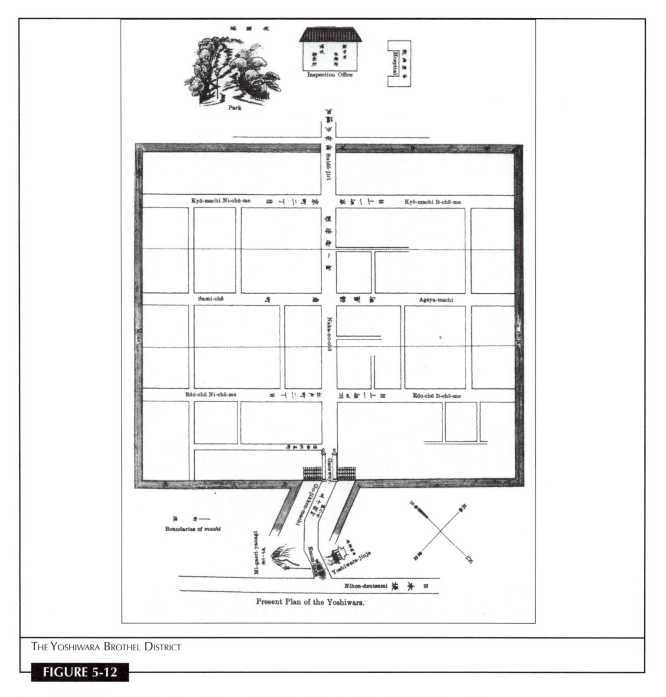

THE YOSHIWARA BROTHEL DISTRICT

FIGURE 5-12

Source: J.E. De Becker, *The Nightless City or the History of the Yoshiwara Yukwaku*, Charles E. Tuttle, Co. Inc., 1971.

available. The destinations of many of these tours have been cities in South Korea, Indonesia, Thailand, Malaysia, and the Philippines (Green 1998). In a recent report, Lin Lim (1998) noted that the sex industry accounts for about 14 percent of the gross domestic product from those countries. In Thailand, almost $300 million is sent by sex workers annually to their poor families. Children's charities estimate that in Asia alone 650,000 children work as prostitutes. Geographic areas that have played host to military bases also generally support high rates of prostitution (Sturdevant and Stoltzfus 1992).

Because of religious or ideological reasons, some jurisdictions strongly curtail prostitution. The Muslim faith condemns prostitution; consequently, most Muslim countries have low rates. Scandinavian countries developed an ideology supportive of equality between the sexes and have strong economies with small differences between the wealthiest and the poorest; thus, they have low rates of prostitution (Hoigard and Finstad 1992). The USSR, China, and Eastern European countries also promoted equality between the sexes, although with less success than Scandinavia. Since the breakup of the USSR, prostitution has skyrocketed in Russia.

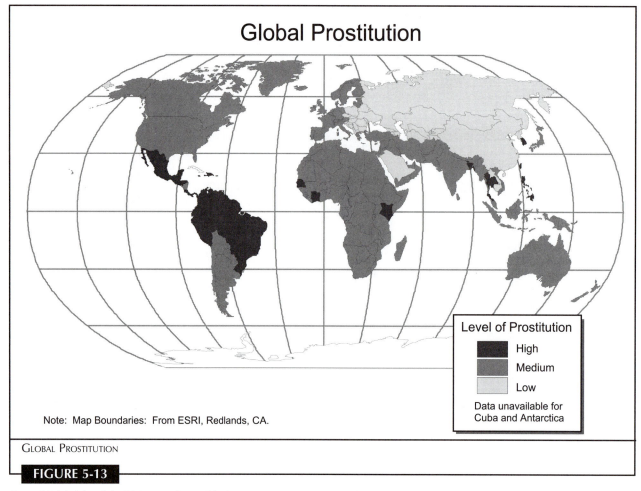

Global Prostitution

Level of Prostitution
- High
- Medium
- Low

Data unavailable for Cuba and Antarctica

Note: Map Boundaries: From ESRI, Redlands, CA.

GLOBAL PROSTITUTION

FIGURE 5-13

Source: Modified from John J. Macionis, *Society: The Basics.* New Jersey: Prentice Hall, 1996, p.148.

Another important factor in explaining prostitution rates around the world is the organization of communal life. In much of Africa south of the Sahara, for example, as well as in India, life is organized around villages where most residents are members of extended kin groups. Africa had low rates of prostitution and AIDS until the breakup of stable communities. Today prostitution and AIDS thrive along the major river systems used by young men in search of jobs. India, too, is experiencing increased internal migration with a concomitant rise in prostitution and AIDS (Statistical Outline of India 1995).

By comparing prostitution rates between countries, we can see how these various factors work in concert to produce either high or low rates. For example, even though the status of women is low (compared to Western societies) in Saudi Arabia, the prostitution rate is low because the government strongly condemns prostitution, and women are not free to engage in it; whereas in the Philippines, poor women have been free and often encouraged to engage in sex work. Before the collapse of the USSR, prostitution was actively discouraged. Men who frequented prostitutes had their photographs displayed on their factories' bulletin boards. At present, both male and female prostitution is rampant and largely unregulated in the former USSR.

Prostitution in a Regional Perspective

The racial, ethnic, and religious composition of the population; population density; extent of urbanization; and regional norms and values all affect the arrest rates for prostitution across the regions of the U.S. These factors are important for understanding differences in both the amount of prostitution and the number of arrests for that offense.

The Federal Bureau of Investigation (FBI) (1996) collects arrest data from a number of jurisdictions throughout the United States and classifies them into 27 categories, including "prostitution and commercial vice." The FBI also constructs a "crime index" taken from the eight "most serious" violent and property crimes. The data in this section that report on income, the percent of crime in rural areas, and the index crime rate are taken from the *Statistical Abstract* (U.S. Department of Commerce 1996). In the following subsections, we examine the arrest rates (number of arrests per 100,000 population) for nine geographic areas of the United States. For the 1996 reporting period, four states, plus the District of Columbia, did not contribute arrest data. Figure 5-14 presents the arrest rates for nine regions for prostitution and commercial vice. Calculations were based on reported arrests for both juveniles and adults. The average arrest rate for prostitution and commercial vice for the entire United States in 1996 was 41.7, in contrast to the crime index rate of 1,081.8 per 100,000 population.

New England

The prostitution arrest rate for this region was 28.2, significantly below the average for the nation. Boston is the premier city in this urbanized region where only 15 percent of the population live outside metropolitan areas. New England residents have the highest average individual income. In addition, this region has the lowest rate for property index crimes and a relatively low rate for violent crimes.

Middle Atlantic

This region is more urbanized than New England with several large cities, including New York City, Newark, Philadelphia, and Pittsburgh. Only 8.8 percent of the population live outside metropolitan areas. While its index crime rate is higher than New England's, it is below the national

average. The prostitution rate, 44.2, is higher than the average for the country. Both Pennsylvania and New Jersey, with smaller populations, arrested about the same number of prostitutes as New York. The average income of people in this region is also above the national average, although some severe pockets of high unemployment exist, particularly in New Jersey.

South Atlantic

This region constitutes a block of states that was part of the Old South and part of what is often referred to as the Bible Belt. Georgia is characterized by a high rate of in-migration, especially to the Atlanta metropolitan area. The states in this region contain a number of large cities and contiguous suburban areas: Atlanta, Raleigh/Durham, Baltimore, Miami, and Washington, D.C. Approximately 20.6 percent of the population live outside metropolitan areas, slightly more than the national average. Also, a significant number of military bases are located in this region. The average income of individuals was $21,781, slightly below the national average. This region has a low prostitution rate (22.5) relative to the national average because both Florida and the District of Columbia did not report data for 1996. Addi-

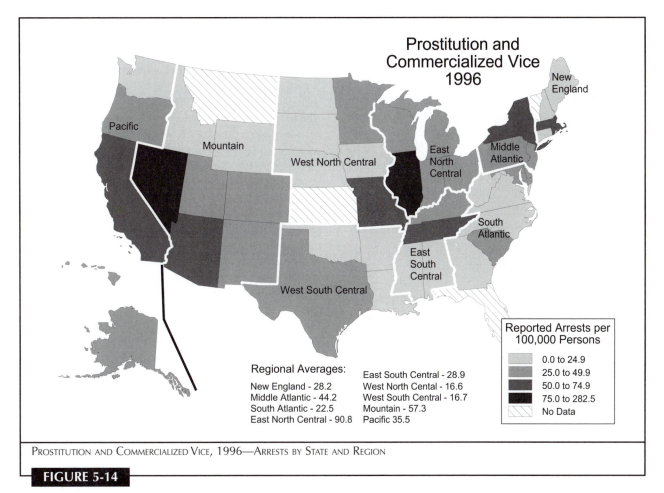

PROSTITUTION AND COMMERCIALIZED VICE, 1996—ARRESTS BY STATE AND REGION

FIGURE 5-14

Source: Federal Bureau of Investigation, *Uniform Crime Reports, 1997.*

tionally, both North Carolina and Georgia reported unusually low rates, 13.0 and 6.3, respectively. These data may reflect law enforcement policies and priorities.

East South Central

Both border states and parts of the deep South are included in this region. These states have also been largely rural in the past, and this region still has the highest percent (42.5) living outside metropolitan areas. Large cities include Nashville, Louisville, Birmingham, and Gulfport. The prostitution rate, 28.9, is only slightly higher than that of the South Atlantic region and significantly lower than the national average. Alabama and Mississippi have a high percentage of people living below the poverty level, and citizens of this region have the lowest average personal income ($16,262).

East North Central

This region contains such large metropolitan areas as Chicago, Detroit, Cincinnati, Indianapolis, and Gary, as well as rural areas in Wisconsin, Michigan, and Indiana. Only slightly more than 20 percent live outside metropolitan areas. Unemployment has often been high because of recent shifts away from heavy industry. The average income is slightly below the national average. The prostitution rate (90.8) is the highest of any of the regions, reflecting both the number of large urban areas and the change in the economy with the resulting underemployment.

West North Central

This region is the American breadbasket and the heart of the Great Plains. Forty-one percent of the population live outside metropolitan areas. With a relatively low population density and few large cities, this region has a low prostitution rate, 16.6. The average income of individuals, at $19,211, is below the national average and the region also has an index crime rate below the national average.

West South Central

In terms of population and urbanization, Texas dominates this region. The region's prostitution rate of 16.7 is largely reflective of Texas and its large cities, such as Dallas, Houston, Galveston, and San Antonio. This region also has an index crime rate above the national average. Only 23.4 percent of citizens live outside metropolitan areas, and the average income, $17,606, is only slightly higher than in the neighboring East South Central region.

Mountain

Even though the mountain states encompass a large geographic area, much of their population lives in a few major urban areas: Phoenix, Boulder, Denver, Las Vegas, and Salt Lake City. Fewer than 30 percent live outside metropolitan areas. A number of military bases are located throughout the region, including those near Las Vegas and Colorado

Springs. This region has experienced a major growth in population, particularly in Arizona, Colorado, and New Mexico. The average personal income of $18,100 is significantly below the national average. However, this region has the highest rate of index crimes, and the prostitution rate, 57.3, is significantly above the average.

Pacific

In this region, California has by far the largest population, most of which is urban or suburban. Further, California has more people serving in military installations than any other state. Hawaii also has a large number of military personnel in residence. California's economy has recently improved as have the economies of Oregon and Washington; their average individual income, $22,382, is slightly higher than the national average. Only 8.5 percent of the population live outside metropolitan areas. This region is also experiencing a high rate of in-migration. The index crime rate is slightly higher than the national rate; however, the prostitution rate, 35.5, is slightly below the national average.

In sum, the arrest rates for prostitution and commercial vice for the nine regions vary between 16.6 and 90.8. Those regions falling below the national average are West South Central, New England, South Atlantic, West North Central, East South Central, and Pacific. Those falling above the national average are East North Central, Mountain, and Middle Atlantic. This amount of variation is the result of the interaction of a number of factors, including idiosyncratic reporting practices and policies within the many jurisdictions whose statistics are used to compile the FBI *Uniform Crime Reports*. However, it is worth noting that all the southern states except Tennessee report rates below the national average, perhaps reflecting, in part, the importance of religious traditions in those regions. The Mountain region reports rates above the national average and is experiencing high in-migration. Large numbers of newcomers often lead to community disruption and destabilization, particularly when the new people have traditions and beliefs different from the older residents.

The East North Central's rate, 90.8, is so significantly higher than the others that it deserves special comment. At one time, this region was the industrial heartland of the United States. Immigrants from Europe and the South poured into the region looking for work and a better life. Although this region has suffered from a shift in the economy, it is still dominated by large cities such as Chicago, Cleveland, Detroit, Milwaukee, Gary, and Cincinnati. The relationship between urbanization and prostitution is dramatic. For cities with 250,000 or more people, the prostitution arrest rate was 150.2, while the arrest rate for cities under 10,000 was 2.2 and for rural counties 1.1 (Federal Bureau of Investigation 1996). Clearly, the fact that this region contains so many large cities is a major factor in explaining its high rate. Prostitution arrests are negatively related to regions with stable populations, few large cities, few military bases, and relatively high incomes.

Prostitution in a Local Perspective

Prostitutes work in a variety of settings: expensive apartments and condominiums, massage parlors, special rooms in strip clubs, hotels, and on the street. Those who work on the street are the most visible, and, consequently, the most likely to cause public disfavor. For that reason, police control efforts are usually focused on street prostitution.

Municipalities have developed several strategies for controlling (or attempting to control) street prostitution. One strategy is to attempt to eliminate it entirely. Efforts along this line involve delegating police to arrest street prostitutes and, occasionally, customers (johns). Laws like "loitering for the purpose of prostitution" are invoked to arrest known prostitutes. Police sometimes masquerade as johns or sex workers. The police may impound johns' cars or publish their names and photographs in the local paper. Additional strategies include laws that affect johns' behaviors. To make it difficult to cruise for sex workers, laws are enacted limiting how slow cars may go or how many times they can circle the same street. These efforts are labor intensive and usually unsuccessful. Sex workers and johns may change locations or "lie low" for a time, but eventually business will resume as usual.

Another approach is to segregate vice to a particular geographic area. Zoning laws are created to restrict "sex and vice" to small geographic areas away from schools, religious institutions, and respectable businesses. Boston's ill-fated "Combat Zone" is an example of that strategy. This approach has two key problems. The area will eventually become so undesirable that potential johns will not enter, forcing prostitutes to go where johns with money are located.

Some municipalities try the opposite zoning strategy. They enact laws that force sex and vice businesses to locate in many different areas so that they are not concentrated in one zone. The idea is that if vice-oriented businesses are distributed over a large area, no area will "tip," that is, develop a concentration of vice shops and street prostitutes. This strategy is difficult to manage because in most cities local businesses and citizens do not want sex shops located next door, or even on the next street. However, in cities such as New Orleans and San Francisco, zones that have traditionally catered to vice have thrived largely unopposed by the local citizenry.

Prostitution control strategies often involve selective enforcement. In deciding how much effort to put into prostitution control, the police weigh a number of issues, including citizen complaints, manpower, media attention, political considerations, and the organization and staffing of police departments. In the 1980s, for instance, an Atlanta neighborhood, Midtown, began to experience gentrification. Gradually, well-to-do white, college-educated professionals started "homesteading" in this transitional area. When they discovered that female, transvestite, and male sex workers walked the streets trolling for customers, they inundated the police department and the mayor's office with complaints. In response, the mayor formed the Mayor's Task Force on Prostitution (MTFOP), with a mandate to develop recommendations for "doing something about" prostitution in Midtown. Twelve of us,

HYPOTHETICAL PROSTITUTION LANDSCAPE

FIGURE 5-15

Organized and Entrepreneurial Crimes

including two city council representatives and Dolores French, a prostitute and president of HIRE (Hooking Is Real Employment), met for over two years. We made a number of recommendations, none of which were enacted. In the meantime, increased police presence plus the growth of escort services and massage parlors reduced the physical presence of sex workers in Midtown. Sex workers are endlessly adaptable; close a neighborhood and they move a few blocks.

While a member of MTFOP, I used arrest data to plot the key prostitution locations in the city. These data al-

lowed us to make generalizations about the physical characteristics of locations where street prostitution is most likely to occur. An ideal physical locality for street prostitution will have the following characteristics:

1. The streets are either two-lane or four-lane thoroughfares, or at most, one street off the major thoroughfare. The street should not end in a cul-de-sac.
2. Hotels, motels, or rooming houses are found on or near the street. Vacant lots are also useful.

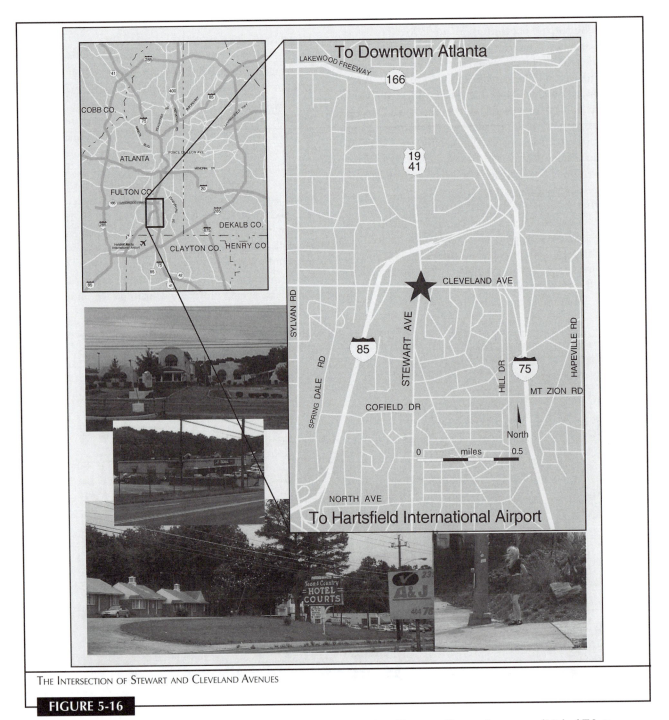

The Intersection of Stewart and Cleveland Avenues

FIGURE 5-16

Sources: Maps courtesy of the Department of Anthropology and Geography, Georgia State University. Photographs courtesy of Michael T. Laitta.

3. Lighted locations where sex workers can stand or sit are found along the street. Low benches are particularly helpful. The john wants to see what the sex worker looks like, and the sex worker wants to see the car tag number and perhaps the driver's license, and wants to check for the presence of a gun, for undercover police officers always wear their guns.

4. The area is relatively prostitute friendly. The presence of sex shops, including strip clubs, bars, massage parlors, and stores selling pornography and sex toys suggests that the local businesspeople will be sympathetic to streetwalkers as long as they do not assault or rip off customers.

Two Atlanta streets that fit the above description are Stewart Avenue and Cypress Street.

Stewart Avenue

Stewart Avenue (recently renamed Metropolitan) is a long street running north-south on Atlanta's south side (Figure 5-16). The character of the street changes. Although it has working-class homes, churches, the Salvation Army's campus, and a community college, one part of the street has been known as a haven for prostitutes for over 30 years. The key area is the intersection of Cleveland Avenue (which runs east-west) and Stewart. Both Cleveland and Stewart are close to two major expressways, Interstates 75 and 85.

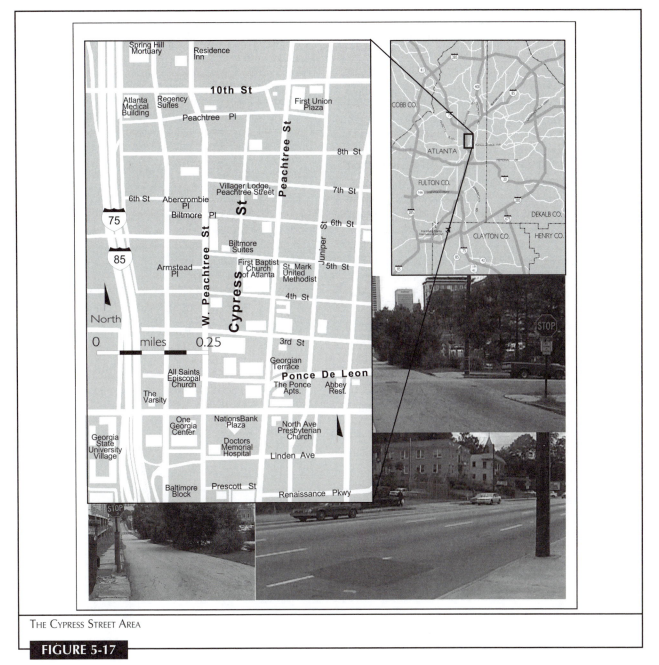

THE CYPRESS STREET AREA

FIGURE 5-17

Sources: Maps courtesy of the Department of Anthropology and Geography, Georgia State University. Photographs courtesy of Michael T. Laitta.

Hartsfield International Airport is south of the area and the city center is north. A number of light industrial districts are located to the west and some residential areas to the east. Until recently, when a john was killed there, the centerpiece of Stewart Avenue was the Alamo Plaza Motel, a 1940s motel with one entrance and a number of cabins located around the center court. Each cabin was rented by one or more prostitutes, and pimps controlled the entrance and egress. Today, the central location is a gas station, which stays lit all night, near the Stewart and Cleveland intersection. Also, a number of motels, strip clubs, and bars dot the general area.

Cypress Street

At one time, Cypress Street was the major male prostitute stroll in the Atlanta area (Boles and Elifson 1994). On a typical night, as many as 50 male prostitutes would be sitting, standing, and strolling along the street while cars drove slowly by. Cypress Street runs north-south parallel to Peachtree Street (Figure 5-17). It is only a few blocks from a major interstate, and the Midtown area is a transitional neighborhood in which gays, straight couples, and the more adventuresome young live. Both female and transvestite sex workers worked on many of the neighboring streets. A gay bar and the first office of AID Atlanta, an advocacy and educational organization for people with AIDS, were located on the south end. The rear of a building, housing the Georgia Department of Public Health, faced the street at the north end. Midway along the length of the street, a small building was rented by a man teaching fencing. A low wall offered seating. A rooming house and several motels were within walking distance, and a fast food restaurant on Peachtree Street offered shelter from rain and snow for the price of a cup of coffee.

Cypress Street, as a center for male prostitution, fell victim to the determined efforts of the city to close it. Before the 1996 Olympics, the city closed the fast food restaurant, encouraged a popular strip club nearby to move, and set up semi-permanent blockades across the street. AID Atlanta moved to a larger location, and the building housing the State Department of Public Health closed. Only the gay club is left. Hustling is now distributed over the city; most hustlers stroll near to gay clubs in Midtown and parts of nearby DeKalb County.

Prostitution flourishes in locations where johns and sex workers intersect—traditionally, around major communication arteries (e.g., rivers, seaports, and thoroughfares). The organization of prostitution is always changing, respond-

ing to new technology. In the past, the automobile, the telephone, and the motel changed the way sex workers and their customers contracted their business. Today, the Internet and the World Wide Web are transforming the business on an international scale. However, much remains the same. Streetwalkers still loiter, and customers still cruise looking for the "right person."

References

Anonymous. 1910-11. *Blue Book.*

Barrera Caraza, Estanislao. 1974. Prostitution in Jalapa: Estudio de Algunos Socioeconomicos. Thesis in *Antropologia*, Universidad Veracruzzana, Jalapa, Veracruz.

Boles, Jacqueline, and Elifson, Kirk. 1994. Sexual Identity and HIV: The Male Prostitute. *The Journal of Sex Research* 31: 39-46.

De Becker, J.E. 1971. The Nightless City or the History of Yoshiwara Yukwaku. 5th ed. Tokyo: Charles E. Tuttle, Co., 1971.

Federal Bureau of Investigation. 1996. *Crime in the United States, Uniform Crime Reports, 1996.* Washington, DC: Government Printing Office.

Green, Richard. 1998. The Sex Tourist and International Law. In James Elias, Vern Bullough, Veronica Elias, and Gwen Brewer, eds. *Prostitution: On Whores Hustlers and Johns.* Amherst, NY: Prometheus Books, p. 473.

Hoigard, Cecilie, and Finstad, Liv. 1992. *Backstreets: Prostitution, Money and Love.* University Park: The Pennsylvania State University Press.

Kamel, G.W. Levi. 1983. *Downtown Street Hustlers: The Role of Dramaturgical Imaging Practices in the Social Construction of Male Prostitution.* Unpublished dissertation, University of California at San Diego.

Lim, Lin. 1998. *The Plight of Women in Asia's Sex Industry.* Report issued by the International Labour Organization. As reported by Paul Majendi, Reuters International.

Parent-Duchatelet. A.J.B. 1857. *De la Prostitution dans la Ville de Paris.* 2nd ed. Paris: J.B. Bailiere de Fils.

Reynolds, Helen. 1986. *The Economics of Prostitution.* Springfield, IL: Charles C. Thomas.

Shumsky, Neil, and Springer, Larry. 1979. *San Francisco's Zone of Prostitution 1880-1934.* Unpublished manuscript.

Statistical Outline of India. 1995. *The Status and Trends of the Global HIV/AIDS Pandemic.* Bombay, India: Tata Press.

Sturdevant, Saudra, and Stoltzfus Brenda. 1992. *Let the Good Times Roll: Prostitution and the U.S. Military in Asia.* New York: The New Press.

Symanski, Richard. 1981. *The Immoral Landscape: Female Prostitution in Western Societies.* Toronto: Butterworths.

United States Department of Commerce. 1996. *Statistical Abstract of the United States, 1996.* Washington, DC: Bureau of the Census.

Modern Maritime Piracy

George J. Demko

Today, many people still imagine pirates as dashing and heroic rogues and piracy as a romantic and daring vocation. Despite the fascinating, fictional characters produced by Robert Louis Stevenson and others, pirates were and are criminals and piracy comprises a set of violent criminal acts. The estimated cost of contemporary maritime piracy and related maritime fraud exceeds $16 billion a year. In 1998, pirates murdered 51 members of ships' crews and wounded 31 (International Maritime Organization 1999). Contemporary piracy is a serious and violent crime that afflicts many areas of the world.

Piracy is defined as "any illegal acts of violence or detention, or any act of depredation, committed for private ends by the crew or the passengers of a private ship or a private aircraft and directed: on the high seas against another ship or a aircraft; or against persons or property on board such a ship or aircraft, persons or property in a place outside the jurisdiction of any State; any act of voluntary participation in the operation of a ship or aircraft with knowledge of facts making it a pirate ship or aircraft; or any act of inciting or of intentionally facilitating an act described above" (United Nations 1983). For the purposes of this essay, the place of the piratical act has been altered to include not only the high seas or international waters, but also the territorial waters of specific countries, including ports, where most piracy occurs today.

Brief Historical Note on Piracy

In the past, all maritime areas of the world have experienced piracy of some type. Historically, some pirates were distinguished from common criminals by the fact that they were raiding other vessels under letters of marque from a sovereign state. This group of maritime marauders, known as "privateers," shared their plunder with the authorities of the states that commissioned them. Much of the romantic and heroic image of pirates stems from that practice (Thompson 1996).

The seventeenth and eighteenth centuries were the "golden age" of piracy, although the practice extends far back into the past. The Vikings were renowned pirates of the Baltic and North Seas. Other famous or infamous pirates include the Muslim raiders of the Barbary Coast of North Africa, the remarkable Chinese pirate Ching Yih on the South China Sea in the late 1700s, and the Caribbean "buccaneers." The last large-scale pirate stronghold was located in the Malay Archipelago off Malaysia and was only broken up after the Opium Wars in the late nineteenth century (Cordingly 1995). Piracy's long and bloody history continues today in acts of robbery, murder, and violence in many regions of the globe.

Acts of Modern Piracy

Although bearing a striking resemblance to piratical violence of the past, modern piracy has grown more daring, more sophisticated, and no less violent. Acts of piracy range from stealing cargo from ships (including mid-sea pumping of oil from tankers) to hijacking of ships, repainting and renaming them, and sailing them off to distant ports to sell both cargo and vessel. On a smaller scale, pirates have attacked small fishing ships, injuring and robbing the crew and stealing the catch. They have boarded refugee vessels and raped and pillaged defenseless escapees from poverty and political repression. Luxury vessels and yachts have also been violently attacked, with passengers murdered and wounded and valuables stolen. Sophisticated fraud related to ships and their cargoes are more modern versions of piracy and difficult to control, given that many of these acts involve shippers and officials (Vantage Systems 1998).

The number of pirate attacks has been increasing, especially since 1990 when 50 incidents were reported globally. Figure 5-18 clearly depicts the significant increase in incidents from 1995 onward, with a peak of 252 in 1997. In 1998, the number of reported incidents reached 210, of which 190 occurred in either territorial waters or in a port. In contrast, only 17 incidents took place in international waters (International Maritime Organization 1999). The data are those reported by the Maritime Safety Committee of the International Maritime Organization, and may well understate the incidence of piracy. Underreporting may be the result of fear of insurance cost increases and the fact that some countries and authorities are loath to provide data that reflect poor security or even complicity with some acts. Crime on the world's coastal and international waters is a significant and growing problem.

Geography of Piracy

Contemporary piracy has a distinct spatial pattern even though most of the world's coasts are afflicted to some degree. In general terms, piracy is greatly facilitated by physical and political conditions. For example, coastal areas with long, narrow navigational channels or dotted with many small islands are prime locations for pirates. The physical conditions create ideal conditions in terms of slowing traffic and providing hiding places for marauders. The Strait of Malacca, most of the Indonesian coast, and the Philippine

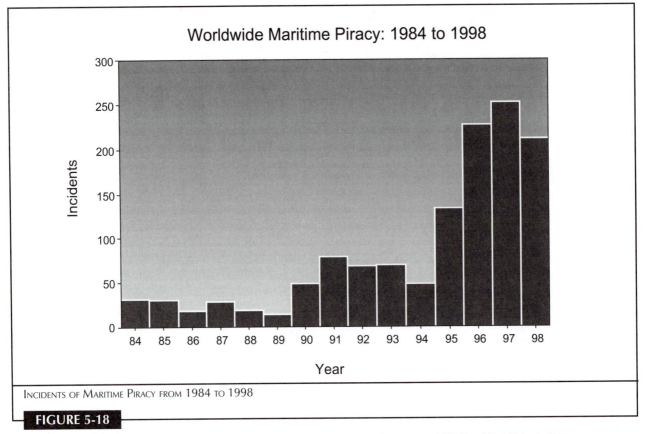

Worldwide Maritime Piracy: 1984 to 1998

INCIDENTS OF MARITIME PIRACY FROM 1984 TO 1998

FIGURE 5-18

Source: Reports on Acts of Piracy and Armed Robbery Against Ships, International Maritime Organization, MSC/Circ.903, 15 March, 1999.

Islands are excellent examples of physical sites vulnerable to piracy. Regions and countries in a state of political chaos or economic instability are similarly excellent locales for pirates. Current examples of such places include Somalia, Indonesia, Sri Lanka, and the west coast of Africa. These countries have been wracked by civil war, internal political struggles, and even anarchy. In addition, many of these countries suffer from poor or nearly absent maritime law enforcement and are characterized by crowded ports and long police response times.

An examination of pirate attacks in seven macro regions of the world clearly pinpoints the South China Sea region as the area with a major concentration of piracy (Figure 5-19). The combination of the South China Sea and the Malacca Strait results in a region where 48 percent of all piracy occurred in 1998, a pattern that has persisted over the past five or six years. This segment of the world has a long history of piracy and merits special attention in terms of piracy prevention measures. South America suffered 38 attacks that are clustered in two areas, one on each coast. The Indian Ocean suffered 25 attacks in one of the world's poorest regions. The map of maritime piracy (Figure 5-20) provides a complete and more detailed view of the spatial distribution of piracy incidents. Overall, the concentration of attacks in the Third World is remarkable and reflects the conditions that favor maritime criminality. A heavy con-

centration of piracy in Southeast Asia is focused on Indonesia, Malaysia, and the Philippines. In the Indian Ocean, Bangladesh, Sri Lanka, and India are focal points of piracy. Africa has two distinct clusters—on the east coast in Somali waters, and on the west coast from Nigeria through Sierra Leone to Liberia and Senegal. In South America, incidents of piracy are focused off the coast of Brazil, on the east coast of Colombia, and off Ecuador in the west. The Nicaraguan-Costa Rican coasts have also been plagued by piracy. Much of the piracy in this area is related to drug traffic, a criminal trade that often uses sea lanes to distribute narcotics (Dominguez 1995). No more than a half dozen attacks took place in European or North American waters, where conditions are much more difficult for pirates to exploit.

Examples of Modern Piracy

As noted above, types of pirate acts vary greatly across the globe. Among the boldest and best organized acts are ship hijackings. In recent years, at least three oil tankers have been taken by pirates in the waters between Indonesia and Malaysia. Similarly, cargo ships carrying grain, electronics, or other valuable cargo have been plundered by pirates off Indonesia and Brazil. Shipping fraud is a more sophisticated type of piracy involving "phantom" ships. For example, in

150

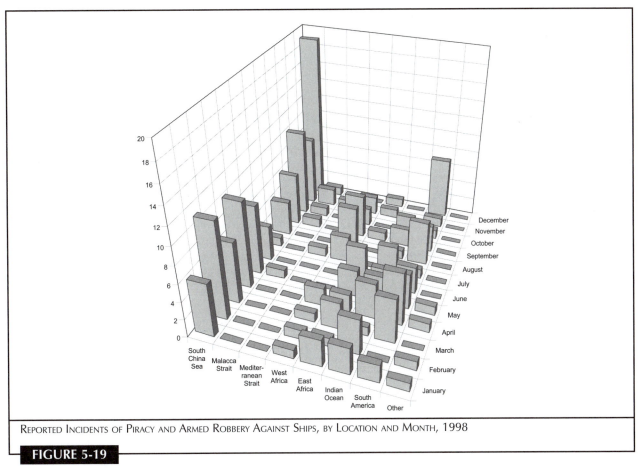

Reported Incidents of Piracy and Armed Robbery Against Ships, by Location and Month, 1998

FIGURE 5-19

Source: Reports on Acts of Piracy and Armed Robbery Against Ships, International Maritime Organization, MSC/Circ.903, 15 March, 1999.

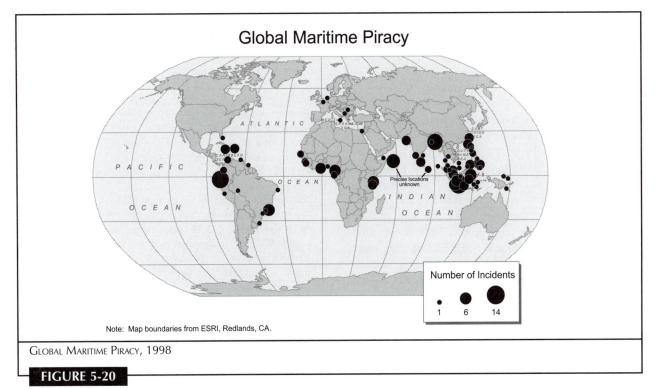

Global Maritime Piracy, 1998

FIGURE 5-20

Source: Reports on Acts of Piracy and Armed Robbery Against Ships, International Maritime Organization, MSC/Circ.903, 15 March, 1999.

1997, a cargo ship was reported sunk in the Atlantic and later discovered without its cargo in Ghana. In such cases, the piracy involves insurance payments and double sale of cargo by corrupt insiders (Vantage Systems 1998).

Small bands of pirates often attack returning fishermen and steal the crews' valuables as well as the catch. These are common problems in the Philippines and off the coast of Ecuador. Somali pirates have kidnapped yacht passengers and even United Nations officials in waters off that country. In Florida, the Caribbean, and the Mediterranean, luxury boats have been boarded by pirates and passengers terrorized, robbed, wounded, and even murdered.

Modern piracy includes a remarkable array of types of banditry and is extremely difficult to predict and control. The problem of control is complicated by the fact that many of the larger vessels are registered under flags of convenience and these countries have minimal capability of responding to (or reporting) acts of piracy. Attacks in international waters are complicated by the fact that no state has legal jurisdiction in such areas. Piracy in ports is often met with indifference, inasmuch as local authorities often deny help, justifying a lack of effort by a claim of no jurisdiction over foreign ships. Legal issues related to law enforcement in maritime piracy are complex and significant.

Anti-Piracy Policies

In 1992, the increasing level of piracy and associated material and human loss led the International Maritime Bureau, a division of the International Chamber of Commerce in Paris, to collaborate with members of the maritime shipping industries and law enforcement agencies to create the Regional Piracy Centre (International Chamber of Commerce 1996). The Centre, headquartered in Kuala Lumpur, Malaysia, and funded by contributions from shippers, insurance companies, and other organizations, acts as an information clearing center for piracy prevention. The Centre provides around-the-clock information, reports of attacks, and news about suspicious vessel movements.

In 1998, the International Maritime Organization (IMO), through the offices of its Maritime Safety Committee, organized a number of regional seminars to develop an international code for the investigation of piracy and armed robbery against ships. The Maritime Safety Committee has published a number of circulars with recommendations to governments for the prevention and suppression of piracy (International Maritime Organization 1999). Since 1995, the Maritime Safety Committee has issued monthly reports of piracy incidents on a regional basis. Because international cooperative action is so recent, much more can be done (International Maritime Organization 1999).

Conclusion

The resurgence of piracy in recent years is a serious and costly global crime. The urgency of the problem has finally been realized by international organizations, governments, and the private sector and is leading to improved information flow and prevention policies. There is a need for programs to heighten awareness and prevention by maritime personnel, law enforcement agencies, and other international bodies. More detailed analysis of locations of incidents and the conditions that promote and facilitate piracy are required to improve the prediction of frequency and locations of incidents and to encourage more effective deployment of resources to confront piracy. More well-defined legal measures regarding maritime fraud are also needed, as is more cooperation among states in piracy research and its prevention. This need is especially true in many developing states with poorly evolved law enforcement capabilities. A need also exists to provide resources and other support for training and equipment to those states where piracy has traditionally been a serious problem and where resources to combat it are inadequate. Governments in many areas must also be convinced that piracy merits a higher law enforcement priority than it has in the past. The cost of piracy is high and growing—a situation that demands greater global awareness and more international cooperation.

References

Cordingly, David. 1995. *Under the Black Flag.* New York: Random House.

Dominguez, Jorge I., ed. 1995. *From Pirates to Drug Lords: The Post-Cold War Caribbean Security Environment.* Albany: State University of New York.

Galvin, Peter R. 1998. *Patterns of Pillage: A Geography of Caribbean-based Piracy in Spanish America, 1536-1768.* Washington, DC: American University Press.

Gosse, Philip. 1932. *The History of Piracy.* New York: Tudor Publishing.

International Chamber of Commerce, Business World (The Electronic Magazine of the ICC). 1996. *The Battle Against Crime on the High Seas.* London, March 7.

International Maritime Organization (IMO) 1999. See their Web site at <http://www.imo/briefing/1999/faxO6.htm>.

International Maritime Organization, Maritime Safety Committee. 1999. *Reports of Acts of Piracy and Armed Robbery Against Ships.* London. Circular 903, March 15.

Johnson, Charles et al. 1998. *A General History of Pirates.* New York: Lyons Press.

Omerad, H.A. 1996. *Piracy in the Ancient World: An Essay in Mediterranean History.* Baltimore: Johns Hopkins Press.

Thompson, Janice E. 1996. *Mercenaries, Pirates, and Sovereigns: State Building and Extraterritorial Violence in Early Modern Europe.* Princeton, NJ: Princeton University Press.

United Nations. 1983. *The Law of the Sea: Official Text of the United Nations Convention on the Law of the Sea with Annexes.* New York: St. Martin's Press.

Vantage Systems, Inc. 1998. See Web site at <http://www.vantage-security.com>.

CHAPTER 6

"Film at 11" Crimes

Chapter 6 is devoted to crimes in the news. The idea behind this chapter was to present essays dealing with crimes of such emotional magnitude that they catch each of us open-mouthed and glued to the television. Although a number of topics fit this description, the ones selected were found most frequently in current news headlines: serial killers, terrorism, hate crimes, and school violence.

Serial killers have filled the public psyche with both terror and fascination since reports of Jack the Ripper surfaced in England in the late 1800s. His murderous prowls through dark London streets have been the focus of cinema, television, and literature. Those who care to track the serial killer of today can, on the Web at APB online <http://www.apbonline.com/serialkiller/atlas/index.html>, which includes an interactive atlas.

This site examines the spatial dimension of cases in three categories: confirmed, suspected, and undetermined. This interactive atlas allows the user to *see* where these crimes occurred on a U.S. map, and a click gives further details regarding specific locations. For instance, the Green River Killer is named for the area in Washington State where most of his victims were found. Other cases indicate that major interstates and highways also appear to be favorite routes of serial killers. Recent news events have highlighted the capture of alleged serial killer Angel Maturino Resendez, who is named the "railroad killer" (Chicago Tribune Online Edition 1999). Serial killers vary in their journey to crime. For instance, the Boston Strangler attacked victims within a certain area of that city whereas Ted Bundy committed murder from the Pacific (Washington) to the Atlantic (Florida).

In his essay "Serial Murder in the United States, 1860-1995," the United Kingdom's Christopher Missen offers a theoretical view of American serial killers from an historical perspective. Having collected data on this topic for the past 25 years, he shares his expert insights into the regional variations found in the U.S.

News reports of the second topic in the chapter, terrorist activity, always seem distant to Americans. Terrorism happens somewhere else. Figure 6-1 depicts the regional variations of international terrorist incidents from 1993 to

1998. Regions in rank order were Western Europe, Latin America, the Middle East, Asia, Eurasia, Africa, and North America. International attacks have claimed U.S. casualties; 1993 was the worst year with 1,004 citizens wounded, while 1996 saw the highest number of deaths (25). The year 1998 saw attacks on U.S. embassies in Kenya and Tanzania (U.S. Department of State 1999).

Although incidents of terrorism have occurred in the U.S., the horror of the Oklahoma City and the New York City Trade Center bombings brought it into the homes of Americans. The realization that it can happen here filled local and national news reports. In his essay, Damon Camp, an expert on domestic terrorism, highlights incidents of both right- and left-wing terrorist groups operating in the U.S. for the past 25 years.

Camp also discusses a topic closely related to terrorism in another essay on "Hate Crimes." Many of the same groups, such as the Ku Klux Klan, overlap the two categories of violence, and Camp describes the distinctions and similarities and gives an account of who is active where. Hate crime is a category that was added to the FBI's *Uniform Crime Reports* after the passage of the Hate Crimes Statistics Act of 1990. This law was amended in 1994 to include crimes motivated by a bias against persons with disabilities, and in 1996 to include church burnings (Federal Bureau of Investigation 1996). The Hate Crimes Prevention Act, passed this year (2000), allows federal investigation of hate crimes resulting in death or bodily injury. According to recent data, most incidents of hate crimes occurred in the residence. Other sites were, in order of frequency, highways, roads, alleys, or streets; schools and colleges; parking areas; and commercial office buildings (Federal Bureau of Investigation 1997).

The final essay in this section is on school violence. During the course of mapping this phenomenon, new incidents had to be added to the "final" graphic. School violence recently has been mapped in the news. ABCNEWS.com displays an interactive map showing the locations of school violence incidents from 1996 through

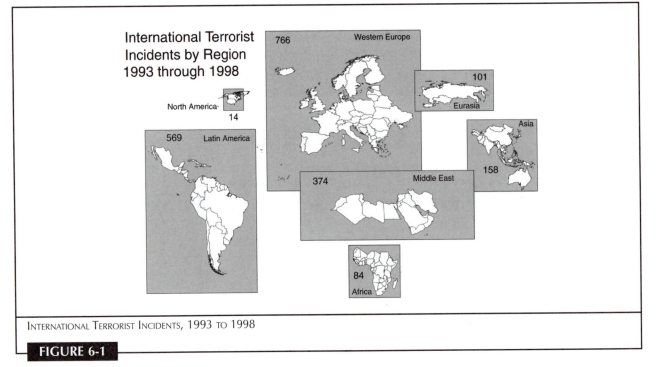

International Terrorist Incidents by Region 1993 through 1998

North America · 14

569 Latin America

766 Western Europe

101 Eurasia

Asia

158

374 Middle East

84 Africa

INTERNATIONAL TERRORIST INCIDENTS, 1993 TO 1998

FIGURE 6-1

Source: U.S. Department of State 1999.

May 1999. Details regarding the nature of the incidents are also provided for the map reader.

School violence is a subject of investigation by the academic community. At the University of Michigan, researchers identified "hot spots" of school violence in both secondary and elementary schools (Garsten 1999). Their findings revealed that violence occurs in "free-zone" areas, or locations with no adult supervision. These public areas include bathrooms, locker rooms, hallways, and school grounds. Another factor was that students outnumbered teachers by a large ratio.

In an educational document on discipline and violence in public schools, city schools reported 95 incidents of serious violence per 100,000 students compared to schools in towns with 28 per 100,000 (U.S. Department of Education 1998). This study also reported that schools in the Northeast were more likely to have controlled access to school buildings (70 percent) compared with schools in the West (46 percent), the Central (48 percent), and the Southeast (52 percent) regions.

Interestingly, most school shootings are located in town settings rather than the large inner-city areas where one expects to find this kind of violence. Another ABC News story describes the differences between the settings (Kreig 1999). Suburban and rural environments are not the safe havens they are perceived to be. One theory is that a young person who does not represent the norm can feel more isolated in a school with a homogeneous population. Kids in suburban schools kill for emotional reasons whereas kids in urban schools kill in self-defense or during the commission of another crime. Another difference is that city schools already have defense mechanisms because of the "expected"

violence, and suburban and rural schools are caught unaware.

In their essay, Pamela Riley and Joanne McDaniel from the Center for the Prevention of School Violence, discuss the evolution of this phenomenon and the problem of weapons on campus. Through case studies for the school years 1997 through 1999, the authors profile the offenders and offer common threads of behavior.

References

ABC News. 1999. *Violence in U.S. Schools.* <http://ABCNews. go.com/sections/us/DailyNews/schoolshootings990420.html>.

APB Serial Killer Bureau. 1999. *Serial Killer Atlas.* <http:// www.apbonline.com/serialkiller/atlas/index.html>.

Chicago Tribune Online Edition. 1999. "Rail Killer" Suspect Faces 2 More Charges. <http://chicagotribune...icle/0,2669,SAV-9908010132,FF.html>.

Colombia's Other Gangsters. 1995. *The Economist*, March 25: 48.

Federal Bureau of Investigation (FBI). 1997. *Uniform Crime Reports.* Hate Crimes Statistics, 1997.<http://www.fbi.gov/ucr/hc97all.pdf>.

———. 1996. *Uniform Crime Reports.* Hate Crime Statistics, 1996. <http://www.fbi.gov/ucr/hc96all.pdf>.

Garsten, Ed. 1999. Researchers Map Out School Violence "Hot Spots." *CNN Interactive*, June 4. <http:/ www.cnn.com/US/9906/04/school.danger.zone/>.

Kreig, Alison. 1999. It Can Happen Here: Are Suburban Schools More at Risk for Violence? <http://abcnews.go.com/sections/us/DailyNews/littleton_suburbkids.html>.

U.S. Department of Education. 1998. *Violence and Discipline Problems in U.S. Schools: 1996-1997.* <http://nces.ed.gov/pubs98/violence/98030003.html>.

U.S. Department of State. 1999. *Patterns of Global Terrorism: 1998.* <http://www.usis.usemb.se/terror/rpt1998/review.html>.

Serial Murder in the United States, 1860-1995

Christopher G. Missen

A serial killer is someone who has instigated and participated in at least three unlawful and unilateral murders over an indeterminate timespan, with a clear cooling-off period separating each one. Serial murderers cannot be agents of the state, or act on anyone else's behalf (Missen 2000).

Only if John and Bobby Kennedy and Martin Luther King were shot by the same assassin, who proved to be a misfit with a grudge—"a lone nut"—could the culprit have been accurately described as a serial killer. If the perpetrator were directly or indirectly carrying out the orders or wishes of the CIA, Cuban fanatics, organized crime, the Teamsters, a Texas oil cartel, or some other group or organization, the label would not be appropriate. If the assailant acted on his or her own initiative, but had some minor connection to a rogue faction within the intelligence community, the killer's proper classification would depend upon the responses of his or her superior(s). Would the assassin's actions be justified, condoned, condemned, or disowned by the person(s) in charge of the service? If the purported chief were disparaging in public, but approving in private, the executioner should not be classed as a serial killer. Only if the assassin's deeds were uncompromisingly rejected and demonstrably disavowed by those in command would the term be justified.

TABLE 6-A

SERIAL KILLERS AND HOMICIDE, 1860-1997

Serial Killers and Homicide

Year	Total Population (x mil.)	Percent Increase/decrease From Previous Decade	Homicides (x 1000)	Percent Increase/decrease From Previous Decade	Serial Killer Cases (Number)	Percent Increase/decrease From Previous Decade	Sexual Killer Cases (Number)	Percent Increase/decrease From Previous Decade	Serial Killers (Number)	Percent Increase/decrease From Previous Decade
1860-9	31		2.8		41		3		56	
1870-9	39	26	8.0	185	42	2	6	100	59	5
1880-9	50	28	6.6	-21	24	-43	4	-33	27	-146
1890-9	63	26	6.0	-9	52	46	10	150	68	152
1900-9	76	21	5.7	-5	62	19	12	20	80	18
1910-9	92	21	7.5	32	66	6	16	33	92	15
1920-9	106	15	8.8	17	115	74	34	113	187	103
1930-9	123	16	18.0	105	147	28	54	59	194	4
1940-9	132	7	12.5	-31	124	-16	65	17	175	-10
1950-9	151	14	8.2	-30	212	71	139	114	287	64
1960-9	179	19	9.6	17	363	71	240	73	448	56
1970-9	203	13	15.8	65	846	133	637	165	991	121
1980-9	227	12	23.0	46	889	5	725	24	1079	9
1990-9	249	10	23.4	2						
1997	267	7		-22						
Percent Change 1860 - 1989	632		721		2068		24,067		1826	

Note: All serial killer data provided by author.

Serial murder is a diverse phenomenon, a generic term encompassing many kinds of episodic homicidal aggression, such as repeated lethal stick-ups, medical murders, snipings, and fraudulent attempts to obtain insurance money, a spouse's estates, and so forth.

In the West today, serial murder has become increasingly identified with recurrent *lust-related* killings, while its many other distinct variants are largely disregarded. Herein, the designation lust-driven (or sexual) serial killer refers to an episodic homicidal assailant, whose murderous series includes at least one killing in which "sexual" features may be discovered at the crime scene, or are yielded up by the victim's body.

In absolute terms, a succession of linked homicides of any sort is an exceptionally rare form of human criminality, even in the U.S., where serial killers are currently responsible for about 800 deaths annually, between 60 and 70 percent of the world's total (Missen et al. 1997; Ressler and Schachtman 1992; Hickey 1991). Less than 500 of the yearly toll of serial murders in the U.S. include evidently sexual features, although approximately 75 percent of present-day American serial killers have committed at least one carnal homicide (Missen et al. 1997) (Table 6-A and Figure 6-2).

Despite their apparent numerical-demographic insignificance, serial sex murderers have become an omnipresent theme in many advanced consumer societies. The U.S. and its cultural satellites seem most affected. Why countries like the United States, the United Kingdom, Germany, France, Australia, Russia, Japan, and Canada should be most prone to the phenomenon, while such others as the Netherlands, Korea, Sweden, Ireland, New Zealand, Italy, and Switzerland have a much lower incidence, or none at all, is an important question. The answer may provide some revealing insights and thereby indicate new approaches to the problem. Similarly, regional variations within the same nation, should they prove significant, may offer additional clarification. Alternatively, such studies may muddy the already murky waters, confusing the issue still further.

The more affected states share certain conditions that do not afflict the opposite grouping, at least not to the same extent. The following factors may explain some of the major deviations:

1. **Significant Counter-Culture:** Because such counter-cultures are usually based upon a complete inversion of prevailing morality, anti-social behavior, deviance, and even the notion of sanity are recognized as relative, arbitrary standards with little absolute validity. In some cultures, this attitude may be ascribed to the pervasive influence of romanticism whereby all feelings, however negative, are deemed legitimate because they were natural. Nature, though often mysterious, cannot be wrong.

2. **High Prison Population:** Although not readily quantifiable, a figure of anything from 0.3 to 0.5 per 100,000 of the general populace—two to three times the West European average—may be considered unusually, even unnecessarily high. The U.S. rate, for instance, is 0.875 per 100,000 (Department of Justice 2000).

3. **Post-Imperial Heritage:** The right to determine the destinies of persons deemed inferior or more primitive, that was at one time taken for granted, may have permeated the national mores of former colonial powers. Some collective habits, such as "lording" it over "subject" peoples, may be hard to break.

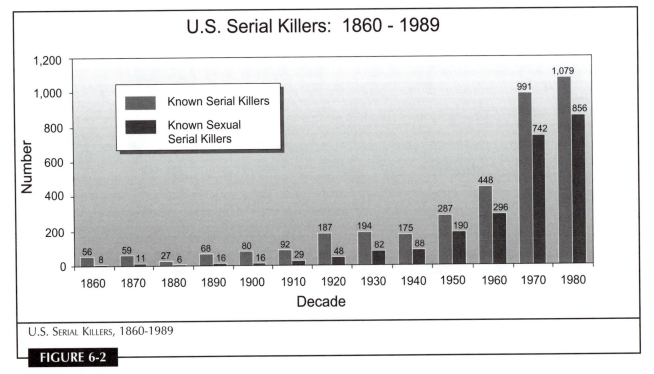

U.S. SERIAL KILLERS, 1860-1989

FIGURE 6-2

Source: Author's research.

4. **Densely Populated Urban Communities:** In such communities, neighborhood solidarity tends to break down, eventually disintegrating completely. It may be replaced by feelings of isolation, alienation, and insignificance, that undermine the individual's sense of identity and self-worth. Perhaps worse still, a culture of anomie may develop in a deprived locality, in which society's norms, standards of conduct, and values are absolutely reversed. Status symbols become taboos and the violation of taboos becomes a status symbol.

5. **Ongoing Socioeconomic Transformation:** While such transformation is often represented as widespread rejection of traditional family and social structures, the driving force behind it tends to be radical changes to the status and role of women, requiring reconstruction of established sexual identities.

6. **Great Expectations of Consumerism:** Consumerism, with its ubiquitous promotion and justification of ever greater consumption, is bound to exclude 20 to 30 percent of the population from "the good life" they see all around them. Anomie results, so the desperation and resentment of those groups and individuals consigned to the economic margins may reach homicidal intensity, as it did in "Little Italy" in New York in the 1930s.

Some or all of these criteria, albeit in modified form, may explain recurrent variations in the prevalence and nature of single and serial homicides, and may characterize a nation's geographically and historically distinct regions, such as the states of the United States. For the purposes of this study, Washington, D.C., is treated as a state. In 1990, the District incarcerated three times as many (1,602 per 100,000) of its citizens proportionately than did the highest state proper (Delaware at 526 per 100,000). Given the excessively high number of serial killers who have committed all or most of their crimes in the District—36 since 1970 (Missen 2000: 44)—some link between these two circumstances may not be beyond the bounds of possibility, although the figures may owe as much to coincidence as to correlation. (Although the 1990 figures given above seem modest by current standards, they show how rapidly the prison population is increasing. In January 2000, U.S. penal facilities reached 2 million inmates, and the rate of incarceration shows no signs of slowing.)

However, these common factors seem to exert a collective or cumulative influence upon nations. The greater the number and prominence of these features within a society, the more conducive the environment for the rearing and shaping of serial sex killers. In a few instances, the absence of just one of these prerequisites seems to have drastically curtailed the incidence of serial murder in a country. New Zealand, for example, lacks most of the above factors and has produced no serial sex killer. Countries having most or all of these aforementioned features seem more prone to sexual serial killers. Whether this susceptibility applies uniformly to all parts of the country, even the most culturally distinct, is less clear.

Like their British and German counterparts, U.S. sexual serial killers seem collectively driven by the same directional currents and patterns (Figure 6-3). In the United Kingdom (U.K.), few if any lust-driven serial killers have journeyed northwards to kill; British serial sex killers usually travel from their native North to kill in their adoptive South.

In the U.S., episodic carnal slayers tend to be born in Michigan (sometimes Ohio, Indiana, Iowa) but to kill in California (less often in Texas or Florida). Both U.S. and U.K. serial killers seldom take lives in the communities where they were born. One possible explantion for these shared geographical habits and almost instinctive homicidal migration routes may be that sexual serial killers are often ambitious, dominant, intelligent individuals. Having failed to live up to their early promise and fallen short of expectations, they in some way associate lust-related murder with upward mobility. Many serial sex slayers demonstrate powerful "glory-seeking" tendencies, having failed to live up to their youthful potential. This kind of control-driven, power-hungry serial killer detests normality and seems unable to accept obscurity. Disenchanted by and alienated from the mainstream that persistently spurned them, they are unable to renounce their desperate need to dominate. Believing they have nothing to lose, repeated carnal homicide becomes their way of retaliating against society. It may become their means of exacting revenge and of making a name for themselves (Leyton 1986; Missen 2000). Fortune-seeking has traditionally actuated the westward trek in the U.S. Desperadoes, misfits, and outlaws headed for the frontier, which symbolized and promised security to the outcast. All or none of these largely subliminal associations discussed may influence the strange directional inclinations of serial killers (Figure 6-3).

Differences: Actual and Anecdotal

Figure 6-4 shows that the number of serial killers has varied considerably from state to state during the years 1860 to 1995. At the beginning of this period, the United States was still expanding, annexing and opening up new territories that would become states. These heterogeneous areas tended to have distinctive characters due to differences of history and geography. These individual identities were so cherished that the catalyst of the Civil War was needed before all these disparate entities became an indissoluble union and a cohesive nation.

These unique political events shaped much of the character and evolution of individual states' attitudes to lawbreaking. In the wake of the Civil War, despite $10,000 rewards and their outlaw status, the James-Younger Gang became folk heroes. The "Yankee" railroads were perceived as the villains, not the marauders who robbed them at gunpoint, killing as and whomever they deemed necessary.

Legendary Texas gunfighter John Wesley Hardin was a revered figure in his native state, celebrated as the "fastest gun in the West." However, records show that more than half of Hardin's reputed 42 victims were defenseless blacks

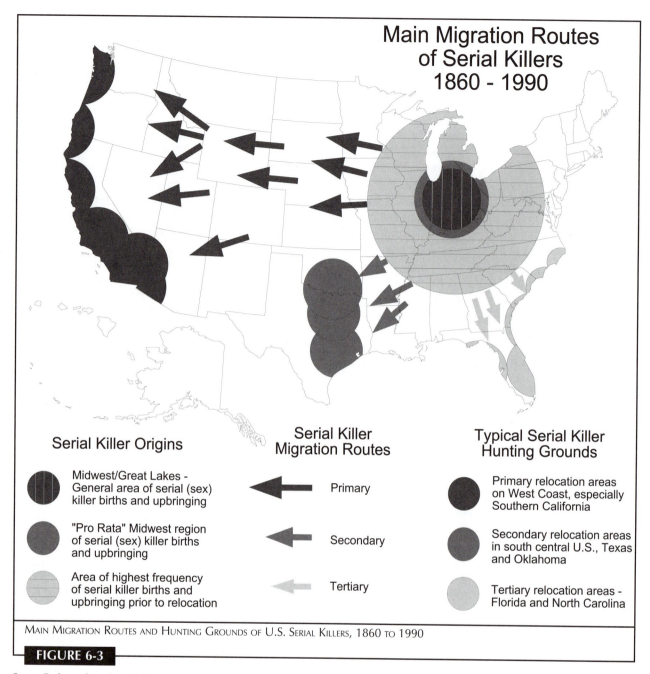

Main Migration Routes
of Serial Killers
1860 - 1990

Serial Killer Origins

- Midwest/Great Lakes - General area of serial (sex) killer births and upbringing
- "Pro Rata" Midwest region of serial (sex) killer births and upbringing
- Area of highest frequency of serial killer births and upbringing prior to relocation

Serial Killer Migration Routes

- ← Primary
- ← Secondary
- ← Tertiary

Typical Serial Killer Hunting Grounds

- Primary relocation areas on West Coast, especially Southern California
- Secondary relocation areas in south central U.S., Texas and Oklahoma
- Tertiary relocation areas - Florida and North Carolina

MAIN MIGRATION ROUTES AND HUNTING GROUNDS OF U.S. SERIAL KILLERS, 1860 TO 1990

FIGURE 6-3

Source: Redrawn from the author's original sketches.

who failed to doff their hats quickly enough, or who did not step off the sidewalk when they saw Hardin coming (Breihan 1961). Hardin's psychopathic racism, in the context of Texas during Reconstruction, did not occasion censure. It was interpreted as a sign of the former Confederate state's unbroken spirit of defiance. Such behavior might well have met an entirely different response had it occurred in contemporaneous Massachusetts. These sorts of variation are readily understood as straightforward responses to collective local experiences.

Such sociologically intelligible differences scarcely require in-depth psychological scrutiny because they hardly touch the kinds of episodic homicide typically associated with serial murder. The repetitive local idiosyncrasies of ha-

bitual lust-driven killers, lifelong poisoners, elusive metropolitan snipers, and persuasive predatory polygamists are more problematic. Why one especially rare, bizarre variant of modern serial murder defies the law of averages by recurring with improbable frequency in one particular state or region is a mystery. Then again, are these supposed peculiarities authentic, or the stuff of folklore?

One of the more credible examples of a conjectural parochial (episodic) homicidal proclivity is the ostensible connection between the State of Wisconsin and cannibalism. Cannibalism of any sort is a rare occurrence. Murdering an actual or potential sex partner to dismember then consume them for sexual stimulation is one of the rarest and most extreme manifestations of carnal violence, en-

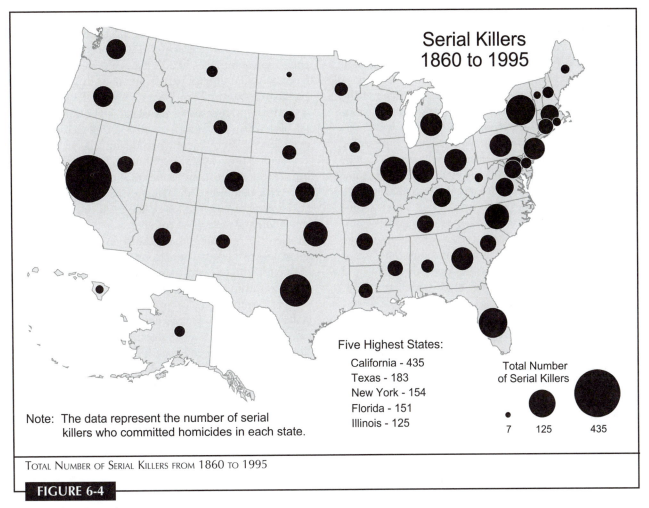

Serial Killers 1860 to 1995

Five Highest States:

California - 435
Texas - 183
New York - 154
Florida - 151
Illinois - 125

Total Number of Serial Killers

7   125   435

Note: The data represent the number of serial killers who committed homicides in each state.

TOTAL NUMBER OF SERIAL KILLERS FROM 1860 TO 1995

FIGURE 6-4

Source: Author's Research.

tailing the violation of a primal taboo. During the entire twentieth century no more than about 30 U.S. cases have been objectively verified.

A disproportionate number of the authenticated instances have taken place in Wisconsin. Ed Gein, the inspiration for Hitchcock's movie of Robert Bloch's book *Psycho*, was a native of Plainfield, Wisconsin. His contemporary successor, the late Jeffrey Dahmer, lived in Milwaukee. Another Wisconsin resident, John Weber, was an abusive husband and serial rapist who harbored a dark passion for his sister-in-law; one day, he ravished her, then cooked and ate part of her. Joachim Madler, married with two teenage children, was a 42-year-old German immigrant and doctor of science, who had settled in Wisconsin in 1967. In 1990, while his family was away for a weekend, this highly respected citizen engineered an encounter with a local adolescent. Exactly what happened is unknown. However, two days later, the boy's severed head, minus the carefully removed brain, was discovered in Madler's dustbin. Traces of brain matter were found in a saucepan. Madler insisted that he merely covered up a shooting accident. These are just four of Wisconsin's more prominent latter-day cannibals; the state has had other lesser known cases. The reasons for this type of killing are unclear, but may be related

to a love of hunting. The skinning and gutting of animals tends to be learned and mastered at an early age, so the know-how is usually present when someone decides to reclassify humans as "fair game."

Another example of a particular kind of homicidal activity connected with a certain state might be the abundance of bizarre, ostensibly motiveless serial murders in California. These recurring homicidal quirks and patterns are not necessarily confined to states. Some seem to represent regional tendencies. For instance, the vast majority of American female serial poisoners since 1860 were born (and usually raised) in the South. Many were born and raised in the Central and Eastern segments of the old Confederacy, the border states of Kentucky and Missouri, and, most frequently, Alabama, Georgia, and the Carolinas. Of perhaps 60 or more classic female mass poisoners, fewer than 10 were born on northern soil.

A similar repetitive regional phenomenon involves those few sexual serial murderers who suddenly depart from the critical intermission period between killings by going "on a rampage." Using a vehicle to move quickly from place to place, heading nowhere in particular, they commit increasingly pointless murders almost daily. An unaccountably large number of these homicidal murderers come from the Midwest, most often from Illinois or Ohio.

What specific factors, either alone or in combination, can convincingly explain why two neighboring states with many common geographic and demographic features have radically contrasting rates of serial murder? Some of the more obvious possible correlates can be excluded. The incidence of serial murder, especially lust-driven serial murder, appears to have little correspondence with the states' general homicide figures. Louisiana had the second highest general homicide level in 1995 and 1997. Virginia was third in 1995 and sixth in 1996. Alabama also ranked among the top five or six in 1994 and 1995. Yet, all three of these southern states have over the past 130 years registered a significant underrepresentation of serial killers, which is even more pronounced for *sexual* serial killers. At the same time, Washington D.C., pro rata usually records the highest or second highest ordinary homicide figures (1996/97/98) and Iowa, judged by the same criteria, is always among the lowest (1994/96). The incidence of serial murder and the numbers of its perpetrators in each state—Washington, D.C., abnormally high and Iowa unusually low—closely mirror the general (one-off) extreme homicide levels recorded by the same two states. These display two different murder rates. In few states is there such an equivalence. In most instances, any correlation is more likely to be one of inverse proportionality.

Prevalence is not an absolute, self-contained factor. A cross-reference to population is needed to establish a standard incidence rate for each state to facilitate meaningful comparisons. California, with a population of roughly 29 million, contains 12-13 percent of all present-day inhabitants of the U.S., well ahead of New York State with just over 18 million and Texas with over 17 million. At the other end of the scale, Wyoming has 468,000 residents; Washington D.C., which is regarded as a small but highly atypical area, has about 630,000 citizens; while North and South Dakota each have under 700,000 residents.

Chronological time must likewise be taken into account. Of U.S. serial murderers who were identified and captured—an estimated 10 to 20 percent of American serial killers are never caught—more emerged during the first six years of the 1970s than the total number documented in all the previous 110 years added together. The 1980s total is approximately 12 percent higher. Seventy-four percent of all the known U.S. serial killers became active in these two decades. If the 1960s are also included, the proportion rises to 83 percent (Missen 2000).

To offset these large differentials, each state's serial murderer total from 1960 to 1990 is divided into its average recorded population for those decades, thereby providing a comparable figure. South Carolina affords a convenient yardstick. Its serial murder total over the designated period is 31; dividing this figure into the state's average population over those 30 years—3,150,000—produces a *comparative* figure of around 1/100,000, a mean against which other states may be gauged. South Carolina also ranks

about mid-way between the highest and lowest states, so serial killer incidence rates may be calculated according to these fixed points. Washington D.C., for instance, with a population *average* of 450,000, if it conformed to the mean (the equivalent of level par) should have had 4 to 5 serial killers over the past 30 to 35 years. The total is actually 37, around 800 percent above the mean, a phenomenal overrepresentation, which suggests that special factors may be at work. If so, they urgently need identification.

Finding the common predisposing characteristics of the high (and low) frequency states may require the development of a new hybrid discipline, which might be termed *psycho-epidemiology*. This discipline might involve the examination and attempted correlation of numerous disparate factors, everything from population density and child abuse rates to the presence of mountain ranges or large tracts of forest in the relevant states. Currently, no one has answers or is even sure of the right questions to ask.

For example, some people's behavior, specifically their violent actions, may be affected by geographical features, such as mountains, forests, volcanoes, deserts, or prairies. The negative influence of winds like the *Mistral, Harmattan,* or *Sirocco* have been well documented over a long period. In southern France, the onset of the *Mistral* invariably coincides with a sudden climb in suicides, homicides, traffic accidents, and mental hospital admissions (Williams 1961; Levi-Strauss 1959). Their mechanism, however, remains undiscovered, so such phenomena have been largely disregarded by conventional science, although the relatively new discipline of Earth sciences may gradually attend to some of these oversights.

Many cultures, including Native American, Chinese, Australian Aboriginal, Hindu, many African traditions, and most ancient civilizations, claimed to be aware of subtle, but powerful natural energies flowing invisibly and mysteriously through the material world as catalysts, changing it, but never changing themselves. The course of one such force determines where the Chinese build their houses, how the homes should be furnished, and where each piece of furniture should be located to allow the energies to circulate favorably and bring good fortune. Cases like Ronald ("Butch") deFeo and the purportedly consecutive *Nightmare on Elm Street* and *Amityville* massacres certainly give pause for thought.

Are these possible contributory factors really so irrational and superstitious? Many scientists might say so. Social scientists examine the individual human, constitutional, cultural, and environmental causes of violence, but no one knows for sure that these are not the marginal influences, while the natural and preternatural phenomena may be the pre-eminent determinants.

Similarly, how and to what degree do individual human susceptibilities, collective values and movements, and different social settings interact with forces of nature? Little research has been done on these possible connections in modern times. Certainly, none of the orthodox explanations for variations in levels of violence is wholly convincing.

Conclusion

If the states of the United States are graded purely quantitatively, the number of serial killers active within their individual borders is broadly in line with absolute population levels. Nevertheless, sundry exceptions and anomalies preclude the formulation of any general rules. Comprehensive explanations, orthodox or unorthodox, for arithmetical disparities in the regional prevalence of both serial killers and their killings are conspicuous by their absence. The topic has scarcely been discussed, let alone examined methodically and the results recorded. This small survey may have helped to establish the facts, which was its main purpose. Now that significant differences have been shown to exist, the next step should be to account for them, using scientific means.

Note

My own research has opened up previously unexplored territory. It has been a protracted, laborious, and time-consuming business, taking up much of the last 25 years. I have located and recorded every American, British, German, etc., serial murder case that I could find in such extant sources as U.S. newspapers, journals, magazines, books, TV shows, trial transcripts, and archives. Each account was independently cross-referenced and finally, in the vast majority of instances, checked with someone close to the case. Among those kind enough to extend their assistance to me were law enforcement officers, staff members of district attorneys' offices, medical examiners and their deputies and technicians, the Library of Congress and its obliging personnel, occasionally friends and family of victims or perpetrators, and, most helpful of all, crime staff reporters, free-lance journalists, and professional crime writers. Without this help, I could not have constructed the world's largest database of serial killers. About 70 percent of the 3,500 or so I have documented committed some or all of their homicides in the U.S.

References

Ashton-Wolfe, Henry. 1927. *Outlaws of Modern Days*. London: Cassell & Company Limited.

Breihan, Carl. 1961. *Great Gunfighters of the West*. New York: John Long Limited (Arrow Books).

Canter, David V. 1994. *Criminal Shadows: Inside the Mind of a Serial Killer*. London: HarperCollins.

Godwin, John. 1978. *Murder USA: The Ways We Kill Each Other*. New York: Ballantyne.

Harris, Marvin. 1962. *Cows, Pigs, Wars and Witches: The Riddles of Culture*. New York: Random House.

Hickey, Eric. 1991. *Serial Murderers and Their Victims*. Pacific Grove, CA: Brooks/Cole.

King, Veronica. 1924. *Problems of American Crime*. London: Heath Cranton.

Levi-Strauss, Claude. 1959. *Totemism*. London: Routledge & Keegan Paul.

Leyton, Elliot. 1986. *Compulsive Killers (in UK—Hunting Humans)*. New York: New York University Press.

Missen, Christopher G. 2000. *Taking Life: A Behavioural Approach to the Classification of Serial Killers*. Virgin (pending).

Missen, Christopher G., Canter, David V., and Samantha Hodge. 1997. Are Serial Killers Special? *Policing Today*, December: 62-69.

Missen, Christopher G., and Samantha Hodge. 1996a. Geographical Facets of Serial Murder. *Journal of Environmental Psycholology*, June.

———. 1996b. *Environmental Range of U.S. Serial Killers*. Transcript of BPS presentation. April.

Nash, Jay Robert. 1973. *Bloodletters and Badmen*. New York: Evans.

Radzinowicz, Sir Leon, and Joan King. 1977. *The Growth of Crime*. London: Hamish Hamilton.

Ressler, Robert, and Tom Schachtman. 1992. *Whoever Fights Monsters*. London: Simon & Schuster (Pocket Books).

Whitman, Howard. 1952. *Terror in the Streets*. New York: The Dial Press.

Williams, Alan. 1961. *Barbousse*. Harmondsworth, Middlesex: Penguin.

Domestic Terrorism

Damon D. Camp

Domestic terrorism, and the impact of terrorist acts upon the political and social forces of everyday life in the United States, have garnered increasing attention over the last several decades. Although concern over terrorism seems to have its own ebb and flow, the problem will continue to be a thorny one that commands constant attention. Almost every major political and social event staged in this and other countries takes into consideration the "terrorism factor." Plans are made, training is conducted, and precautions are undertaken to thwart a potential "terrorist" attack. Agencies respond to the threat of terrorists in a host of ways, taking both reactive and pro-active measures. In addition, legislation has attempted to prevent certain acts through proscription, and to deter and punish via prosecution and conviction.

However, caught in the web of these various measures is an array of constitutional and other issues. The concept of the "traditional terrorist" has been expanded to encompass far more than the Marxist or Nihilist group with "overthrow" on its mind. Currently, the concept includes a wide array of groups that use terror to promote their political cause or even to reach more hedonistic goals.

Modern Terrorism

Modern terrorism is characterized by three elements: (1) violence or the threat of violence is used to intimidate, (2) random attacks on "innocent" non-combatants create a sense of terror, dread, and intense fear, and (3) this fear is used to force persons in authority to respond in ways that are contrary to the norm (National Advisory Commission 1976). The Federal Bureau of Investigation (FBI) defines terrorism in a similar fashion: "The unlawful use of force or violence to intimidate or coerce a government, the civilian population, or any segment thereof, in furtherance of political or social goals" (Federal Bureau of Investigation 1991: 25).

Domestic terrorism in this country can be divided into four categories. The first two include the major political movements: the Right Wing and the Left Wing. The third category contains a variety of "issue-oriented groups" that represent everything from Armenian nationalism to environmental protectionism. The fourth classification embodies a wide range of "cults," which are mainly religious in nature, and an assortment of "gangs," which range from those whose members ride motorcycles and terrorize small towns to street gangs whose members terrify neighborhoods. All are different and far too numerous to examine in detail. However, as Figure 6-5 indicates, all four classes have an impact on American lifestyles. The geographic distribution of terrorist incidents from 1990 through 1996 appears to be random, occurring sporadically in various regions of the country. However, the West's three incidents rank it higher than the other regions, if only marginally. The South and the Midwest have two each and the Northeast only one.

This is clearly represented in the April 19, 1995, Oklahoma City bombing as well as in the bombings in Tacoma in 1993 and in Spokane in 1996. Evidence of left-wing terrorism can be found in Urbana, Illinois, in 1993 and in Fresno, California, in 1991. Issue-oriented groups, such as the Animal Liberation Front and the Mexican Revolutionary Movement, are represented as well. Finally, cult activity, like that of David Koresh and the Branch Davidians in Waco, Texas (not shown in Figure 6-5), also occurred as did much gang-related violence. A general review of each category along with an examination of recent activities of specific groups should provide a representation of the phenomenon.

Right-wing extremism contains the largest assortment of groups and poses perhaps the greatest threat today. The bombing of the Alfred P. Murrah Federal Building in Oklahoma City in April 1995 (Kushner 1998) as well as the search for alleged bomber Eric Robert Rudolph (Pressley 1999) underscore the currency and significance of the threat posed by the Right Wing.

The "Far Right," as it is often called, represents probably the largest collection of domestic violent extremist groups in the country. Members of the extreme "Right" are not new to domestic terrorism. For example, the Ku Klux Klan (see essay on "Hate Crimes" in this chapter), in its various forms, has been involved in American politics since the late nineteenth century. According to the Anti-Defamation League, membership in the Klan has declined, although its notoriety and the attention paid to its actions has not (Anti-Defamation League 1996). Also included in this general area are Neo-Nazi organizations and other white supremacist groups. While these are clearly aligned with the political Right, many also possess particular extremist views.

Left-wing groups, like their conservative counterparts, have been on the American scene for decades and are veterans at promoting extremist views. Their orientation is mainly Marxist. Many of the groups in this category are loosely connected with activists from the 1960s, and they engage in a wide range of behaviors. Since 1980, the number and intensity of leftist groups has appeared to increase.

The belief systems of Far Left groups are more diverse than their right-wing counterparts and vary greatly from

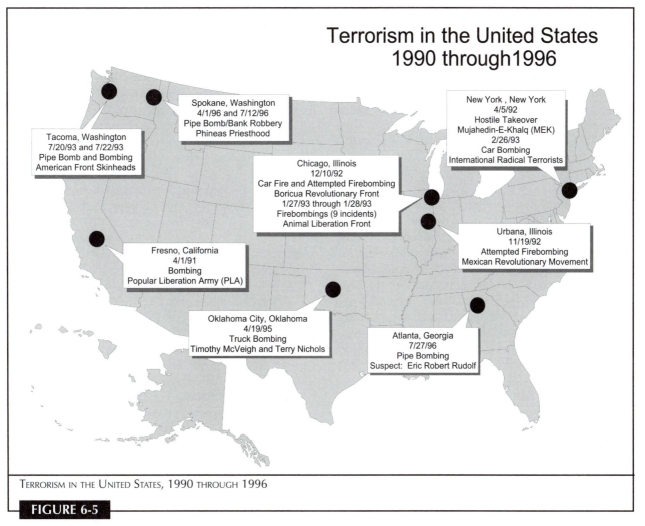

Terrorism in the United States 1990 through1996

Tacoma, Washington
7/20/93 and 7/22/93
Pipe Bomb and Bombing
American Front Skinheads

Spokane, Washington
4/1/96 and 7/12/96
Pipe Bomb/Bank Robbery
Phineas Priesthood

New York , New York
4/5/92
Hostile Takeover
Mujahedin-E-Khalq (MEK)
2/26/93
Car Bombing
International Radical Terrorists

Chicago, Illinois
12/10/92
Car Fire and Attempted Firebombing
Boricua Revolutionary Front
1/27/93 through 1/28/93
Firebombings (9 incidents)
Animal Liberation Front

Urbana, Illinois
11/19/92
Attempted Firebombing
Mexican Revolutionary Movement

Fresno, California
4/1/91
Bombing
Popular Liberation Army (PLA)

Oklahoma City, Oklahoma
4/19/95
Truck Bombing
Timothy McVeigh and Terry Nichols

Atlanta, Georgia
7/27/96
Pipe Bombing
Suspect: Eric Robert Rudolf

TERRORISM IN THE UNITED STATES, 1990 THROUGH 1996

FIGURE 6-5

Source: Terrorism in the United States, 1996. Federal Bureau of Investigation.

group to group. However, common threads seem to run through most radical leftist organizations. Most are extremely anti-government; they are fervent revolutionaries; and many groups focus on a specific issue or set of concerns. They object to many of the same governmental and political entities that their conservative counterparts oppose, but for different reasons.

Whereas right-wing groups seek to diffuse federal power, and to a degree state power, to thereby localize control, left-wing organizations strive to replace current structures with socialist/communist forms of government. Extremists on the Left believe that the current government is corrupt and founded on capitalist principles that perpetuate domination by an elite upper class. Furthermore, leftists subscribe to the belief that the majority of the people are subjected to rules and regulations that subjugate them to positions that are tantamount to servitude (Klehr 1988).

Those on the extreme Left also believe that the system is so corrupt and so infected with capitalism that a complete overhaul in government is required. This belief leads to the second common thread that runs through most Far Left groups—a fervent devotion to revolution that is often almost a religion. Essentially, being a revolutionary means

a general rejection of the government in power and a belief that it should be overthrown. Many traditional left-wing proponents viewed themselves as "revolutionaries" at war with the "establishment." In the mid-1970s, when members of the Weather Underground Organization (WUO) were being pursued by law enforcement officers across the nation, the WUO made an "underground" film that had the producer interviewing Kathy Bodine, Bernadine Dohrn, Billy Ayers, and others. During that film, they described themselves as revolutionaries at war with the U.S. government (Smith 1994).

The Weather Underground claimed responsibility for a series of violent attacks during the late 1960s and early 1970s, including a number that occurred in Chicago: violence connected to the 1968 Democratic Convention; the bombing of a police monument on October 6, 1969; and the "Days of Rage," October 8-10, 1969. The Days of Rage involved three nights of rioting, millions of dollars of damage, and the arrest of 75 WUO members whose collective bail was in excess of $2.5 million (Collier and Horowitz 1982). Other WUO activities entailed an attempted bombing of the judge presiding over the trial of the Chicago Seven (which included Black Panther Bobby Seale, who was alleged to be responsible for inciting the 1968 Democratic Convention riots) and a successful bombing of the U.S. Capitol in March 1971 (Castellucci 1986).

The third common characteristic of many left-wing groups is that they are often issue or "cause" specific. In some cases, the motive may be broad-based and focus on structural changes in government. In others, the focus may be on a concern such as the independence of a political entity. Furthermore, some groups may focus on a specific issue, such as animal rights, nuclear energy, or environmental pollution.

Like their right-wing counterparts, most groups on the Far Left promote their views through rhetoric and are mostly nonviolent (Klehr 1988). However, activists on the Left have engaged in criminal behavior and acts of violence to further their cause. The FBI has linked violent terrorist activities to a variety of left-wing groups, including the Communist Workers Party, the Revolutionary Communist Youth Brigade, the May 19th Communist Organization, the Black Brigade, the United Freedom Fighters, the New Afrika Freedom Fighters, the Armed Resistance Unit, and the Red Guerrilla Resistance (Federal Bureau of Investigation 1985).

Although little violent activity was attributed to the Left Wing in the 1990s, this does not mean that members of the radical Left are dormant. Several former fugitives who were once associated with the WUO have surfaced and turned themselves in to the authorities. The most recent was Jeffrey Powell, who after 25 years on the run, surrendered on January 6, 1994. Powell, who was one of several WUO members involved in the "Days of Rage" in Chicago in 1968, was fined $500, assessed $210 in court costs, and placed on probation for 18 months (Davis 1994). Just four months earlier, Katherine Ann Power surrendered in Boston after being on the run for 23 years (Former Fugitive Says Life on the Run Was Unbearable 1994). A Brandeis University student in the 1960s who became involved in radical leftist anti-war activities, Ms. Power drove the getaway car in a 1970 Boston bank robbery where a police officer was killed (Ex-Fugitive Trades Self-Imprisonment 1993). She pleaded guilty to manslaughter charges and was sentenced to an eight-year prison term (United Press International 1994). Ms. Power gained additional notoriety when interviewed from her jail cell by Barbara Walters for a segment of ABC's *20/20* (The Fugitive 1994).

Patronage and Special Interest Groups

In addition to the Left and Right Wing, a number of organizations engage in terrorist activities that are often political in nature but that are not easily characterized as either Left or Right. These groups can be divided further into two distinct categories: patronage groups and special interest groups.

Patronage groups generally consist of organizations interested either in seeking a forum from which to promote their crusade or in providing direct support for their cause. However, they use the United States as a "platform" to voice their views or attack their enemies. The first sub-category includes government-oriented organizations (either pro or anti) that promote independence for Puerto Rico (Macheteros and FALN) and other nations (White 1991). Other groups support the Armenian cause, oppose Libya or Iran, or are anti-Cuban, such as the Alpha 66 and Omega 7 associations (Polland 1988). The above groups could best be classified as "forum seekers" who use free-speech opportunities in the United States to oppose the policies of other nations; they use this country as a stage to voice their views.

While these groups have particular political objectives, other similar groups are more difficult to classify because their thrust is more pro-cause or pro-people than pro- or anti-government. Groups like the Jewish Defense League/American Revenge Committee and Jewish Direct Action typify this type of "support group." The American Indian Movement (AIM) could also be so classified. Like their government-targeted counterparts, they too are difficult to classify as either Right Wing or Left Wing. However, their cause is often specific. Some of these groups have been classified as terrorist. During the early 1980s, the FBI (1985) considered the Jewish Defense League (JDL) to be one of the most active terrorist groups in the country.

The JDL was founded in New York City by Rabbi Meir Kahane in 1968 to protest Soviet mistreatment of Jews, to protect elderly and other Jewish citizens against anti-Semites, and to support the Jewish state of Israel (Polland 1988). In response to the New York City teachers' strike of 1968, which pitted predominately Jewish teachers against militant blacks wanting to gain greater control over their schools, the JDL made headlines by marching though the streets with baseball bats. Ostensibly marching to protest attacks on elderly Jews, the JDL blossomed in membership (Friedman 1988). During its first years of existence, the JDL carried out a series of demonstrations against the Soviet Union, Arabs, and the Black Panthers. Between 1977 and 1986, JDL members were alleged to be involved in over 40 acts of terrorism (Vetter and Perlstein 1991).

It is believed that disruption of the Middle East peace talks was behind the bombing of the World Trade Center in New York City in 1992. Extremists connected to a New Jersey Muslim cleric planted a bomb that killed six people, injured over a thousand others, and did millions of dollars in damage. Although not directly linked to any known extremist organization, the bombing was considered a terrorist attempt to protest U.S. support for Israel and the Middle East peace process. On March 4, 1994, four Arabs were convicted in a New York federal court of conspiracy, assault, and various weapons charges and face life terms for their involvement in the bombing (Neumeister 1994). The fundamentalist Muslim leader connected to the bombing, Sheik Omar Abdel-Rahman, still awaits trial for a related plot to bomb several other buildings and tunnels in the New York City area (Plevin 1994).

Special interest groups form around issues such as abortion, AIDS, and the environment. Distinctive issues cause either the formulation of new interest groups or create a focal point upon which established groups may focus their attention. Normally, such groups engage in peaceful, legal activities to voice their support or opposition for a particular cause. However, like patronage groups, they also sometimes engage in criminal and terrorist activities.

An example of issue-group activism is Earth First!, an environmentalist organization formed in 1980 (Parfit 1990). Embracing the philosophy of "deep ecology" (no living creature has a greater claim to its natural habitat than the next), Earth First! began a campaign to disrupt the efforts of loggers and developers. Using a technique known as "monkey-wrenching" or "ecotage," group members have been accused of pulling up survey stakes, wrecking earth-moving equipment, and spiking trees (Murphy and McCulloch 1991).

Members of Earth First! were also linked to a 1990 car bomb incident in Oakland, California. Judi Bari and Darryl Cherney were injured when a bomb exploded in their car. Police believed that the two, who were the main organizers of a series of demonstrations set for that summer, had constructed a pipe bomb that detonated prematurely (Deringer 1990). Earth First! claimed that the two leaders were targets of an attack. Bari and Cherney have since filed a multi-million-dollar lawsuit against agents of the FBI and a number of local California agencies responsible for inquiring into the bombing. The suit asks for monetary damages and an injunction compelling federal authorities to fully investigate the case (Deringer 1991).

Another type of special interest group is represented by a collection of pro-life radicals, most notably, Operation Rescue, Lambs of Christ, and Rescue America. Opposing abortion on moral or religious grounds, these groups normally have three primary goals: (1) shutting down abortion clinics, (2) drawing attention to the issue in the press, and (3) paralyzing the criminal justice system by forcing it to deal with massive numbers of demonstrators (Nathanson 1989).

Pro-life radicals have been responsible for numerous deadly threats (Faux 1990), bombings (McKeegan 1992), and numerous other terrorist acts. Figure 6-6 shows incidents of violence against abortion providers that occurred between 1984 and 1998. Since 1977, over 23,000 documented incidents of violence were perpetrated against abortion providers, including 6 murders, 39 bombings, 150 arsons, 104 assaults, 131 death threats, and 712 acts of vandalism (National Abortion Federation 1998). Violent acts against abortion providers have topped 100 in each of the last seven years and peaked in 1993 at 437.

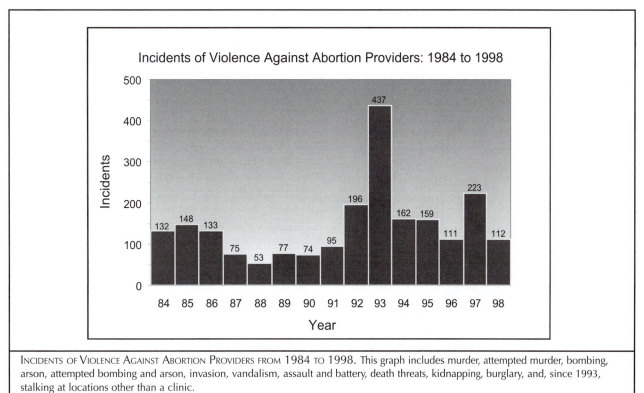

INCIDENTS OF VIOLENCE AGAINST ABORTION PROVIDERS FROM 1984 TO 1998. This graph includes murder, attempted murder, bombing, arson, attempted bombing and arson, invasion, vandalism, assault and battery, death threats, kidnapping, burglary, and, since 1993, stalking at locations other than a clinic.

FIGURE 6-6

Source: National Abortion Federation, 1998.

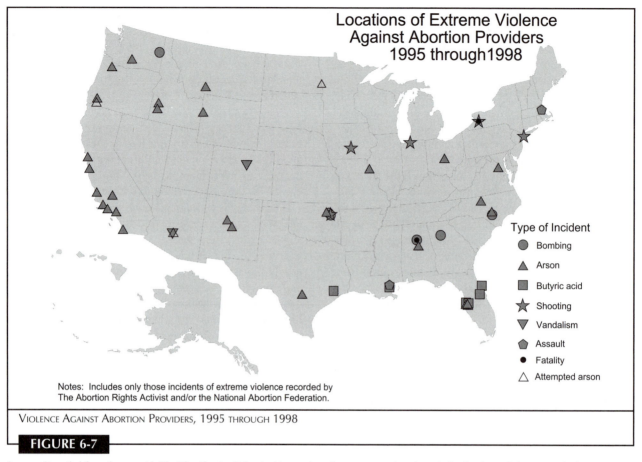

Locations of Extreme Violence
Against Abortion Providers
1995 through 1998

Type of Incident

● Bombing
▲ Arson
■ Butyric acid
★ Shooting
▼ Vandalism
⬟ Assault
• Fatality
△ Attempted arson

Notes: Includes only those incidents of extreme violence recorded by
The Abortion Rights Activist and/or the National Abortion Federation.

VIOLENCE AGAINST ABORTION PROVIDERS, 1995 THROUGH 1998

FIGURE 6-7

Sources: Compiled from data provided by *The Abortion Rights Activist* at <http://www.cais.com/agm/main/index.html> and the National Abortion Federation at <http://www.prochoice.org>.

Figure 6-7 tracks violence against abortion providers. These acts of violence have been spread throughout the country with a heavy concentration of arson in the West, especially in California. Butyric acid attacks along the Gulf Coast, specifically in Florida, Louisiana, and Texas, illustrate a regional cluster. Shootings are prevalent in the Northeast and North Central part of the country. Table 6-B provides the reader with additional geographic and temporal information on each incident.

Perhaps the most notorious of these incidents was the murder of Dr. David Gunn outside a Pensacola abortion clinic. Michael Griffin was accused of killing Dr. Gunn during an anti-abortion demonstration at the Pensacola Women's Medical Services Clinic on March 10, 1993. Griffin, who allegedly admitted shooting Gunn to a police sergeant, later was tried for first degree murder ("I Shot Him," Police Quote Abortion Foe 1994).

A final example of an activist special interest group is the AIDS Coalition to Unleash Power (ACT-UP). Founded in 1987 by Larry Kramer (Cowley 1990), ACT-UP claims some 40 chapters, and has as its goal the use of direct action to end the AIDS crisis (Kenkelen 1989). Documented activities of ACT-UP include the disruption of Catholic masses and defacing church property (Kenkelen 1989), disruption of the filming of the movie *Basic Instinct*, and vandalism of the director's home (Leo 1992).

Cult and Gang Terrorism

Unlike the issue groups or members of right- or left-wing extremist organizations, cult and gang followers are generally more egocentric than altruistic in nature. Often adhering to unusual doctrines, these individuals justify their actions not by political righteousness, but rather by devotion to a way of life.

Numerous groups and movements can be categorized as cults and gangs that represent domestic extremism and that have their own belief system. However, certain common characteristics bond these various groups together. These common characteristics include extreme religious or hedonistic beliefs; restrictive group membership, often including an elaborate initiation procedure; and the use of violence and terrorism to enforce internal control as well as external obedience.

Religious groups that fit this description abound. One such group is the Black Separatists (Figure 6-8). They are found in 18 states, with Massachusetts and California having the highest number. The map shows heavy concentrations in the South and Northeast. Another example is the black religious group that follows Yahweh ben Yahweh, formally Hulon Mitchell, Jr., of Oklahoma, who claims to be the Messiah of the lost black tribe of Israel. The Yahwehs,

TABLE 6-B

VIOLENCE AGAINST ABORTION PROVIDERS, 1995 THROUGH 1998

VIOLENCE AGAINST ABORTION PROVIDERS			
STATE	CITY	TYPE	DATE
Alabama		arson	Jul-97
Alabama	Birmingham	bomb, murder, attempted murder	Jan-98
Arizona	Tempe	vandalism	Sep-96
Arizona	Phoenix	attempted arson	Dec-98
California	Ventura	arson	Feb-95
California	Santa Barbara	arson	Feb-95
California	San Luis Obispo	arson	Feb-95
California	Santa Cruz	arson	Feb-95
California	San Francisco	arson	Feb-95
California	North Hollywood	arson	Mar-97
California	Bakersfield	arson	Mar-97
California	San Diego	arson	Apr-98
Colorado	Denver	vandalism	Mar-95
Florida	St. Petersburg	arson	Aug-95
Florida	St. Petersburg	arson	Aug-95
Florida	St. Petersburg	arson	Nov-95
Florida	Orlando	butyric acid	May-98
Florida	Daytona Beach	butyric acid	May-98
Florida	Miami	butyric acid	May-98
Florida	Clearwater	butyric acid	May-98
Florida	St. Petersburg	butyric acid	May-98
Georgia	Atlanta	bomb	Jan-97
Idaho	Boise	arson	May-96
Idaho	Boise	arson	Jul-96
Indiana	South Bend	shooting	Jan-95
Iowa	Des Moines	shooting	Sep-95
Louisiana	New Orleans	attempted murder	Dec-96
Louisiana	New Orleans	butyric acid	Jul-98
Massachusetts	Brookline	assault	Mar-95
Michigan	Warren	shooting	Apr-95
Missouri	Hannibal	arson	Nov-96
Montana	Bozeman	arson	Apr-97
New Mexico	Albuquerque	arson	Jan-95
New Mexico		arson	Feb-95
New York	Long Island	shooting	Jan-95
New York	Amherst	shooting, murder	Oct-98
North Carolina	Greensboro	arson	May-97
North Carolina	Fayetteville	arson	Sep-98
North Carolina	Fayetteville	bomb	Oct-98
North Dakota	Fargo	attempted arson	Apr-98
Ohio	Columbus	arson	Aug-98
Oklahoma	Broken Arrow	bomb	Sep-96
Oklahoma	Tulsa	arson	Jan-97
Oklahoma	Tulsa	bomb	Jan-97
Oklahoma	Tulsa	shooting	Feb-97
Oregon	Grants Pass	arson	Aug-95
Oregon	Grants Pass	attempted arson	Jan-96
Oregon	Portland	arson	May-97
Texas	San Antonio	arson	Jan-98
Texas	Houston	butyric acid	Jul-98
Virginia	Falls Church	arson	Feb-97
Washington	Spokane	bomb	Jul-96
Washington	Yakima	arson	May-97
Wyoming	Jackson	arson	Sep-95

Sources: Compiled from data provided by *The Abortion Rights Activist* at <http://www.cais.com/agm/main/index.html> and the National Abortion Federation at <http://www.prochoice.org>.

established in Miami, Florida, in 1979, claim more than 20,000 members nationwide in more than 45 cities. Their Temple of Love has amassed business and real estate holdings of over $8 million since 1981. Although the group has been credited with cleaning up drug-plagued neighborhoods and numerous community projects, they also have been accused of committing bizarre murders and mutilations. Yahweh ben Yahweh was sentenced to 18 years in federal prison for fire-bombing and murder (Florida Sect Leader Convicted 1992).

Finally, certain gang activity could well be considered violent extremism. Dangerous motorcycle gangs, such as the "Outlaws," the "Hell's Angels," and the "Pagans," easily fit into this category. They totally reject generally accepted social lifestyles and embrace instead a hedonistic existence. Dangerous motorcycle gangs have been known to terrorize entire communities, kill police officers, run drugs, and launder money, among other things. They rely on their unusual lifestyles and terrifying persona to intimidate outsiders. They entrust internal discipline to a rigid code of conduct that metes out harsh punishments for disobedience and death for disloyalty.

Street gangs operate in a similar fashion but tend to rely more heavily on violence and terrorism to force compliance with their demands. Like outlaw biker gangs, they embrace counter cultural goals and lifestyles, and have rigid "entrance" requirements. This type of domestic extremism is perhaps best exemplified in the characteristics of Asian gangs or tongs, which are involved in gambling, extortion, prostitution, and drug trafficking (Ko-lin 1990).

Responding to Domestic Terrorism

Over time, domestic terrorism has passed through three stages of importance: no problem, major problem, and a situational problem. Prior to the 1950s, domestic extremism occasioned little or no concern. While there was great fear of potential foreign infiltration, little attention was given to internal disruption. Federal and state intelligence networks were established to deal primarily with external threats. By the 1960s, a well-grounded federal system existed and, with the beginning of a national intelligence network, state and local units were established. This system, which allowed the FBI to take the lead in creating and maintaining files on local left- and right-wing groups and individuals, provided a mechanism by which intelligence information could be gathered, stored, and retrieved electronically, and exchanged among law enforcement agencies. The result was a highly sophisticated networking system (for that time) that was capable of tracking individuals across the nation. After Watergate and the Senate Intelligence Hearings, this apparatus was dismantled for the most part. As a result of the Freedom of Information Act and the Privacy Act and several court decisions such as *U.S. v. U.S. District Court* (1972), the entire domestic terrorism intelligence system in the U.S. underwent a radical change.

This change resulted in, among other things, an apparent dividing of the territory among federal, state, and local agencies. At present, federal agencies concentrate on groups perpetrating federal crimes and this concentration seems to be along traditional jurisdictional lines. The FBI,

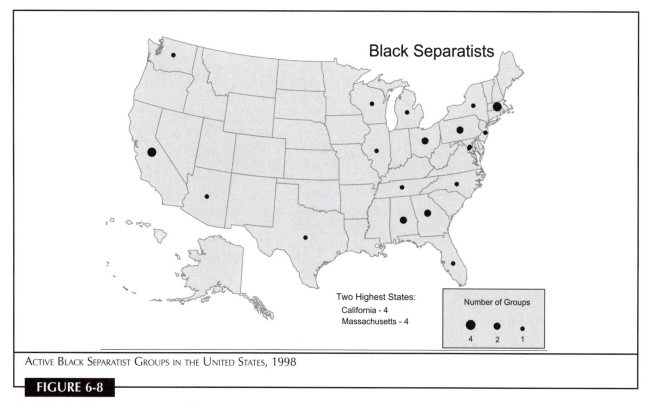

Two Highest States:
California - 4
Massachusetts - 4

Number of Groups

4   2   1

ACTIVE BLACK SEPARATIST GROUPS IN THE UNITED STATES, 1998

FIGURE 6-8

Source: Southern Poverty Law Center available online at http://www.splcenter.org/splc.html.

for example, was instrumental in the eventual arrest of a number of individuals in various groups.

State agencies, on the other hand, have been investigating various local right- and left-wing groups, particularly Neo-Nazi and Klan elements. Local agencies do little broad-based intelligence gathering. However, many are beginning to concentrate on traditional quasi-terrorist groups as well as more nontraditional ones. This change is due largely to the expansion of the view of terrorism to include a wide range of violent extremism. Many larger police departments have "specialists" who deal variously with the local Ku Klux Klan, or related groups, as well as with traditional left-wing activists. Extending a watchful eye to these extremist groups is justified by their rhetoric, affiliations, and potential.

Some law enforcement specialists now concentrate on terrorists *per se*, such as satanist groups, bikers, and certain issue-oriented groups. Sources are developed and intelligence is gathered on group activities. As a result, when the Klan marches in a small Georgia community, enforcement officials outnumber demonstrators sometimes 10-to-1.

Legislative efforts in this area seem to be divided into two major categories. One category deals with traditional criminal statutes and the other concerns special "hate crime" laws. At present, few federal "anti-terrorism" laws exist, mainly proscriptions against specific acts of terror. When legislation of this nature is passed, it normally appears in one of two forms, policy dealing with broad terrorist enterprises or legislation focusing on terrorist acts. In the first instance, the U.S. Congress has passed or amended several pieces of legislation that prohibit certain trade or assistance practices with countries fostering terrorism (Alexander and Nanes 1986).

By the mid 1970s, 16 states were identified by the National Governors' Association (1979) as having some type of anti-terrorist legislation. These state laws either enhanced the penalty for an existing crime or created specialized language for general conduct, such as making terrorist threats (Georgia Code Ann. 1974). While both of these types of measures drew attention to the problem of terrorism, neither provided much legislative assistance in combating the problem.

This lack of specific legislation may have been due to the theoretical underpinnings of our system. Because of its heavy reliance on due process and its philosophical orientation toward concepts such as the presumption of innocence and propriety (Newman 1986), the system has discouraged specialized legislation and selective enforcement. Therefore, proscribing against extremist views and actions like racism, anti-Semitism, and even anti-government rhetoric has been slow.

Instead of relying on these special types of measures, the agents of the criminal justice system have had to depend on legislation based primarily on general proscribed conduct. However, when the system has attempted to prosecute extremists for "terrorism-like" behavior, it has been far less successful. Incarceration not only may not discour-age extremism, but also may actually contribute to its early growth and foster its development.

However, efforts to reduce the effects of extremism have not been useless. A number of states in recent years have adopted statutes geared toward deterring certain types of terroristic behavior. Often at the urging of the Anti-Defamation League (ADL) of B'nai B'rith, these laws, which bar what are collectively known as "hate crimes" or "bias crimes," are often patterned after ADL model statutes. However, much of the legislation so categorized is neither new, nor is it really aimed at the type of extremist behavior discussed here.

Conclusions

Considerable concern is focused on the potential use of weapons of mass destruction and on a repeat performance of the bombings that occurred in New York and Kansas City. The potential for nuclear terrorism increases as the stability of the former Soviet Union decreases, providing the oil-rich Middle East terrorist with a place to acquire apocalyptic weapons. Biological and chemical agents are relatively easy to acquire or develop. The essential ingredients needed to make truck bombs, like those used in the World Trade Center and Oklahoma City bombings, can be purchased openly. Web sites on the Internet provide simple directions for making serin gas, pipe bombs, and other deadly devices.

With the possibility of terrorism on a mass scale, government agencies are preparing for the worst and focusing on dangerous groups. The geographic display of information on terrorist groups may assist in these efforts by identifying heavy concentrations of activity and locations of home bases.

References

Alexander, Y., and A.S. Nanes, eds.1986. *Legislative Responses to Terrorism*. Dordrecht, The Netherlands: Martinous Nijhoff Publishers.

Anti-Defamation League. 1996. *Danger: Extremism*. New York: Anti-Defamation League.

Bromley, D. 1991. The Satanic Cult Scare. *Culture and Society* 50: 55-66.

Castellucci, J. 1986. *The Big Dance*. New York: Dodd Mead & Co.

Coates, J. 1987. *Armed and Dangerous*. New York: Noonday Press.

Collier, P., and D. Horowitz. 1982. Doing It: The Inside Story of the Rise and Fall of the Weather Underground. *Rolling Stone*, September 30: 19-100.

Cowley, G. 1990. ACT-UP Acts Out: Crossing the "Revulsion Threshold." *Commonwealth*, September 14: 476.

Davis, R. 1994. Days of Rage More Like a Convulsion That Became a Blip in History. *Chicago Tribune*, January 8: 3.

Deringer, E. 1991. Earth First Leaders Sue Authorities over Oakland Blast; Police Accused of Not Looking for Bomber. *San Francisco Chronicle*, May 22: A17.

———. 1990. Earth First! as "Not Scared" Anti-Logging Group Says Bomb Was Planted, Won't Deter Efforts. *San Francisco Chronicle*, May 24: A4.

Ex-Fugitive Trades Self-Imprisonment. 1993. *St. Louis Post-Dispatch*, September 17: 1A.

Faux, M. 1990. *Crusaders: Voices from the Abortion Front*. Syracuse, NY: Carol Press.

Federal Bureau of Investigation, FBI Terrorist Research and Analytical Unit. 1991. *Terrorism in the United States: 1990*. Washington, DC: U.S. Department of Justice.

———. 1985. *Analysis of Claimed Terrorist Incidents in the U.S.: 1981-1985*. Washington, DC: U.S. Department of Justice.

Florida Sect Leader Convicted. 1992. *Facts on File World News Digest*, June 11: 428 B1.

Former Fugitive Says Life on the Run Was Unbearable. 1994. Orlando Sentinel, February 11: 12A.

Friedman, R.I. 1988. Kahane's Good Jewish Boys. *The Nation*, January 16: 45-48.

The Fugitive. 1994. ABC News, *20/20* (February 11).

Georgia Code Ann. §§16-11-37, 1974.

"I Shot Him," Police Quote Abortion Foe. 1994. *Chicago Tribune*, March 2: 7N.

Kenkelen, B. 1989. Protesting Gay Activists Up the Ante. *National Catholic Reporter*, December 22: 3.

Klehr, H. 1988. *Far Left of Center*. New Brunswick, NJ: Transaction Books.

Ko-lin, Chin. 1990. *Chinese Subculture and Criminality*. New York: Greenwood Press.

Kushner, H.W. 1998. *The Future of Terrorism: Violence in the New Millennium*. Thousand Oaks, CA: Sage Publications.

Leo, J. 1992. The Politics of Intimidation. *U.S. News & World Report*, April 6: 24.

Magnuson, E. 1989. In a Rage Over AIDS: A Militant Protest Group Targets the Catholic Church. *Time*, December 25: 33.

McKeegan, Michele. 1992. *Abortion Politics: Mutiny in the Ranks of the Right*. New York: Free Press.

Murphy, M., and J.I.B. McCulloch. 1991. Gulf War Reveals Environmental Terrorist Threat. *National Underwriter, Property & Casualty/Risks and Benefits Management* 95(17): 9, 44-47, 52.

Nathanson, B. 1989. Operation Rescue: Domestic Terrorism or Legitimate Civil Rights Protest? *The Hastings Report*, Nov.-Dec.: 28-32.

National Abortion Federation. 1998. <http://www.prochoice.org/violence/98vd.html>.

National Advisory Commission on Criminal Justice Standards and Goals. 1976. *Report of the Task Force on Disorders and Terrorism*. Washington, DC: U.S. Government Printing Office.

National Governors' Association. 1979. *Domestic Terrorism*. Washington, DC: U.S. Government Printing Office.

Neumeister, L. 1994. 4 Convicted in Trade Center Bombing. *The Atlanta Journal/Constitution*, March 5: 6A.

Newman, D.E. 1986. *Introduction to Criminal Justice*. New York: Lippincott.

Parfit, M. 1990. Earth Firsters! Wield a Mean Monkey Wrench. *Smithsonian* 21(1): 184-204.

Plevin, N. 1994. Worshipers at N.J.-area Mosque Angry Over Bombing Verdicts. *The Atlanta Journal/Constitution*, March 5: 6A.

Polland, J.M. 1988. *Understanding Terrorism: Groups, Strategies, and Responses*. Englewood Cliffs, NJ: Prentice-Hall.

Pressley, S.P. 1999. Carolinians Doubt Rudolph Is Hiding in Their Mountains; Suspect Thought to Evade Manhunt Via Stealth. *The Washington Post*, March 31: A103.

Smith, B. 1994. *Terrorism in America: Pipe Bombs and Pipe Dreams*. Albany: State University of New York Press.

United Press International (UPI). 1994. January 6, Chicago.

U.S. vs. U.S. District Court for the Southern District of Michigan, 407 U.S. 297, 1972.

Vetter, H.M., and G.R. Perlstein. 1991. *Perspectives on Terrorism*. Pacific Grove, CA: Brooks/Cole.

Walker, S.P. 1980. *Popular Justice*. New York: Oxford University Press.

White, J.R. 1991. *Terrorism: An Introduction*. Pacific Grove, CA: Brooks/Cole.

Yahweh Sect Murdered Randomly, Brutally, Prosecutor Says. 1992. *Chicago Tribune*, January 8: 12C.

Hate Crimes

Damon D. Camp

One of the major components of domestic terrorism is a phenomenon often collectively identified as *hate crime*. Although the concept has no generally accepted definition, most experts agree that hate crime deals with criminal behavior motivated by bigotry and hatred. Additionally, hate crime focuses on the symbolic status of the victim and the motives of the perpetrator (Hamm 1994). The *Uniform Crime Reports* state that the most frequently reported hate crime is intimidation and that most hate crime victims are individuals (Federal Bureau of Investigation 1996). Typically, they have been victimized because of their race, religion, or ethnicity. Recently, V. Jenness and K. Broad (1997) have suggested that hate crime should be expanded to include bias-related crime that has been spawned by other factors, including gender, political belief systems, and sexual orientation.

Regardless of the motivational category, hate crime represents what might be considered "normal" criminal behavior that has been singled out as particularly reprehensible because it is motivated by bias and is meant to intimidate or *terrorize* the victim. It is characterized by the manner in which society responds to the problem and normally involves the imposition of enhanced criminal penalties. While hate crime can occur in a variety of circumstances and entail a wide range of motivations, by far the vast majority of activity in this area has involved perpetrators who are ultra-right-wing extremists.

The Far Right

Far Right extremism generally consists of ultra conservative beliefs that include one or more of the following: anti-government views, pro-Christianity, and racial and ethnic purity. For example, many right-wing domestic groups focus much of their attention on the "Zionist Occupation Government" or ZOG. This view, which espouses the belief that the United States government is actually run or controlled by the international banking industry, which is in turn dominated by wealthy Jews, is most notably found in the teachings of the Identity Church Movement. However, various other positions and groups espouse these same anti-government sentiments, including most Klan organizations and other white supremacy groups.

Many right-wing groups rely on Christianity in general and Christian Identity in particular for justification. The Identity Church Movement is central to a number of such organizations. Members of this movement believe that the true Israel, or "Holy Land," is the United States. Founded on the principle of Anglo-Israelism, which surfaced in En-

gland in the latter part of the nineteenth century, this concept was "re-born" under Reverend Wesley Swift, founder of the Christian Defense League (Anti-Defamation League 1983).

Christian identity groups can be found all over the country (Figure 6-9). Heavier concentrations are found in certain regions—the Midwest, Pacific Northwest, and South. These groups tend to gravitate toward areas that are rugged, rural, and isolated. This geographic distribution fits with their separatists beliefs and their survivalist, para-military orientation.

While many right-wing extremist groups hold religious views that are tied to Christianity in general, or the Identity Church Movement in particular, almost all are significantly racially or ethnically biased. The most notable are the Ku Klux Klan and the Aryan Nations. Other lesser known groups, such as the Euro-American Alliance, Inc., the Institute for Historical Review, and the National Alliance, also cling to white supremacy beliefs. Mostly anti-black, these groups, along with the National Association for the Advancement of White People (NAAWP), the White Patriots Party, and the National States Rights Party, espouse anti-Semitic doctrines. These white supremacist views coupled with deep religious/pro-Christian beliefs permeate right-wing extremism and are often used collectively to justify discriminatory acts based on the former (Anti-Defamation League 1996). In addition to these common threads, a number of other less common tendencies tie many of these right-wing organizations together. These other ties include survivalism, para-militarism, Neo-Nazism, and Holocaust Revisionism.

Survivalists generally focus their efforts on preparing for an anticipated "Doomsday" or Armageddon. Many believe that a major race war will break out after a United Nations takeover of the United States. Furthermore, only those who are prepared to resist and defend themselves will survive the racial and economic chaos. Groups such as the Christian-Patriots Defense League; the Covenant, the Sword, the Arm of the Lord; the Citizens Emergency Defense System; and the Posse Comitatus, along with several other Identity Church affiliates, are among those that ascribe to survivalism. They prepare for the apocalypse by stockpiling food, weapons, and other supplies in remote locations (Coates 1995).

Those who espouse survivalist theory usually also promote para-military training. Training facilities and entire encampments designed to promote para-militarism, like the Arkansas compound of the Covenant, the Sword, and the

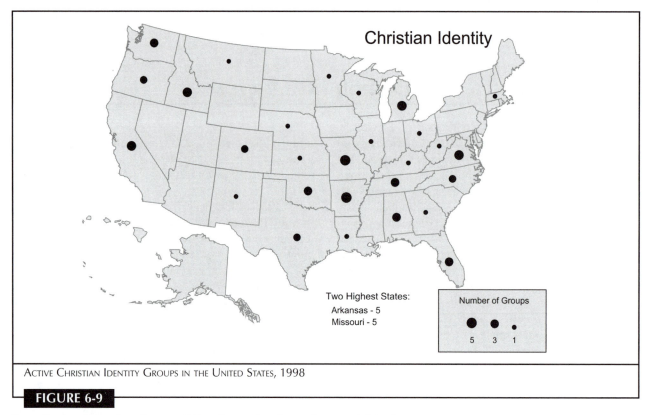

Christian Identity

Two Highest States:
Arkansas - 5
Missouri - 5

Number of Groups

5   3   1

ACTIVE CHRISTIAN IDENTITY GROUPS IN THE UNITED STATES, 1998

FIGURE 6-9

Source: Southern Poverty Law Center available online at <http://www.splcenter.org/splc.html>.

Arm of the Lord, have surfaced all across the country. In addition, military fatigues seem to have become the uniform of the day as displayed by a number of factions of the Ku Klux Klan and other groups such as the Heritage Library (Dees 1996).

Several domestic groups adopt beliefs that are related to Neo-Nazism. While predominantly anti-Semitic and anti-black, these groups also often display swastikas, wear Nazi-related uniforms, and promote ideas related to Fascism and Nazism. Domestic groups within this category include the National Socialist Party of America/American Nazi Party, the National Socialist League, the National Socialist Liberation Front, the National Socialist Movement, the National Socialist White Worker's Party, and the National Alliance.

Neo-Nazi groups can be found throughout the country (Figure 6-10). The largest concentration of these groups is in the Great Lakes region. This concentration may be due in part to the industrial base in that region and the notion that Neo-Nazi groups appeal to working class individuals who may feel that they have been victimized by a "welfare state" or by industrial downsizing. Other significant clusters are located in California, Oregon, and Washington in the West and Texas, Florida, and North Carolina in the South.

Closely aligned with and often a part of Neo-Nazism is Holocaust Revisionism, a systematic denial of the Holocaust. Based somewhat on Arthur Butz's *The Hoax of the Twentieth Century*, Holocaust Revisionists claim that top U.S. officials were involved in a hoax to turn public opinion against Hitler's Germany. Groups supporting this principle include the National Alliance, the Liberation Movement of the German Reich, the National Socialist White People's Party, the Euro-American Alliance, Inc., and the National States Rights Party. The Institute for Historical Review, a vocal supporter of Holocaust Revisionism, at one time offered $50,000 for proof of the Holocaust (Anti-Defamation League 1983).

These right-wing extremist organizations are often collectively referred to as "hate groups" and their prevalence is evident (Figure 6-11). They can be found in 44 states and in some jurisdictions they number in the 20s and 30s, with Florida and California having the highest numbers. At least some hate-oriented organizations are located in every region, with the Great Plains having the lowest occurrence of hate groups.

Hate Group Activities

Hate groups engage in a broad range of activities. Although they offer a wide range of political rhetoric and circulate one or more varieties of publications, most do not actively engage in overt violence. However, they preach and teach hatred and violence. Regular publications range from *The White Patriot* of the Knights of the Ku Klux Klan to the *Aryan Nations Newsletter*. Typical headlines include "Blacks Average 15 I.Q. Points Lower than Whites" (1986) from *The Thunderbolt* of the National States Rights Party and "Anti-

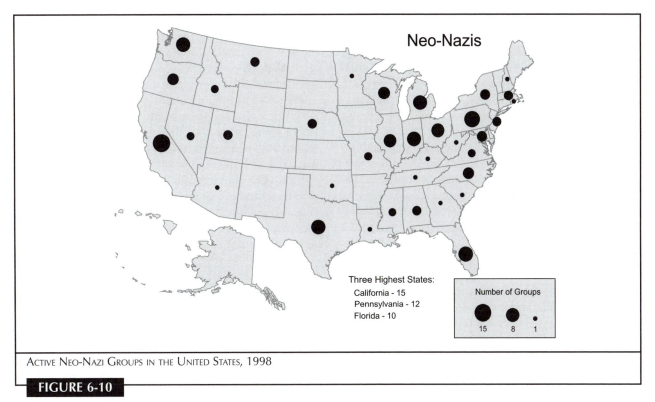

Neo-Nazis

Three Highest States:

California - 15
Pennsylvania - 12
Florida - 10

Number of Groups

15   8   1

ACTIVE NEO-NAZI GROUPS IN THE UNITED STATES, 1998

FIGURE 6-10

Source: Southern Poverty Law Center available online at <http://www.splcenter.org/splc.html>.

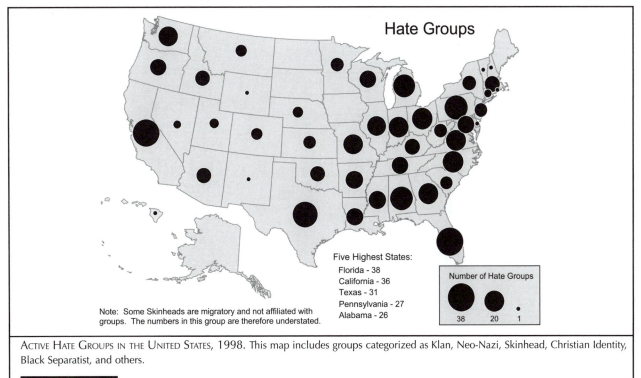

Hate Groups

Five Highest States:

Florida - 38
California - 36
Texas - 31
Pennsylvania - 27
Alabama - 26

Number of Hate Groups

38   20   1

Note: Some Skinheads are migratory and not affiliated with groups. The numbers in this group are therefore understated.

ACTIVE HATE GROUPS IN THE UNITED STATES, 1998. This map includes groups categorized as Klan, Neo-Nazi, Skinhead, Christian Identity, Black Separatist, and others.

FIGURE 6-11

Source: Southern Poverty Law Center available online at< http://www.splcenter.org/splc.html>.

White Quota Drives Contractor Out of Business" (1984) from *NAAWP News*, a publication of the National Association for the Advancement of White People. Right-wing groups also have established a computerized network that links various organizations and individuals through personal computers. Through this network, they maintain communication, exchange files on opponents, and circulate materials (Lowe 1986).

These groups also produce recruitment flyers and, in some instances, training manuals and other para-military documents such as the tactical manuals published by The Covenant, the Sword, and the Arm of the Lord (CSA). Other materials relate to philosophical positions or specific issues like the pamphlet entitled "Get America Up in Arms" by William P. Falls and published by the Christian-Patriots Defense League.

Some right-wing members do engage in criminal violence. For example, The Order, a splinter Aryan Nations group, was allegedly involved in one or more armed car robberies in Oregon. They were responsible for the 1984 assassination of radio talk-show personality Alan Berg, and member David Tate killed a Missouri state trooper (Coates 1995). A year earlier, Posse Comitatus leader Gordon Kahl killed two U.S. marshals when they came to arrest him for a weapons charge and he then killed an Arkansas sheriff in the shoot-out that ensued on his capture (Corcoran 1990). Other right-wing violence includes numerous cross burnings, racially motivated assaults, and various acts of vandalism.

Many of these incidents have been linked to "Skinheads," a term used to identify a category of similar groups whose origin can be traced to Great Britain during the height of the "punk rock" era. Made up mostly of young, conservative people, they frequently identify themselves as Neo-Nazis. They often shave their heads, wear "jackboots" and leather jackets, and promulgate a philosophy of white supremacy and racial bigotry.

While not all Skinheads are Neo-Nazi racists, some of these groups have been linked to numerous attacks. In November 1988, a group of Skinheads in Portland, Oregon, attacked an Ethiopian immigrant and beat him to death. Three were convicted of murder. Subsequently, Tom Metzger, the head of the California-based White Aryan Resistance (W.A.R.), and his son John, lost a multi-million-dollar lawsuit when a jury found that they had influenced the attack by promoting violence among the group responsible (Ellis 1990).

Racist Skinhead groups can be found in almost every region of the country (Figure 6-12). California and Arizona have the largest number with seven each. This concentration may be due in part to the activities of Tom Metzger and W.A.R. Other significant locations include Kansas, Minnesota, Pennsylvania, Alabama, and Florida.

Perhaps the most infamous hate group is the Ku Klux Klan, which is not a single group but an array of extremist organizations that have adopted the name. Currently, several Klan "federations" exist, including the United Klans of America and the New Order, Knights of the Ku Klux Klan (Anti-Defamation League 1996). Also active are a number of independent Klans and at least two large groups—the Invisible Empire, headquartered in Louisiana, and the

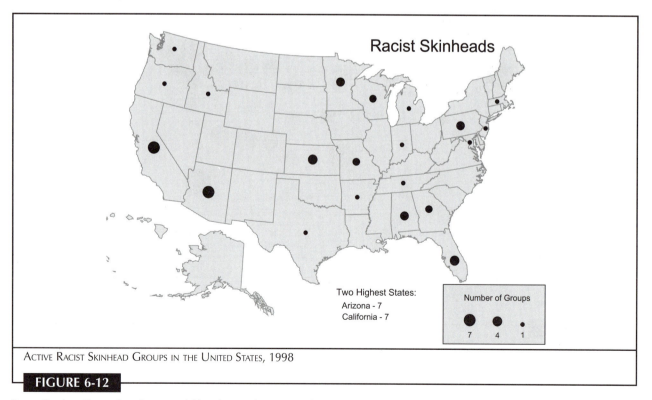

ACTIVE RACIST SKINHEAD GROUPS IN THE UNITED STATES, 1998

FIGURE 6-12

Source: Southern Poverty Law Center available online at <http://www.splcenter.org/splc.html>.

Knights of the Ku Klux Klan with its home in Alabama. The Klan can be found in over 30 states, but Klan activity is predominately concentrated in the South and Midwest (Figure 6-13). Texas, Alabama, North Carolina, and Virginia have the highest number of Klan groups, although the Ku Klux Klan can also be found in New England.

Crime and violence surrounding numerous Klan groups have also been prevalent in the recent past. Often this violence is a reaction to demonstrations against bigotry, such as the march in Forsyth County, Georgia, in 1987. Klan members and supporters hurled bottles and rocks at demonstrators. As a result of the attack, a lawsuit was filed, and subsequently won by the victims, and a judgment of almost $1,000,000 was entered against the counter-demonstrators. In late 1991, two men, a Grand Dragon for the Tennessee KKK and a member of the Aryan Nations, were indicted on federal civil rights charges for allegedly shooting into a synagogue in June 1990 (Grand Dragon of Tennessee KKK Indicted 1991).

Violence also can erupt when the Klan marches, as was seen in January 1992 in Denver, Colorado, where some 100 Klansmen marched to the state capitol and were confronted by an estimated 1,000 counter-marchers.

> After the rally, a crowd of about 1,000 people throwing bottles, bricks and snowballs attacked the school bus on which police tried to spirit the Klan members out of the Capitol area. Protesters also damaged five police cars, overturning one. . . . Later, youths ran down a nearby shopping district and ransacked a sports clothing store, punching two store employees. (Rovin 1992: 42)

Some Klansmen have even expanded their activities in an attempt to further their cause. Southern White Knights Grand Dragon Gregory Walker was arrested on federal drug and firearms charges when he attempted to sell both to a Georgia Bureau of Investigation undercover officer in May 1992. Walker was believed to be selling narcotics to finance the Southern White Knights, a small splinter group in the state (Scruggs 1992). Members of the Klan also continue to engage in cross burnings. In January 1992, 13 members of the Louisiana Ku Klux Klan were sentenced for burning nine crosses in Shreveport in May 1991. Among the perpetrators were the top two leaders of the state's largest Klan organization (Hines 1992).

The influence of the Klan, Skinheads, and other right-wing extremists is not confined to the United States. A Ku Klux Klan group in southern England has ties to the Invisible Empire Knights of the KKK in the U. S. (Roy 1992). In Montreal, Canada, 30 Skinheads and 3 Klansmen were arrested in January 1992 for possession of fire bombs (Molotov cocktails) not far from a metro station. Links have been found between German extremist groups and the American KKK (Kabel 1992). German officials announced the discovery of the link in August 1992 after police in the city of Rostock fought Neo-Nazi demonstrators for four straight nights (*Atlanta Journal/Constitution* 1992). Klan organizations are known to be in Berlin and a number of smaller German cities. Right-wing attacks on mostly foreign émigrés soared to almost 1,500 in Germany in 1992. It is estimated that right-wing radicals currently outnumber left-wing extremists in Germany (Kabel 1992).

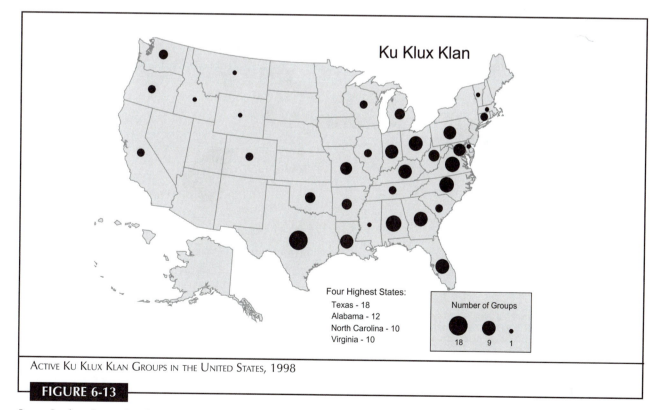

ACTIVE KU KLUX KLAN GROUPS IN THE UNITED STATES, 1998

FIGURE 6-13

Source: Southern Poverty Law Center available online at <http://www.splcenter.org/splc.html>.

In the United States, hate crimes against persons and property have affected every region of the country (Figure 6-14). Georgia and Oklahoma reported the greatest number of incidents in 1997. Other states reporting a high per capita number of hate crimes are located in the Far West and the Great Lakes region, as well as in New England. Responses to the problem have been far reaching. Differing adherence to reporting standards from state to state may explain some unexpected results. For example, Georgia is relatively high whereas the rest of the South is low in rates of reported victims.

Response to Hate Crime

Much of the violence perpetrated by the Right Wing manifests itself in hate crime that has prompted many jurisdictions to respond to the problem through legislation. A number of states in recent years have adopted statutes geared toward deterring certain types of terrorist-like behavior. Often passed at the urging of the Anti-Defamation League (ADL) of B'nai B'rith, these laws, which address what are collectively known as "hate crimes" or "bias crimes," are sometimes patterned after ADL model statutes. However, much of the legislation so categorized is neither new, nor really aimed at the type of extremist behavior discussed in this essay.

Virtually every state has some type of hate crime legislation. Over half the states have laws based at least in part on the ADL model. Some, however, have statutes that are limited in scope. In all, they describe a collection of proscribed behavior that can initially be divided into three groups: criminal laws, enhanced civil remedies, and reporting/training statutes.

The largest of these categories—criminal laws—can be divided into two broad categories. The first concerns institutionalized violence. Here states have banned a wide range of vandalism, including the desecration of venerated places or objects. Some states, like Alabama (Ala. Code § 13A-11-12, 1988) and Delaware (Del. Code Ann. tit. 11 § 1331, 1987), limit their statutes to places of worship and public monuments, flags, and symbols. Others include a broad range of places, such as cemeteries and schools. These statutes are geared toward general acts of vandalism against specific targets, and while they may be used to prosecute violent extremists, that does not seem to be their purpose at passage. A few states, however, have passed broad-based institutional vandalism statutes that do target extremists (Camp 1990).

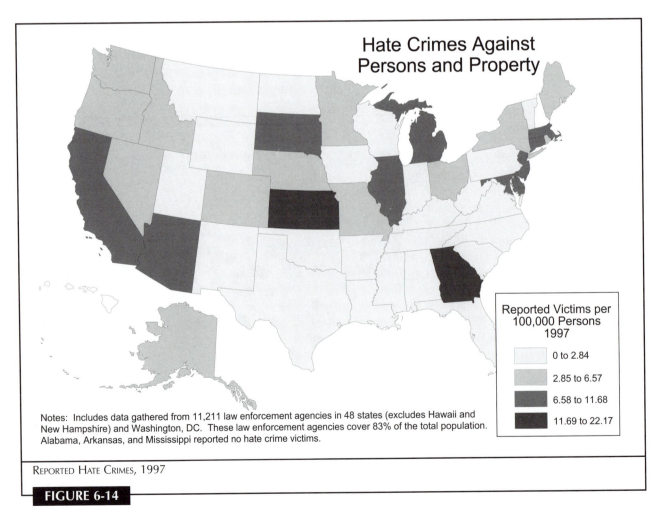

Notes: Includes data gathered from 11,211 law enforcement agencies in 48 states (excludes Hawaii and New Hampshire) and Washington, DC. These law enforcement agencies cover 83% of the total population. Alabama, Arkansas, and Mississippi reported no hate crime victims.

Hate Crimes Against Persons and Property

Reported Victims per 100,000 Persons 1997

- 0 to 2.84
- 2.85 to 6.57
- 6.58 to 11.68
- 11.69 to 22.17

REPORTED HATE CRIMES, 1997

FIGURE 6-14

Source: FBI *Uniform Crime Reports, Hate Crime Statistics 1997.*

The second broad category of criminal legislation concerns intimidation or harassment. More than half the states have passed such statutes, but most target extremist-oriented behavior. Some have restrictive laws that deal primarily with disturbing religious ceremonies. Others outlaw public cross burning and three prohibit the display of swastikas under certain circumstances. Some states also have a limited prohibition on the use of masks or hoods. Several states have broad-based harassment statutes (Camp 1990).

Many of these intimidation statutes provide for enhanced penalties where assault or criminal trespass is motivated by racial or religious bias. Some states with such statutes provide for punishments at the felony level, with misdemeanor penalties the rule in jurisdictions where intimidation is limited to the disturbance of religious services (Camp 1990). Virtually every state with this type of legislation targets hate crimes based on race, religion, or color. Eleven states target harassment as the basis of sexual orientation and nine states provide enhanced penalties for the harassment of the handicapped (Jenness and Broad 1997).

Enhanced penalty provisions of many hate crime laws have generated the most controversy. Statutes provide for stiffer penalties for traditional crimes (such as assault) when they are motivated by hate or bias against a statutorily identified group. The central element in these statutes is the intent of the perpetrator. Proponents of these provisions, like V. Jenness and K. Broad (1997), rely on a "but for" rationale to justify why someone should be punished more severely than normal for assaulting a person because of a certain characteristic, such as race, ethnicity, gender, or sexual preference. They suggest that "but for" some hate motivation, a given crime would not have occurred and thus an enhanced penalty is justified. But this view presupposes that no crime would have been committed without bias on the part of the perpetrator, and therein lies the problem. While this rationale may support an institutionalized vandalism statute, it does not vindicate an enhanced penalty hate crime law. One would have to argue that a certain assault or robbery would not have occurred but for the presence of some special characteristic of the victim, e.g., race, ethnicity, or sexual orientation, and so the perpetrator should be punished more severely than normal. This view presupposes that without the presence of this characteristic, no crime would have been committed, a leap in logic proponents do not address.

The second group of statutes relates to civil actions, where two different approaches also exist. Most jurisdictions provide for some special civil remedy that most often comes in the form of extended parental liability. In 38 jurisdictions, parents can be held liable for the damages caused by their children. An increasing number of states, however, are providing enhanced civil remedies. In Idaho, for example, the legislature created a new cause of action for "malicious harassment" and provided for special and general damages, including those for emotional distress and attorney fees (Idaho Code § 18.7903 1987). Some experts have called upon Congress to expand the federal RICO

(Racketeer-Influenced and Corrupt Organizations) statute to include civil remedies for victims of violent extremism. Such action would allow potential recovery on the establishment of a pattern of violent behavior (Blakey and Perry 1990).

The final group of statutes involves certain administrative procedures or requirements. In many jurisdictions, law enforcement agencies are required to collect hate crime statistics. In some cases, this mandate is by executive order rather than by statute. Most of these data collection requirements have surfaced in the past five years and virtually all contain the same basic elements: a state agency is designated to collect, analyze, and disseminate information on crimes motivated by racial, religious, or ethnic basis. Congress passed the Hate Crimes Statistics Act in 1990; it requires the attorney general to collect such data for a five-year period beginning in 1991 (24 U.S.C. § 534 1990). In addition, several jurisdictions, like Minnesota, are requiring the establishment of training courses designed to assist law enforcement officers in identifying and responding to bias-motivated crimes (Minn. Stat. § 626, 8451 1989). However, data reporting problems surface when officers do not properly label hate crimes or when departments ignore the reporting requirements.

Bias-related prohibitions have not been limited to the state house. With the rising tide of racism being reported on college campuses, several colleges and universities have adopted policies designed to remedy the problem (France 1990). One such policy was adopted by the University of Michigan and was successfully challenged in federal court by a graduate teaching assistant (*Doe v. University of Michigan* 1989). The policy provided sanctions for speech and conduct that stigmatized or victimized "individuals or groups on the basis of race, ethnicity, religion, sex, sexual orientation, creed, national origin, ancestry, age, marital status, handicap, or Vietnam-era veteran status" (*Doe v. University of Michigan* 1989: 853). The court issued a permanent injunction against all speech-related sanctions, ruling that in this area the policy was contrary to the First Amendment to the U.S. Constitution, but the court denied an injunction request concerning the policy's regulation of physical conduct.

These responses have heightened public awareness of the problems and have encouraged the criminal justice community to increase its efforts to deal with hate crime. Although some concern has been expressed over the justification for enhanced penalties, these legislative efforts have by and large met with success in the courtroom and with the public.

Conclusions

Hate crimes are characterized by criminal behavior motivated by bigotry and hatred, and are usually perpetrated by individuals and groups positioned politically on the Far or Extremist Right. Generally, they hold anti-government views, are pro-Christianity, and practice racial and ethnic biases. Although these groups can be found in most parts of the United States, some regional clusters describe the hatred landscape. Active Christian Identity groups are located primarily in Missouri, Arkansas, and states in the Northwest. Neo-Nazi groups favor the American Midwest as well as Florida and Texas. Racist Skinheads are clustered in California and Arizona, but can be found in lesser numbers in Minnesota, Florida, Kansas, and Missouri. Ku Klux Klan groups dominate the eastern half of the country. Hate groups in general are more prevalent east of and along the Mississippi River, and in states along the Pacific. The United States legal system and the public appear in favor of enhanced punishments for hate crimes.

References

Anti-Defamation League. 1996. *Danger: Extremism*. New York: Anti-Defamation League.

———. 1986a. *Extremism Targets the Prison*. New York: Anti-Defamation League of B'nai B'rith.

———. 1986b. *Special Edition*. (October). New York: Anti-Defamation League of B'nai B'rith.

———. 1983. *Extremism on the Right: A Handbook*. New York: Anti-Defamation League of B'nai B'rith.

Anti-White Quota Drives Contractor Out of Business. 1984. *NAAWP News 33*: 3.

Atlanta Journal/Constitution. 1992. August 26: A9.

Blacks Average 15 I.Q. Points Lower Than Whites. 1986. *The Thunderbolt 313*: 4.

Blakey, G.R., and T.A. Perry. 1990. An Analysis of the Myths That Bolster Efforts to Rewrite RICO and the Various Proposals for Reform. *Vanderbilt Law Review 43*: 933-79.

Camp, D.D. 1990. Domestic Terror: The Impact of Anti-Hate Group Legislation. Presented at the Annual Meeting of the Southern Criminal Justice Association, New Orleans, LA, October.

Coates, J. 1995. *Armed and Dangerous*. New York: Noonday Press.

Corcoran, J. 1990. *Bitter Harvest, Gordon Kahl and the Posse Comitatus: Murder in the Heartland*. New York: Viking Press

Dees, M. 1996. *Gathering Storm: America's Militia Threat*. New York: HarperCollins.

Deringer, E. 1991. Earth First Leaders Sue Authorities Over Oakland Blast; Police Accused of Not Looking for Bomber. *San Francisco Chronicle*, May 22: A17.

———. 1990. Earth First! Is "Not Scared" Anti-Logging Group Says Bomb Was Planted, Won't Deter Efforts. *San Francisco Chronicle*, May 24: A4.

Doe v. University of Michigan, 721 F. Supp. 852 (E.D. Mich., 1989).

Ellis, D. 1990. Suits Against White Sheets. *Time*, October 1: 136.

Federal Bureau of Investigation (FBI). 1996. *Uniform Crime Reports*. Washington, DC: US Dept. of Justice, Government Printing Office.

France, S. 1990. Hate Goes to College. *ABA Journal 76*: 44–49.

Georgia Code Ann. §§16-11-37, 1974.

Grand Dragon of Tennessee KKK Indicted for Racial Violence. 1991. *U.S. Newswire*, December 20.

Hamm, M.S. 1994. *Hate Crime: International Perspectives on Causes and Controls*. Cincinnati: Anderson Publishing Company.

Hines, G. 1992. Man Sentenced in Cross Burnings. *Gannett News Service*, January 31.

Jenness, V., and K. Broad. 1997. *Hate Crime: New Social Movements and the Politics of Violence*. Hawthorne, NY: Aldine de Gruyter.

Kabel, M. 1992. Neo-Nazi Violence Soars in United Germany. *Reuters Library Report*, August 13.

Lowe, D. 1986. *Computerized Networks of Hate*. New York: Anti-Defamation League of B'nai B'rith.

Richwine, D. 1982. Turkish Import Store Hit by Bomb. *United Press International*, March 23.

Rovin, A. 1992. Klan Rally Sparks Violence at Denver King Celebration. *Los Angeles Times*, January 21: 14.

Roy, A. 1992. KKK Exposed in Britain. *Sunday Telegraph*, June 7: 20.

Scruggs, K. 1992. Klansman Faces Drug, Firearm Charges. *Atlanta Journal and Constitution*, May 20: D2.

School Violence

Pamela Riley
Joanne McDaniel

The 1997-1998 and 1998-1999 school years were marked by heightened concern about the problem of school violence. School bells became alarm bells as scenes of students shot by classmates appeared regularly on news broadcasts. Just as one tragic incident faded from the television screen, another one seemed to occur. The shootings at Columbine High School in Littleton, Colorado, happened just as everyone was hoping that the 1998-1999 school year would be free of incidents.

During the 1997-1998 school year, four incidents resulted in multiple deaths and focused attention on the problem of violence occurring on school property. Although this phenomenon encompasses other weapons, concern in 1997-1998 focused on the role of firearms because all the incidents involved this weapon type. Each incident involved perpetrators who carried out an act of violence at their own school. Additionally, each perpetrator was a young male whose behavior much earlier in his life was a warning sign.

Historical Background

Despite increased news coverage, violent acts taking place on school property were not new in 1997-1998. Concern about this problem in recent years began to emerge in the late 1970s when the U.S. Department of Education published *Violent Schools–Safe Schools*. The study, released with others that indicated an increase in violent incidents on school property, highlighted the fact that students were more likely to be victims of crime at their own schools than at any other place (U.S. Department of Health, Education, and Welfare 1977).

Many studies of school violence in the 1980s continued this theme and focused on the likelihood of student victimization at school. National crime victimization surveys found younger teens (ages 12-15) more likely to be victims of crime at school than older teens. Regardless of the age of victims, crimes were less likely to involve weapons than street crime in which young people were victims (National Crime Victimization Survey 1991).

This trend changed in the late 1980s and early 1990s. Government studies found that more students had experienced violent crimes at school, many involving weapons. As a result, many more students were reported carrying weapons for self-protection. A survey in 1991 determined that almost 20 percent of students reported that they had carried some type of weapon to school (Weapon-Carrying Among High School Students 1991). A study from the University of Michigan estimated that students carried 270,000 guns to school each day (Standing Up to Violence 1995). Over a two-year period, 1992-1994, 105 school-associated violent deaths occurred, with 75 percent involving some type of firearm (School-Associated Violent Deaths in the United States 1996).

While overall the number of incidents of school violence appeared to hold constant through this period, concern about the problem of school violence grew as incidents seemed to intensify in severity. The noted increase in the number of weapons on school property undoubtedly contributed to the increase in violent incidents. Whereas students previously used feet and fists, they were now more likely to use knives and guns.

Responding to the heightened concern about weapons on school property, the Gun-Free Schools Act (GFSA) was enacted in 1994. The GFSA requires that each state receiving federal funds via the Elementary and Secondary Education Act must have a state law that requires all school districts in the state to expel from school for at least one year any student who brings a firearm onto school property. States are required to report this information annually to the secretary of education. The requirements put forth by the GFSA are important because they generate the only national report that attempts to provide data on school crime incidents such as weapon carrying. Other than what is required by the GFSA, fewer than half the states collect data on such crime. A high degree of variability exists in the data on school violence incidents, and the lack of uniformity in definitions makes general comparisons difficult.

Two years of reporting for the GFSA have been completed to date. According to the U.S. Department of Education, data from the school year 1995-1996 were problematic in terms of quality. Data from the school year 1996-1997 reveal an estimated total of 6,093 students expelled from school for bringing a firearm or other weapon to school (Figure 6-15). Of those expelled, 56 percent were high school students, 34 percent were junior high or middle school students, and 9 percent were elementary school students. The types of weapons brought to school were delineated by 47 states. Wyoming and Hawaii had no expulsions for that school year. Fifty-eight percent were handguns, 7 percent were rifles, and the remaining 35 percent were "other" types of firearms such as bombs, grenades, starter pistols, and rockets (U.S. Department of Education 1998a).

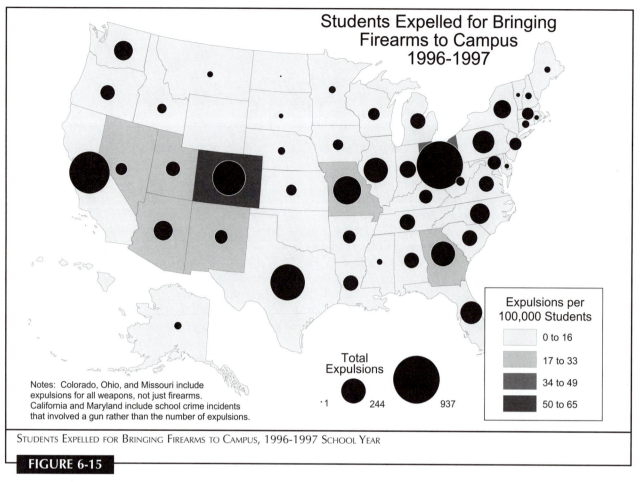

Students Expelled for Bringing Firearms to Campus 1996-1997

Expulsions per 100,000 Students
- 0 to 16
- 17 to 33
- 34 to 49
- 50 to 65

Total Expulsions
·1   244   937

Notes: Colorado, Ohio, and Missouri include expulsions for all weapons, not just firearms. California and Maryland include school crime incidents that involved a gun rather than the number of expulsions.

STUDENTS EXPELLED FOR BRINGING FIREARMS TO CAMPUS, 1996-1997 SCHOOL YEAR

FIGURE 6-15

Source: Report on State Implementation of the Gun-Free Schools Act—School Year 1996-97. Prepared for the U.S. Department of Education, Office of Elementary and Secondary Education and Planning and Evaluation Service. Contract No. EA94052001. Available at <http://www.ed.gov/pubs/gunfree>.

Ohio, California, and Colorado appear to have exceptionally high rates of expulsions, but inferences from this map must be made caustiously (Figure 6-15). For instance, Ohio, Colorado, and Missouri count expulsions for all weapons, not just firearms. Statistics from California and Maryland are school crime incidents involving a gun rather than the number of expulsions. Texas had a high number of expulsions for only firearms on campus. The geographical variations may have a number of possible theoretical explanations, aside from the previously discussed ones of definition and data variability. For example, some of the differences in the numbers of expulsions may be related to differences in philosophical approaches to discipline in various parts of the country. Or, in some places, educators may be more likely to expel students than in others. Additional research is needed to identify specific reasons.

Although the U.S. Department of Education released a study in early 1998 entitled *Violence and Discipline Problems in U.S. Public Schools: 1996-1997,* which attempts to describe what is taking place, it does not provide state-to-state comparisons. At best, with reference to geographic patterns, it reveals that urban fringe schools were not significantly different from those in cities. These schools are at least twice as likely to report serious violent crime as

those in towns and in rural locations (U.S. Department of Education 1998b). In this report, violent crime involves many weapon types. Therefore, conclusions regarding differences between cities/urban fringes and towns/rural areas must be approached cautiously with reference to firearms.

With efforts to increase the penalties associated with bringing firearms to schools, the number of firearms being reported is still startling. For school year 1997-1998, the Parents' Resource Institute for Drug Education (PRIDE) found nearly a million students admitted to taking guns to school. Of these, 37 percent claimed to have carried a gun to school once, 18 percent said they had carried a gun two to five times, and 45 percent claimed to have carried a gun six or more times. Of those who said they carried guns, 59 percent were white, 18 percent were black, 12 percent were Hispanic/Latino, 3 percent were Asian, and 3 percent were Native American. These students, according to the PRIDE survey, were less likely to live with both parents, less likely to make good grades, and more likely to be in trouble with the police and to join gangs.

The good news from the PRIDE survey is that the percentage of students who admitted to carrying guns has fallen by 36 percent over the last five years from 6 percent in school year 1993-1994 to just under 4 percent in 1997-1998. The bad news is that 51 percent of the students who carried guns said they had threatened to harm a teacher and 63 percent said they had threatened to harm another student (Parents' Resource Institute for Drug Education 1998).

Four Incidents, 1997-1998

In four instances during the school year, threats against fellow students were carried out: Pearl, Mississippi; Paducah, Kentucky; Jonesboro, Arkansas; Springfield, Oregon. The locations of these incidents now stand as examples of the horror that can result when school violence erupts (Figure 6-16). Four schools, 47 wounded, 12 dead, and 5 boys allegedly responsible for it all. Littleton, Colorado, has the highest number of fatalities (15), far outnumbering the remaining incidents. Jonesboro, Arkansas, ranks second in number of fatalities (5) followed by Paducah, Kentucky (3). The geographic pattern during these school years shows a clustering in the South with random occurrences in other regions across the country. One striking conclusion is that none of these locations is a large urban area; each is a rela-

tively small town or city: Springfield, OR (pop. 41,621); Jonesboro, AR (pop. 31,530); Paducah, KY (pop. 29,315); Littleton, CO (pop. 28,631); Fayetteville, TN (pop. 7,559); Edinboro, PA (pop. 6,324); and Bethel, AK (pop. 3,576).

The first of the shootings took place at Pearl High School in Pearl, Mississippi. The morning of October 1, 1997, after beating and stabbing his mother to death, Woodham brought a hunting rifle to school and shot two female students, one his former girlfriend, at close range. He continued to shoot until he was out of bullets. Then he reloaded and shot again. Eventually, nine classmates were hit; two died. Originally thought to be part of a larger conspiracy of violence planned to be carried out at the school, Luke Woodham was ultimately deemed solely responsible for the shooting spree that took place. Eight months after the shooting, Woodham stood trial, was found guilty, and sentenced to life in prison.

As the first shooter in the series of incidents that marked the 1997-1998 school year, Woodham provides a starting point for highlighting commonalities found among all the

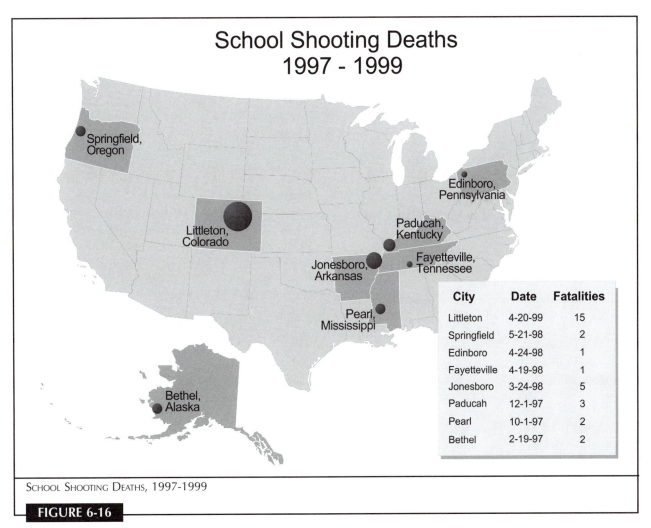

City	Date	Fatalities
Littleton	4-20-99	15
Springfield	5-21-98	2
Edinboro	4-24-98	1
Fayetteville	4-19-98	1
Jonesboro	3-24-98	5
Paducah	12-1-97	3
Pearl	10-1-97	2
Bethel	2-19-97	2

SCHOOL SHOOTING DEATHS, 1997-1999

FIGURE 6-16

Sources: Center for the Prevention of School Violence. 313 Chapanoke Road, Suite 140, Raleigh, NC 27603 and Cable News Network online at <http://www.cnn.com>.

perpetrators. In addition to all the shooters being males, they all had histories of not "fitting in" at school, they all had access to guns, and each had talked about harming others. Two had even brought guns to school before the shooting sprees occurred.

Described in a Louisville *Courier-Journal Extra* as "A boy almost no one seemed to know," Woodham isolated himself from others. He did not participate in school activities and did not excel academically. In interviews with psychologists while awaiting trial, Woodham revealed that he felt different from others and that he did not have any friends. He reported being the victim of bullying and, while in middle school, was suspended several times for fighting with classmates. In writings from his private journals, Woodham revealed his hatred of others and described how he beat his "dear dog Sparkle" to death. On the day before the shooting, Woodham told an acquaintance he intended to kill his mother, former girlfriend, and other people. The friend did not take him seriously.

The second shooting incident was similar. Michael Carneal, a 14-year-old freshman at Heath High School in Paducah, Kentucky, opened fire on a group of classmates with a .22 caliber semiautomatic handgun at the start of a school day. The 911 call logged after the shooting, as reported by Associated Press, reveals the terror of the moment.

> **Operator:** 911, what is your emergency?
>
> **Caller:** Ah, we just heard, ah, I think, gunfire. This is Barbara McGinty [the school's assistant principal].
>
> **Operator:** Ok, where's the shots fired?
>
> **Caller:** At the high school, at the lobby.
>
> **Operator:** Where? Where? In the lobby of the high school?
>
> **Caller:** In the lobby of the high school.
>
> **Operator** (shouting to another person): Brant! Brant! Shots fired in the lobby of the high school. At Heath . . . .

Carneal fired 10 rounds into a student prayer group before being subdued. When the shooting ended, three students lay dead and five were wounded.

Carneal, like Woodham, often was isolated from others and considered himself an outcast. Two times prior to the shooting incident, he carried guns to school and showed them off to classmates. One of these incidents occurred just five days before the murders. Allegedly, he showed the gun to "some kids who were going to beat him up." At the time of the shooting, Carneal was carrying five guns. A search of Carneal's bedroom after the shooting resulted in the discovery of numerous boxes of ammunition. The guns were allegedly stolen.

Stolen guns also played a role in the shooting that occurred in Jonesboro, Arkansas. In this incident, two alleged shooters, 13-year-old Mitchell Johnson and 11-year-old Andrew Golden, opened fire on classmates after triggering a false fire alarm. Four handguns and three high-powered rifles, all taken from Golden's grandparents' home, were the weapons used by these boys.

Wearing camouflage fatigues and toting the guns, Johnson and Golden hid in the woods that adjoin school property. As their classmates filed out the back of the sixth-grade classroom building for the fire drill, the boys began firing dozens of shots. A news report of the incident revealed that the boys were "so determined" and "so ruthlessly efficient" that they scored "15 hits in less than a minute, five of them fatal" (The Boys Behind the Ambush 1998). In addition to the five dead, one teacher and four students, ten students were wounded.

The day before the shooting, Johnson was reported to have told no fewer than 16 classmates that he "had a lot of killing to do." According to police reports, Golden made similar statements a few months before the shooting. For both boys, talk of shooting was part of the world in which they lived. Both had grown up around guns and were, according to the Louisville *Courier-Journal Extra*, "known for a love of shooting."

A fascination with guns and other weapons characterized the boy responsible for the fourth school shooting. Like Woodham and Carneal, Kip Kinkel, a 15-year-old freshman at Thurston High School in Springfield, Oregon, started a typical school day with terror and bloodshed. Shortly before the eight o'clock school bell rang, Kinkel opened fire on a cafeteria crowded with hundreds of students. Carrying three guns and using a .22 caliber rifle, Kinkel killed two students and wounded 25 others before being subdued by a member of the school wrestling team. The day before the shooting, Kinkel had been suspended for bringing a gun to school. The morning of the shooting, before coming to school, Kinkel had killed his parents.

Kinkel's gun possession the day before the incident was not the only warning sign he provided. He was known to have written papers for school in which he described violent scenes. His preoccupation with explosives had prompted his parents to seek professional help for him. Much like the boys in the other incidents, Kinkel spoke of killing other people. One classmate said in a news report in the Raleigh *News and Observer* that Kinkel "always said that it would be fun to kill someone."

Littleton, 1998-1999

The tragedy at Columbine High School in Littleton, Colorado, was the only multiple homicide incident to occur during the 1998-1999 school year. Again, young men with access to firearms and a history of warning signs disrupted the sense of calm and relief that many were experiencing with reference to the problem of school violence. The magnitude of the violence at Littleton leaves no doubt that further understanding is needed to determine the underlying causes of this phenomenon. The common factors linking these individual case studies are evident. They were all young males who had access to guns. They also had given warning signs through their words and behaviors to those around them that they intended to harm others prior to the incidents. Each incident discussed in this essay provides an opportunity for reflection.

Conclusion

Schools and communities throughout the country are enhancing their efforts to make schools safer and more secure. Legislation that limits young people's access to firearms is an issue gaining increased attention. Educators hope to enter the next century with strategies that are directed toward prevention, intervention, and crisis response. The U.S. Department of Education's document, *Early Warning—Timely Response,* offers a guide showing schools how to approach safety issues.

The geographic aspect of the data in this essay helps to identify areas of concern. Through the mapping, we have discovered an interesting characteristic to these school shootings—they are happening in small cities and towns previously thought to be safe, secure environments. This finding will help direct future research into an examination of environmental factors, such as socio-cultural influences, which may be contributing to this pattern.

References

The Boys Behind the Ambush. 1998. *Newsweek,* 6 April.

National Crime Victimization Survey. 1991. *National Crime Victim Survey for 1991* (NCJ-131645). Washington, DC: U.S. Government Printing Office.

Parents' Resource Institute for Drug Education (PRIDE). 1998. *Almost a Million Students Carry Guns and Other Problems to Class.* <http://www.pride surveys.com>. Sept. 8, 1998.

School-Associated Violent Deaths in the United States, 1992-1994. 1996. *Journal of the American Medical Association* 275: 1729-33.

Standing Up to Violence. 1995. *Phi Delta Kappan Special Report.*

U.S. Department of Education. 1998. *Early Warning—Timely Response.* Washington, DC: U.S. Government Printing Office.

———. 1998a. *Report on State Implementation of the Gun-Free Schools Act—School Year 1996-97: Final Report.* Washington, DC: U.S. Government Printing Office.

———. 1998b. *Violence and Discipline Problems in U.S. Public Schools: 1996-1997.* Washington, DC: U.S. Government Printing Office.

U.S. Department of Health, Education, and Welfare. 1977. *Violent Schools—Safe Schools: The Safe School Study Report to the Congress.* Washington, DC: U.S. Government Printing Office.

Weapon-Carrying Among High School Students: United States. 1991. *Morbidity and Mortality Weekly Report* 40: 681-84.

CHAPTER 7

Mental Mapping

One of the distinguishing aspects of the study of geography is that geographers like maps of all kinds, from traditional paper maps, such as topographic maps, statistical maps, and even road maps, to "virtual" maps that appear on computer screens. Furthermore, geographers like to inquire about and explore environments and how they are represented on maps. An interesting extension of this inquiry is maps that are held in the minds of people. According to Robert Lloyd (1973), who has studied this aspect of mapping for years,

> Geographers have always aspired to represent environments on maps and have been concerned by how effectively these maps communicate information about environments. It is this desire to communicate this spatial information effectively that has caused geographers to be interested in the cognitive processes people use when interacting with cognitive maps.

Because most people have mental images of their environments, this holds true for the criminal as well, as shown by David Canter and Samantha Hodge later in this chapter.

Those who specialize in studying this cognitive process have termed these mental environmental images "mental maps." One of the pioneering works employing mental maps was Kevin Lynch's *The Image of the City* (1960). Lynch investigated urban environments. By examining the mental maps of urban residents and then by developing composite images, he was able to identify certain physical elements in the environment that affect people's *spatial* behavior. At that time, no thought was given to the mental maps of criminals.

Subsequent work on mental and cognitive mapping took other approaches to the study of these map images. Peter Gould and Rodney White first published their book *Mental Maps* in 1974; it displayed fascinating looks into the perceptions of places. For instance, students from several locations across the country were asked questions such as where they would like to live. Their preferences were mapped to find that their perceptions of a place had everything to do with their desire to live there. In 1977, Roger

Downs and David Stea (*Maps in Minds*) defined inner space as a representation of the geographical environment as it exists within a person's mind and this environment is the world that people believe it to be.

Cognitive mapping is an abstraction that includes all cognitive abilities of persons that allow them to collect, organize, store, recall, and manipulate information about their spatial environments. The importance here is that *cognitive mapping* is a process, whereas a *cognitive map* is a product. The latter is an organized representation of some part of one's spatial environment. When called upon to do so, we can generally reconstruct a cognitive map by sketching. A cognitive map also may be called a *mental map*.

Through intensive study of many individuals, one can piece together a composite mental map. These composite mental maps are thought to represent shared images of environments by different actors in the field. One of the more provocative studies using composite mental maps was done by Stanley Milgram and reported by Susana Duncan (1977) in "Mental Maps of New York," a paper published in the *New York Times Magazine*. Professor Milgram commented, "I'm interested in the New York City mapped in our minds." In Milgram's research, different areas of New York City were labeled "Snob Appeal," "Away From It All," and "Sweet Solitude" to capture the popular terminology of the residents of New York. These were based on composite mental images.

Of interest from a crime perspective, is that Milgram also studied places of fear in New York. For example, he found that no fewer than 10 percent of his respondents admitted to fright "almost anywhere and everywhere" in New York City. For example, the six most feared places in New York were, in order: (1) Harlem, (2) South Bronx, (3) Lower East Side, (4) Times Square, (5) Bedford Stuyvesant, and (6) Central Park. Most cities probably could have a similar composite mental image drawn for them. In a college classroom study conducted by Borden Dent, individual students' mental maps were used to develop a composite picture to determine *where* in the City of Atlanta were the areas they *perceived* as most dangerous at twelve o'clock midnight. The most feared place was around the Atlanta/Fulton County Stadium, essentially in the heart of downtown Atlanta. It did not matter that this was or was not the *real* center of danger in downtown, what was important was that the images, collective in this case, determined when or where these people did not travel. A map from a more recent study of fear in Atlanta was presented in the essay "Brief History of Crime Mapping" in Chapter 1.

Another interesting facet of mental maps is that research has shown repeatedly that these mental images are usually not correct in terms of such dimensions as location, distance, and time. We have all experienced getting lost when we have poorly formed mental maps. Likewise, everyone has probably experienced that it seems to take longer going to an unwanted appointment than it does coming home from one. Most people have all experienced difficulty in finding their way in unfamiliar environments, especially in visiting urban areas where the street pattern is irregular or perhaps radial. Imagine visiting Washington, D.C., in a car on a Monday morning at Dupont Circle, trying to find an unknown address (especially if you live in or grew up in a city with a rectangular street pattern). You have no well-formed mental map to guide you. Mental maps are forged through personal experience and development. People are sometimes surprised to go home to those environments in which they grew up to find that a pond or a hill is not nearly as big as they remembered it to be.

Generally, the mental maps in people's heads are shaped by their awareness of home and distant places, and by beliefs about them. Mental maps are characterized in the following way: generally, near places are preferred over far places, unless much information is known about the far place. Individuals tend to increase the size of familiar places and decrease the sizes of all others. People with similar experiences tend to give similar answers to questions about the environment and produce comparable maps. Uniform life experiences often yield similar life expectations, and mental maps shape our spatial behavior. Finally, people carry around in their heads mental maps of early childhood environments, more often than not with errors.

Until recently, little intensive research has been done on the mental maps of criminals. Because research has shown that mental maps shape our spatial behavior, one may suspect that the criminal's mental map does the same. In high-speed police chases around large cities, drivers of the chased stolen vehicle may appear to be "going in circles," most likely because they did not have a good mental map of the area. Professor David Canter from the University of Liverpool's Centre for Investigative Psychology has pioneered research into this field. Along with Samantha Hodge, he shares his research with us in the essay on "Criminals' Mental Maps."

Two other interesting essays in this chapter are Patricia Gilmartin's "Cognitive Maps and the Fear of Crime," and Leslie Edwards' "Maps in Detective Fiction." These three essays will provide an interesting array of the extent and possibilities that lay ahead for those who wish to look further into this exciting area of mapping.

References

Downs, Roger M., and David Stea. 1977. *Maps in Minds*. New York: Harper & Row Publishers.

Duncan, Susana. 1977. Mental Maps of New York. *New York Magazine*, December 19.

Gould, Peter, and Rodney White. 1986. 2nd ed. *Mental Maps*. Boston: Allen & Unwin.

Lloyd, Robert A. 1973. *Images of Survival*. New York: Dodd, Mead.

Lynch, Kevin. 1960. *The Image of the City*. Cambridge, MA: Technology Press.

Sigler, L. 1993. Cognitive Processes and Cartographic Maps. In Tommy Garling and Reginald G. Golledge, eds. *Behavior and Environment: Psychological and Geographical Approaches*. New York: North-Holland, pp. 141-49.

Criminals' Mental Maps

David Canter
Samantha Hodge

Many people have noted that criminals tend to offend in a limited area and that area tends to be close to where they live. The basis of penal reform in the nineteenth century was precisely to remove people from their areas of criminal activity, which were regarded as supporting their crime-oriented lifestyles. The first fully documented account of the geographical localization of criminals is usually regarded as the work of the Chicago School of sociologists (Shaw 1942). Subsequently, with the development of empirical criminology, especially in the 1970s and 1980s, a variety of studies drew attention to the limits on criminal mobility (Capone and Nicholas 1976; Pettiway 1982). These studies of criminal localization paralleled broader developments in what became known as *Environmental Psychology*. This examination of how people make sense of and relate to their surroundings led to the development of the concept of "mental maps," those internal representations of the world that we all use to find our way around and make decisions about what we will do and where. The importance of the mental map can be traced at least to the writings of C.C. Trowbridge (1913), who called them "Imaginary Maps," but it received new impetus from the writings of various psychologists, notably F.C. Bartlett (1932) and an urban planner, K. Lynch (1960).

These psychological ideas provided one form of explanation for the limitations on the geographical mobility of criminals, as well as most other people, by suggesting that it was their limited mental maps that structured their activities. Awareness of the possibility of such limited psychological structures rather than the vagaries of local geography encouraged researchers to examine how locations of crimes could be modelled generally as schematic systems rather than as particular geographical instances (Brantingham and Brantingham 1981; Constanzo et al. 1986). A growing body of research attempts to develop general principles that will characterize the geographical patterns of individual offenders in many places rather than aggregate patterns of samples or populations of offenders in particular locations (Canter and Larkin 1993). These principles have been found to have practical significance in helping solve crime (Canter 1994) as well as for the broader theoretical issues to which they contribute.

This work points to the personal mental representation of locations as the basis for the selection of the location for offence activities. This mental representation is often referred to, a little inaccurately, as a "mental map." A considerable amount of research over the last 30 years has demonstrated that such internal representations only approximate the maps with which geographers are familiar. They are more akin to a summary of a person's knowledge and experience of a place, being distorted by many of the processes involved in committing experiences to memory and, later, in retrieving them. However, precisely because of these psychological distortions, such maps help us to understand how people conceptualize their surroundings and the activities that take place there.

Criminological Cognitive Cartography

Because the mental representations criminals have of the locations in which they commit their crimes are rarely examined, the suppositions that form the basis of many debates in environmental criminology have yet to be tested. For example, routine activity theory would indicate that offenders' mental maps of the locations in which they commit their crimes would be seamlessly linked to the areas in which they carry out other activities. By contrast, a perspective that emphasises crime emerging out of awareness of opportunities might be expected to give more salience to the routes and paths that people follow when carrying out their crimes. Alternatively, crimes that are a dominant part of an offender's life might be expected to dominate their conceptualizations of places and be the primary focus of the maps they draw.

Interesting questions also concern the sorts of details that offenders may recall or choose to symbolize in their representations of their geographical experiences. Do these indicate a studied examination of their surroundings or a haphazard, opportunistic approach to their selection of locations in which to offend? Of course the nature of the crime may be expected to relate to how the environment is conceptualized by the offender. Crimes that are closely tied to particular locations, such as burglaries, may be hypothesized to have stronger geographical structures than those that follow the possibilities for finding vulnerable victims, such as rape. Furthermore, some crimes may be location specific, such as targeting a specific warehouse, while others can take place wherever the opportunity presents itself. In all these cases, the question arises as to whether the offender has some mental representation that reflects the selection of crime locations and that possibly helps to enhance the geographical focus of his or her crimes.

Contributors' Note: We are grateful to Jonathan Boehm for collecting some of the maps used here.

186

Exploring Urban Images

The exploration of essentially, subjective, internal, mental representations is notoriously difficult, but this has not stopped psychologists and other social and behavioral scientists from making approximations for the way people cognitively structure their transactions with the world. One procedure that has been widely used actually owes its scientific origins to urban planner Kevin Lynch (1960). He asked people to draw sketch maps of their cities as a way of exploring their mental representations or "images," as he called them, of those cities. His early studies of Boston, Jersey City, and Los Angeles have encouraged many other people to follow his lead, in the main because of the distorted and limited maps that people draw. These distortions and limitations are seen as indicators of the cognitive processes that shape people's transactions with their surroundings.

Of course, as was illustrated in some detail years ago (Canter 1977) and has subsequently been elaborated with great precision (Kitchen 1994), a number of methodological difficulties arise from basing psychological models solely on "sketch maps." The skills of the producer may distort what he or she draws. The ability to understand the nature of the exercise may relate to cartographic training and the precise details of the instructions may have a strong influence. However, important aspects of the respondents' conceptual system are clearly indicated by what they choose to draw and how they choose to draw it when asked to "draw a map from memory" of any particular area.

Considerable potential for understanding criminals' ways of thinking about their crimes and the locations in which they commit them lies in asking them to "draw a map that indicates where you have committed crimes." What follows are some illustrations of the results of such explorations. They indicate the potentials for this line of research. At the present time, these results are presented as indications of the possibilities for such a methodology in the hope that they will stimulate others to develop them further.

Icons of Experience

The instructions to "draw a map" assume some understanding of the mapping process. In the British education system, children are given such exercises throughout their school career. It may start at the age of 7 or 8 with being required to draw a map (or more accurately a plan) of their classroom, or to draw a map of their route to school. British offenders can thus be assumed to have some idea of what is required from an early age. In the explorations we have carried out, we have never found individuals who did not understand the instructions, even though they may have found it challenging to follow those instructions in relation to their own criminal activity. Therefore, when a respondent chooses to interpret the instructions in an unexpected way, it is worth considering the implications of that reaction.

An interesting illustration of this is Figure 7-1. J, who had a heroin habit from the age of 14, drew this figure. He had a long history of drug dealing, burglary, car theft, and other crimes all over England. He would often spend 24 hours away from home on a burglary spree, travelling along country roads over great distances to commit crimes. Drawing a map of these activities would clearly be demanding for any person. J therefore had to choose some aspect of his criminal activity to represent. He chose to draw a number of sketches of particular locations without any indication of the links between them, perhaps illustrating something of his haphazard approach to his criminal activities.

Figure 7-1 is especially instructive. He chose to draw a bird's eye view of a particularly dangerous moment in a car chase. He wrote on the "map" the words "many car chases all over most Areas." The drawing has strongly emphasized skid marks and even the numbering on the top of a police car. The drawing captures the excitement that J obviously feels in the chase and serves to illustrate the importance of the component of adventure he finds in his criminal activities.

J's "map" also indicates the metaphorical qualities of attempts to represent the locational qualities of thoughts and feelings. This is worth bearing in mind even when a map appears to be an attempt at some cartographic exactitude. It is really just one set of symbols that aims at reconstructing experience. The geographical cross-reference in the symbols will always refer to or mask many other psychological associations. Of course, care must be taken in treating the drawings offenders produce as a "projective" technique, like a Rorschach inkblot. But as Lynch (1960) stressed, sketch maps and related drawings may often function as a fruitful focus for a more extended interview, exploring the emotions and conceptualizations associated with the image produced. J's drawing, therefore, serves to illustrate that even the most impoverished attempt at a sketch

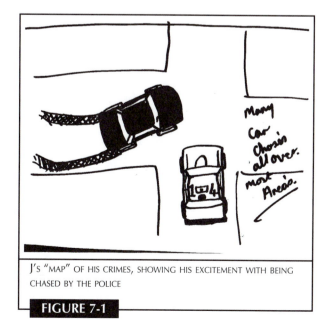

J's "MAP" OF HIS CRIMES, SHOWING HIS EXCITEMENT WITH BEING CHASED BY THE POLICE

FIGURE 7-1

map may emphasize important aspects of offenders' relationships to their crimes and the targets they select.

Routes to Crime

Figure 7-2 is clearly just a set of routes that might be sketched out by a delivery employee seeking to make a note of the journeys that need to be made to various drop-off points. The names on the map are small towns and cities in the north of England. The numbers are those that designate the main inter-city highways (motorways as they're called in the UK, hence M6, M65). The times are the journey times from the base in Liverpool. In some senses, that is what this sketch is, although for F, it was the routes she took to go shop-lifting, taking from stores rather than delivering to them.

For her, stealing from well-known department stores was treated as if it were a job. She stole to order. This is her collection route. People asked her for specific goods then she went off to steal them. She visited the well-known chain stores in the knowledge that they would have what she wanted, preferring those in the smaller towns because their security was more lax. A mother with seven grandchildren, she rarely visited the places on her map except on "business." She just parked in the central car park near the stores where she did her thieving, leaving each load in the car while she moved on to the next shop, and then returned straight home.

F's mental image of crime scenes is a set of opportunities distributed throughout a network of available small towns. The reliability of goods on offer in chain stores across the country means that the only thing she needs to know is whether any small town boasts a Woolworth's or Marks & Spencer. If it does, then the town name implies a standard pattern of activity. She would even steal from the shops in a standard sequence that she had developed over her years of theft.

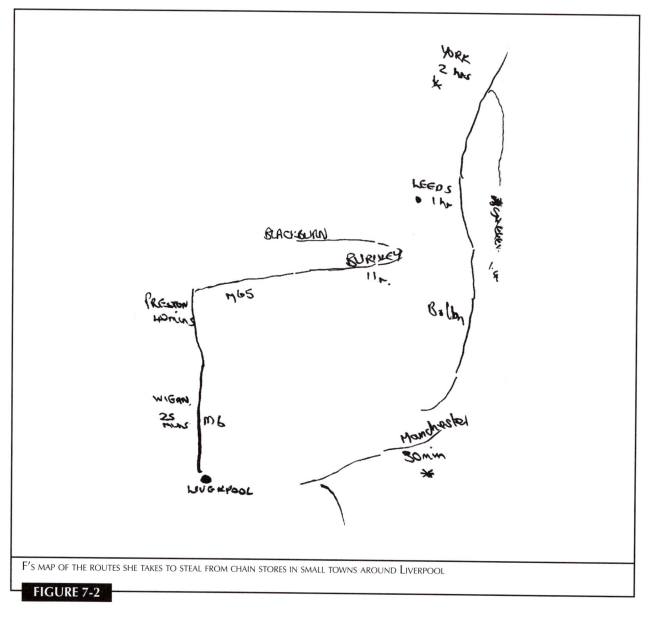

F's MAP OF THE ROUTES SHE TAKES TO STEAL FROM CHAIN STORES IN SMALL TOWNS AROUND LIVERPOOL

FIGURE 7-2

F gives no details of Liverpool, where she is based, or the link roads from her home in Liverpool to the motorways. She just sets off on the road to crime. She reported that she would never steal in her local shopping center, in part because she only goes there on her "days off" from work, and also because she does not want to risk losing membership in her local golf club if she should be caught.

Designations of Locality

When crime is an integral part of the offender's day-to-day activities, the sketch maps that are drawn can be taken as indicators of how they see the structure of their local world. This view can be seen clearly in D's map (Figure 7-3), which is not untypical for young, prolific burglars. D's home is in the middle of the map, but the Grand Union Canal to the right distinctly demarcates the area he chooses to draw. A more direct representation of the no-man's land into which a criminal will not venture to commit crimes could not be drawn.

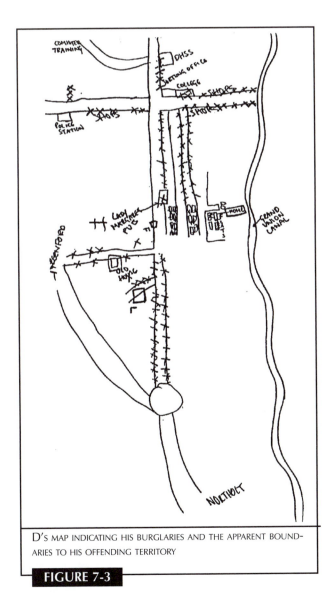

D'S MAP INDICATING HIS BURGLARIES AND THE APPARENT BOUND-ARIES TO HIS OFFENDING TERRITORY

FIGURE 7-3

In contrast, the area around D's home is marked in some detail. The salient locations in it, his local pub, which interestingly forms the center of the map, the DHSS (Department of Health and Social Security) office where he gets his welfare checks, and the police station are all marked as well as the sets of tower blocks that create the area in which he has an apartment. But what is particularly noteworthy is his memory of the locations in which he has carried out a burglary, each carefully marked with a cross. The prolific crosses are clearly on the main routes he takes between this home and the DHSS office and out towards the main road junction that defines for him the edge of his domain.

D's map reveals a dense world of criminal opportunity. The crosses that mark his crime sites are not casually placed there. The thinner pattern of crosses around the "old house," and on the way to the police station, show that he has carefully marked actual sites. The street in which he has burgled virtually every house or shop is also marked, showing the assiduousness with which he has broken into every place on both sides of the road. This map reveals a burglar for whom all the properties that he has easy access to are feasible targets for his criminal activities. But this is also a constrained world, bounded by the limits of his familiarity, the police station, the DHSS office, and the canal.

Sometimes young burglars like D produce maps with even more detail, proud to mark on every building the particular form of security devices and burglar alarms it has. For these people, the sketch map reveals the plan of work that shapes their deeds. It can almost be regarded as an action plan that will be drawn on in the future as well as a record of what they have enjoyed doing in the past.

Indications of Involvement

When the crimes become an all-embracing drive that takes over the offender's life, then the sketch maps the offenders draw can be chilling in the sense they give of dominating the offender's life. Figure 7-4 was drawn by a man in his mid-20s to indicate the locations in which he had raped 14 different women, all strangers to him, over a period of a few months.

P has taken the trouble to mark on the locations of his assaults their chronological order as well as indicating with an X the location of his home during the period he was attacking these strangers. It is remarkable, not to say unnerving, to see how closely this schematic pattern reflects the model put forward by D. Canter and P. Larkin (1993) on the basis of the crime locations of serial rapists in the south of England. The home is clearly at the conceptual center of P's map. He is also aware of a process in which his first attack is some distance from his home, but then a wave of attacks happen in the closer area around his home, which he has bounded with a line. He then sees himself moving out from that location, after his sixth crime, to a further region before moving back again for the eleventh and twelfth and further on again for the thirteenth, before attacking closer to home for the fourteenth, where he was caught.

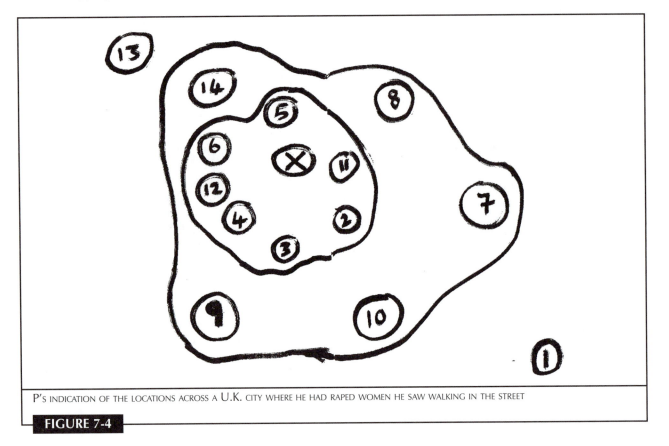

P's INDICATION OF THE LOCATIONS ACROSS A U.K. CITY WHERE HE HAD RAPED WOMEN HE SAW WALKING IN THE STREET

FIGURE 7-4

After his initial rape of a girlfriend, he took to following women as they left railway stations on their way home, attacking them as they walked through areas where there was no one to witness his assault. For P, the whole of the city around where he lived became his stalking ground, moving from one locality to another in case he was recognized. The sequence shows clearly that he would never carry out more than a couple of assaults in adjacent localities before moving on to somewhere distinctly different. He was aware of doing that and felt he had been caught because he moved back to an area where he had committed crimes earlier and where the police were therefore waiting for him.

The lack of any other detail in P's map than the rape sites and his home show how important these assaults became in defining his existence. He could move anywhere he liked and find possible victims. The only thing that brings significance to a location appears to be whether he carried out an attack there. Within this framework he seems to have a notion of boundaries that relate the offence to his home location. This gives the impression of his being aware that he had been moving into unknown territory, although he puts a lot of space between his first assault and any of the others.

Conclusions: The Values of Imaginary Maps

The four examples presented here were selected to illustrate the ways in which criminal activity can be more fully understood if the mental representations that criminals have of where they commit their crimes are explored. Asking offenders to draw maps of where they commit their crimes does reveal some interesting insight into their approach to their offending. However, the sketch maps on their own without any other background information can be misleading. They are best as a focus for an interview that explores the criminal's lifestyle and offending career.

Nonetheless, despite the difficulties inherent in exploring what is going on in the minds of criminals, this brief examination of their mental representations shows that there is another side to the maps that can fill an atlas of crime. These maps are the products of the amalgamated activities of many individuals. Without knowing how those individuals see the geography of their crime, the maps produced by cartographers can only be seen as a relatively superficial account of the effects of criminals' actions with only indirect hints of their causes.

By understanding the limited horizons of some criminals, the way others shape their lives around their criminal activities, and the dominant roles that others assign to the routes and pathways to criminal opportunities, it is possible to begin to see the psychological processes that underpin an atlas of crime. Development of this work will help us understand not just the way criminals' mental geography shape their activities but how such processes shape the transactions that we all have with our surroundings.

References

Bartlett, F.C. 1932. *Remembering*. Cambridge: Cambridge University Press.

Brantingham, P.J., and P.L. Brantingham. 1981. *Environmental Criminology*. Prospect Heights, IL: Waveland Press.

Canter, D. 1994. *Criminal Shadows*. London: HarperCollins.

———. 1977. *The Psychology of Place* London: Architectural Press.

Canter, D., and P. Larkin. 1993. The Environmental Range of Serial Rapists. *Journal of Environmental Psychology* 13: 63-69.

Capone, D.L., and W. Nicholas, Jr. 1976. Urban Structure and Criminal Mobility. *American Behavioral Scientist* 20: 199-213.

Constanzo, D.B, W.C. Halperin, and N. Gale. 1986. Criminal Mobility and the Directional Component in Journeys to Crime. In R.M. Figlio, S. Hakim, and G.F. Rengert, eds. *Metropolitan Crime Patterns*. Monsey, NY: Willow Tree Press.

Kitchen, R.M. 1994. Cognitive Maps: What Are They and Why Study Them? *Journal of Environmental Psychology* 14, 1-19.

Lynch, K. 1960. *The Image of the City*. Cambridge, MA: MIT Press.

Pettiway, L.E. 1982. Mobility of Burglars and Robbery Offenders. *Urban Affairs Quarterly* 18 (2), December: 255-70.

Shaw, C. 1942. *Juvenile Delinquency and Urban Areas* Chicago: University of Chicago Press.

Trowbridge, C.C. 1913. On Fundamental Methods of Orientation and "Imaginary Maps." *Science* 38 (990): 888-97.

Cognitive Maps and the
Fear of Crime

Patricia Gilmartin

Do any of the following scenarios seem familiar?

"Dang! I forgot to pick up my prescription on the way home! I need the medicine, but it's dark now, do I dare go out and get it?"

"Yes, Robbie, you can go ride your bike with Kris, but don't go near that neighborhood across Hunter Street."

"You're traveling to Colombia? Be careful; that's a dangerous place!"

They do for most people. Each one expresses a fear of crime linked to a specific place or time, which may influence one's behavior. Most of us have in our heads rather detailed cognitive maps of places where the risk of being a victim of crime is relatively high. These cognitive maps may range in scale from the national or even international to one's own neighborhood. They may be accurate or inaccurate, detailed or impressionistic, but they are important for several reasons. Perhaps most fundamentally, cognitive maps of where criminal activity is likely to occur serve a survival function by warning us away from those places and thus have a direct impact on our spatial behavior. In addition to influencing our overt actions, cognitive maps affect our sense of well-being or apprehension associated with specific places. And because cognitive maps of crime are somewhat different for different groups of people, they demonstrate the differential effects of crime (or the perception of it) for those groups. One of the earliest and still-classic studies of how people perceive and react to the danger of crime was centered on a black neighborhood in inner Philadelphia (Ley 1974). Three gangs of teenagers had divided the neighborhood spatially into territories or turfs, which they controlled and defended from incursions from rival gang members. The gangs' activities ranged from just obnoxious to the overtly violent, and seemingly minor incidents could erupt suddenly into major confrontations, contributing to an atmosphere of tension and uncertainty within the neighborhood. Residents of the neighborhood identified crime, especially juvenile and gang-related crime, as the community's most serious problem (Ley 1974).

Fear of these juvenile gangs influenced people's spatial behaviors within their neighborhood in a variety of ways. For gang members, it meant limiting their mobility to the few blocks comprising their gang's territory. For other, non-gang teenagers, the gangs' control of the spatial environment led to high numbers of student transfers to other school districts and to high absentee rates for students who were fearful of walking through gang turfs to get to school. Teenagers also abandoned neighborhood amenities, such as parks and movie theaters, rather than travel through dangerous gang turfs to get to them. Younger children were also affected by their parents' cognitive maps of crime in the neighborhood. About a quarter of the residents surveyed said they would either not permit a seven-year-old to leave the house or to range more than two doors away; 93 percent said they would not let the child leave his or her home block (Ley 1974).

Figure 7-5 summarizes residents' cognitive maps of danger in their neighborhood. The map reveals an "acute differentiation of space" (Ley 1974: 220), reflecting the perceived risk or "stress" associated with places where gang members hung out and where drug dealing was concentrated. While certain areas, streets, and intersections are perceived as being dangerous, the apparent threat can subside within distances as short as a block.

It seems logical that in moving through their neighborhood, residents would seek to avoid the most dangerous places, and such proved to be the case. When residents were queried about routes they would take at night between given points within the neighborhood, almost a third of them refused to even consider walking any route at night. The others' answers reflected a sensitivity to the perceived stress patterns within the neighborhood. As shown in Figure 7-6, people formulated indirect routes, which often added considerable length to the distance, rather than traverse high-crime areas. Participants may have been well aware that their chosen route was not the shortest, most direct path, but in another study, researchers found that people estimated route distances to be longer through areas which they perceived to be dangerous than through those thought to be relatively safe (Mattson and Rengert 1995).

David Ley's study shows that place, space, and environment contain meanings that affect people's behaviors and attitudes. Ley concluded that, "the behavioral environment emerges as the most salient both in perception and in decision making. When inner city residents ascribe properties to space . . . their spatial image is more likely to be colored by behavioral than by physical characteristics" (Ley 1974: 229).

How accurate, in general, are people's cognitive maps of crime? The answer to this question depends, in part, on the scale at which one asks the question. At the macro

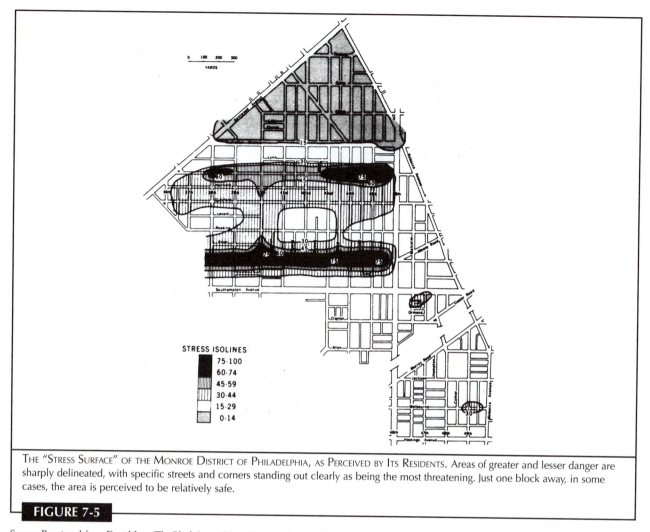

THE "STRESS SURFACE" OF THE MONROE DISTRICT OF PHILADELPHIA, AS PERCEIVED BY ITS RESIDENTS. Areas of greater and lesser danger are sharply delineated, with specific streets and corners standing out clearly as being the most threatening. Just one block away, in some cases, the area is perceived to be relatively safe.

FIGURE 7-5

Source: Reprinted from David Ley, *The Black Inner City as Frontier Outpost.* Washington, DC: Association of American Geographers, 1974, p. 221.

level—cities, regions, states, and countries—people may have an overall impression about the relative safety and crime rates in those places, but such generalizations overlook the variability within macro-scale spaces and, thus, are rather inaccurate. Even at the level of a small area within a city—a six-by-eight block neighborhood in Vancouver—considerable inaccuracies have been found (Brantingham et al. 1986). In this study, residents overestimated the actual characteristics of criminal behavior within their neighborhood on three of the four measures used. In another study, where the researcher measured the perceived risk of personal crimes in 10 Minneapolis neighborhoods, residents' perceptions of the danger from such crimes were found to be significantly correlated with the actual crime rates (McPherson 1978).

It is not uncommon for people's fear of crime to exceed actual crime rates, a phenomenon that some researchers have linked to perceived physical and social incivilities in an area (Perkins et al. 1992; Perkins et al. 1993; Taylor 1989). Social incivilities include such things as public drunkenness and drug-dealing, prostitution, and loitering, while physical incivilities encompass vacant buildings, overgrown

vegetation, abandoned automobiles, graffiti, and the like. Studies have shown that people's fear of crime and perceptions of incivilities are correlated to actual measurements of physical incivilities (Perkins et al. 1992).

The accuracy of cognitive maps of crime also may be a product of "ecological labels" that some people attach to certain areas. Ecological labels are "expectations of particular behavioral patterns that people attach to specific places . . . . [P]eople impute reputations to specific places, treat those reputations as if they were based in actual factual events, and adjust their behavior in those places to accommodate the expectations drawn from the imputation. [In extreme cases,] the imputation of an ecological label eventually changes the character of a labeled place so that its factual aspects—the kind of people found and the sorts of events that occur there—come to match the content of the label" (Brantingham et al. 1986: 143). An example of ecological labeling was found in a study of perceptions of crime in Akron, Ohio (Pyle 1980). The researcher's most consistent finding was that suburbanites perceived the downtown area to be generally unsafe and their suburbs to be mostly crime-free, overlooking sections of both areas that

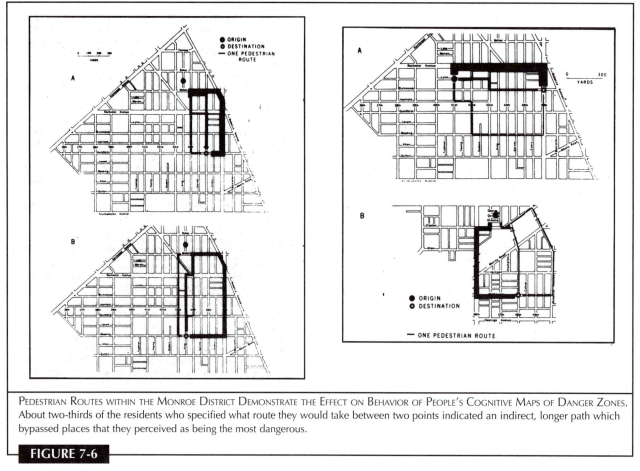

PEDESTRIAN ROUTES WITHIN THE MONROE DISTRICT DEMONSTRATE THE EFFECT ON BEHAVIOR OF PEOPLE'S COGNITIVE MAPS OF DANGER ZONES. About two-thirds of the residents who specified what route they would take between two points indicated an indirect, longer path which bypassed places that they perceived as being the most dangerous.

FIGURE 7-6

Source: Reprinted from David Ley, *The Black Inner City as Frontier Outpost.* Washington, DC: Association of American Geographers, 1974, pp. 224–25.

did not match their generalized labels. Another investigation showed that people's perception of the safety of central Philadelphia was correlated not with actual crime rates and familiarity with the city but with the ethnicity of the population (Rengert and Pelfrey 1997).

Group Differences in Cognitive Maps of Crime

Numerous studies have shown that, in general, women have cognitive maps of violent crime that are both quantitatively and qualitatively different from men's. Compared to men, women are much more fearful of being crime victims, have different perceptions of what environments pose the greatest risk to their personal safety, and, in response, limit or alter their spatial mobility more than men. James Garofalo (1979) found, for example, that the most important variable in explaining people's fear of crime was gender (followed by the actual crime rate, age, personal experience with victimization, and evaluation of the local police). In another study that was part of a national crime survey, several thousand Britons were asked whether they would feel unsafe walking in their neighborhood after dark. The percentage of women under the age of 60 who said they would

feel unsafe was four to six times greater than the proportion of men (Smith 1989). Similarly, in another inquiry involving users of three parks in the U.S. Midwest, 90 percent of the women surveyed, compared to only 8 percent of the men, reported feeling unsafe, and the proportion of women who reported avoiding areas of the park was five times greater than for men (Westover 1985: 415). (For other studies documenting women's greater fear of crime see Nasar and Fisher 1993: 197; Pyle 1980: 230; Riger et al. 1978; Riger 1981; Valentine 1989; Warr 1984; and Wittl 1993.)

Whereas familiarity with a place can lead men to feel more safe, this is not necessarily true of women, as shown in a study in which college students were asked to indicate which parts of the city they thought would be unsafe to walk in after midnight (Smith and Patterson 1980). A summary of their responses is shown in Figure 7-7. The women's mental maps showed four concentrations of fear, one of which was the university, the area with which they were the most familiar. The men were most apprehensive about areas in which they had relatively little experience, such as the mental hospital and the downtown area. When questioned about their perception of danger around their own residences, the women, more often than the men, indicated that threatening conditions exist much closer to their homes.

> [I]n fact several of the women indicated that the most dangerous area in the city was actually in their neighborhood . . . . This was much less evident for the men in the sample, most of whom felt that the dangerous parts of the city were spatially separated from them . . . . In general men feel that they are unlikely to be involved in crimes, and the crimes that do occur will probably be located in a part of the city they are not familiar with. (Smith and Patterson 1980: 212)

Similar findings emerged from another study of students' perceptions of safety on a university campus. Male students' perceptions of safety rose with familiarity (measured as the length of time they had lived on campus) and with mobility (the number of locations they visited each week), whereas women students did not develop an increased sense of safety on campus, whether they lived there one year or four, and regardless of their level of mobility (Wittl 1993).

Specific differences have been found in the kinds of environments perceived as dangerous by men and women. Based on a study of students' perceptions of their university campus, Wittl concluded as follows:

> Females feel unsafe in areas where an attacker could hide and surprise them, and in open areas where they might not be heard yelling. Males feel more unsafe in social or competitive areas, areas where they might encounter conflict or a confrontation . . . . Females fear being a victim and look to other people as a defense against harm. Males on the other hand view other individuals or groups as a potential source of threat. (1993: 52-53)

Other areas identified as threatening to women include closed spaces with limited exits; areas poorly lighted at night; large, open spaces, such as parks, which are often deserted at night; and environments affording places where attackers could conceal themselves (Nasar and Fisher 1993; Valentine 1992: 92).

In response to the fear of crime, people adjust their spatial mobility patterns so as to avoid or minimize the perceived risk, as we saw earlier in Figure 7-6. Since women are more apprehensive about crime than men, it seems logical that their movements would be more affected by that fear, and such does seem to be the case. Women have been found to adopt significantly more self-protective behaviors than men (Riger et al. 1978), including, at the extreme end of the response continuum, not going anywhere alone or not going out alone at night (Riger 1981; Valentine 1992: 95; Westover 1985: 416). Other behavioral adaptations reported by women include avoiding public transportation, avoiding specific places at certain times of the day or night, traveling in groups rather than alone, and adopting multiple protective behaviors (Smith 1989: 209-10; Nasar and Fisher 1993: 198). Riger concluded that, "While some precautionary behavior may keep women alert and on guard, the overall impact of restrictions seems crippling and costly" (1981: 64).

In contrast to the research cited above, one study found that women perceived central Philadelphia to be safer than men did (Rengert and Pelfrey 1997). However, several methodological differences between these authors' study and earlier ones make direct comparisons of results problematic. For example, Rengert and Pelfrey gathered respondents' perceptions of daytime rather than nighttime conditions, and they did not take into account familiarity with the areas. (They did look for correlations between familiarity and fear of crime at the group level—overlooking any interactions with gender that may have existed—but found none.) Overall, relatively little research has been done regarding gender differences in cognitive maps of fear. Further research might clarify how factors such as daytime versus nighttime conditions, types of environment (college campus, urban centers, parks, neighborhoods, private vs. public spaces, etc.), and individual differences in respondents (race, class, age, and the like) affect people's fear of crime and their responses to it.

While research regarding gendered perceptions of crime is sparse, studies pertaining to elderly populations are even more rare. Most inquiries concerning the effects of age on people's fear of crime have shown that the elderly perceive themselves to be at greater risk of victimization than do younger people (Eve and Eve 1984; Garofalo 1979; Kennedy and Silverman 1985; Pyle 1980; Smith 1989; Stutz 1976). One author maintains, however, that when one controls statistically for gender and community factors in the fear of crime, differences based on age disappear (Ferraro 1995). Aside from their absolute levels of fear, the cognitive maps of crime of the elderly reveal spatial patterns in areas they believe to be dangerous. A study of the spatial mobility of poor, non-welfare, elderly men living in a downtown San Diego hotel showed that several factors, including health problems and the expense of owning a car or hiring a taxi, limited the men's mobility. Within the limits of these general conditions, however, the men also adjusted their movements to avoid what they perceived as dangerous areas near the hotel (Figure 7-8) (Stutz 1976). The numbers on the isolines in Figure 7-8 show the proportion of the men who would be likely to go to or through the areas around their hotel in a week's time. Far from being random, their movements show a definite east-west bias. Only 20 percent of the men would go even a block south of their hotel because Market Street is perceived as a "stressful and unsafe" area. To the north, Broadway acts as a similar barrier to movement. About 70 percent of their mobility is within an area about two blocks wide (east to west) and three blocks north of their hotel.

Various analyses of reasons for the fear of crime by the elderly conclude that their fear is, in part, a "symbolic" fear related to general feelings of physical vulnerability, powerlessness, fear of the future, and a lack of political, social, and economic resources (Berg and Johnson 1979; Eve and Eve 1984; Skogan 1978; Smith 1989). Mark Warr (1984) surmised that there are age-related differences in the per-

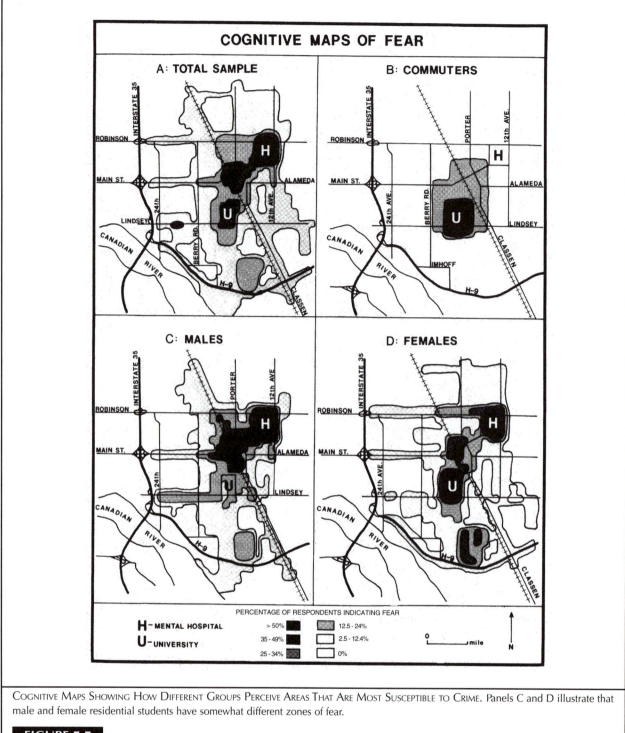

COGNITIVE MAPS SHOWING HOW DIFFERENT GROUPS PERCEIVE AREAS THAT ARE MOST SUSCEPTIBLE TO CRIME. Panels C and D illustrate that male and female residential students have somewhat different zones of fear.

FIGURE 7-7

Source: Reprinted from Christopher J. Smith and Gene Patterson, Cognitive Mapping and the Subjective Geography of Crime. In Daniel Georges-Abeyie and Keith Harries, eds. *A Spatial Perspective.* New York: Columbia University Press, 1980, p. 213.

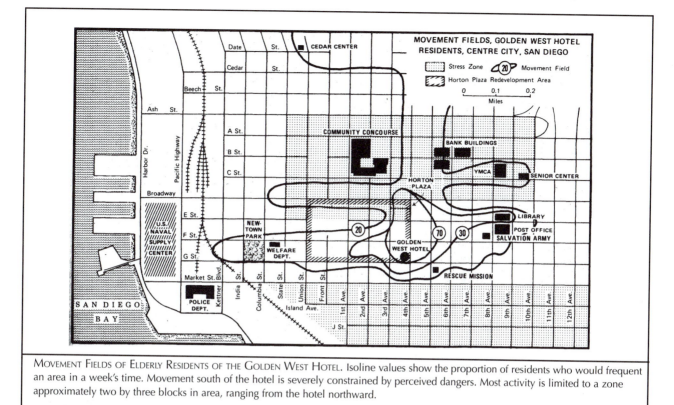

MOVEMENT FIELDS OF ELDERLY RESIDENTS OF THE GOLDEN WEST HOTEL. Isoline values show the proportion of residents who would frequent an area in a week's time. Movement south of the hotel is severely constrained by perceived dangers. Most activity is limited to a zone approximately two by three blocks in area, ranging from the hotel northward.

FIGURE 7-8

Source: Reprinted from Frederick Stutz, Adjustment and Mobility of Elderly Poor Amid Downtown Renewal. *Geographical Review* 55 (1976): 398.

ceived seriousness of certain crimes and that older people have higher levels of fear, in general—not only of crime.

In observing the differences discussed above in the fear of crime as a function of gender and age, it is important to note the interaction between the two. While the fear of crime has been found to be higher for women at all ages and to increase with age for both genders, the increases are greater for men than for women. In one study, six times as many women as men at ages 16-45 expressed concern about their safety (42 percent versus 7 percent), while at ages above 60 the differences had declined to about double (60 percent for women compared to 27 percent for men (Smith 1989; see also Baumer 1985; Ferraro 1995). Susan Smith concluded that, "Certainly fear is most widespread amongst the elderly, but gender retains its salience as a predictor of fear amongst all age groups" (1989: 205).

The preceding discussion contains considerable irony arising from the discrepancy between the rates of actual crimes against certain populations and their perception of their own risk of victimization. Statistics show that the elderly are least likely of all age groups to be victims of violent crime, and yet older citizens fear crime more than younger people. Women are at less risk of violence than men—especially in younger age groups—but women's worries about victimization are several times greater than men's. Young men are the ones most likely to be victims of violent crime, and yet they are the least concerned about it (Garofalo 1979; Riger et al. 1978; Riger 1981; Smith 1989). Gill Valentine

(1992) also has pointed out that women are fearful of public places and unknown men, while the greatest violence done to women occurs in private spaces (their own homes) by men whom they know. This exaggerated or misplaced fear of victimization within certain populations has been called the "paradox of fear" (Warr 1984: 700). If this paradox could be resolved somehow, perhaps groups who underestimate their risk of being a crime victim would develop more cautious behavior patterns, and those who overestimate their risks would be less fearful as they move about their world.

Conclusion

"The power to discriminate between . . . a safe and dangerous space is assimilated at an early age. Survival depends on the ability to learn safe [spatial] configurations" (Ley 1974: 212). As Ley observed, accurate cognitive maps of crime risk are critical to our safety because they inform us about places that are dangerous and to be avoided. Inaccurate perceptions of crime patterns can either lead us unwittingly into hazardous zones or, conversely, cause us to avoid safe areas. In the latter case, the viability of businesses, neighborhoods, urban areas, and public amenities may be jeopardized if people avoid them in the mistaken belief that they are dangerous. For the individual, exaggerated levels of fear of crime unduly constrain spatial mobility and constitute a needless source of anxiety.

In this essay, I have discussed several factors that can affect people's cognitive maps of crime. One, of course, is the actual spatial pattern of criminal activity, but that alone is inadequate to explain the nuances of individuals' perceptions. Ecological labeling also plays a role, as do certain attributes of the places themselves, such as poor nighttime illumination and pockets of concealment where attackers may hide. Psychological factors involving general feelings of powerlessness or vulnerability, as experienced by women and the elderly, also can contribute to exaggerated levels of fear of crime. Time is another factor; it interacts with place in patterning maps of fear because many locations seem safe during daylight hours but become places to be avoided after dark.

In spite of what may seem like a relatively good base of knowledge about cognitive maps of fear, researchers have really only just begun to identify the relevant elements of such maps and the interrelationships among them. Much more research is needed on the topic. A better understanding of how people visualize the spatial patterning of crime could lead to more accurate cognitive maps and enable professionals, such as law enforcement officials, architects, and city planners, to create public spaces that will both discourage criminal activity and be perceived as safe and comfortable places.

References

Baumer, T.L. 1985. Testing a General Model for Fear of Crime: Data from a National Sample. *Journal of Research in Crime and Delinquency* 22: 239-55.

Berg, W.E., and R. Johnson. 1979. Assessing the Impact of Victimization. In W.W. Parsonage, ed. *Perspectives on Victimology*. Beverly Hills, CA: Sage Publications, pp. 58-71.

Brantingham, Paul, Patricia Brantingham, and Diane Butcher. 1986. Perceived and Actual Crime Risks. In Robert Figlio, Simon Hakam, and George Rengert, eds. *Metropolitan Crime Patterns*. Monsey NY: Criminal Justice Press, pp. 139-59.

Eve, Raymond, and Susan Brown Eve. 1984. The Effects of Powerlessness, Fear of Social Change, and Social Integration on Fear of Crime Among the Elderly. *Victimology: An International Journal* 9: 290-95.

Ferraro, Kenneth. 1995. *Fear of Crime: Interpreting Victimization Risk*. Albany: State University of New York Press.

Gallup Organization. 1989. Most Important Problem. *The Gallup Report*, March/April.

Garofalo, James. 1979. Victimization and the Fear of Crime. *Journal of Research in Crime and Delinquency* 16: 80-97.

Kennedy L.W., and R.A. Silverman. 1985. Significant Others and Fear of Crime Among the Elderly. *Journal of Aging and Human Development* 20: 241-56.

Ley, David. 1974. *The Black Inner City as Frontier Outpost: Images and Behavior of a Philadelphia Neighborhood*. Washington, DC: Association of American Geographers.

Mattson, Mark, and George Rengert. 1995. Danger, Distance, and Desirability: Perceptions of Inner City Neighborhoods. *European Journal on Criminal Policy and Research* 3: 70-78.

McPherson, Marlys. 1978. Realities and Perceptions of Crime at the Neighborhood Level. *Victimology: An International Journal* 9: 319-28.

Nasar, Jack, and Bonnie Fisher. 1993. "Hot Spots" of Fear and Crime: A Multi-Method Investigation. *Journal of Environmental Psychology* 13: 187-206.

Perkins, D., J. Meeks, and Ralph Taylor. 1992. The Physical Environment of Street Blocks and Resident Perceptions of Crime and Disorder: Implications for Theory and Measurement. *Journal of Environmental Psychology* 12: 21-34.

Perkins, D., A. Wandersman, R. Rich, and Ralph Taylor. 1993. The Physical Environment of Street Crime: Defensible Space, Territoriality, and Incivilities. *Journal of Environmental Psychology* 13: 29-49.

Pyle, Gerald F. 1980. Systematic Sociospatial Variation in Perceptions of Crime Location and Severity. In Daniel Georges-Abeyie and Keith Harries, eds. *Crime: A Spatial Perspective*. New York: Columbia University Press, pp. 219-45.

Rengert, George, and William Pelfrey, Jr. 1997. Cognitive Mapping of the City Center: Comparative Perceptions of Dangerous Places. In David Wiesburd and Tom McEwan, eds. *Crime Mapping and Crime Prevention*. Monsey, NY: Criminal Justice Press, pp. 193-217.

Riger, Stephanie. 1981. On Women. In Dan Lewis, ed. *Reactions to Crime*. Beverly Hills, CA: Sage Publications, pp. 47-65.

Riger, Stephanie, Margaret Gordon, and Robert Le Bailly. 1978. Women's Fear of Crime: From Blaming to Restricting the Victim. *Victimology: An International Journal* 3: 274-84.

Skogan, Wesley. 1978. *The Fear of Crime among the Elderly, Research into Crimes Against the Elderly (Part II)*. Joint Hearing before the Select Committee on Aging and the Committee on Science and Technology. U.S. House, 95th Congress, second session.

Smith, Christopher J., and Gene Patterson. 1980. Cognitive Mapping and the Subjective Geography of Crime. In Daniel Georges-Abeyie and Keith Harries, eds. *Crime: A Spatial Perspective*. New York: Columbia University Press, pp. 205-18.

Smith, Susan J. 1989. Social Relations, Neighborhood Structure, and the Fear of Crime in Britain. In David Evans and David Herbert, eds. *The Geography of Crime*. London: Routledge, 193-227.

Stutz, Frederick. 1976. Adjustment and Mobility of Elderly Poor Amid Downtown Renewal. *Geographical Review* 55: 391-400.

Taylor, Ralph. 1989. Toward an Environmental Psychology of Disorder: Delinquency, Crime, and Fear of Crime. In Daniel Stokols and Irwin Altman, eds. *Handbook of Environmental Psychology*, Vol. 2. New York: John Wiley, pp. 951-86.

Valentine, Gill. 1992. London's Streets of Fear. In Andy Thornley, ed. *The Crisis of London*. London: Routledge, pp. 90-102.

———. 1989. The Geography of Women's Fear. *Area* 21: 385-90.

Warr, Mark. 1984. Fear of Victimization: Why Are Women and the Elderly More Afraid? *Social Science Quarterly* 65: 681-702.

Westover, Theresa. 1985. Perceptions of Crime and Safety in Three Midwestern Parks. *The Professional Geographer* 37: 410-20.

Wittl, Donna Leigh. 1993. *Conditions of Night Safety: Spatial Patterns and Group Similarities*. M.A. Thesis, Department of Geography, Miami University, Oxford, Ohio.

Maps in Detective Fiction

Leslie Edwards

Maps and detective novels have much in common. Both synthesize data, or clues, to create meaningful patterns; both pull their readers into different worlds; and both by their very natures embody tensions between the known and the unknown, and between truth and deception. If detectives are in a sense wayfarers searching for truth (or, at any rate, an answer to whodunit), maps often help them find their way—and on a more picturesque route. Maps are valuable complements to the detective novel. They amplify the impact of the genre in most of its many facets, whether "puzzle" mysteries that emphasize the pleasures of untangling a problem, novels that plumb the darker aspects of crime and psyche, or narratives that explore different cultures and identities (Westlake 1998; McCracken 1998).

A major role of maps in detective novels is to provide unique insights into the detection process. Scott McCracken (1998: 53) has suggested that detective novels involve "the logical process of perceiving in clues a significance that reveals an explanatory logic where at first there appears to be the fact of an unexplained, violent death." Slowly, a pattern emerges in what initially seems to be an obscure, irrational act. Agatha Christie's Poirot articulates this process in *The Mysterious Affair at Styles*.

> "We will arrange the facts, neatly, each in his proper place. We will examine—and reject. Those of importance we will put on one side; those of no importance . . . blow them away! One fact leads to another—so we continue. Does this fit in with that? This next little fact—no! Ah, that is curious! There is something missing—a link in the chain that is not there. . . . And that curious fact, that possibly paltry little detail that will not tally, we put it here!" He made an extravagant gesture with his hand. (1991: 35)

Yet pattern finding is not always linear; it is not always a matter of links in a chain. Maps help detectives in perceiving non-linear, spatial patterns. Alan MacEachren (1994: 2) noted that "maps are tools that can prompt insight, reveal patterns in data, and highlight anomalies. The goal is to help us notice something." Tony Hillerman vividly articulated this in *Coyote Waits*.

> Leaphorn swiveled in his chair to face the map that dominated the wall behind his desk. It was a magnified version of the "Indian Country" map produced by the Automobile Club of Southern California. . . . For years he had sprinkled it with coded pins using it, so he said, to reinforce his memory. Actually, Leaphorn's memory was remarkable and needed no reinforcement. He used the map in his endless hunt for patterns, sequences, order—something that would

bring a semblance of Navajo *hohzho* to the chaos of crime and violence. (1992: 150)

Detectives often draw maps to impose order and pattern upon the logistical aspects of the crime scene to figure out how the murder was committed and who was in a position to commit it. For example, in Arthur Upfield's *Mystery at Swordfish Reef* (1988), the detective (Bony) created a map that was vital to determining who was near the crime scene (Figure 7-9). Eyes closed, Bony later envisioned the map.

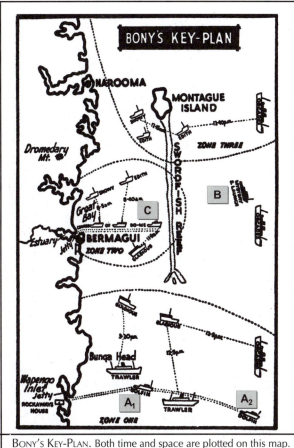

BONY'S KEY-PLAN. Both time and space are plotted on this map. The detective, Bony, deduced that the Dolfin (A1 and A2), disguised itself as a gray steam launch (B) and then traveled undetected in the fog to sink the Do-Me (C).

FIGURE 7-9

Source: Arthur W. Upfield, *The Mystery of Swordfish Reef.* New York: Simon and Schuster, 1988. Used with the permission of the Tessa Sayle Agency. © Bonaparte Holdings Pty., 1939.

Contributor's Note: While this paper will emphasize novels in which a professional or amateur detective solves a crime, other sub-genres of crime fiction, such as thrillers, spy novels, novels of suspense, and police procedurals will also be referenced.

In this pseudo darkness he was able to throw upon the screen of his mind the picture of that key plan evolved by Blade and himself from the maps completed by the launchmen and from information received. On this plan the sea had been forced to retain the tracks of five motor launches, a small steam launch, a trawler and an overseas liner. He continued to have faith that here was hidden a clue of vital importance once he obtained a lead indicating it. (164).

Just as Bony's map captured intangible tracks in water, the map in *Murder on Safari* (Huxley 1989) depicted another intangible: the wind, which was crucial to identifying the murderer because it governed who could hear the bullet. In Christianna Brond's *Tour de Force* (1996), the murderer switched identities with the victim. The stark logic of the map helped Cockrill realize that a switch must have occurred.

He got to work with paper and pencil. The senorita had last been seen at 4:30 (he stubbed with a nicotined forefinger at a rough plan of the hotel and gardens whose perspective grew progressively wider as its details and the glasses of the aguardienta multiplied). At that time all the. . . suspects. . . were gathering together on the beach. . . . he was prepared to say that not for one single moment had any of them been out of his sight. (105)

Sherlock Holmes, rather than drawing a crime scene map, absorbed the huge amount of information available on an ordnance map before pursuing the Hound of the Baskervilles, as he described to Watson.

"I have been to Devonshire."

"In spirit?"

"Exactly. My body has remained in this arm-chair; and has, I regret to observe, consumed in my absence two large pots of coffee and an incredible amount of tobacco. After you left I sent down to Stanford's for the Ordnance map of this portion of the moor, and my spirit has hovered over it all day. I flatter myself that I could find my way about."

"A large-scale map, I presume?"

"Very large." (Doyle 1981: 714)

Beyond the logistics of the crime scene, detectives also use maps to track down criminals, corpses, and stolen goods. Maps are, above all else, transmitters of knowledge (Dent 1993: 3) and detectives use maps of all sorts with striking insights. Peter Wimsey's knowledge of the London sewer map enabled him to predict where a corpse would appear (Sayers and Walsh 1998). Jim Chee followed a gas well-service route map to find a stolen backhoe (Hillerman 1990). Sharavi hacked into a Department of Motor Vehicles file to find an address, then used a Thomas Guide map to locate it geographically (Kellerman 1998). Neil Hammel deciphered the beeper code language of Albuquerque teenager culture and consulted a map to find the scene of the killer's rendezvous.

When I flipped the beeper right side up I got 17701117 which could be Main [177 is M; 01 is A, 1 is I, 17 is N]. . . my eyes returned to the map and wandered around the North Valley until they landed on the Main Canal, which flows from the Sandia Reservation to the South Valley. This Main could be reached by starting at the lateral that flowed by Patricia's house and following the ditch network. (Van Gieson 1998: 199)

Sonny Baca searched an old Spanish land grant map when hunting for a criminal who was about to dynamite a truck carrying nuclear waste, and keyed into symbolism important to the criminal.

"He could follow an arroyo to the highway and never be seen," Sonny said. "He would go east toward the rising sun on the day of the summer solstice. The sun would stand still."

He looked at Rita. "On the day of the summer solstice, the suns stands still, then begins its journey south," she intoned.

"The explosion will make fire, the sun standing still," Sonny kept repeating, the mantra increasing the tension he felt. "It's here," he whispered, and looked closely at the names of the arroyos on the map. "Arroyo del Oso, Calazas Arroyo, Arroyo de las Gallinas, Arroyo del Sol [of the Sun]." He stopped and felt his heart skip a beat. "That's it!" he shouted. (Anaya 1996: 312)

And a map's visual hierarchy made the criminal's escape strategy pop out in *Murder in Memoriam*, when a new map with bright yellow and orange highways replaced an antique wall map in police headquarters.

He played a canny game, suspecting the first thing we'd do would be to check all points on route. It was a good bluff, choosing the long way around. . . . Who would of thought of a guy being so smart as to drive an extra 600 kilometres to blur his tracks? It nearly worked! It was the Departmental Supplies Section of Haute-Garonne that put us right, by accident! They had the nice idea of replacing our old wall map with one where the motorways are almost phosphorescent. (Daeninckx 1991: 168)

Maps can also reveal motive. An ordnance map unveiled the first glimmers of the enemies' motives in the classic spy thriller, *The Riddle of the Sands*. The hero devoured the information on the map of Friesland, Germany (Figure 7-10), in the dim light of a railroad carriage, and tangled thoughts began to sort themselves out.

One of the threads of my skein, the canal thread, tingled sympathetically, like a wire charged with a current. Standing astraddle on both seats, with the map close to the lamp, I greedily followed the course of the "tief" southward. . . . For the first time that day there came to me a sense of genuine inspiration. (Childers 1987: 282)

In Eric Ambler's comic novel *The Light of Day* (1962), a map would also provide clues to the motive, if it could be obtained. The narrator, a reluctant, self-interested spy, regretted telling his spy-masters about the map he had seen in the enemies' hands when he was forced to take extraordinary risks to find it: "I was annoyed with myself. I should

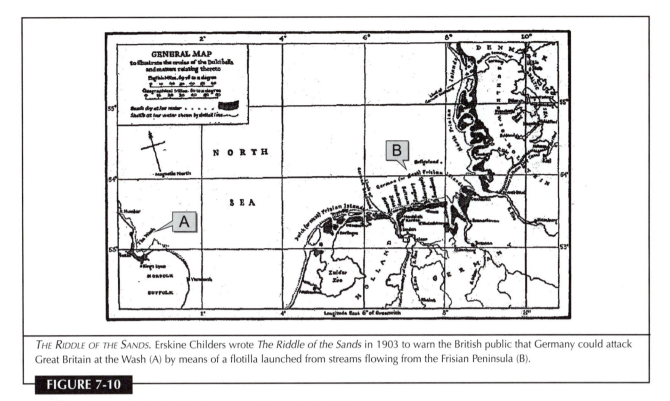

THE RIDDLE OF THE SANDS. Erskine Childers wrote *The Riddle of the Sands* in 1903 to warn the British public that Germany could attack Great Britain at the Wash (A) by means of a flotilla launched from streams flowing from the Frisian Peninsula (B).

FIGURE 7-10

Source: Erskine Childers, *The Riddle of the Sands.* London: Penguin Books, 1987.

have known better. Any sort of map is catnip to intelligence people" (148).

In all these cases, deciphering the maps enhanced the pleasures of puzzle solving. Indeed, skilled map-readers and detectives share the satisfaction of figuring out how and why, no matter the context. In *Mother Nature,* a geologist detective searched through maps and found the motive for murder in a zoning code. However, identifying other patterns on the map eclipsed the find.

> I traced Santa Rosa and Piner Creeks, which emptied their waters directly into the Laguna right near the old Ferris place. The Army Corps of Engineers had straightened them and ramped their banks into an engineering-approved angle designed to deliver water downhill faster so that during heavy rains the upper end of the drainage—in this case the City of Santa Rosa—wouldn't flood. But everything downstream from these creeks would. Faster. Deeper. And carrying more sand, gravel, brush, old tires, couches, and runaway Buicks. So if the Laguna, Mark West Creek, and the Russian River ever backed up at the same time some thousand-year freakish amount of water charged down the channelized creeks, the Laguna could flood to a higher level. Maps are such fun. (Andrews 1998: 264)

Another use of maps in detective novels, rather than as a tool for the detective, is to orient the reader to the characters' movements within the setting. Maps often convey information more economically and thoroughly than can the text on its own.

> Writers may be especially attracted to maps because they are so well acquainted with the limitations of written communication in. . . the space-time continuum. Written lan-

guage is linear. . . . Maps, on the other hand, involve far less transcription from reality and less formatting than idioms do. Maps appeal in a natural and logical way to our visual sense. (Muehrcke and Muehrcke 1974: 318-19)

Thus, a village map was placed in *The Ice House* (Walters 1992) as a type of "dynamic media" to amplify the "through line" of the plot (Muller 1998: 179). Following the characters in detective novels on maps provided in the books, readers are able to descend into a cave system in New Mexico (Figure 7-11; Barr 1998); go through the mazes of ancient Chinese and Italian monasteries (Van Gulik 1983; Eco 1983); navigate South Florida inlets (White 1993); orient to the Anasazi country of New Mexico (Hillerman 1990); penetrate Venetian lagoons (Dibdin 1994); explore Copenhagen and Greenland (Høeg 1994); and perambulate through English villages (George 1996) or medieval England (Peters 1997). Crime can happen anywhere, anytime.

In some cases, depiction of a new place or culture can take precedence over examination of crime and criminals, providing both new knowledge and escape from the workaday world. H.R.F. Keating (1981: 12) declared that it is "people in their settings" that provides the irresistible fascination of the mystery. Rudolfo Anaya said of his series that he was "more interested in conveying a cultural context, a tradition, a history," than he was with the conventions of the mystery genre (Dick and Sirias 1998: 178). The reader's immersion in setting can be enhanced by the map's style. Civil War Richmond comes to life in *Dead March* through a reproduced map of 1869 Richmond (MacMillan 1998); cal-

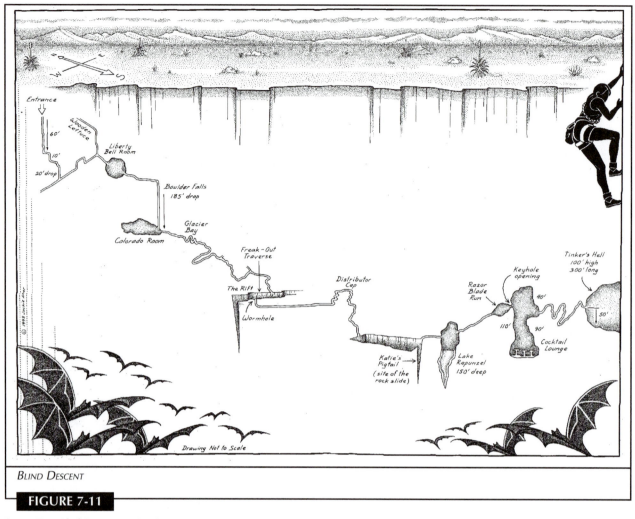

BLIND DESCENT

FIGURE 7-11

Source: From *Blind Descent*. By Nevada Barr, copyright © 1988 by Nevada Barr. Used by permission of G.P. Putnam's Sons, a division of Penguin Putnam, Inc.

ligraphic strokes evoke Chinese culture in the Judge Dee series (e.g., van Gulik 1977); detailed line drawings evince the (seemingly) secure world of Agatha Christie's St. Mary Mead (Riviere and Naudin 1997); flying geese suggest Nantucket in *Dark Nantucket Noon* (Langton 1981); and a shadow looms over a street map of New York in *The Interceptor* (Herschlag 1998). Also, an advance review indicates that the exotic allure and adventure that maps can convey, as well as the challenges of deciphering them, will play an important role in an upcoming work by Aruturo Pérez-Reverte, which involves sunken galleons, "18th century map-making and problems of longitude and latitude." (Gussow 1999: B-4).

Imaginative map reading by characters to convey mood and character insight is another type of map use in detective novels. Muehrcke and Muehrcke (1974: 320) described imaginative map reading as follows: "A map is both more and less than itself, depending on who reads it. . . . To a person who uses his imagination, a map is greater than itself, for it evokes images and emotions not apparent on the piece of paper that is called a map." In *The Moor*, a charac-

ter emotionally animates a map of Dartmoor, expressing the foreboding she feels.

> This was, judging by the few roads and fewer dwellings, one of the most deserted areas of the entire moor, a place thick with the Gothic script mapmakers use to indicate antiquities: hut circles, stone rows, stone avenues, tumuli, and ancient trackways, as well as an ominous scattering of those grass-tuft symbols that indicate marshland. There were no orange rows for miles, or even the hollow lines of minor roads, only densely gathered contour lines, numerous streams and the markings for "rough" pasture. A howling wilderness, indeed. (King 1998: 45)

Similarly, the detective in *Plum Island* conjures up ominous danger from a map of an island where secret animal disease research is conducted.

> When you see this island on maps and navigation charts, most of the time there aren't any features shown on the island—no roads, no mention of Fort Terry, nothing except the words, "Plum Island—Animal Disease Research— U.S. Government—Restricted." And the island is usually colored yellow—the color of warning. Not real inviting, not even on a map. . . . And if you go so far as to picture the

place you get this Poe-like image of the ultimate dim Thule, a dark landscape of dead cattle and sheep, bloating and rotting on the fields, vultures feeding on the carrion, then dying themselves from the infected flesh. (DeMille 1997: 95)

In *Map of Mistrust*, an intelligence agent symbolically reads an airline map that depicts flight routes as characterizing geographic zones of mistrust created by hostile nations (MacKinnon 1948). In *God in Concord*, characters reveal their true nature in the way they imaginatively read maps. A real estate magnate placed maps of different scales on his map table to "focus the zoom lens of his interest swiftly, rushing down from far away to stare at single souls laid bare. . . . Today their attention was directed at Concord, Massachusetts, [where they were planning to covertly install a hazardous waste site]" (Langton 1993: 4-5). Juxtaposed with this rapacious view, Homer Kelly in the next chapter "was studying a map of Concord. His was an old one. . . . Looking at the map, consulting Thoreau's journal, Homer could imagine the mid-nineteenth century town. Daily he studied the record of Thoreau's explorations of his native village. Daily he set off to see the places for himself, looking for the wellsprings of Thoreau's prose (Langton 1993: 7).

Maps, then, go beyond the transmittal of the concrete when they are embellished graphically or read with imagination. Further departing from the factual, maps can be deceptive. Mark Monmonier (1991: 2) noted that "[m]aps, like speeches and painting, are authored collections of information, and are also subject to distortions arising from ignorance, greed, ideological blindness or malice," qualities often central to the detective novel. In *Plum Island* (with echoes of Poe's *The Gold Bug*), the murderer created a false map showing Captain Kidd's treasure buried on his own property. In plumbing the crime, a character expounded as follows upon the inherent untrustworthiness of old maps:

There was a real problem with geographic place names in the New World. Some English sea captains had only Dutch maps, some had maps showing the wrong name for an island or river, for instance, and the spelling was atrocious, and some maps simply had blanks and some had purposely misleading information. A pirate's treasure map, which could be drawn from a chart, could start with some inaccuracies. And you have to remember there are not many authentic treasure maps in existence today, so it's hard to draw any conclusions about the general accuracy of buried-treasure maps. (DeMille 1997: 322)

Similarly, in *Bombay Ice*, a novel rich in cartographic metaphors, the narrator contemplates mapmakers' treatment of Bombay's indeterminate boundaries in ways that seem to also echo the changing nature and outward appearance of the novel's characters.

Old maps of Bombay are unreliable, charts of a city which doesn't exist anymore—or never did. Cartographers here

have always disagreed on where land stopped and liquid began. In the seventeenth century, when the future metropolis consisted of no more than seven islands emerging reluctantly from a tidal swamp, every mapmaker altered and reinvented the geography, as if those islands were mere visions based on an insubstantial fabric whose shape could change to suit the audience. (Forbes 1999: 6)

Good guys deceive with maps, too. In *Nobody Wore Black*, Jane believes she is choosing a vacation spot with a random pinprick on a map, but actually her detective husband Dagobert is manipulating her to travel to the crime scene (Ames 1951). And Nancy Drew created a fake version of a treasure map to foil her adversaries in *The Quest of the Missing Map*.

"When Irene and Fred Brown followed me that day and I was afraid they might steal the precious paper, I mailed it to Dad at his office. Just before that I made a sketch of it, but I deliberately made all the instructions appear backward." Nancy adjusted the map to the bright sunlight. Thus viewed, with the directions showing through it, the diagram appeared in its true order. (Keene 1942: 209)

Maps can also be deceptive in that they make the world seem simpler than it is. Muehrcke and Muehrcke (1974: 319) observed that "[m]aps cannot be both revealing and complete. Thus the mapping process is one of evaluation, selection, and emphasis, which leads to simplification of the detail and intricacy of the real world. If it were complete, it would be too true to be useful." Monmonier (1991: 1) observed, "[T]here's no escape from the cartographic paradox: to present a useful and truthful picture, an accurate map must tell white lies." Muehrcke and Muehrcke (1974: 319) noted Josephine Tey's acknowledgment of this limitation in *The Man in the Queue* (1927: 138), where the detective realizes "from bitter experience that the very best map-reader had to suffer some severe shocks when he comes face to face with reality."

That reality was painfully clear to an engineer in *The Interceptor*, who struggled with the failings of New York sewer maps drawn up under the 1930s Works Project Administration (WPA)—"[T]hose maps. . . were not truly complete the day they were drawn"(Herschlag 1998: 75). Similarly, in *Rift*, a naïve young woman journeyed through the African Rift Valley, dependent upon a government-issued map that misrepresented unpaved, rutted roads as finished highways. Travel from place to place, deceptively easy on the map, was in reality an agonizing wait to procure transportation to the next disease-ridden, drought-stricken town (Figure 7-12). Further, the map was often wrong and incomplete.

"Let's have a look at your map," Graham said when he came to join me. We pored over it. There was the route: Arba Mintch, Gardulla, Gidole, Conso, Yabega, Mega, Moyale. Gardulla, Gidole: the names swam in and out of focus. "I don't trust maps anymore," I said.

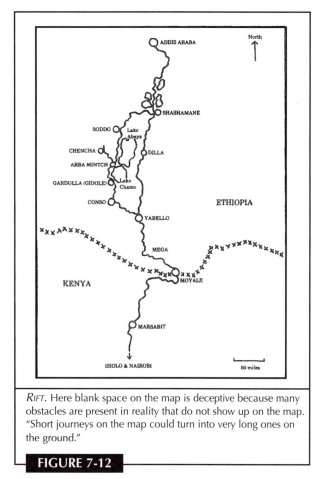

Rift. Here blank space on the map is deceptive because many obstacles are present in reality that do not show up on the map. "Short journeys on the map could turn into very long ones on the ground."

FIGURE 7-12

Source: Liza Cody, Rift. New York: Penguin Books, 1989, p. 100. From *Rift* © Liza Cody 1988. Reproduced by permission of Felicity Bryan and Liza Cody.

"They don't tell the whole story, do they?" he agreed. "Where's Dorsu, for instance? And another thing—these hot springs old Latybalu was boasting about. Where are they?" (Cody 1989: 142)

The unmapped is dangerous. A victim was murdered on a trail "too new to show on the map" in *The Dark Place* (Elkins 1994: 1). Desire lines, the informal paths created by people taking short cuts as they "desire," are not on maps and were metaphors for people's hidden, cruel impulses in the novel *Desire Lines* (Kline 1999). In *A Small Target*, a character observed that, "There are no reliable maps for the wilderness of the soul" (Andreae 1996: 204). The map in the book is disconcertingly barren; its contour lines seem disconcertingly skewed. It is a map of an unknown place, just as, upon confronting the killer (in one of the map's blank spaces), the protagonist senses an unknown psychological state.

Although I was only a hundred or so feet above the clearing, it was like climbing into another dimension, a place where inchoate rules flickered and shifted with the light, where honest nouns and verbs were more dangerous than indulgent half-lies. (Andreae 1996: 223)

In the *Ruined Map*, this inchoate inner world is brought to full realization. Physical maps are used as metaphors of cognitive maps, symbolizing personal integration and the ability to function within recognizable social and physical boundaries and landmarks. One map the detective had was wrong, another was "too simple compared to the actual town" (Abe 1993: 269). Just as his physical maps did not work, his social cognitive maps dissolved in the uncertainties of his relations to others, and his mental maps of the physical world were destroyed by amnesia. K. Lynch described the need for functioning mental maps as follows:

We are supported by the presence of others and by special way-finding devices: maps, street numbers, route signs, bus placards. But let the mishap of disorientation occur, and the sense of anxiety and even terror that accompanies it reveals to us how closely it is linked to our sense of balance and well-being. The very word "lost" in our language means much more than simple geographical uncertainty: it carries a tone of utter disaster (Downs and Stea 1977: 5).

The "ruined map" then, was the detective's mind, destroyed by betrayal, injury, and the total loss of trust in others.

Yet, if maps can be used in detective novels in encountering the dark and vulnerable parts of the human psyche from which horrendous criminal acts spring and victims suffer, they are also, in the hands of masters of the craft, vehicles for witty romps through the landscape. In *Dead Men's Morris* (Mitchell 1986), the map depicts the places contained in the lines of a traditional Morris dance that was danced from site to site in the Oxfordshire countryside. Chapter headings (and the detective, Dame Beatrice Lestrange Bradley) follow the map that follows the dance (Figure 7-13). In the *Moving Toyshop* (Crispin 1988), Gervase Fen ponders a toyshop that transmogrifies overnight into the longstanding Winkworth's grocery. (The accompanying map shows the peripatetic toyshop, not Winkworth's.) And the exaggerated notations in the map in *The Gyrth Chalice* (Allingham 1989) capture the almost farcical high spirits that sometimes characterize Marjory Allingham's work.

Thus, maps serve detective novels in a stunningly full realization of their range: pattern conveyors, works of art expressing culture and emotion, invaluable tools, promoters of deception, jarringly incomplete betrayers of our trust, and imaginative works providing fun and escape. No wonder, then, that Internet ads for Delano Ames' *Nobody Wore Black* (1951) prominently proclaim "Map" to lure readers to the purchase (Figure 7-14).

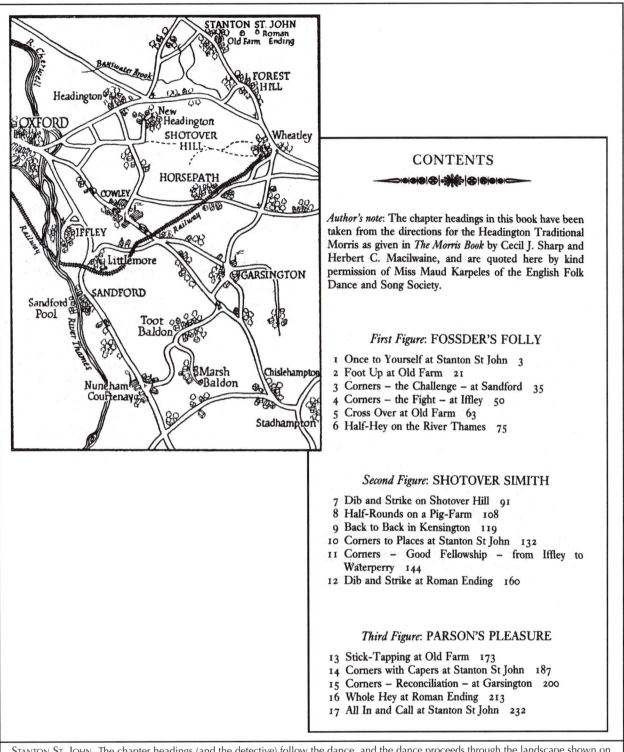

CONTENTS

Author's note: The chapter headings in this book have been taken from the directions for the Headington Traditional Morris as given in *The Morris Book* by Cecil J. Sharp and Herbert C. Macilwaine, and are quoted here by kind permission of Miss Maud Karpeles of the English Folk Dance and Song Society.

STANTON ST. JOHN. The chapter headings (and the detective) follow the dance, and the dance proceeds through the landscape shown on this map from *Dead Men's Morris*.

FIGURE 7-13

Source: Gladys Mitchell, *Dead Men's Morris.* London: Michael Joseph, 1986.

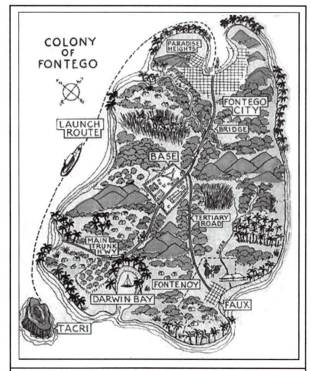

NO MASK FOR MURDER. The Delano Ames map, originally in color, appeared on a Dell paperback mystery. During the late 1940s and early 1950s, a heyday for paperback cover art, Dell Books published many pulp crime novels that featured maps on the back. Besides helping readers through a twisted plot, the maps advertised some of the thrills on offer inside. "Mapbacks" proved to be popular with readers and are still a favorite of paperback collectors today. Ruth Belew was one of the leading illustrators of mapbacks, including No Mask for Murder.

FIGURE 7-14

Source: Text and map reprinted with the permission of the Epicurious Web site <http://travel.epicurious.com/travel/d_play/03_gallery/maps/masked.html>.

References

Abe, Kobo. 1993. *The Ruined Map*. New York: Kodansha America, Inc.

Allingham, Marjory. 1989. *The Gyrth Chalice Mystery*. New York: Avon Books.

Ambler, Eric. 1962. *The Light of Day*. New York: Alfred A. Knopf.

Ames, Delano. 1951. *Nobody Wore Black (Death of a Fellow Traveler)*. New York: Dell Publishing Company.

Anaya, Rudolfo. 1996. *Zia Summer*. New York: Warner Books.

Andreae, Christine. 1996. *A Small Target*. New York: St. Martin's Press.

Andrews, Sarah. 1998. *Mother Nature*. New York: St. Martin's Press.

Barr, Nevada. 1998. *Blind Descent*. New York: G.P. Putnam's Sons.

Brand, Christianna. 1996. *Tour de Force*. New York: Carroll & Graf Publishers, Inc.

Childers, Erskine. 1987. *The Riddle of the Sands*. London: Penguin Books.

Christie, Agatha. 1991. *The Mysterious Affair at Styles*. New York: Berkley Books.

Cody, Liza. 1989. *Rift*. New York: Penguin Books.

Crispin, Edmund. 1988. *The Moving Toyshop*. London: The Penguin Group.

Daeninckx, Didier. 1991. *Murder in Memoriam*. London: Serpent's Tail.

DeMille, Nelson. 1997. *Plum Island*. New York: Warner Books, Inc.

Dent, Borden. 1993. *Cartography: Thematic Map Design*. 3rd ed. Dubuque, IA: Wm. C. Brown Publishers.

Dibdin, Michael. 1994. *Dead Lagoon*. New York: Vintage Books.

Dick, Bruce, and Silvio Sirias. 1998. *Conversations with Rudolfo Anaya*. Jackson: University Press of Mississippi.

Downs, R. M., and D. Stea. 1977. *Maps in Minds: Reflections on Cognitive Mapping*. New York: Harper & Row.

Doyle, Arthur Conan. 1981. *The Hound of the Baskervilles*. London: Octopus Books Limited.

Eco, Umberto. 1983. *The Name of the Rose*. San Diego: Harcourt, Brace Jovanovich.

Elkins, Aaron. 1994. *The Dark Place*. New York: The Mysterious Press.

Forbes, Leslie. 1999. *Bombay Ice*. New York: Bantam Books.

George, Elizabeth. 1996. *In the Presence of the Enemy*. New York: Bantam Books.

Gussow, Mel. 1999. The Pen Is Mighty, but Oh, that Sword. *The New York Times*, July 13, pp. B-1, B-4.

Herschlag, Richard. 1998. *The Interceptor*. New York: The Ballantine Publishing Group.

Hillerman, Tony. 1992. *Coyote Waits*. New York: HarperCollins Publishers, Inc.

———. 1990. *A Thief of Time*. New York: HarperCollins Publishers, Inc.

Høeg, Peter. 1994. *Smilla's Sense of Snow*. New York: Dell Publishing.

Huxley, Elspeth. 1989. *Murder on Safari*. New York: The Penguin Group.

Keating, H.R.F. 1981. *Murder Must Appetize*. New York: The Mysterious Press.

Keene, Carolyn. 1942. *The Quest of the Missing Map*. New York: Grosset & Dunlap.

Kellerman, Jonathan. 1998. *Survival of the Fittest*. New York: Bantam Books.

King, Laurie R. 1998. *The Moor*. New York: Bantam Books.

Kline, Christina Baker. 1999. *Desire Lines*. New York: William Morrow and Company, Inc.

Langton, Jane. 1993. *God in Concord*. New York: Penguin.

———. 1981. *Dark Nantucket Noon*. New York: Penguin Books.

Lynch, K. 1960. *The Image of the City*. Cambridge, MA: M.I.T. Press.

MacEachren, Alan M. 1994. *Some Truth with Maps: A Primer on Symbolization and Design*. Washington, DC: The Association of American Geographers.

MacKinnon, Allan. 1948. *Map of Mistrust*. New York: Unicorn Press.

McCracken, Scott. 1998. *Pulp: Reading Popular Fiction*. New York: St. Martin's Press.

McMillan, Ann. 1998. *Dead March*. New York: Penguin Putnam Inc.

Mitchell, Gladys. 1986. *Dead Men's Morris*. London: Michael Joseph.

Monmonier, Mark. 1991. *How to Lie with Maps*. Chicago: The University of Chicago Press.

Muehrcke, Phillip C., and Meuhrcke, Juliana O. 1974. Maps in Literature. *The Geographical Review* 3: 317-38.

Muller, Adrian. 1998. Minette Walters, Interview by Adrian Muller. In E. Gorman and M. H. Greenberg, eds. *Speaking of Murder*. New York: Berkley Prime Crime.

Peters, Ellis. 1997. *The Rose Rent*. New York: The Mysterious Press.

Riviere, Francois, and Naudin, Jean Bernard. 1997. *In the Footsteps of Agatha Christie* North Pomfret, Vermont: Traflagar Square Publishing.

Sayers, Dorothy. L., and J. Paton Walsh. 1998. *Thrones, Dominations*. New York: St. Martin's Paperbacks.

Tey, Josephine. 1927. *The Man in the Queue*. London: Peter Davies.

Upfield, Arthur W. 1998. *The Mystery of Swordfish Reef*. New York: Simon & Schuster.

Van Gieson, Judith. 1998. *Ditch Rider*. New York: HarperCollins Publishers, Inc.

Van Gulik, Robert. 1983. *The Haunted Monastery*. New York: Charles Scribner's Sons.

———. 1977. *The Chinese Lake Murders*. Chicago: The University of Chicago Press.

Walters, Minette. 1992. *The Ice House*. London: Macmillan London Limited.

Westlake, Donald. E. 1998. Introduction D.E. Westlake, ed. *Murderous Schemes*. Oxford: Oxford University Press.

White, Randy Wayne. 1993. *The Heat Islands*. New York: St. Martin's Press.

CHAPTER 8
Criminal Justice

According to some experts, the criminal justice system is a misnomer (Albanese 1999). It is not a system at all, but a collection of independent agencies created to manage the aftermath of crime commissions. The essays in Chapter 8 cover law enforcement, community policing, crime scene sketches, police and Geographic Information Systems (GIS), and capital punishment. Other topics, though not included, also deserve a mention, such as prisons and juvenile justice. Therefore, maps depicting the spatial dimension of prisoners and juveniles arrested across the U.S. are offered in this introduction.

The criminal justice process begins with an investigation by police and ends with punishment for the perpetrator. Law enforcement began in this country as an informal patrolling of communities by volunteer watchmen (Friedman 1993). With the growing urbanization of American society, policing needed to become more organized and professional to establish order and control expanding criminal activity. Today, law enforcement is divided into three levels: local, state, and federal. Local police consist of municipal officers, county sheriffs, and special agents (e.g., university, airport, and parks officers). It is still the largest component of law enforcement in terms of number of officers (Albanese 1999). Figure 8-1 shows heavy concentrations of sworn officers for 1996 in Alaska, Louisiana, New Hampshire, and Nevada. Some counties in Maine, South Dakota, and Texas also have high rates of police officers. State police patrol roads and highways that connect cities and towns and enforce state laws. Every state has a police force except for Hawaii (Albanese 1999). Federal agents investigate violations of congressional laws. Agencies responsible for this type of police work include the Federal Bureau of Investigation (FBI), Drug Enforcement Agency (DEA), Immigration and Naturalization Service (INS), and the Bureau of Prisons, among others.

The correctional system is also organized on local, state, and federal levels. After offenders are arrested and processed through the courts, some are placed in jails or prisons to serve the terms of their punishment. State facilities hold the majority of prisoners incarcerated in the U.S. (Albanese 1999). Figure 8-2 shows that California, Texas, New York, and Florida had the largest numbers of prisoners in both state and federal custody in 1996. Race and ethnic divisions reveal that African Americans were incarcerated in greater numbers than any other group in many states along the East Coast and in parts of the South and Midwest. Whites occupied more prison space than other groups in the Great Plains and the Pacific Northwest. The spatial anomaly, California, almost has an equal number of each group, but Hispanics represent the largest by a slight margin. These facilities were built for the imprisonment of adult offenders, but what about juvenile offenders, who are traditionally kept separate from adult criminals? Viewed as inappropriate for children, hot, overcrowded, and isolated correctional facilities create environments believed to cause aggression. (Lewis 1992).

The realization that children are committing "adult" crimes has stirred issues regarding juveniles as criminals. A recent poll asked teenagers whether juveniles who are 13 years old should be tried as adults for violent crimes; 56 percent supported an adult trial while 37 percent favored juvenile court (U.S. Department of Justice 1998). The National Center for Juvenile Justice (1999) reported that approximately 2.8 million juveniles (under 18 years of age) were arrested in 1997, a decrease of 1 percent from 1996. Figure 8-3 shows spatial patterns of juvenile arrests by county. Wisconsin appears to have relatively high rates statewide, particularly in the southeastern and northeast central parts of the state. Other counties of significance are located in the Dakotas, Nebraska, Georgia, Arkansas, Louisiana, Texas, Utah, Colorado, Idaho, and Washington.

As has been demonstrated with prisoners and juvenile arrests, geographic techniques can be applied to the study of criminal justice topics. The two disciplines can be combined in many other ways, several of which are presented by the contributors to this chapter. Robert Kaminski, Eric Jefferis, and Chanchalat Chanhatasilpa apply their statistical skills to the essay "A Spatial Analysis of American Po-

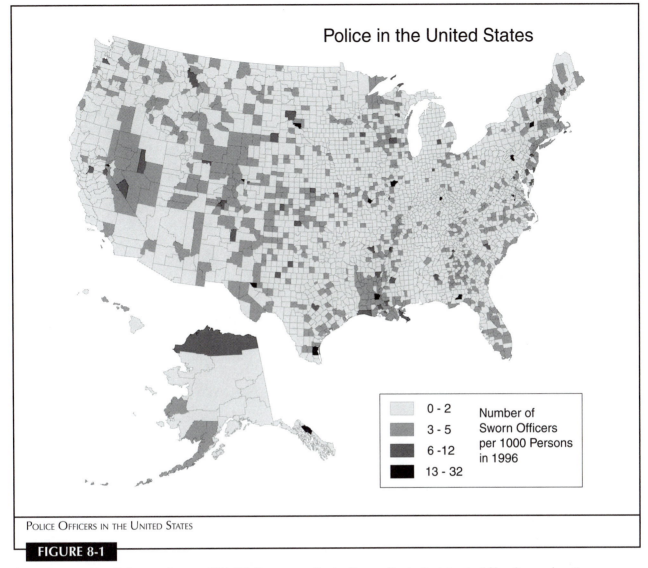

Police in the United States

	Number of Sworn Officers per 1000 Persons in 1996
0 - 2	
3 - 5	
6 -12	
13 - 32	

POLICE OFFICERS IN THE UNITED STATES

FIGURE 8-1

Source: Directory of Law Enforcement Agencies, 1996. U.S. Department of Justice. Bureau of Justice Statistics. Available online at <http://www.icpsr.umich.edu>.

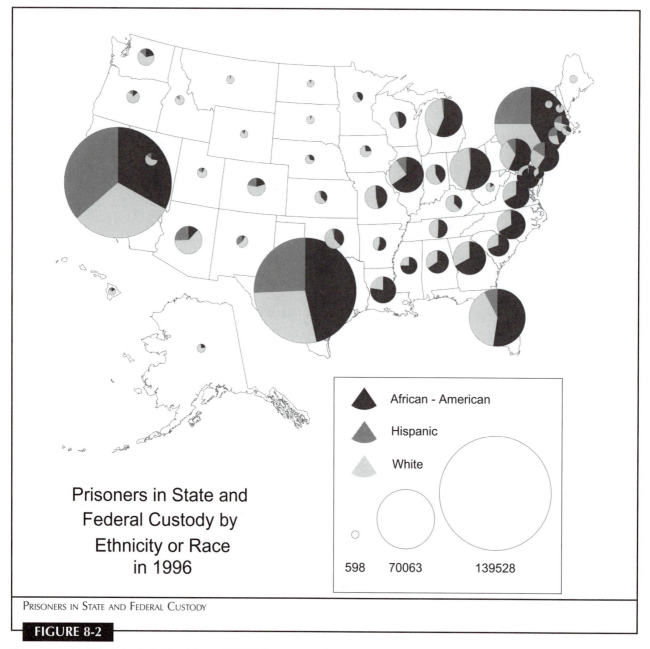

Prisoners in State and
Federal Custody by
Ethnicity or Race
in 1996

African - American

Hispanic

White

598   70063   139528

PRISONERS IN STATE AND FEDERAL CUSTODY

FIGURE 8-2

Source: Correctional Populations in the United States, 1996. U.S. Department of Justice. Bureau of Justice Statistics. Available online at <http://www.ojp.usdoj.gov/bjs/abstract/cpius96.htm>.

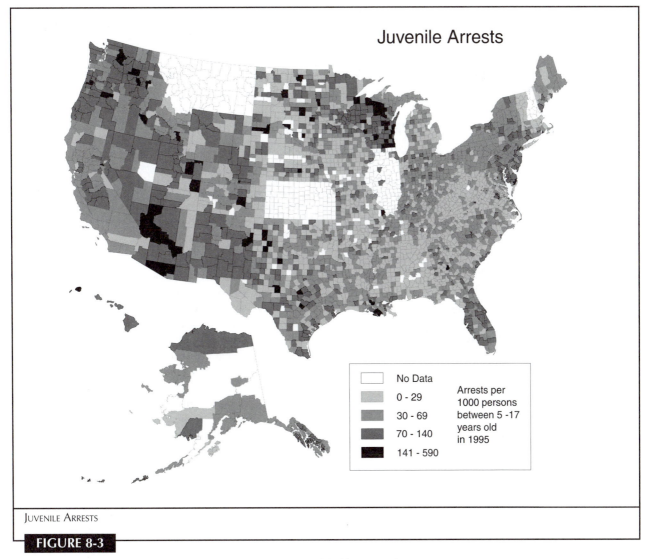

JUVENILE ARRESTS

FIGURE 8-3

Source: Geospatial & Statistical Data Center. Available online at <http://fisher.lib.Virginia.edu/crime>.

lice Killed in the Line of Duty." William Ackerman introduces the reader to law enforcement strategy on a local level in "The Concept of Community Policing and a Case Study of Lima, Ohio." In his essay on the "Crime Scene Sketch," Jerry Chisum describes the various methods used by police artists. Elaine Hallisey Hendrix describes the use of Geographic Information Systems in the everyday work of police departments across the country. The chapter concludes with a geography of capital punishment by Keith Harries, who examines the spatial evolution of one of the most controversial criminal justice issues facing the nation.

References

Albanese, J.S. 1999. *Criminal Justice*. Boston: Allyn and Bacon.

Federal Bureau of Investigation (FBI). 1996. *Uniform Crime Reports*. <http:www.fbi.gov>.

Friedman, L.M. 1993. *Crime and Punishment in American History*. New York: BasicBooks.

Lewis, D. 1992. From Abuse to Violence: Psychophysiological Consequences of Maltreatment. *Journal of the American Academy of Child and Adolescent Psychiatry*. <http:// www.pbs.org/wgbh/pages/frontline/shows/little/readings/lewis.html>.

National Center for Juvenile Justice. 1999. *Juvenile Justice Facts and Figures*. <http://ojjdp.ncjrs.org/ojstatbb/qa001.html>.

U.S. Department of Justice. 1998. *Sourcebook of Criminal Justice Statistics 1997*. Table 2.45. <http://www.albany.edu/sourcebook/>.

A Spatial Analysis of American Police Killed in the Line of Duty

Robert J. Kaminski
Eric S. Jefferis
Chanchalat Chanhatasilpa

Cultural explanations for homicide and other crimes have a long history, and substantial theoretical and empirical work has focused on cultural/subcultural differences to explain variation in violent behavior among racial/ethnic groups, gangs, southerners, and others (Corzine, Huff-Corzine, and Whitt 1999; Gastil 1971; Hackney 1969; Wolfgang and Ferracuti 1967). For example, the subculture-of-violence thesis devised by M.E. Wolfgang and F. Ferracuti (1967: 161) was a combination of theories developed to bring together "psychological and sociological constructs to aid in the explanation of the concentration of violence in specific socio-economic groups and ecological areas." Wolfgang and Ferracuti argued that some segments of society adopt distinct subcultures that include pro-violent values. The subculture provides greater normative support for violence in "upholding such values as honor, courage, and manliness," which increases the probability of violent responses when threats to such values are presented (Corzine, Huff-Corzine, and Whitt 1999: 43). The southern subculture-of-violence thesis (Gastil 1971; Hackney 1969) posits that "southerners have a greater predisposition for violence because southern regional culture permits or demands violent responses to a situation in which one's honor, family, or possessions are challenged or assaulted" (Parker, McCall, and Land 1999: 108). Based on this theoretical framework, one would expect to observe significant clustering of violent crime in the South relative to other areas of the United States.

A considerable amount of empirical research has examined the relationship between civilian homicide rates and geographic location in the South. Most studies find either statistically significant effects in the expected direction or null effects (Land, McCall, and Cohen 1990; Parker, McCall, and Land 1999). Although comparatively less research has been done on homicides of law enforcement officers, simple tabular analyses show that the South typically experiences a greater-than-expected number of police killings, even when controlling for regional variation in levels of violent crime, arrests, population, and number of officers employed (Cardarelli 1968; Federal Bureau of Investigation 1992, 1997; Fridell and Pate 1997; Geller and Scott 1992).

Other research has employed multiple linear regression to test whether various social, cultural, and structural features of cities or states are associated with killings of police (Bailey 1982; Bailey and Peterson 1987, 1994; Chamlin 1989; Fridell and Pate 1995; Peterson and Bailey 1988). None of these features consistently exhibited statistically significant associations in the expected direction. In fact, among the majority of covariates examined, null findings were the rule rather than the exception, including geographic location in the South.[1]

Unfortunately, research on the risk factors associated with killings of police has been fraught with methodological shortcomings, making it difficult to conclude with any degree of certainty which factors are or are not associated with the risk of being killed in the line of duty. For instance, the research employing tabular analyses failed to include statistical tests of significance to determine whether the number or rate of killings of police in the South is significantly greater than would be expected by chance alone.

Limitations of other studies include the failure to control for base rate activities (Garner and Clemmer 1986; Sherman 1980), the use of biased samples (King and Sanders 1997), the inappropriate application of the multiple linear regression model to rare-event count outcomes (Kaminski 1997),[2] and the failure to control for spatial autocorrelation.[3]

An additional limitation of the extant research examining regional variation in killings of police is that the analyses were restricted to testing whether counts or rates of homicides were significantly greater in the South relative to one or more other geographic areas. The prior research, therefore, was unable to test whether significant clustering exists at lower levels of aggregation (e.g., at the county level), a limitation overcome in the analysis that follows.

The purpose of this essay is to examine the spatial distribution of American state and local law enforcement officers feloniously and accidentally killed in the line of duty.

Contributors' Note: We thank Ashton Flemmings, Bureau of Justice Assistance, for access to the Public Safety Officers' Benefit program data. Points of view are those of the authors and do not necessarily represent the views of the U.S. Department of Justice or the National Institute of Justice. Direct all correspondence to Robert J. Kaminski, National Institute of Justice, 810 7th Street, NW, Washington, DC 20531.

This analysis is accomplished in two ways. Simple graduated symbol maps are used to illustrate the county-level distribution of deaths as counts and also normalized by the underlying population distribution. To test for geographical variation in line-of-duty deaths, a "spatial scan statistic" is used to identify statistically significant spatial clusters of incidents. Choropleth, as well as multi-class qualitative, maps are used to depict those counties and regions with higher than expected mortality rates.

Although the focus of this essay is felonious killings of police, the authors are unaware of previous research that examined the spatial distribution of accidental line-of-duty deaths, aside from basic descriptive statistics (Federal Bureau of Investigation 1997b). This essay explores, therefore, the distribution of accidental deaths with descriptive graduated symbol maps and cluster analysis procedures.

Data

The data on line-of-duty deaths come from the Public Safety Officers' Benefits (PSOB) program, administered by the Bureau of Justice Administration (BJA).[4] For our purposes, we are interested only in eligible cases involving felonious killings or accidental deaths of law enforcement officers with arrest powers serving state or local agencies within the 50 states.[5]

For the period under study (1985-1997), 1,478 line-of-duty death cases filed with the PSOB program were eligible for benefits; 745 of these involved intentional killings of officers (50.4 percent), while the remaining 733 were accidental line-of-duty deaths.[6]

Method

The PSOB data were geocoded by zip code and then aggregated to the county level using the ArcView-GIS package.[7] Data were aggregated to the county level for two reasons: (1) population estimates were unavailable for the entire country by zip code, and (2) line-of-duty deaths of law enforcement officers are statistically rare events, particularly at the zip code level, a fact that makes analysis at a lower level of aggregation difficult.

First, to visually describe the spatial distribution of incidents, graduated symbols fixed upon county geographic centers (centroids) were created to represent simple counts of the number of felonious killings and accidental deaths (Figures 8-4 and 8-6, respectively). In addition, the number of felonious killings and accidental deaths normalized

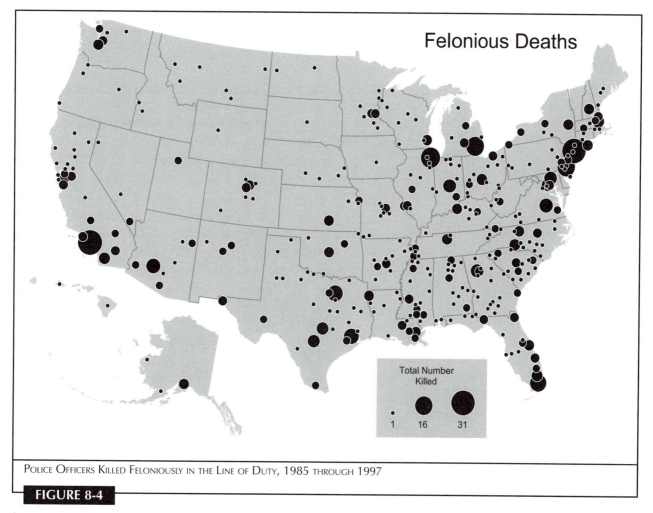

POLICE OFFICERS KILLED FELONIOUSLY IN THE LINE OF DUTY, 1985 THROUGH 1997

FIGURE 8-4

Source: Bureau of Justice Assistance, Public Safety Officer Benefit Program.

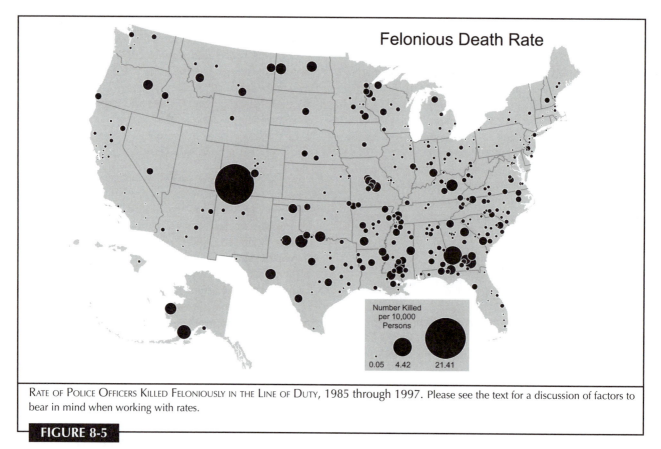

RATE OF POLICE OFFICERS KILLED FELONIOUSLY IN THE LINE OF DUTY, 1985 through 1997. Please see the text for a discussion of factors to bear in mind when working with rates.

FIGURE 8-5

Sources: Bureau of Justice Assistance, Public Safety Officer Benefit Program and U.S. Census of Population and Housing, 1990.

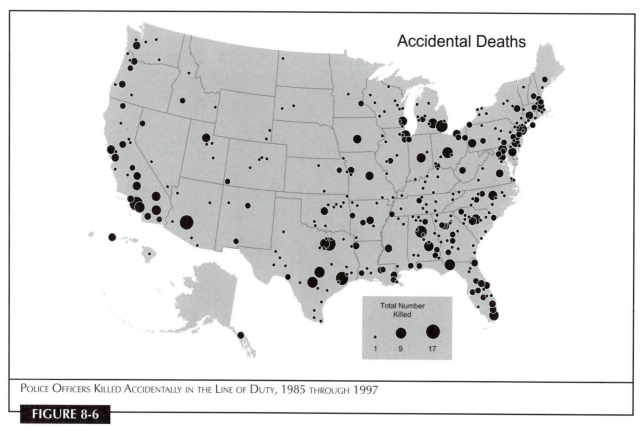

POLICE OFFICERS KILLED ACCIDENTALLY IN THE LINE OF DUTY, 1985 THROUGH 1997

FIGURE 8-6

Source: Bureau of Justice Assistance, Public Safety Officer Benefit Program.

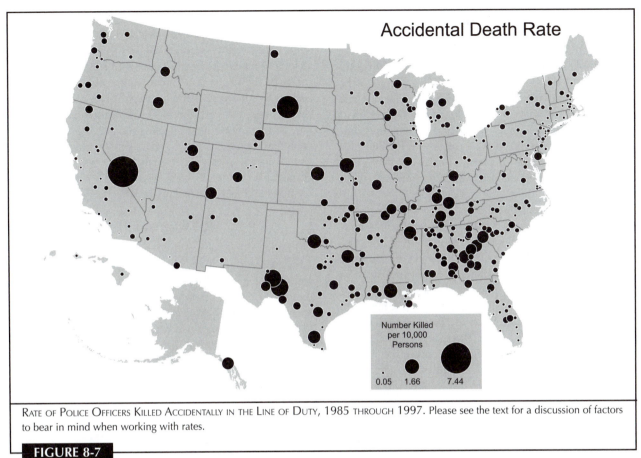

Accidental Death Rate

Number Killed per 10,000 Persons

0.05   1.66   7.44

RATE OF POLICE OFFICERS KILLED ACCIDENTALLY IN THE LINE OF DUTY, 1985 THROUGH 1997. Please see the text for a discussion of factors to bear in mind when working with rates.

FIGURE 8-7

Sources: Bureau of Justice Assistance, Public Safety Officer Benefit Program and U.S. Census of Population and Housing, 1990.

by county population are provided in Figures 8-5 and 8-7, respectively. All maps for this essay were created using the MapViewer software package.

Second, to identify areas with statistically significant clusters of incidents, we employed the *spatial scan statistic* as implemented in SaTScan (Kulldorff 1997; Kulldorff and Nagarwalla 1995). Useful methods for the analysis of the spatial clustering of extremely rare events have been used by epidemiologists for decades. These methods allow an analyst to determine, for instance, whether diseases cluster naturally due to chance alone or because of some underlying spatial risk factor. In addition to avoiding ad hoc procedures to test for spatial clustering of rare outcomes, the main benefits of the spatial scan statistic are that it allows for inferential tests and it is not restricted to clusters that conform to predefined administrative or political borders (Kulldorff 1997; Kulldorff and Nagarwalla 1995). Although the spatial scan statistic was developed for epidemiological cluster analyses, given their statistically rare occurrence, it has direct applicability to the study of police deaths.

To identify areas with clusters of incidents that cannot be explained simply by an uneven population distribution, the spatial scan statistic requires that the underlying population distribution be known. Zip code level data, there-

fore, were aggregated to the same level of analysis for known 1990 population data, in this case the county. The spatial scan statistic operates on the assumption that the number of cases in each area is Poisson distributed.[8] Under the null hypothesis of spatial randomness, the expected number of cases in each window is proportional to its population size. In this way, the spatial scan statistic adjusts for uneven population distributions.

As applied to the identification of statistically significant clusters, SaTScan imposes a circular scan window centered on each county centroid throughout the study region. For each centroid, the window varies in size from zero to an upper limit imposed by the user. The upper limit indicates the maximum proportion of the population study area to be included in the window. To allow for the identification of significant clusters as large as the most populous region of the country, we limited the size of the largest possible cluster to 32 percent of the nation's total population.[9] Theoretically, this method results in an infinite number of distinct scan windows, with differing sets of neighbors within the circles, each of which is a possible cluster candidate.[10] Therefore, unlike in the prior research on police killings, significant clusters in the current study can range in size from a single county to an entire region of the country.

Findings

Count and Rate Distributions

Figure 8-4 illustrates the spatial distribution of 729 felonious killings of law enforcement officers, as reported to the PSOB program from 1985 through 1997. As expected, the graduated symbol map indicates that metropolitan areas tend to experience the most fatalities. The map draws immediate attention to the New York, Los Angeles, and Chicago areas. Simple count maps such as this show the overall dispersion and frequency of events, but tell little about risk to police.

A vastly different distribution appears in Figure 8-5, where we show the number of felonious killings standardized by the county population. Most interesting, the concentrations in New York, Los Angeles, and Chicago seem to disappear. The southern region—spanning from Georgia to Texas—appears to have an unusually high mortality rate compared to the rest of the nation. However, rate maps can be misleading when rare events are being considered or populations are highly variable (Bailey and Gattrell, 1995: 301). For example, the symbol representing the highest mortality rate occurs in Hinsdale County, Colorado, which corresponds to a single incident in a county with a 1990 population of only 467.

The spatial distribution of accidental deaths of officers (n=711) is illustrated by Figure 8-6. The overall distribution appears more evenly dispersed than the incidents of felonious killing shown in Figure 8-4 (except for large blank areas in the Plains states), but again, urban areas tend to experience more accidental deaths. When standardized by county population (Figure 8-7), the South and counties in the mountainous West appear to experience the highest accidental mortality rates. Again, the limitations of simple rate maps are evident in that the largest symbol represents Esmeralda County, Nevada, which had a 1990 population of 1,344 and recorded one police officer accidentally killed.

SaTScan Analysis

Although the presentation of count and rate maps are important first steps in understanding the spatial distribution of officer deaths, more sophisticated analytical methods are required to determine whether apparent clusters are "real" or whether they could have occurred by chance alone. The spatial scan statistic provides such a test, the results of which are provided in Table 8-A. Separate analyses were conducted on both felonious killings and accidental deaths. Approximate locations of four statistically significant clusters were identified during each analysis.

TABLE 8-A

SIGNIFICANT CLUSTERS OF FELONIOUS AND ACCIDENTAL DEATHS

	National	Most Likely Cluster	Secondary Cluster 1	Secondary Cluster 2	Secondary Cluster 3
Panel A: Felonious Killings					
# of counties	3140	1	1	1093	2
Area population (1990 Census)	248,709,873	1,487,536	502,824	65,756,702	266,362
Observed # of cases	729	30	15	270	9
Expected # of cases	----	4.36	1.47	192.74	0.78
Incidence rate (per 100,000 population)	0.293	2.02	2.98	0.41	3.38
Odds ratio	----	6.88	10.17	1.40	11.53
Log likelihood ratio	----	32.68	21.40	19.60	13.83
p-value	----	.001	.001	.001	.004
Panel B: Accidental Deaths					
# of counties	3140	645	2	147	1
Area population (1990 Census)	248,709,873	37,312,992	453,331	11,151,829	63,579
Observed # of cases	711	194	11	63	5
Expected # of cases	----	106.67	1.30	31.88	0.18
Incidence rate (per 100,000 population)	0.286	0.52	2.43	0.56	7.86
Odds ratio	----	1.82	8.49	1.98	27.51
Log likelihood ratio	----	35.34	13.89	12.52	11.77
p-value	----	.001	.004	.007	.017

Notes for *Panel A* (Felonious Killings): The Most Likely Cluster is New York County, NY; Secondary Cluster 1 is Camden County, NJ; Secondary Cluster 2 includes much of the Southeastern United States; and Secondary Cluster 3 includes Hanover and Richmond County, VA.
Notes for *Panel B* (Accidental Deaths): The Most Likely Cluster encompasses a large portion of the South; Secondary Cluster 1 includes Richland and Lexington County, SC; Secondary Cluster 2 involves much of the West; and Secondary Cluster 3 is Cole County, MO.

Felonious Killings

The analysis identified New York County (Manhattan) as the most likely cluster,[11] with a mortality rate 588 percent higher than the rest of the United States[12] (odds ratio=6.88).[13] Camden County, New Jersey, identified as secondary cluster 1, has a mortality rate 917 percent higher than the rest of the country (odds ratio=10.17). A large portion of the South was identified as secondary cluster 2 with a mortality rate 40 percent higher than the rest of the county (odds ratio=1.40), while the Richmond-Hanover, Virginia, cluster (secondary cluster 3) has a mortality rate over 1,000 percent higher than the rest of the United States (odds ratio=11.53). Panel A in Table 8-A presents findings from the SaTScan analysis of felonious killings. Areas identified as primary and secondary clusters of felonious killings are illustrated as a two-class qualitative map in Figure 8-8.

Accidental Deaths

The southern region was identified as the most likely cluster with an accidental mortality rate 82 percent higher than the rest of the United States (odds ratio=1.82). The Lexington-Richland cluster, with a mortality rate 749 percent higher (odds ratio=8.49), was identified as secondary cluster 1. A large portion of the western United States was identified as secondary cluster 2, with a mortality rate nearly 100 percent higher than the rest of the country (odds ratio=1.98). Finally, Cole County, Missouri, was identified as secondary cluster 3, with a mortality rate over 2,600 percent higher than the rest of the nation. Results from this analysis are presented in Table 8-A (Panel B), and statistically significant clusters are shown in Figure 8-9.

Discussion

Previous research and theory has posited that the southern United States experiences an unusually high rate of homicide in the general population (Corzine, Huff-Corzine, and Whitt 1999; Gastil 1971; Hackney 1969; Wolfgang and Ferracuti 1967). To date, however, empirical support for this position has been somewhat mixed (Land, McCall, and Cohen 1990; Parker, McCall, and Land 1999). Policing researchers have assumed that higher levels of homicide in the South translate into a higher risk of officers being killed feloniously in the line of duty. The relationship between unit location in the South and higher police officer mortality rates, however, is not well supported by previous research (Bailey and Peterson 1987; Peterson and Bailey 1988; Fridell and Pate 1995).

The results of the analysis presented here, while not incongruent with the southern subculture-of-violence thesis, suggest that areas other than the South also present

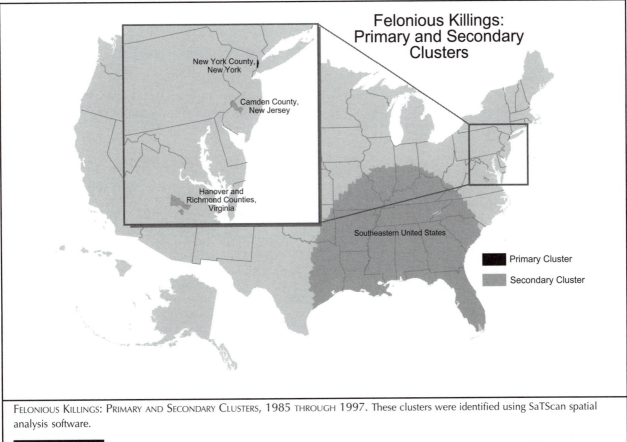

FELONIOUS KILLINGS: PRIMARY AND SECONDARY CLUSTERS, 1985 THROUGH 1997. These clusters were identified using SaTScan spatial analysis software.

FIGURE 8-8

Source: Bureau of Justice Assistance, Public Safety Officer Benefit Program.

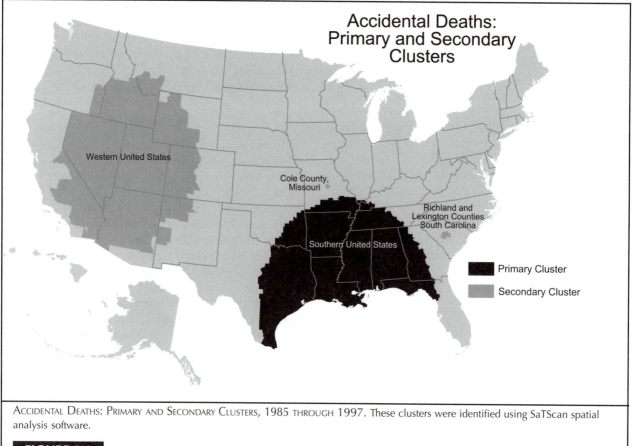

ACCIDENTAL DEATHS: PRIMARY AND SECONDARY CLUSTERS, 1985 THROUGH 1997. These clusters were identified using SaTScan spatial analysis software.

FIGURE 8-9

Source: Bureau of Justice Assistance, Public Safety Officer Benefit Program.

significant risk to officers in terms of being killed feloniously. For instance, two areas in the Northeast were identified as statistically significant clusters (New York County and Camden County, New Jersey). Mortality rates in these areas are substantially higher than the rates observed in the southern cluster.[14]

Regarding accidental line-of-duty deaths, the analysis also revealed significant clustering in the southern United States. Besides the identification of two smaller clusters, the analysis revealed an additional large cluster in the West. Future research will delve further into the causes of these clusters.

A substantial overlap of clusters of felonious killings and accidental deaths was identified in the South. The unusually high rates observed in the South suggest that some factor (or factors) other than a southern subculture of violence may explain both of these clusters. On the one hand, because felonious killings cluster significantly in the South, the findings presented here provide some indirect support for the southern subculture-of-violence thesis. On the other hand, because accidental deaths also cluster in the South, alternative explanations may exist, including (but not limited to) regional variation in (1) the quality of trauma care systems (Bonnie et al.1999; Doerner 1988), (2) law enforcement agency policies or practices (Kaminski 1998), and (3)

economic conditions (Loftin and Hill 1974). The testing of these and other rival hypotheses will be the focus of future research aimed at explaining the geographical distribution of police mortality rates.

Endnotes

1. Three of the six multivariate studies on killings of police included an indicator of southern region (Bureau of the Census classification). Two of the studies found no statistical association (Peterson and Bailey 1988; Fridell and Pate 1995), while one study found weak support for a relationship in that location in the South was significant in only two of twelve annual cross-sectional models estimated (Bailey and Peterson 1987).

2. Count variables, such as homicides, are frequently treated as though they are continuous and modeled improperly using linear multiple regression (Liao 1994: 70). Applying least squares regression to model rare-event counts is inappropriate because it may produce non-constant variance and negative predictions of the number of events (Crawley 1993: 226; Gardner, Mulvey, and Shaw 1995: 392-93; King 1989: 763). Further, least squares analysis of count data is inefficient and can produce inconsistent and biased estimates (King 1989: 763; Long 1997: 217).

3. Spatial autocorrelation can occur when the enumeration units being analyzed (e.g., states, MSAs, cities) share boundaries that result in a structure to the data. Units that share physical

boundaries or are closer to each other are likely more similar than units not sharing physical boundaries or those that are farther away from each other. Thus, geographic data may often fail to meet the assumption of normal-theory statistical methods that the observations be independent of one another. The consequence is that the errors will not be independent—a condition for valid hypothesis tests. The consequences of spatial autocorrelation are the same as in temporal autocorrelation, i.e., in the linear regression model the standard errors will be biased, and t statistics used to test the null hypothesis may seriously overstate the statistical significance of an effect. This can lead to the mistaken conclusion that variables are related when they are not (Odland 1988).

4. The PSOB Act was enacted by Congress in 1976 to assist in the recruitment and retention of law enforcement officers and firefighters by providing financial benefits to financially dependent survivors of officers killed in the line of duty and for officers permanently and totally disabled in the line of duty. No benefit is paid if the death or disability was caused by the intentional misconduct, grossly negligent conduct, or suicide by the public safety officer, if the officer was voluntarily intoxicated at the time of death or permanent disability, or if the death or permanent disability resulted from stress, occupational illness, or a chronic, progressive, or congenital disease (such as heart or pulmonary disease), unless there is a traumatic injury that is a substantial contributing factor in the death or permanent and total disability. These cases are classified as either denied from benefits or withdrawn from consideration. *Law enforcement officers* include, but are not limited to, police, corrections, probation, parole, and judicial officers. Public agencies include any department or agency that falls under the jurisdiction of the United States (federal), any U.S. state (state), any U.S. county or city (local), the District of Columbia, the Commonwealth of Puerto Rico, and any U.S. territory or possession.

5. Excluded from the analysis are officers employed by federal agencies, sheriffs' agencies without a law enforcement function, and officers from Puerto Rico and other U.S. territories.

6. The cases used in this study represent all applications for benefits approved by the PSOB program for the years 1985 through 1997. The year of application does not always coincide with the year of an officer's death.

7. The geocoding process achieved a 98 percent "hit rate." In other words, 98 percent of all cases were successfully attached to a geographic coordinate and appear on the maps presented.

8. SaTScan allows the user to specify either a Poisson or Bernoulli (binomial) distribution.

9. The Southern Census Region is the most populated, accounting for approximately 32 percent of the total U.S. population.

10. A thorough description of the spatial scan statistic is beyond the scope of this essay; see Kulldorff (1997) and Kulldorff and Nagarwalla (1995) for details.

11. SaTScan calculates a likelihood function for each location and size of the scan window, testing the null hypothesis that the incidence rate within the window is not significantly different from the area outside the window. The "most likely cluster" is the scan window area identified as having the greatest likelihood ratio. "Secondary clusters," which do not overlap the "most likely cluster" or one another, are also identified and ranked according to their likelihood ratio.

12. Because Manhattan has an influx of people during the day that is probably disproportionate to other counties, the day-

time population might be a better approximation of officer risk than the number of residents.

13. The odds ratio is defined as the ratio of a/b to c/d, where a is the total United States population, b is the total number of observed events occurring within the United States, c is the population of the relevant cluster, and d is the observed number of events occurring within the relevant cluster. Thus, the odds ratio for the most likely cluster is calculated as (248, 709, 873/729)/1,487, 536/30) = 6.88. SatScan actually reports the relative risk rather than the odds ratio, which is defined as the ratio $a/(a+b)$ to $c/(c+d)$. Technically, the relative risk is appropriate only when one has two binomial variables obtained from a prospective, but not a retrospective, study (Kuzma, 1984); hence our reason for reporting odds ratios. Note, however, that when the outcome of interest is rare the odds ratio approximates the relative risk (Hosmer and Lemeshow, 1989), and in this study their values are virtually identical.

14. The southern cluster likely includes areas with low mortality rates, which may account for the relatively low overall incidence rate reported for the South in Panel A.

References

Adams, J. 1995. *Risk*. London: UCL Press Limited.

Bailey, T.C., and A.C. Gattrell. 1995. *Interactive Spatial Data Analysis*. Essex, England: Longman Group Limited.

Bailey, W.C. 1996. Less-Than-Lethal Weapons and Police-Citizen Killings in U.S. Urban Areas. *Crime and Delinquency* 42(4):535-52.

———. 1984. Poverty, Inequality, and Homicide Rates: Some Not So Unexpected Findings. *Criminology* 22: 531-50.

———. 1982. Capital Punishment and Lethal Assaults Against Police. *Criminology* 19(4): 608-25.

Bailey, W.C., and R.D. Peterson. 1994. Murder, Capital Punishment, and Deterrence: A Review of the Evidence and an Examination of Police Killings. *Journal of Social Issues* 50(2): 53-73.

———. 1987. Police Killings and Capital Punishment: The Post-Furman Period. *Criminology* 25(1): 1-25.

Bonnie, R.I., C.E. Fulco, and C.T. Liverman, eds. 1999. *Reducing the Burden of Injury: Advancing Prevention and Treatment*. Washington, DC: National Academy Press.

Cardarelli, A.P. 1968. An Analysis of Police Killed by Criminal Action: 1961-1963. *Journal of Criminal Law, Criminology, and Police Science* 59: 447-53.

Chamlin, M.B. 1989. Conflict Theory and Police Killings. *Deviant Behavior* 10: 353-68.

Chapman, S.G. 1998. *Murdered on Duty: The Killing of Police Officers in America*, 2nd ed. Springfield, IL: Charles C. Thomas.

Cook, P.J., and M.H. Moore. 1999. Guns, Gun Control, and Homicide. In M.D. Smith and M.A. Zahn, eds. *Homicide: A Sourcebook of Social Research*. Thousands Oaks, CA: Sage Publications.

Corzine, J., L. Huff-Corzine, and H.P. Whitt. 1999. Cultural and Subcultural Theories of Homicide. In M.D. Smith and M.A. Zahn, eds. *Homicide: A Sourcebook of Social Research*. Thousands Oaks, CA: Sage Publications.

Crawley, M.J. 1993. *GLIM for Ecologists*. Cambridge, MA: Blackwell Scientific Publications.

Creamer S.J., and G.D. Robin. 1972. Assaults on Police. In Samuel G. Chapman, ed. *Police Patrol Readings*, 2nd ed. Springfield, IL: Charles C. Thomas.

Doerner, W.G. 1988. The Impact of Medical Resources on Criminally Induced Lethality: A Further Examination. *Criminology* 26(1):171-79.

Federal Bureau of Investigation. 1997a. *In the Line of Fire: Violence Against Law Enforcement.* Washington, DC: U.S. Department of Justice.

————. 1997b. *Law Enforcement Officers Killed and Assaulted, 1977.* Washington, DC: U.S. Department of Justice.

————. 1992. *Killed in the Line of Duty: A Study of Selected Felonious Killings of Law Enforcement Officers.* Washington, DC: U.S. Department of Justice.

Fridell, L.A., and A.M. Pate. 1997. Death on Patrol: Killings of American Law Enforcement Officers. In Roger G. Dunham and Geoffrey P. Alpert, eds. *Critical Issues in Policing: Contemporary Readings.* 3rd ed. Prospect Heights, IL: Waveland Press, Inc.

————. 1995. *Death on Patrol: Felonious Killings of Police Officers.* Final report submitted to the National Institute of Justice, Washington, DC.

Gardner, W., E.P. Mulvey, and E.C. Shaw. 1995. Regression Analyses of Counts and Rates: Poisson, Overdispersed Poisson, and Negative Binomial Models. *Psychological Bulletin* 118(3): 392-404.

Garner, J., and E. Clemmer. 1986. *Danger to Police in Domestic Disturbances: A New Look.* Research in Brief. Washington, DC: National Institute of Justice.

Gastil, R.D. 1971. Homicide and a Regional Culture of Violence. *American Sociological Review* 36: 412-27.

Geller, W.A., and M.S. Scott. 1992. *Deadly Force: What We Know.* Washington, DC: Police Executive Research Forum.

Hackney, S. 1969. Southern Violence. *American Historical Review* 39: 906-25.

Hosmer, D.W., and S. Lemeshow. 1989. *Applied Logistic Regression.* New York: John Wiley and Sons.

Kaminski, R.J. 1998. Toward an Organizational-Exposure Model of Police Officer Victimization. Paper presented at the American Society of Criminology, Washington, DC, November 11-14.

————. 1997. Analyzing the Structural Determinants of Killings of Police: Does Method Matter? Paper presented at the American Society of Criminology, San Diego, CA, November 18-22.

King, G. 1989. Variance Specification in Event Count Models: From Restrictive Assumptions to a Generalized Estimator. *American Journal of Political Science* 33(3): 762-84.

King, W.R., and B.A. Sanders. 1997. Nice Guys Finish Last: A Critical Review of *Killed in the Line of Duty. Policing: An International Journal of Police Strategies and Management* 20: 392-407.

Kleinbaum, D.G. 1994. *Logistic Regression: A Self-Learning Text.* New York: Springer-Verlag.

Kulldorff, M. 1997. A Spatial Scan Statistic. *Communication in Statistics: Theory and Methods* 26(6):1481-96.

Kulldorff, M., and N. Nagarwalla. 1995. Spatial Disease Clusters: Detection and Inference. *Statistics in Medicine* 14: 799-810.

Kuzma, Jan W. 1984. *Basic Statistics for the Health Sciences.* Mountain View, CA: Mayfield Publishing Company.

Land, K.C., P.L. McCall, and L.E. Cohen. 1990. Structural Covariates of Homicide Rates: Are There Any Invariances Across Time and Social Space? *American Journal of Sociology* 95: 922-63.

Liao, T.F. 1994. *Interpreting Probability Models: Logit, Probit, and Other Generalized Linear Models.* Sage University Paper Series on Quantitative Applications in the Social Sciences, 07-101. Thousand Oaks, CA: Sage.

Loftin, C., and R.H. Hill. 1974. Regional Subculture and Homicide: An Examination of the Gastil-Hackney Thesis. *American Sociological Review* 39: 714-24.

Long, S.J. 1997. *Regression Models for Categorical and Limited Dependent Variables.* Thousand Oaks, CA: Sage Publications.

Odland, J. 1988. *Spatial Autocorrelation.* Scientific Geography Series, Vol. 9. Beverly Hills, CA: Sage Publications.

Parker, K.F., P.L. McCall, and K.C. Land. 1999. Determining Social-Structural Predictors of Homicide. In M. Dwayne Smith and Margaret A. Zahn, eds. *Homicide: A Sourcebook of Social Research.* Thousand Oaks, CA: Sage Publications.

Peterson, R.D., and W.C. Bailey. 1988. Structural Influences on the Killing of Police: A Comparison with General Homicides. *Justice Quarterly* 5(2): 207-33.

Sherman, L.W. 1980. Perspective on Police and Violence. *The Annals* 452: 1-12.

Slovic, P., Baruch Fischhoff, and S. Lichtenstein. 1990. Rating the Risks. In T.S. Glickman and M. Gough, eds. *Readings in Risk.* Washington, DC: Resources for the Future.

Williams, F.P., III, and M.D. McShane. 1988. *Criminological Theory.* Englewood Cliffs, NJ: Prentice Hall.

Wolfgang, M.E., and F. Ferracuti. 1967. *The Subculture of Violence.* Beverly Hills, CA: Sage Publications.

The Concept of Community Policing and a Case Study of Lima, Ohio

William V. Ackerman

In the late 1960s, crime began to increase sharply in the United States and to impact smaller communities (Ackerman 1998a). Between 1967 and 1980, the overall rate of violent crime per 100,000 population went up by 135.6 percent and property crime increased by 95.6 percent (Figure 8-10). Property crime peaked in 1980, declined until 1984, and then increased again from 1985 to 1991. After 1991, property crime began a steady decline; in 1996, it reached a level slightly below the mean for the 1967-1996 period. Violent crime increased steadily from 1967 until 1980, declined slightly until 1983, and then increased again, peaking in 1991. Violent crime has declined since 1991 but remains above the mean for the 1967-1996 period.

The impact of rapidly increasing crime across the city-size spectrum motivated public officials and police departments to reevaluate existing deployment strategies to deal with crime and public safety. The most common approach to policing in the United States had resulted in a system of highly centralized, militaristic, reactive departments. Such deployment models, characterized by radio dispatched patrol units operating out of automobiles, kept officers largely detached from citizens. It was increasingly clear that such strategies were neither reducing crime nor allaying public fear of crime (Goldstein 1979 and 1987; Kratcoski and Dukes 1995). The concept of community policing arose from dissatisfaction with traditional policing methods.

Perhaps the best generalized definition of community policing is offered by Robert Trojanowicz and Bonnie Bucqueroux (1990: 5): "Community policing is a new philosophy of policing, based on the concept that police officers and private citizens working together in creative ways can help solve contemporary community problems related to crime, fear of crime, social and physical disorder, and neighborhood decay." A guiding assumption is that identifying and solving problems is preferable to continually reacting to them (Bureau of Justice Assistance 1997).

However, in spite of substantial interest in and widespread implementation of community policing, it has no single definitive form (Police Executive Research Forum 1996). The concept means different things to different people, and different proponents of the strategy emphasize different aspects while using the same terminology (Bayley 1988 and 1994; Goldstein 1987 and 1990; Wilson and Kelling 1989; Eck and Spelman 1987; Trojanowicz and Bucqueroux 1990; Manning 1988; Green and Mastrofski 1988; Klockars 1988). Mark Moore (1992) suggests that the ambiguity of the concept is an asset because it stimulates a wide pattern of experimentation. Definitional problems notwithstanding, police agencies are increasingly engaged in a diverse set of practices united by the philosophy that the police and public need to become better partners to more effectively control crime and disorder (Police Executive Research Forum 1996). In the 1990s, community policing became the dominant strategy of crime prevention in the United States. The concept is strongly endorsed by politicians and has been incorporated into legislation. The 1994 Crime Bill provided for 100,000 new police officers, specifying that they had to be engaged in community policing (Cordner 1998). Implementation has expanded to the extent that Trojanowicz and Bucqueroux (1992) estimate that two-thirds of all police departments serving communities with populations greater than 50,000 are either now employing community policing or planning to implement it in the near future.

A review of the literature on community policing suggests two important implementation perspectives (Skolnick and Bayley 1986; Goldstein 1987; Bayley 1994). The deployment perspective focuses on removing officers from patrol cars and placing them "on the beat," i.e., in physical proximity to community residents, especially in densely populated inner-city, high-crime neighborhoods (Police Foundation 1981). The argument for this strategy is that officers more familiar with neighborhoods can learn more about local needs and problems, focus more directly on those problems, better distinguish between offenders and law-abiding citizens, be recognized by and gain the confidence of residents, and develop better cooperation with community members, businesses, and government agencies (Couper and Lobitz 1991; Wycoff and Skogan 1994). As a result, they are presumably better able to prevent crime and disorder.

For the second perspective, community revitalization, Wesley Skogan (1990) finds a relationship between community decay and increasing levels of disorder, crime, fear of crime, and disinvestment. The idea here is to prevent the deterioration of neighborhoods by having the police evaluate fear-inducing neighborhood characteristics and work with government agencies and citizens to properly maintain infrastructure.

Contributor's Note: I gratefully acknowledge the useful comments of Professor Kelly Anspaugh and the research assistance of Ms. Rebecca Zell.

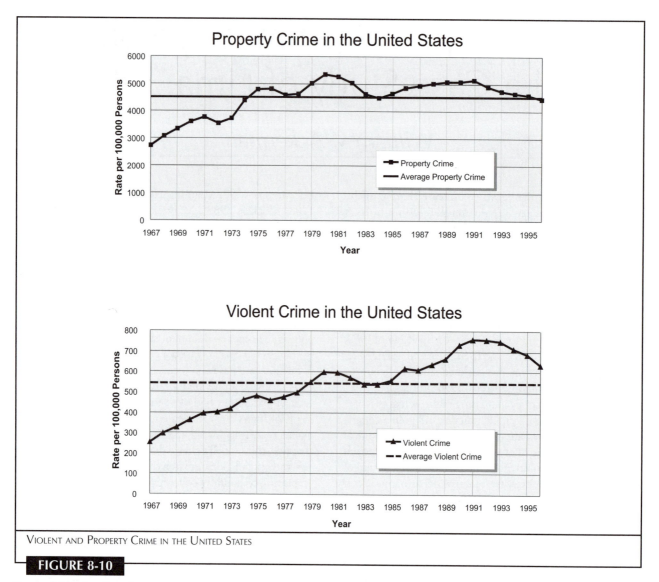

VIOLENT AND PROPERTY CRIME IN THE UNITED STATES

FIGURE 8-10

Source: FBI *Uniform Crime Reports,* 1967-1996.

To best meet the definition of community policing as a strategy based on police officers and private citizens working together to solve problems (Trojanowicz and Bucqueroux 1990), police departments need to combine the above perspectives to varying degrees and implement them in communities (or parts of communities) determined by well-documented needs. Although community policing alone is unlikely to solve all the problems associated with the contemporary urban environment, the strategy, when combined with strong code enforcement, the work of neighborhood associations, and genuine community revitalization, can be extremely effective. With this in mind, community policing needs to be considered as a dynamic operational practice that evolves over time to reflect changing community, organizational, and political needs. Several cities across the United States have implemented community policing, and useful information can be gained from a brief analysis of their implementation strategies and results.

Community Policing in Selected U.S. Cities

A number of cities across the United States have adopted community policing and numerous studies have been made to evaluate results (Bureau of Justice Assistance 1997; Police Executive Research Forum 1996; Wycoff and Skogan 1994; Sadd and Grinc 1994; and Weisel and Eck 1994). This research includes 21 cities distributed across the United States and Canada that cover a wide spectrum of population size. Space does not here permit an in-depth evaluation of findings from these studies, but the studies suggest some important factors to consider in the implementation and evaluation of community policing. First, comparative studies of widely divergent communities with different implementation strategies are probably not useful in evaluating the overall effectiveness of community policing. Success or failure is contingent upon conditions within individual cities. Second, results indicate that successful programs involve neighborhood residents, businesses, key governmental agencies, and the media. Third, in some neighborhoods in some cities, social disorder has risen to the level that adequate norms and values specifying appropriate public behavior are lacking and core groups upon which to build a strong anti-crime movement are non-existent. Community policing in such areas will likely fail (Kessler and Duncan 1996). However, in marginal areas, the fear of crime is reduced by seeing police officers on foot patrol working out of neighborhood sub-stations. In cases where officers have developed sustained cooperation with community groups and fostered self-help, levels of social disorder and physical decay have declined (Skogan 1994).

Because community policing is best evaluated within the local context, Lima, Ohio, is presented here as an excellent example of a smaller city that has experienced a serious crime problem, and a community that has witnessed substantial violent crime reduction since the adoption of community policing.

Community Policing in Lima, Ohio

Lima, a city of approximately 45,000 inhabitants in northwestern Ohio (Figure 8-11), suffered substantial job loss during the massive deindustrialization of the 1970s and 1980s. As a result, levels of poverty, unemployment, and crime, as well as the number of single-parent families, increased and became more concentrated in older, downtown neighborhoods.

Property crime in Lima began to increase between 1978 and 1979, reached a peak in 1980, and by 1985 declined to a level below the mean for the 1976-1997 period. Follow-

LIMA, OHIO

FIGURE 8-11

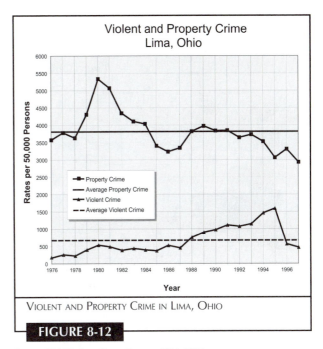

VIOLENT AND PROPERTY CRIME IN LIMA, OHIO

FIGURE 8-12

Source: FBI *Uniform Crime Reports,* 1976-1997.

ing a slight increase in 1989, property crime has generally declined, and in 1997 reached the lowest rate for the 1976-1997 period. Violent crime began to increase in 1988 and increased steadily until 1995. Violent crime declined sharply in 1995 and has continued to decline since (Figure 8-12).

Crime in Lima is concentrated in low socioeconomic status neighborhoods in and proximate to the Central Business District (CBD). These neighborhoods are characterized by poverty, unemployment, single-parent families, and minority populations (Figure 8-13). Lima's violent crime rate per 50,000 inhabitants increased 108.9 percent from the mean for 1976-1984 to that of 1985-1994, and, in the latter period, Lima ranked third among Ohio cities in rate of violent crime per 50,000 inhabitants (Ackerman 1998b). Already overwhelmed by the economic upheaval and resulting social disorganization associated with deindustrialization, community leaders did not react immediately to increasing rates of violent crime (Ackerman 1998a, 1998b).

However, by early 1994, it was becoming increasingly apparent to police officials and community leaders that traditional policing methods were not adequately addressing Lima's rapidly escalating violent crime. In April 1994, the mayor and chief of police decided to evaluate the concept of community policing for possible implementation in Lima. One officer was assigned to research the concept. Site visits were made in four states to evaluate existing community-oriented policing programs. Late in 1994, community officials decided to adopt community policing and implement it city-wide (Blass 1998).

Implementation was begun in early 1995 and a 90-day timeline was established to accomplish three goals. The first was to introduce the concept within the police department.

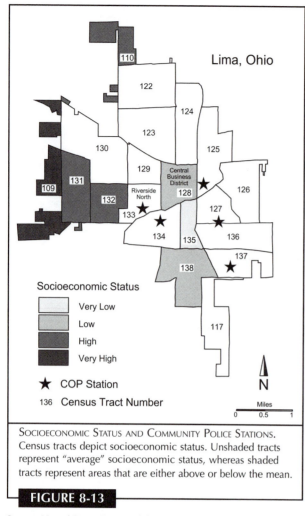

Socioeconomic Status and Community Police Stations. Census tracts depict socioeconomic status. Unshaded tracts represent "average" socioeconomic status, whereas shaded tracts represent areas that are either above or below the mean.

FIGURE 8-13

Sources: United States Bureau of the Census, 1990 and City of Lima Police Department.

This was accomplished in a manner that included all officers, staff, and civilian employees. The second goal was to train police department personnel by employing an outside consultant with expertise and experience in community policing. The last goal was to introduce the concept to the community and to explain the necessity of relationship building between neighborhoods, business leaders, government officials, and the police (Blass 1998).

A committee of police personnel, neighborhood specialists from the Office of Community Development, and members of the community-at-large was formed to oversee the implementation process. This committee selected Lima neighborhoods in which to locate COP (neighborhood police) stations. Selection criteria included a number of factors but essentially depended on the existence of a diverse community with an existing and active neighborhood association and individual residents who were committed to saving their neighborhood. Riverside North was selected as the pilot project. It is located in census tract 133, just west of and proximate to the low socioeconomic status, high-crime CBD (Figure 8-13). Early results from the Riverside North deployment were per-

ceived as positive, and five additional COP Stations were opened in or near Lima's low-status, high-crime neighborhoods by April 1997. Additional COP stations in surrounding neighborhoods have been requested but are not yet established (although high priority) due to budget constraints and staff availability (Garlock 1998).

Evaluating the Impact of Community Policing in Lima

The inability to control for external factors related to crime reduction prevents precise cause-and-effect analysis of the impact of community policing in Lima. However, it is possible to evaluate trends for the community and to compare these to national averages for similar-sized cities. It is also possible to evaluate trends in specific Lima neighborhoods targeted by community policing.

Between 1988 and 1996, crime declined across the United States by an average of 12.8 percent. In cities with populations between 25,000 and 49,999, the average reduction was 11.2 percent. Between 1988 and 1997, Lima experienced a reduction in crime of 29.1 percent, and a decline in violent crime of 32.5 percent (Federal Bureau of Investigation 1967-1997). Two factors associated with Lima's crime reduction point to the efficacy of community policing. First, the rate of reduction is substantially greater than the national average and that for peer group cities. Second, a notable decline in Lima's rate of property crime and violent crime followed the initiation of community policing. This trend is especially apparent with respect to violent crime (Figure 8-12).

Stronger evidence of the probable effectiveness of community policing is provided by evaluating changes in rates of crime for Lima census tracts, specifically those proximate to or containing neighborhood COP stations (Figure 8-13). These stations are located either within or proximate to the low-socioeconomic status, high-crime parts of the city (Figures 8-14 and 8-15). Rates of violent and property crime by census tract were generated from data provided by the Lima Police Department for 1988 and 1997. The year 1988 was selected as a base year for comparison for three reasons. First, much of the groundwork for the successful implementation of community policing began with Lima's neighborhood associations, which were well-organized and active by 1988 and, due to block-watch programs and cooperation with police, had probably helped reduce property crime in Lima (Figure 8-12). Second, in 1988 property crime was at the mean for the 1976-1997 period and violent crime was just slightly above that mean. Therefore, changes in crime rates are not overstated because they are compared to long-term averages, not peak rates. Third, comparing 1988 to 1997 emphasizes the persistent geographical pattern of crime in Lima and provides a better time-frame for the evaluation of the impact of community-oriented policing.

Property crime in 1988 was most pronounced in the CBD (tract 128) and just to the south in tract 135 (Figure 8-14). This pattern was expected based on theory and is

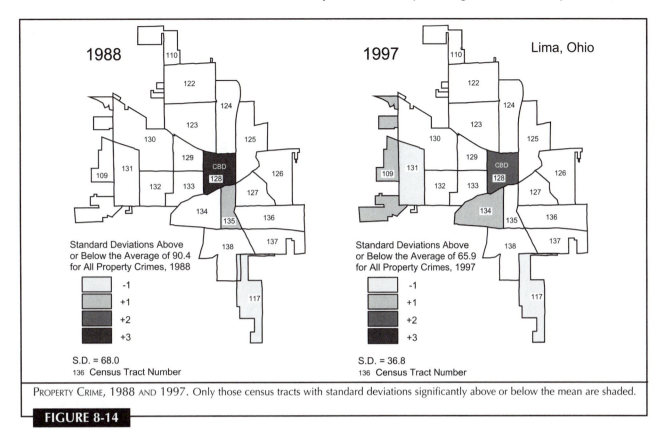

PROPERTY CRIME, 1988 AND 1997. Only those census tracts with standard deviations significantly above or below the mean are shaded.

FIGURE 8-14

Source: Crime by census tract provided by City of Lima Police Department.

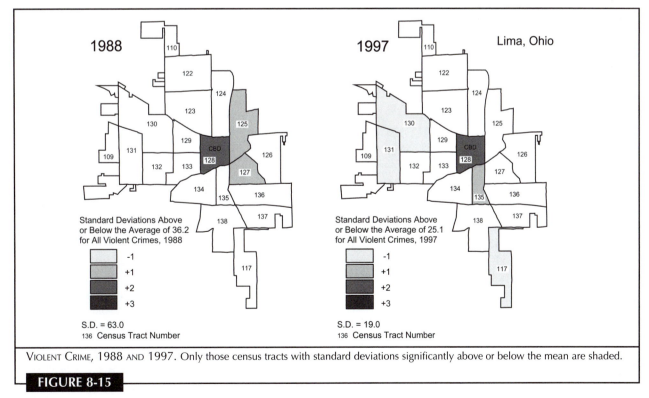

VIOLENT CRIME, 1988 AND 1997. Only those census tracts with standard deviations significantly above or below the mean are shaded.

FIGURE 8-15

Source: Crime by census tract provided by City of Lima Police Department.

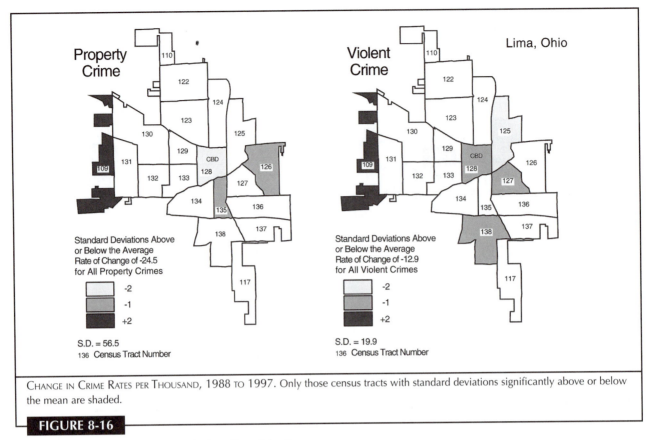

CHANGE IN CRIME RATES PER THOUSAND, 1988 TO 1997. Only those census tracts with standard deviations significantly above or below the mean are shaded.

FIGURE 8-16

Source: Crime by census tract provided by the City of Lima Police Department.

related to socioeconomic characteristics of these neighborhoods (Ackerman 1998a, 1998b). Although the overall locational pattern of property crime changed little by 1997 (Figure 8-14), rates of property crime declined substantially throughout the CBD area. Tract 128 dropped from plus three standard deviations above the mean for the city to plus two. Tract 135 is no longer significantly above the city-wide mean. Tracts 128 and 135 witnessed percentage declines in property crime of 48.8 percent and 45.2 percent, respectively, between 1988 and 1997. Tract 134 lowered its rate of property crime by 22.7 percent. However, the decline lagged behind the average for Lima, and, as a result, tract 134 ranked one standard deviation above the city's mean in 1997.

Violent crime in 1988 was most pronounced in the CBD (tract 128) and in census tracts 125 and 127 just east of the CBD (Figure 8-15). The 1997 pattern suggests that violent crime, while declining overall, has become increasingly concentrated in downtown census tracts 128 and 135 (Figure 8-15). Between 1988 and 1997, rates of violent crime per capita declined in 18 of Lima's 20 census tracts. Tracts 125 and 127 experienced a reduction of one standard deviation, a percentage reduction of 64.5 percent and 55.6 percent, respectively. Tracts 117, 130, and 131 declined from the city-wide mean in 1988 to minus one standard deviation in 1997. Tract 135, although witnessing an overall reduction of 7.2 percent, now ranks one standard deviation

above the city mean as a result of witnessing a lower rate of decline than the average for Lima.

The rate of change of property crime from 1988 to 1997 (Figure 8-16) illustrates an interesting pattern. Perennial CBD problem tracts (126, 125, and 135), heavily targeted by COP stations, experienced rates of decline of one or two standard deviations, reductions of 58.8, 38.6, and 45.2 percent, respectively. However, tract 109, on Lima's west side, increased by two standard deviations. This is a percentage increase of 272.5.

Rates of change of violent crime are mapped in Figure 8-16 and demonstrate the success Lima has experienced in reducing violent crime rates in and around the CBD. Tracts 127, 128, and 138 experienced rates of decline equal to one standard deviation. These figures represent percentage declines of 55.6, 39.4, and 56.8 percent, respectively. Tract 125 witnessed a rate of decline of two standard deviations, a percentage decline of 64.5. Tract 109 on Lima's west side experienced an increase of plus two standard deviations. A similar pattern was noted with property crime and is probably the result of crime displacement from downtown locations. Although the absolute increase seems small, from 4.3 per 1,000 to 29.1 per 1,000, it represents an increase of more than 500 percent. Evidence of crime displacement is not uncommon (Ackerman 1998a; Brown and Oldakowski 1986; Brown 1982); however, such developments should alert neighborhood associations, police, and residents to the potential problem. It should also serve as a warning to proximate suburbs and communities that crime is mobile and that good neighborhood organization, cooperation with police, and constant vigilance is required to control crime.

Summary

Community policing is increasingly proposed as the solution to crime and a number of related serious social problems affecting communities in the United States. Success rates vary and it is premature to consider community policing a panacea. Those responsible for implementing policing strategies should be aware that simply adopting community policing to reduce crime and related social problems is not sufficient to make it successful. Social problems are complex and do not lend themselves to simple explanations or solutions. However, it appears that community policing, by focusing on and attempting to eliminate the underlying causes of crime rather than reacting to the symptoms of crime, holds great potential to help reduce a number of community problems related to crime, fear of crime, social and physical disorder, and blighted neighborhoods. The effectiveness of the strategy depends on public officials and citizens cooperating to identify needs and problems and will be most effective in cities where the police, citizens, social agencies, political leaders, and the media are committed to solving serious social problems in all neighborhoods.

Lima, Ohio, has witnessed substantial reduction in crime following the implementation of programs related to the overall concept of community policing. Given the inability to control for a wide range of economic and social conditions, it is not possible to say with certainty that the reduction in crime in Lima is the result of community policing. However, one can make a strong circumstantial case that it is. Political leaders, the police department, social agencies, neighborhood associations, and the media are all involved in the success of the program. The people involved believe that it is working and are committed to the strategy. Perhaps most important, crime rates are declining, and declining most rapidly in what have historically been the most crime-ravaged neighborhoods.

References

Ackerman, William V. 1998a. Socioeconomic Correlates of Increasing Crime Rates in Smaller Communities. *The Professional Geographer* 50: 372-87.

————. 1998b. The Spread of Crime to Smaller Ohio Cities and the Spatial Distribution of Crime in Lima, Ohio. *The Justice Professional* 10: 265-89.

Bayley, David H. 1994. International Differences in Community Policing. In Dennis P. Rosenbaum, ed. *The Challenge of Community Policing: Testing the Promise.* Thousand Oaks, CA: Sage.

————. 1988. Community Policing: A Report from the Devil's Advocate. In Jack R. Greene and Stephen D. Mastrofski, eds. *Community Policing: Rhetoric or Reality.* New York: Praeger.

Blass, Mike. 1998. Lima Police Department, Lima, OH. Personal Interview, November 19, 1998.

Brown, Marilyn A. 1982. Modelling the Spatial Distribution of Suburban Crime. *Economic Geography* 58(3): 247-61.

Brown, Marilyn A., and Raymond K. Oldakowski. 1986. The Changing Morphology of Suburban Crime. *Urban Geography* 7: 46-62.

Bureau of Justice Assistance. 1997. *Crime Prevention and Community Policing: A Vital Partnership.* Washington, DC: U.S. Department of Justice.

Cordner, Gary W. 1998. Community Policing: Elements and Effects. In Geoffrey P. Alpert and Alex Piquero, eds. *Community Policing: Contemporary Readings.* Prospect Heights, IL: Waveland.

Couper, David C., and Sabine H. Lobitz. 1991. *Quality Policing: The Madison Experience.* Washington, DC: Police Executive Research Forum.

Eck, J.E., and W. Spelman. 1987. Who Ya Gonna Call? *Crime and Delinquency* 34: 1.

Federal Bureau of Investigation. 1967-1997. *Uniform Crime Reports.* Washington, DC: U.S. Department of Justice, U.S. Government Printing Office.

Garlock, Gregory. 1998. Chief of Police, Lima, Ohio. Information provided in Personal Interview, November 23, 1998.

Goldstein, Herman. 1990. *Problem Oriented Policing.* New York: McGraw Hill.

————. 1987. Toward Community Oriented Policing: Potential, Basic Requirements and Threshold Questions. *Crime and Delinquency* 33: 6-30.

————. 1979. Improving Policing: A Problem-Oriented Approach. *Crime and Delinquency* 25: 236-58.

Green, Jack R., and Stephen D. Mastrofski. 1988. *Community Policing: Rhetoric or Reality.* New York: Praeger.

Kessler, David A., and Sheila Duncan. 1996. The Impact of Community Policing in Four Houston Neighborhoods. *Evaluation Review* 20: 627-69.

Klockars, Carl B. 1988. The Rhetoric of Community Policing. In Jack R. Greene and Stephen D. Mastrofski, eds. *Community Policing: Rhetoric or Reality.* New York: Praeger.

Kratcoski, Peter C., and Duane Dukes. 1995. Perspectives on Community Policing. In Peter C. Kratcoski and Duane Dukes, eds. *Issues in Community Policing.* Cincinnati: Anderson.

Manning, Peter K. 1988. Community Policing as a Drama of Control. In Jack R. Greene and Stephen D. Mastrofski, eds. *Community Policing: Rhetoric or Reality.* New York: Praeger.

Moore, Mark H. 1992. Community Policing. In Michael Tonry and Norval Morris, ed. *Modern Policing.* Chicago: University of Chicago Press.

Police Executive Research Forum. 1996. *Themes and Variations in Community Policing.* Washington, DC: Police Executive Research Forum.

Police Foundation. 1981. *The Newark Foot Patrol Experiment.* Washington, DC: Police Foundation.

Sadd, Susan, and Randolph Grinc. 1994. Innovative Neighborhood Oriented Policing: An Evaluation of Community Policing in Eight Cities. In Dennis P. Rosenbaum, ed. *The Challenge of Community Policing: Testing the Promises.* Thousand Oaks, CA: Sage.

Skogan, Wesley G. 1994. The Impact of Community Policing on Neighborhood Residents. In Dennis P. Rosenbaum, ed. *The Challenge of Community Policing: Testing the Promises.* Thousand Oaks, CA: Sage.

————. 1990. *Disorder and Decline: Crime and the Spiral Decay in American Neighborhoods.* New York: Free Press.

Skolnick, Jerome H., and David H. Bayley. 1986. *The New Blue Line: Police Innovations in Six American Cities*. New York: Free Press.

Trojanowicz, Robert C., and Bonnie Bucqueroux. 1992. *Toward Development of Meaningful and Effective Performance Evaluations*. Michigan State University, East Lansing, MI, National Center for Community Policing.

————. 1990. *Community Policing: A Contemporary Perspective*. Cincinnati: Anderson.

Weisel, Deborah Lamm, and John E. Eck. 1994. Toward a Practical Approach to Organizational Change: Community Polic-

ing Initiatives in Six Cities. In Dennis P. Rosenbaum, ed. *The Challenge of Community Policing: Testing the Promises*. Thousand Oaks, CA: Sage.

Wilson, J.Q., and G.L. Kelling. 1989. Making Neighborhoods Safe: Sometimes Fixing Broken Windows Does More to Reduce Crime than Conventional Incident-Oriented Policing. *The Atlantic* Monthly 263: 46-53.

Wycoff, Mary Ann, and Wesley G. Skogan. 1994. Community Policing in Madison: An Analysis of Implementation and Impact. In Dennis P. Rosenbaum, ed. *The Challenge of Community Policing: Testing the Promises*. Thousand Oaks, CA: Sage.

Crime Scene Sketch

W. Jerry Chisum

In Edgar Allan Poe's *The Murders in the Rue Morgue*, the detective Monsieur Auguste Dupin states, "I wish you to glance at the little sketch I have here upon this paper." His sketch of "'dark bruises, and deep indentations of finger-nails,' upon the throat of Madamoiselle L'Espanaye" demonstrated that the hand that made the prints was not human. This was a small crime scene sketch that was used to prove a point. Edgar Allan Poe wrote this story, which is claimed to be one of the first mystery stories, in 1841. That it contains one of the earliest references to crime scene sketches in the literature imprints the significance of the technical aspects of detection.

Introduction

The crime scene sketch may be a rough drawing made at the scene or it can be a polished document prepared for court using a computer-aided drawing (CAD) program. The sketch is an integral part of crime scene investigation. It is invaluable in courtroom presentations. The sketch is used to assist in understanding the locations and relationships that exist between items of evidence. It eliminates the detail and clutter that exist in a photograph.

The sketch has two basic uses. First, it is used to *rebuild* the crime scene. It allows persons who have not been at the scene to visualize the location and relationships. The investigator uses the sketch to familiarize fellow officers with the relationships between items at the crime scene and the attorney uses the sketch to show a jury. In so doing, they are rebuilding the crime scene. While photographs show the detail of the scene, the sketch eliminates the clutter and shows only the important items. The sketch ties the photos together, allowing the jurors to understand the location of the important items in the crime scene.

Investigators use the crime scene sketch to validate the stories of the witnesses or suspects. The scene dimensions are frequently critical in determining whether the witnesses were really able to see what they claim. The sketch supplements photos and video, clarifying the location of the evidence and the relationships among items.

A second function of the sketch is for *reconstruction* of the crime. Reconstruction is the determination of the actions or positions of the participants within the scene. The reconstruction of the crime requires accurate measurements. The reconstruction analyst must understand the size limitations at the scene to interpret bloodstain patterns. The measurements relating to bullet holes or powder patterns must be accurate for the trajectory analyses to be correct. The actions of the participants in a crime are frequently illustrated on the sketch. An example would be the location and movements of the shooter based on the trajectories of multiple shots.

Legal Requirements

To be accepted in court, the sketch must meet the same legal requirements as any other piece of evidence. Someone must be available to authenticate the sketch. If the sketch is not the original, the witness must testify that it truly and accurately represents the original. The witness must know the circumstances under which the sketch was produced and that it is an accurate representation of reality.

To ensure the admissibility of the sketch into a court of law, the following notations should be put on the sketch:

- Name of the person doing the original sketch
- Name of the person preparing the final sketch
- Case number
- Date of original sketch
- Location or address
- Approximate scale

A rough sketch is "not to scale." In a finished sketch, the scale is identified as "approximate." Without the word "approximate," the drawing is assumed to be exact and measurements could be made on it. These measurements may not agree with actual measurements made at the scene and the sketch may lose its legitimacy.

While not a legal requirement, a direction is needed to clarify directions in the minds of other persons; this does not have to be north. Many people (jurors) do not know the compass points, so to identify north to them has no meaning. They do understand "the front of the house" or "the street" or "the corner." These explanations are legitimate direction identifiers.

Types of Sketches

Several types of sketches are used for crime scene illustration. The crime scene sketch artist should consider which type of sketch is most appropriate for the particular crime scene.

Overview

The most familiar and most used sketch is the overview. This sketch is made as if one were looking down on the crime scene from above. It is essentially a map (Figure 8-17). In the figures, numbers are used to refer to items of evidence, capital letters to reference points, small letters to non-removable evidence, and Greek letters to cross-section cuts.

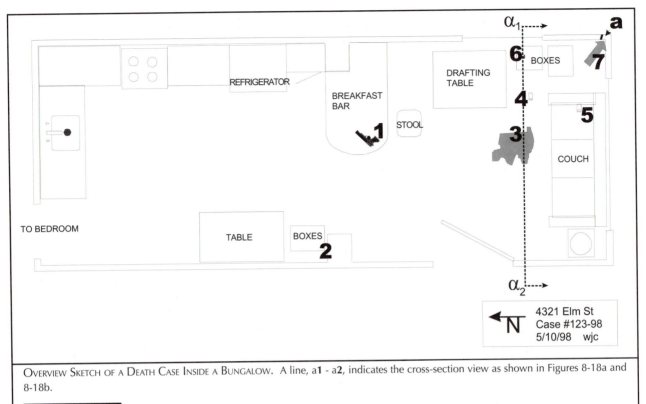

OVERVIEW SKETCH OF A DEATH CASE INSIDE A BUNGALOW. A line, a**1** - a**2**, indicates the cross-section view as shown in Figures 8-18a and 8-18b.

FIGURE 8-17

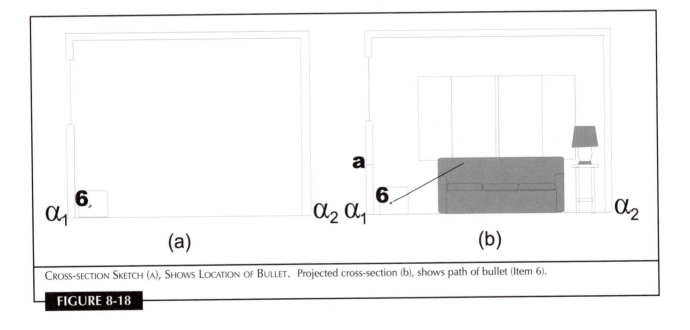

CROSS-SECTION SKETCH (A), SHOWS LOCATION OF BULLET. Projected cross-section (b), shows path of bullet (Item 6).

FIGURE 8-18

Cross-Section

Drawing the intersection of items that intersect a vertical plane through a room or scene gives a true cross-section sketch (Figure 8-18). This is seldom what is drawn. Usually what is drawn as a cross-section sketch is a vertical projection of the furniture and other items; this is a projected cross-section (Figure 8-18a). This is useful to show the relative heights of items or to show stains on the walls or bullet trajectories. If one or more projected cross-sections are attached to the overview, an exploded sketch is created.

Exploded

"Exploding" the overview sketch to show the walls and even the ceiling increases the utility. To explode the sketch, you lay out the walls (Figure 8-19). Imagine a room being a box, draw in the windows and doors, now cut the box along the vertical corners and lay the box flat. This method allows the map to include vertical components. This sketch is useful when showing bullet holes or stains on the walls.

Elevation

Elevation sketches show the side of the building or a "cross-section" of the terrain (Figure 8-20). These sketches illustrate heights and relative landscape features that assist the observer in understanding the items the artist thought were important.

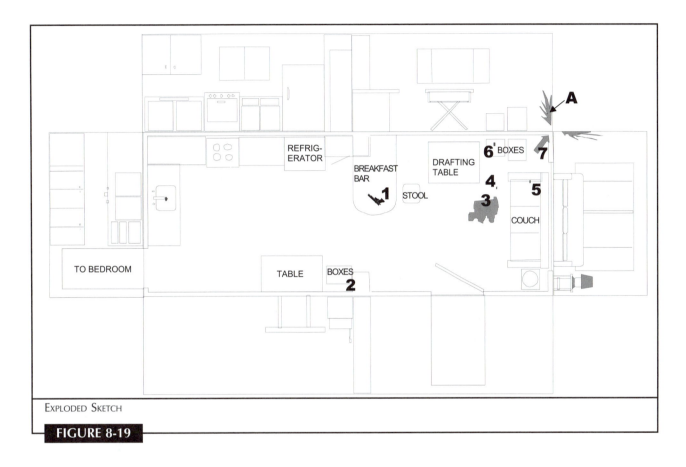

EXPLODED SKETCH

FIGURE 8-19

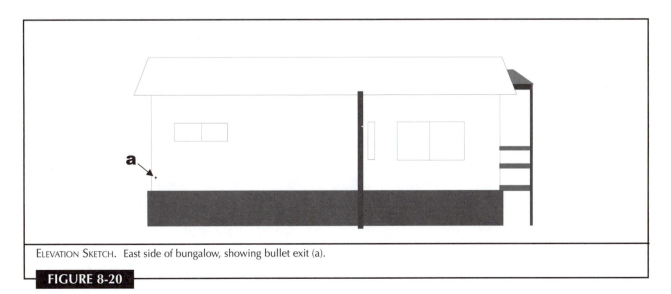

ELEVATION SKETCH. East side of bungalow, showing bullet exit (a).

FIGURE 8-20

Perspective

A perspective sketch is a representation of the third dimension on paper (Figure 8-21). A "vanishing point" is set by the sketch artist. All lines leading away from the viewer converge upon that point. Some accident scenes benefit from this rendition but it is seldom used for court presentations in homicides or other criminal cases.

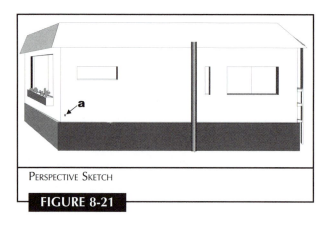

PERSPECTIVE SKETCH

FIGURE 8-21

Reference Systems

The sketch artist must decide from which points to measure in recording the scene. While "permanent" is a relative term, the objects used as reference points should be expected to remain a few years. The computer and CAD programs have had considerable impact upon what is used for a reference.

When entering measurements into the sketch, only the room dimensions should be on the sketch. Sketch artists who put lines on the sketch to show what was measured and then add the measurements to the line will find that they may not be able to read their sketches when the case goes to court. Someone other than the artist will not be able to understand such sketches. To avoid the messiness, clutter, and confusion of all these lines, a legend or table is used. The distances to the items are in this table, which lists the evidence item numbers and a short description of the item. The same table can be used for any of the reference systems. This concept is illustrated in each of the figures showing the various systems.

Rectangular Coordinates

The walls of the room are commonly used to measure the locations of items. The sketch artist selects two perpendicular adjacent walls having the least amount of furniture that may impede the measurements (Figure 8-22). The distance from the object to each wall is measured. The potential error in this method lies in the estimation of right angles at the juncture of the wall and the tape measure. The rectangular coordinate system is easy to transfer to computer drawings of the scene. The jury can also easily understand this system.

Baseline

The baseline method is similar to the rectangular coordinate system. However, only one wall is used for an indoor sketch, a curb line is used for an accident scene, and an

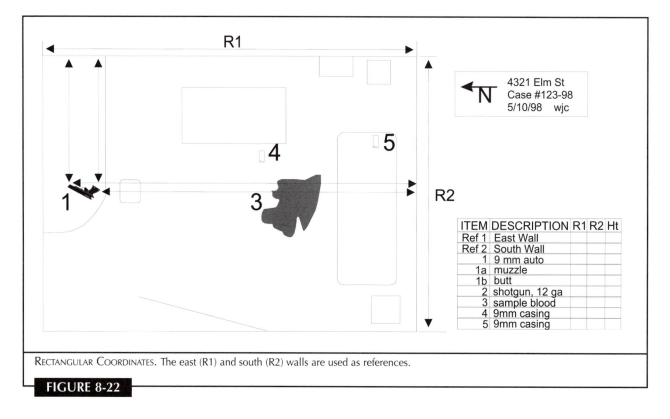

ITEM	DESCRIPTION	R1	R2	Ht
Ref 1	East Wall			
Ref 2	South Wall			
1	9 mm auto			
1a	muzzle			
1b	butt			
2	shotgun, 12 ga			
3	sample blood			
4	9mm casing			
5	9mm casing			

RECTANGULAR COORDINATES. The east (R1) and south (R2) walls are used as references.

FIGURE 8-22

imaginary line (or a long tape measure) is used for outdoor scenes. A "baseline" tape measure is laid against the wall (curb) and a second tape measure is used to measure the distance from the object to that tape (Figure 8-23). The distance along the baseline tape at the intersection point is recorded. Baseline measurements are frequently used in traffic accidents. The method is also useful when several objects, such as cartridge casings, are located near a wall. This method also suffers from the estimation of right angles. The baseline method is also easily imported to the computer and is easily understood.

Triangulation

The most accurate method of making measurements using tape measures is triangulation. The three sides of the triangle fix the location of the object in the sketch. The corners of the room (Figure 8-24) or two fixed objects are used as reference points. Properly used, this method can also be the quickest and easiest for obtaining measurements. Two tape measures are affixed to the reference points and the tapes are crossed over the point to be measured. Measurements obtained by triangulation are difficult to transfer to

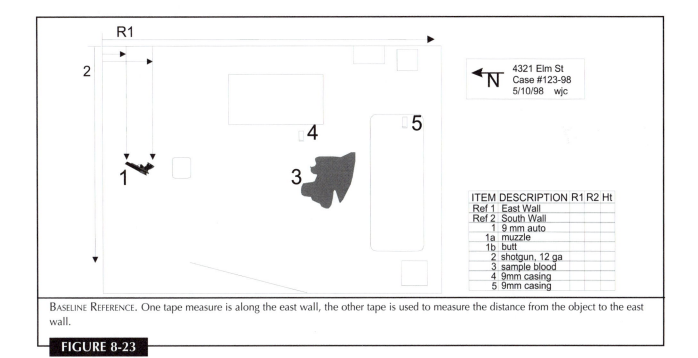

BASELINE REFERENCE. One tape measure is along the east wall, the other tape is used to measure the distance from the object to the east wall.

FIGURE 8-23

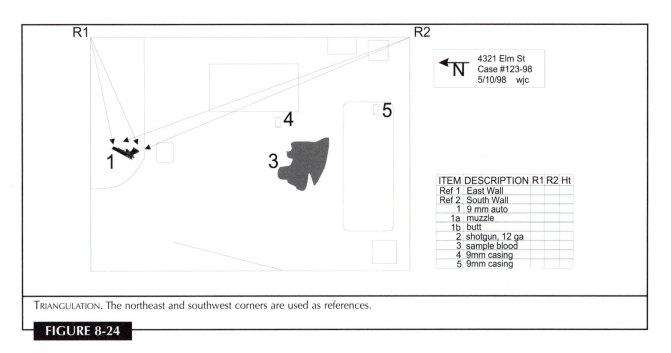

TRIANGULATION. The northeast and southwest corners are used as references.

FIGURE 8-24

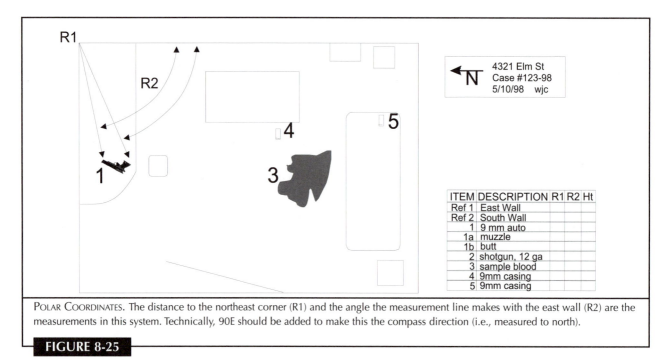

ITEM	DESCRIPTION	R1	R2	Ht
Ref 1	East Wall			
Ref 2	South Wall			
1	9 mm auto			
1a	muzzle			
1b	butt			
2	shotgun, 12 ga			
3	sample blood			
4	9mm casing			
5	9mm casing			

POLAR COORDINATES. The distance to the northeast corner (R1) and the angle the measurement line makes with the east wall (R2) are the measurements in this system. Technically, 90E should be added to make this the compass direction (i.e., measured to north).

FIGURE 8-25

a computer sketch, requiring arcs to be drawn and erased for each point. Triangulation is not as easily understood by the layperson.

Polar Coordinates

The least common system of measurement for the crime scene sketch artist is the polar coordinate system. This method requires the measurement of angles as well as distances (Figure 8-25). While this method can be used effectively for large outdoor scenes covering many miles, it is not practical for indoor use. The measurements can be accurate, but the method is not easily understood.

Artificial Reference Points

When in a remote location or in a location where the nearest "permanent" points are a long distance relative to the size of the crime scene, artificial reference points may be used. Two stakes are placed into the ground at one side of the crime scene at a reasonable distance apart. These stakes become the reference points for triangulation, or a tape measure between them becomes the baseline. The location of the stakes can be determined by measuring to distant objects. Alternatively, a Global Positioning System (GPS) reading and the location by compass direction of landmarks can determine the location of the stakes. It is seldom necessary to return to a remote location. Laboratory analysis may indicate, however, that additional evidence may have been overlooked.

Measurement Systems

A sketch is of limited value without some idea of the scale; therefore, measurements must be made. Several methods of measuring are available. If the wrong measurement

method is used, the distances will be in error. The various methods of measurement are illustrated in Figure 8-26. The measurement between two evidence items is used to show how the various measurements are made.

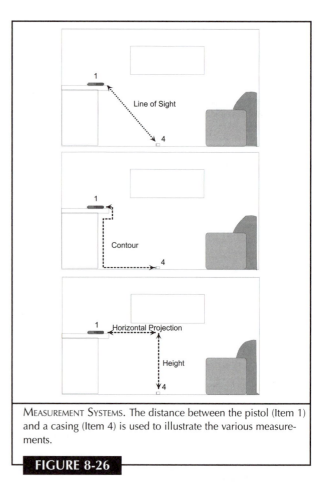

MEASUREMENT SYSTEMS. The distance between the pistol (Item 1) and a casing (Item 4) is used to illustrate the various measurements.

FIGURE 8-26

Line of Sight

Line of sight is the most common method of measuring. It is the shortest distance between two objects. This measurement can be visualized by picturing a bee flying from one point to another (beeline). This is also the most commonly misused method; the measurements made using this method fail to take into account the relative heights of objects. These measurements are only correct if they are made for an elevation sketch. If line-of-sight measurements are used on an overhead sketch, serious errors can occur.

Contour

Contour measurements follow the terrain. When reading a map for the distance between two cities, the mileage is the distance a vehicle travels. Pacing the distance from a landmark to the scene or using a rolling tape measure are legitimate uses of contour measurements. Instead of the beeline analogy above, this type of measurement is analogous to the movement of an ant between two points. The contour measure is not used on indoor crime scenes.

Horizontal Projection

For the overview sketch, the horizontal projection is the correct measurement method. These distances are shorter than the line-of-sight measurements because they do not account for a third dimension. To correctly measure a crime scene, the tape measure must be level. The measurement from an object on a table means the tape must be brought to table height. Otherwise, a plumb must be used to ensure the measurement on the tape is directly over the object. Failure to do so results in errors.

Height

The heights of all items of evidence should always be recorded. Police sketch artists frequently fail to record heights. The movement of furniture and other objects can render these measurements unattainable after the scene is vacated. The height is the third side of the triangle formed by the horizontal projection and the line-of-sight measurements. The heights of the furniture and other items help illustrate the freedom of movement of the participants in the crime or the views of witnesses.

Finished Sketches

In the past, the crime scene artist had to be a draftsperson to produce large versions of a sketch rendered to scale. If no one in the agency was available, the services of a drafting firm were used, sometimes at great expense. The computer has changed the manner in which drawings are made.

A number of two- and three-dimensional drawing programs are available for rendering the final sketch on a computer. Programs designed for law enforcement include symbols for various weapons, stains, footprints, and other items frequently found at crime scenes. Use of one of the CAD or drawing programs has enabled the production of clear, understandable crime scene sketches, by even the smallest agency, without the expense of a drafting firm.

References

Federal Bureau of Investigation. *Crime Scene Sketching*. Manual by the FBI Training Division, (date unknown).

Poe, Edgar Allen. 1991. *Murders in the Rue Morgue*, 1841, World Library's Greatest Books Collection on CD, World Library Inc. Garden Grove, CA.

Rynearson, J.M., and W.J. Chisum. 1989. *Evidence and Crime Scene Reconstruction*. Shingletown, CA: Rynearson.

Police Department Use of Geographic Information Systems for Crime Analysis

Elaine Hallisey Hendrix

Today many police departments use Geographic Information Systems (GIS) to aid in the performance of a number of tasks, such as calls for police assistance, emergency response planning, determination of police beats, the study of changes in crime patterns over time, and a host of other applications. This essay focuses on police agency use of GIS for *crime analysis*, as described in Chapter 3 for the essay on detection of chop shops.

A major component of a GIS is the ability to produce maps. Mapping data enables crime analysts, beat patrol officers, and the general public to interpret information in new ways. Patterns and relationships that are based upon location are much more apparent in a graphic display of data than in traditional reports or tables. As J. Thomas McEwen and Faye Taxman (1995: 280) state,

> Without a mapping system, department personnel tend to analyze crime problems on the basis of incident characteristics such as time of day, day of week and method of entry, with insufficient attention to the spatial aspects of crimes. These spatial aspects are important because they focus on clustering of events in locations, the time of the day of occurrence and the linkage among events.

Many of the essays in this volume analyze geographic patterns of various crimes over large areas. The maps in this essay depict smaller areas, reflecting the fact that most police departments generally focus on the analysis of crime in cities or counties.[1]

What Is a Geographic Information System?

GIS technology is applied to a number of different disciplines, including urban planning, environmental studies, real estate, epidemiology, and policing. In this essay, the examples used to define GIS will reflect policing applications.

A Geographic Information System may be defined as a process in which geographic, or locational data are acquired and compiled into a digital database consisting of both base maps and the characteristics, or attributes, of the base map features. The geographic data are then analyzed in some fashion, using statistical spatial analysis, visual analysis, or both, and the results are presented either graphically as maps or charts, or in text form (Dent 1998).

A GIS database, comprising maps and attributes of the map features, is usually expressed in one of two data models: vector or raster. In the vector data model, features on the earth, such as the locations of reported burglaries, streets, or census boundaries, are represented as points, lines, or polygons. The characteristics of the features are stored in spreadsheets in which individual records are linked to individual features (Figure 8-27). The raster data model subdivides the study area into a grid made up of square cells, or pixels. Each cell, covering a small geographic area, contains a single attribute value (Figure 8-28).

Each data model has advantages and disadvantages. The vector model, for example, displays maps in a format that is familiar to the general public—vector maps look like the "real" world. In addition, a vector database can store numerous map features and attributes using a relatively small amount of computer space. On the other hand, vector-based GISs can be somewhat imprecise when analyzing certain types of data. For instance, several problems arise when an analyst has the software count the number of points, representing burglaries, located within police beat polygons to determine the total number of burglary incidents within each beat. Crimes may be clustered along major roadways, which are often the boundaries of beats and other enumeration units. If a crime occurs on a boundary, to which beat is it assigned? In addition, the varying sizes of the beats, in conjunction with the possibility that burglaries may be clustered in certain areas within each beat instead of evenly dispersed throughout, give the analyst a distorted summary of the data. If the analyst divides the incident count for each beat by the area of each beat to calculate a density, the density is still just an average for what may be a large, diverse area.

The small, uniform cell size of a raster-based GIS does not present these dilemmas. Raster-based GISs are useful for mapping data that vary continuously over a surface, such as crime densities. Rasters, however, tend to be large files and output displays are difficult to interpret unless there is some vector overlay, such as a street map, for the map-reader's geographic reference. Each data model has other advantages and disadvantages with respect to geographic analysis, but the list is too extensive to discuss here. Suffice it to say, the GIS software industry has responded to the

Map Features

Attributes of Map Features

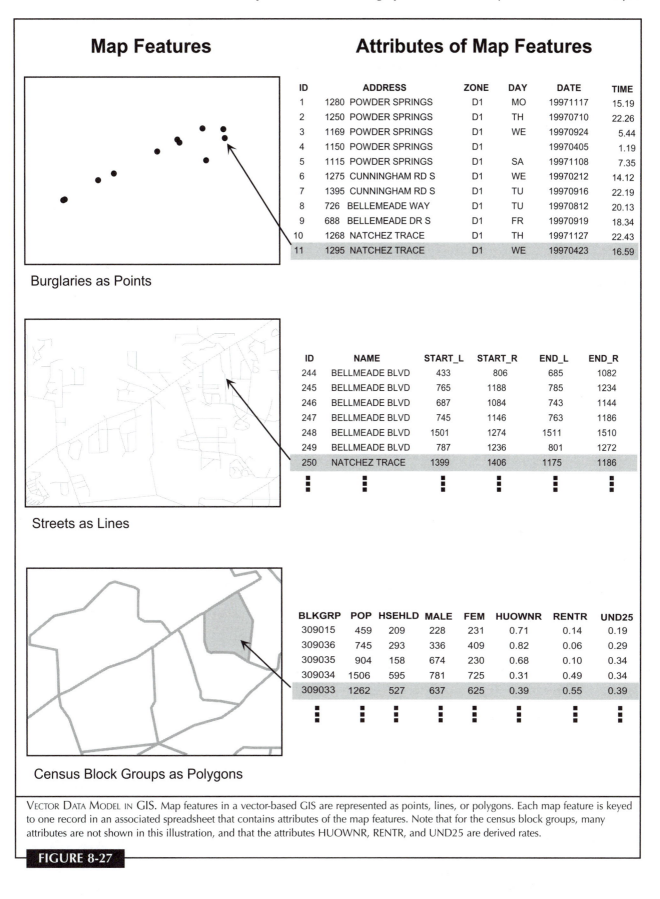

Burglaries as Points

ID	ADDRESS	ZONE	DAY	DATE	TIME
1	1280 POWDER SPRINGS	D1	MO	19971117	15.19
2	1250 POWDER SPRINGS	D1	TH	19970710	22.26
3	1169 POWDER SPRINGS	D1	WE	19970924	5.44
4	1150 POWDER SPRINGS	D1		19970405	1.19
5	1115 POWDER SPRINGS	D1	SA	19971108	7.35
6	1275 CUNNINGHAM RD S	D1	WE	19970212	14.12
7	1395 CUNNINGHAM RD S	D1	TU	19970916	22.19
8	726 BELLEMEADE WAY	D1	TU	19970812	20.13
9	688 BELLEMEADE DR S	D1	FR	19970919	18.34
10	1268 NATCHEZ TRACE	D1	TH	19971127	22.43
11	1295 NATCHEZ TRACE	D1	WE	19970423	16.59

Streets as Lines

ID	NAME	START_L	START_R	END_L	END_R
244	BELLMEADE BLVD	433	806	685	1082
245	BELLMEADE BLVD	765	1188	785	1234
246	BELLMEADE BLVD	687	1084	743	1144
247	BELLMEADE BLVD	745	1146	763	1186
248	BELLMEADE BLVD	1501	1274	1511	1510
249	BELLMEADE BLVD	787	1236	801	1272
250	NATCHEZ TRACE	1399	1406	1175	1186

Census Block Groups as Polygons

BLKGRP	POP	HSEHLD	MALE	FEM	HUOWNR	RENTR	UND25
309015	459	209	228	231	0.71	0.14	0.19
309036	745	293	336	409	0.82	0.06	0.29
309035	904	158	674	230	0.68	0.10	0.34
309034	1506	595	781	725	0.31	0.49	0.34
309033	1262	527	637	625	0.39	0.55	0.39

VECTOR DATA MODEL IN GIS. Map features in a vector-based GIS are represented as points, lines, or polygons. Each map feature is keyed to one record in an associated spreadsheet that contains attributes of the map features. Note that for the census block groups, many attributes are not shown in this illustration, and that the attributes HUOWNR, RENTR, and UND25 are derived rates.

FIGURE 8-27

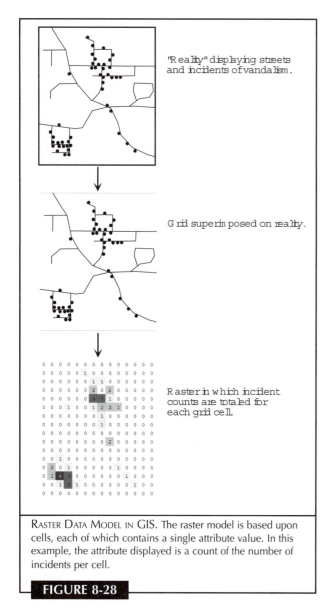

"Reality" displaying streets and incidents of vandalism.

Grid superimposed on reality.

Raster in which incident counts are totaled for each grid cell.

RASTER DATA MODEL IN GIS. The raster model is based upon cells, each of which contains a single attribute value. In this example, the attribute displayed is a count of the number of incidents per cell.

FIGURE 8-28

it occur? The software indicates that the highest count is four and displays the single cell in the southwest corner.

One of the hallmarks of a GIS is the ability to overlay different map layers, or themes, to study the relationships among the various layers (Figure 8-29). For example, the layers from Figure 8-27, burglaries, streets, and census block groups, encompassing the same geographic area, are digitally superimposed. From visual inspection, the analyst sees that a number of burglaries have occurred along the boundaries of several census blocks, which also happen to represent a major street. The analyst may determine that the reason for this pattern is that this major thoroughfare offers burglars easy access and a quick getaway.

Additionally, several incidents are clustered within a northeastern census block group. The analyst may want to determine if there is a relationship between the relatively large number of burglaries and the demographics, or population characteristics, of this block group. Are there a large number of renters or moderately expensive homes in this area, for instance? Are there a large number of young males? This example shows only a small number of block groups, so it is easy for the analyst to determine through visual inspection within which block group these points fall. After the block group is identified, the analyst can inspect the block group attribute table to determine the local demographic composition.

When working with hundreds or thousands of points and polygons, this is not such a simple task without using GIS-based point-in-polygon analysis. Point-in-polygon analysis, a commonly used GIS operation in the study of crime, joins the attributes of the two layers, the crime incident point layer and the polygon layer, to enable the analyst to identify demographic patterns that may contribute to high or low crime rates. The GIS software determines within which polygon each point is located, based on geographic coordinates such as longitude and latitude, and then joins the attributes of polygon layers to the attributes of their corresponding point(s).

differing analytical qualities of the data models by creating GIS software packages that incorporate both vector and raster capabilities, allowing the analyst to move from one model to another, as required.

GIS Analysis

Using either data model, an analyst can pose questions of the geographic database. Working with the burglary data in Figure 8-27, for instance, a crime analyst may enter the following query: At which locations did burglaries occur on a Tuesday? The software highlights the points with IDs of 7 and 8. In a second query, the analyst points to a census block group, the highlighted block group, for example, and asks the following question: What is the population of this polygon? The software displays the population figure as 1,262. Working with Figure 8-28, the analyst poses the following question: What is the highest count and where does

GIS Data Sets

Referring again to Figure 8-29, the analyst may also add additional map layers showing locations of high schools or liquor stores to determine if the distribution of burglaries is related to these features. The Illinois Criminal Justice Information Authority (ICAM) has identified map layers necessary for a GeoArchive, a GIS database useful in crime analysis, investigation, and community problem solving (Block 1997: 48). These layers, which serve to define the environment, include street maps; public transit routes and stops; the locations of schools, community organizations, emergency facilities, parks, public housing, places holding liquor licenses, etc.; land use maps (e.g., whether a parcel is residential, commercial, or vacant); demographics (e.g., census population characteristics); public health data (e.g., mortality rates, fatal firearm accidents); locations of crime incidents; gang territories; and police jurisdictions.

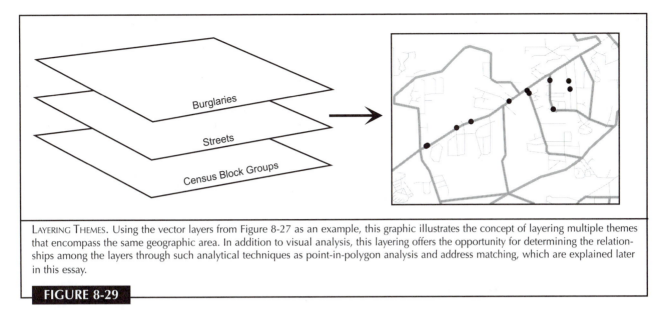

LAYERING THEMES. Using the vector layers from Figure 8-27 as an example, this graphic illustrates the concept of layering multiple themes that encompass the same geographic area. In addition to visual analysis, this layering offers the opportunity for determining the relationships among the layers through such analytical techniques as point-in-polygon analysis and address matching, which are explained later in this essay.

FIGURE 8-29

Many of the layers listed above are available from various government agencies. Local government agencies often maintain digital databases of land use, transit, and other types of data. The U.S. Bureau of the Census maintains an extensive database, TIGER, which contains a detailed street base and demographic data for the entire United States.

Other data sets, such as incident maps, require custom construction. Today, most medium and large police departments use computer-aided dispatch (CAD) and records management systems (RMS)[2] that store and maintain call-for-service, incident, arrest, and other data (Rich 1995). A byproduct of this routine police activity is geocoded data or data with the potential for geocoding. Geocoding, also known as address matching, address geocoding, or pin mapping, is the process by which street addresses or intersections are assigned point locations. It is analogous to the old police practice of placing colored pins on maps to represent crime incidents. Map layers comprised of geocoded crime incidents are an important component of a GIS database because these layers enable law enforcement agencies to identify crime hot spots, or clusters of crime activity.

Most address matching is performed using a street base, such as that shown in Figure 8-27, which includes address ranges in the associated attribute table (Olligschlaeger 1997). Referring to Figure 8-27, START_L is the beginning of the street numbering sequence on the left side of the road and START_R is the beginning of the street numbering sequence on the right side of the road. END_L is the end of the street numbering sequence on the left and END_R is the end of the street numbering sequence on the right. The police department records a call stating that a burglary has taken place at 1295 Natchez Trace (Figure 8-30). Using the street base, the mapping software locates a point on the left side of Natchez Trace because the odd numbered addresses are on the left side of the street. The point falls a little more than half way between the END_L

value of 1175 and the START_L value of 1399 for Natchez Trace.

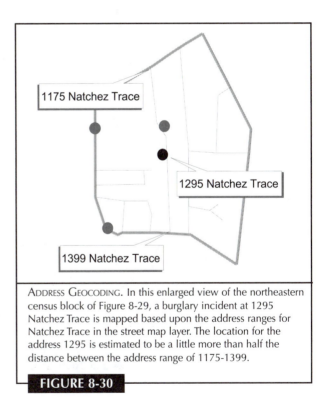

ADDRESS GEOCODING. In this enlarged view of the northeastern census block of Figure 8-29, a burglary incident at 1295 Natchez Trace is mapped based upon the address ranges for Natchez Trace in the street map layer. The location for the address 1295 is estimated to be a little more than half the distance between the address range of 1175-1399.

FIGURE 8-30

Applications of GIS Technology

The Crime Mapping Research Center (CMRC) of the National Institute of Justice conducted a nationwide crime mapping survey over 15 months beginning in March 1997 to determine which law enforcement agencies use GIS technology (Mamalian and La Vigne 1999). The survey targeted 2,768 police departments, with 2,004 responding. The CMRC found that only about 13 percent of departments currently use computerized crime mapping. Interest is growing, however, with almost 20 percent of departments not presently using GIS reporting that they have allocated funds for implementing the technology within the next year. Thirty-six percent of departments with more than 100 sworn officers use GIS, in contrast to smaller departments where only 3 percent use this technology. Of the agencies using GIS, 88 percent employ commercially available software primarily on personal computers. MapInfo, ArcView, and ArcInfo are the most commonly used GIS software packages.

Hot Spot Analysis

According to the CMRC survey, GIS technology has numerous applications. Automated pin mapping is the most frequently used analysis technique with 72 percent of departments performing incident geocoding. Eighty-six percent of departments that conduct hot spot analyses of crime locations visually identify hot spots. Twenty-five percent use software to identify hot spots.

Although visual identification of hot spots works fairly well, the analyst might miss points that are close together or on top of each other. The use of new computer tech-

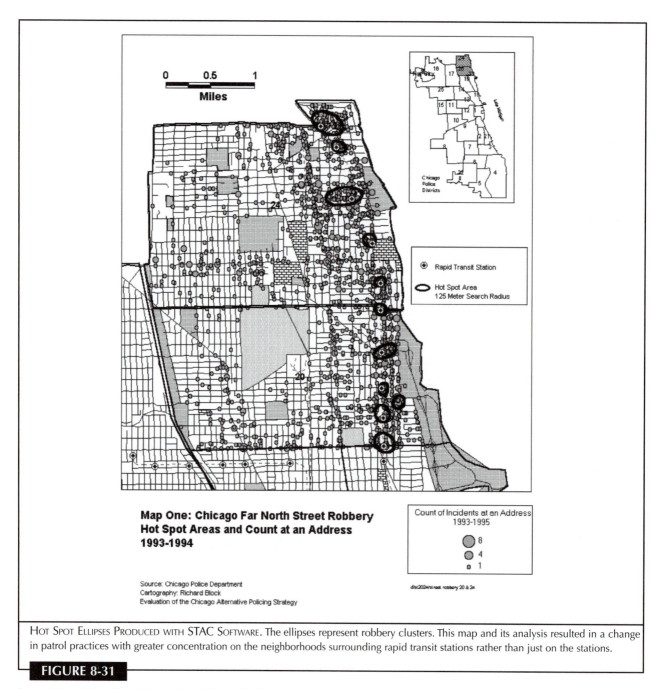

Map One: Chicago Far North Street Robbery Hot Spot Areas and Count at an Address 1993-1994

Source: Chicago Police Department
Cartography: Richard Block
Evaluation of the Chicago Alternative Policing Strategy

HOT SPOT ELLIPSES PRODUCED WITH STAC SOFTWARE. The ellipses represent robbery clusters. This map and its analysis resulted in a change in patrol practices with greater concentration on the neighborhoods surrounding rapid transit stations rather than just on the stations.

FIGURE 8-31

Source: Richard Block, The Environs of Rapid Transit Stations: A Focus for Street Crime or Just Another Risky Place? In R.V. Clarke, ed. *Preventing Mass Transit Crime.* Monsey, NY: Criminal Justice Press, 1996. Reprinted with permission of Criminal Justice Press.

niques in the study of the distribution of point data has raised the level of analytic capabilities. In the 1980s, the Illinois Criminal Justice Information Authority developed the Spatial and Temporal Analysis of Crime (STAC) package to aid in the identification of hot spots (Block 1995). STAC contains a number of tools for statistical analysis, but the most commonly used is the hot spot identifier. Through complex point cluster analysis, the software determines the areas containing the most densely clustered points and draws ellipses around these areas (Figure 8-31).

In addition to STAC, hot spots can be analyzed in a number of other ways. Raster-based GISs are able to create shaded density maps based upon small cells instead of more artificial, less precise areas, such as police jurisdictions (Figures 8-32A to 8-32D). Another method is to create contour maps, in which lines of equal value representing point densities are connected. Some software packages allow for three-dimensional display of point density data as shown in Figure 8-32D.

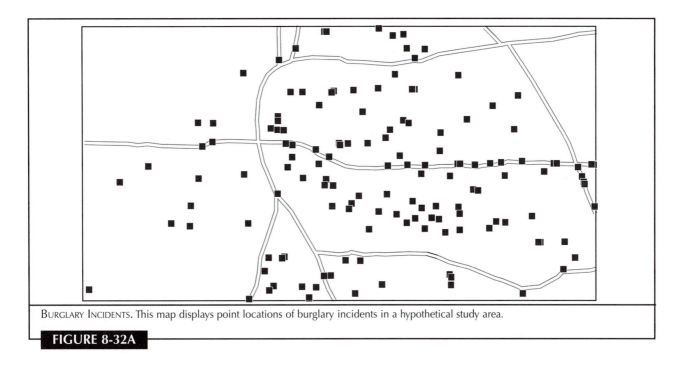

BURGLARY INCIDENTS. This map displays point locations of burglary incidents in a hypothetical study area.

FIGURE 8-32A

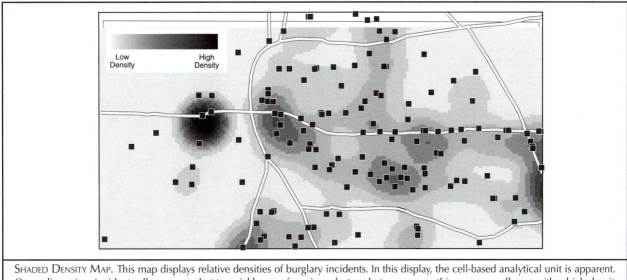

SHADED DENSITY MAP. This map displays relative densities of burglary incidents. In this display, the cell-based analytical unit is apparent. Geocoding crime incidents allows an analyst to quickly scan for crime clusters, but, as seen on this map, a small area with a high density in the western portion of the study area might have been missed with simple observation. A number of burglaries occurred at one address, an apartment complex, so that points were layered one on top of another, obscuring many crime incidents.

FIGURE 8-32B

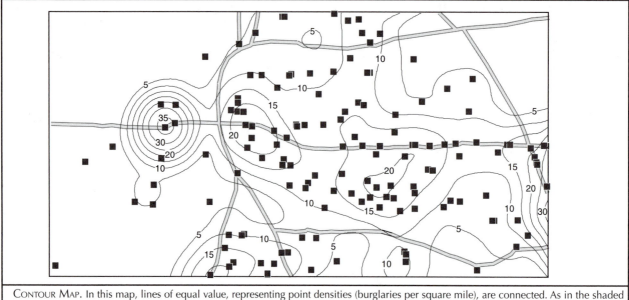

CONTOUR MAP. In this map, lines of equal value, representing point densities (burglaries per square mile), are connected. As in the shaded density map, note the peak at the apartment complex in the western portion of the hypothetical study area.

FIGURE 8-32C

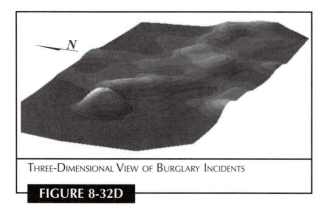

THREE-DIMENSIONAL VIEW OF BURGLARY INCIDENTS

FIGURE 8-32D

Hot spot identification is such a vital aspect of crime analysis that the CMRC is conducting a systematic comparison of the available spatial analysis software packages. This study will examine the "(1) ease of use, (2) accuracy, (3) consistency, (4) face validity, (5) utility for statistical analyses, (6) flexibility, and (7) underlying algorithms" of various spatial analysis software packages (CRMC *Research Portfolio* 1998: 1).

Crime Mapping Applications

Hot spot analyses, as well as other analysis techniques, are consolidated to enable law enforcement agencies to perform useful operations. Listed below are the most common ways GIS crime mapping applications are used by police departments. Examples of actual case studies using this applications are discussed on the following pages.

• Inform police officers and investigators of crime incident locations
• Make resource allocation decisions

• Evaluate police department interventions
• Inform residents about crime activity and changes in their community
• Identify repeat calls-for-service

The Shreveport, Louisiana, Police Department has used GIS for crime analysis for over 10 years (Reno 1998). In one case study, the Shreveport Crime Analysis Unit used maps to perform the first four applications listed above. Burglary incidents were address geocoded so that the analyst could determine if burglary incidents in police district 4 had a pattern (Figure 8-33A). The analyst found that the main concentration of burglaries, located inside the ellipse, was adjacent to a high school indicating a possible truancy problem. The map, as well as other information, was distributed to officers to inform them of the burglary locations. The department increased patrol personnel in the targeted area and community liaison officers met with high school officials to inform them of the increased deployment. After the truancy problem was corrected and high school age burglary suspects arrested, the analyst created new maps to evaluate the effectiveness of police intervention. The sample map (Figure 8-33B) displays a clear reduction in burglaries near the high school.

An innovative approach increasingly used to inform the community about crime activity is online crime mapping. A number of police departments have implemented Internet Web sites that offer interactive mapping. At these sites, citizens select an area of interest, either from a map displaying local areas, such as neighborhoods or police beats, or from a list of areas. There is usually an option to select the type of crime for which information is desired and whether the display is to be in the form of a table or a map of crime distribution (Figure 8-34A–C). Listed below are several examples of police Web sites that enable citizens to gather information regarding crime in their neighborhoods. A fairly large number of police departments use Internet technology to communicate with citizens in this way and the numbers are increasing.

- Chicago Police Department <http://www.ci.chi.il.us/CommunityPolicing/Statistics/Statistics.html>
- Charlotte-Mecklenburg Police <http://www.ci/charlotte.nc.us/cipolice/index.htm>
- Berkeley Police Department <http://police.ci.berkeley.ca.us>

- Mesa Crime Analysis Unit <http://www.ci.mesa.az.us/police/crime_analysis_unit.htm>

There has been some debate that such a public forum for the dissemination of this information raises privacy issues, particularly regarding the privacy of crime victims (CRIMEMAP-L 1999).[3] Presently, most law enforcement agencies are aware of the potential for abuse in both online mapping and crime mapping in general. Many agencies avoid releasing explicit details, such as exact addresses, on crime

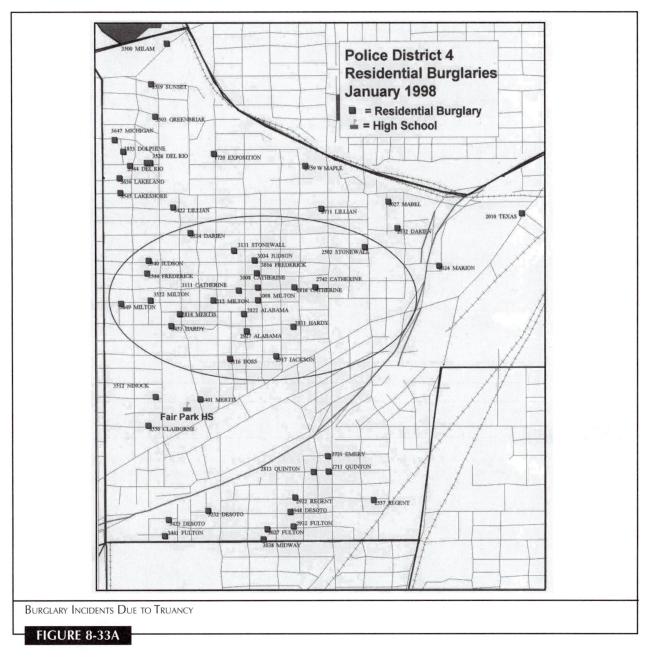

BURGLARY INCIDENTS DUE TO TRUANCY

FIGURE 8-33A

Source: Susan Reno, Using Crime Mapping to Address Residential Burglary. In N.G. La Vigne and J. Wartell, eds. *Crime Mapping Case Studies: Successes in the Field.* Washington, DC: Police Executive Research Forum, 1998. Reproduced with the permission of the Police Executive Research Forum.

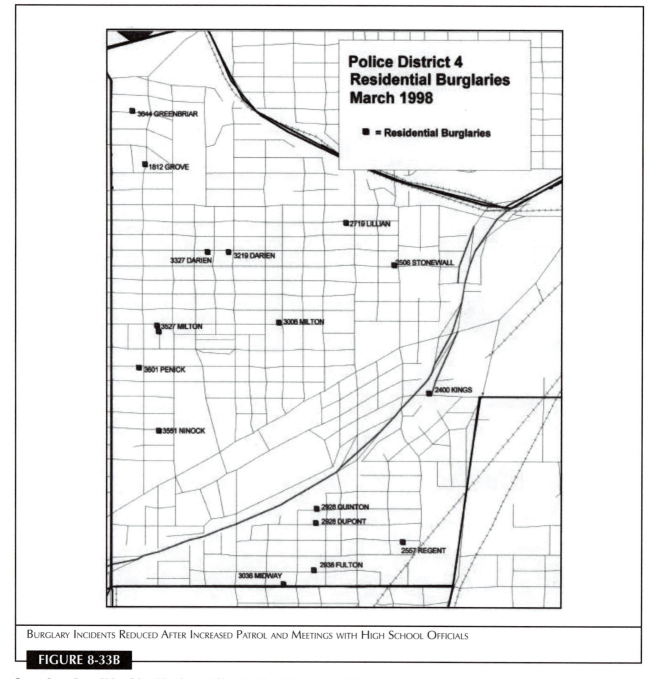

BURGLARY INCIDENTS REDUCED AFTER INCREASED PATROL AND MEETINGS WITH HIGH SCHOOL OFFICIALS

FIGURE 8-33B

Source: Susan Reno, Using Crime Mapping to Address Residential Burglary. In N.G. La Vigne and J. Wartell, eds. *Crime Mapping Case Studies: Successes in the Field.* Washington, DC: Police Executive Research Forum, 1998. Reproduced with the permission of the Police Executive Research Forum.

locations and victims. Some departments, however, distribute such data freely in the belief that this is public information. Crime mapping and the resulting privacy issues, as well as the potential for misusing data, such as the illegal practice of redlining (a form of discrimination in which home-loan funds or insurance opportunities are withheld from areas considered poor economic risks), are currently generating intense discussion among law enforcement officials.

In addition to the more common uses of GIS by police departments, the technology is also used for other purposes, such as modeling-type applications that are focused on either predicting serial crimes using probabilities, or estimating where a serial criminal may live or work based on variables recorded at the crime scenes. In Los Angeles, for example, police successfully predicted the location of a robbery based upon data collected after previous purse snatchings committed by a serial robber known as the "Motorcycle Bandit." In this case, a Los Angeles police officer used a method that required the collection of information regarding the time of day of each incident, the number of days between incidents, and the location of each incident (Geggie 1998). The data were analyzed using complex spatial statistics and the results, rectangles representing 68- and 95-percent probability of the occurrence of the next robbery, were drawn electronically on a map. Unfortunately, the Motorcycle Bandit escaped in rush hour traffic after a brief pursuit, but no similar purse snatchings have been recorded in the area.

Criminal Geographic Targeting (CGT), or geographic profiling, another modeling-type application of GIS based on the premise that people follow geographic patterns in their daily lives, is a computerized technique used for predicting the location of a serial offender's home. CGT is used in conjunction with psychiatric profiling and other investigative techniques, combining point-pattern analysis with journey-to-crime research (Rossmo 1998). A number of geographic variables, including where the victim was found, access routes to the crime scene, where the victim's personal items were found, and local land use, are gathered and analyzed (CMRC FAQ 1999). The data are displayed in a probability surface in which the higher the point on the surface, the higher the likelihood the serial criminal resides there (Figure 8-35). This method, which allows police to focus investigations in areas where the serial criminal is likely to live, has been applied to many cases, including that of the Hillside Stranglers in Los Angeles, British Columbia's Abbotsford murders, and Ontario's Paul Bernardo homicides.

Conclusion

As discussed above, GIS is currently used for a variety of tasks, including mapping and analyzing hot spots, disseminating information to the public, and, more creatively, for predictive modeling. Clearly, Geographic Information Systems technology is a valuable tool for crime analysis. GIS enables police to analyze the *spatial* patterns of crime and to display locational information graphically. With the increased availability of low cost hardware and software, as well as the increased awareness among law enforcement agencies of the capabilities of this technology, the use of GIS for crime analysis will become more prevalent in the future.

Endnotes

1. Law enforcement officials have begun to recognize the importance of analyzing *regional* spatial data. Crimes and crime trends often encompass multiple jurisdictions. Data sharing and information exchange among jurisdictions is, therefore, important to understanding and preventing crime. The Greater Atlanta Data Center (GADC) is one such recently established cooperative effort (Sposato 1999). GADC comprises five metropolitan Atlanta county jurisdictions (Clayton, Cobb, Dekalb, Fulton, and Gwinnett), as well as the City of Atlanta and all the city police jurisdictions in Cobb County. The goals of GADC, as stated on their Web site, are to (1) increase the accessibility of information by providing the means to visualize and integrate crime data using GIS software; (2) improve dissemination of information through support for secure input, storage, and retrieval of crime-related data; (3) provide the ability to retrieve, analyze, and integrate shared information relevant to public safety; and (4) institute partnerships among local law enforcement agencies and educational institutions to provide technical support in the area of GIS (Greater Atlanta Data Center 1999).

2. In GIS applications other than those related to crime mapping, the acronym CAD refers to computer-aided drafting. The acronym RMS refers to root mean square, a type of statistical measurement.

3. In early January 1999, Bryan Vila, an associate professor at the University of Wyoming, posted a query regarding crime mapping and privacy issues to CRIMEMAP-L, an online discussion group composed of crime analysts, researchers, geographers, and others. A lively, thought-provoking discussion ensued. Currently, there are no archives for CRIMEMAP-L, but as a subscriber, I have saved most of the responses to Vila's comments.

References

Block, Carolyn Rebecca. 1997. The GeoArchive: An Information Foundation for Community Policing. In D. Weisburd and T. McEwen, eds. *Crime Mapping and Crime Prevention*. Monsey, NY: Criminal Justice Press.

————. 1995. STAC Hot-Spot Areas: A Statistical Tool for Law Enforcement Decisions. In C.R. Block, M. Dabdoub, and S. Fregly, eds. *Crime Analysis through Computer Mapping*. Washington, DC: Police Executive Research Forum.

Block, Richard. 1996. The Environs of Rapid Transit Stations: A Focus for Street Crime or Just Another Risky Place? In R.V. Clarke, ed. *Preventing Mass Transit Crime*. Monsey, NY: Criminal Justice Press.

Canter, Philip. 1995. State of the Statistical Art: Point-Pattern Analysis. In C.R. Block, M. Dabdoub, and S. Fregly, eds. *Crime Analysis through Computer Mapping*. Washington, DC: Police Executive Research Forum.

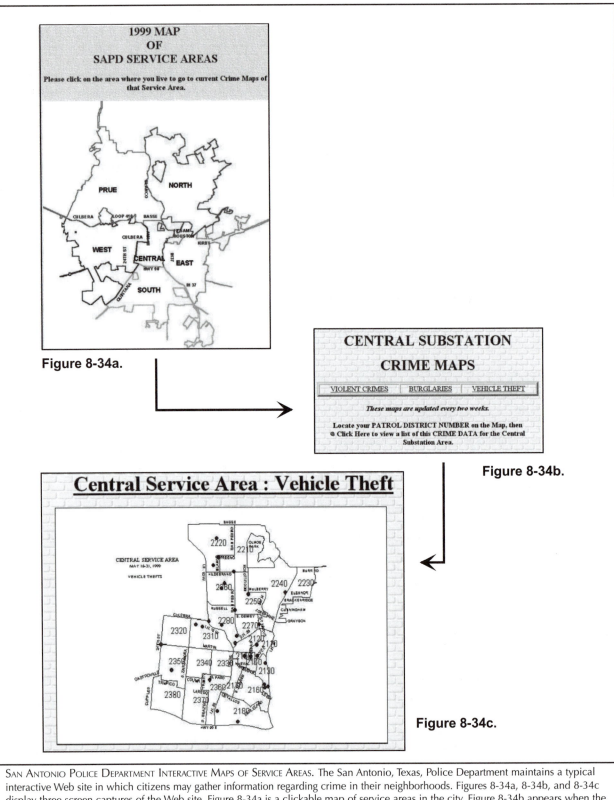

Figure 8-34a.

Figure 8-34b.

Figure 8-34c.

SAN ANTONIO POLICE DEPARTMENT INTERACTIVE MAPS OF SERVICE AREAS. The San Antonio, Texas, Police Department maintains a typical interactive Web site in which citizens may gather information regarding crime in their neighborhoods. Figures 8-34a, 8-34b, and 8-34c display three screen captures of the Web site. Figure 8-34a is a clickable map of service areas in the city. Figure 8-34b appears when the "Central Service Area" is clicked. Figure 8-34c is displayed when "Vehicle Theft" is chosen. The black dots on Figure 8-34c represent vehicle thefts for a two-week period, in this case two weeks in May 1999. Although these screen captures are displayed here in black and white, the Web site is in color. In addition to maps, the SAPD also offers online public access to detailed tabular crime information.

FIGURE 8-34

Source: <http://www.ci.sat.tx.us/sapd/maps.htm>. Graphics used with permission.

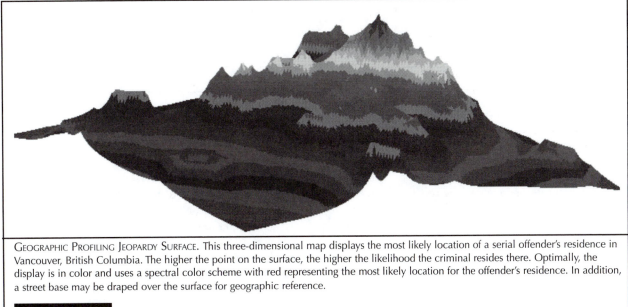

GEOGRAPHIC PROFILING JEOPARDY SURFACE. This three-dimensional map displays the most likely location of a serial offender's residence in Vancouver, British Columbia. The higher the point on the surface, the higher the likelihood the criminal resides there. Optimally, the display is in color and uses a spectral color scheme with red representing the most likely location for the offender's residence. In addition, a street base may be draped over the surface for geographic reference.

FIGURE 8-35

Source: Graphic provided by D. Kim Rossmo, Detective Inspector, Geographic Profiling Section, Vancouver Police Department.

CRIMEMAP-L. 1999. Online postings. January. <http://www.ojp.usdoj.gov/cmrc/faq/welcome.html>.

CRMC FAQ. 1999. Crime Mapping Research Center. National Institute of Justice. June. <http://www.ojp.usdoj.gov/cmrc/faq/profile.pdf>.

CRMC Research Portfolio. 1998. Crime Mapping Research Center. National Institute of Justice. December 14. <http://www.ojp.usdoj.gov/cmrc/research/welcome.html>.

Dent, Borden. D. 1998. *Cartography: Thematic Map Design.* 5th ed. Dubuque, Iowa: WCB/McGraw Hill.

Geggie, Paul. 1998. Mapping and Serial Crime Prediction. In N.G. La Vigne, N.G. and J. Wartell, eds. *Crime Mapping Case Studies: Successes in the Field.* Washington DC: Police Executive Research Forum.

Greater Atlanta Data Center. 1999. June 18. <http://www.kennesaw.edu/burruss_inst/gadc/index.htm>.

Mamalian, Cynthia A., and Nancy G. La Vigne. 1999. *The Use of Computerized Crime Mapping by Law Enforcement: Survey Results.* National Institute of Justice. January. <http://www.ojp.usdoj.gov/nij>.

McEwen, J. Thomas, and Faye S. Taxman. 1995. Applications of Computer Mapping to Police Operations. In J.E. Eck and D. Weisburd, eds. *Crime Prevention Studies, Volume 4.* Monsey, NY: Criminal Justice Press; Washington, DC: Police Executive Research Forum.

Olligschlaeger, Andreas M. 1997. Artificial Neural Networks and Crime Mapping. Policing in Crime Mapping and Crime Prevention. In D. Weisburd and T. McEwen, eds. *Crime Mapping and Crime Prevention.* Monsey, NY: Criminal Justice Press.

Reno, Susan. 1998. Using Crime Mapping to Address Residential Burglary. In N.G. La Vigne and J. Wartell, eds. *Crime Mapping Case Studies: Successes in the Field.* Washington DC: Police Executive Research Forum.

Rich, Thomas. 1995. *The Use of Computerized Mapping in Crime Control and Prevention Programs.* National Institute of Justice. July. <http://www.ojp.usdoj.gov/nij>.

Rossmo, D. Kim. 1998. *A Primer on Criminal Geographic Targeting.* International Association of Law Enforcement Intelligence Analysts. <http://www.ialeia.org/09011.shtml>.

Sposato, Alisa, Director of the Greater Atlanta Data Center. Telephone interview, June 16, 1999.

Vancouver Police Department (Canada), Geographic Profiling Section–Rigel Software. 1999. April. <http://www.city.vancouver.bc.ca/police/structure/op-support/geo/orion.html>.

Williamson, Doug, Sara McLafferty, Victor Goldsmith, John Mollenkop, and Phil McGuire. 1999. A Better Method to Smooth Crime Incident Data. ArcUser. February. <http://www.esri.com/news/arcuser/0199/crimedata.html>.

Capital Punishment

Keith Harries

Like crime, justice in its various manifestations varies at the international, interstate, interurban, and intraurban scales. Variations in justice are due to variations in laws between jurisdictions and to the exercise of discretion by police, prosecutors, and courts. The result is a patchwork of outcomes in which identical behaviors on the part of people with comparable personal backgrounds are liable to result in extraordinary differences in punishments. At the extreme, these variations include the ultimate injustice, the execution of an innocent person. Extreme inconsistency was exemplified in 1999 when Pope John Paul II visited Missouri and Governor Mel Carnahan agreed to grant his request to commute the sentence of execution for Darrell Mease, a triple murderer, whose guilt was not in question. Soon afterwards, the governor rejected a request for clemency from Roy Roberts, convicted of killing a prison guard, but whose case seemed to be filled with evidentiary weakness. Roberts was executed. In the words of a *Washington Post* editorial, "Gov. Carnahan ended up granting clemency in a case with no significant question of innocence and denying clemency in a case where questions remain about the evidence. Who gets executed should not, in a sane criminal justice system, depend on the pope's travel schedule" (Who Gets Executed? 1999).

If political expediency precipitated an inconsistency in Missouri, the impetus for a capital injustice in Illinois was the need for a quick arrest. Four journalism students at Northwestern University in Evanston, Illinois, investigated the case of 15-year death row inmate Anthony Porter, and ultimately obtained his release. The evidence against Porter was dismantled under scrutiny, suggesting that police had arrested a "convenient" suspect who had a long criminal record. Political fall-out in this case was sufficient to lead to a moratorium on capital punishment in Illinois. Altogether, some 75 erroneously convicted persons have been released from death rows since the reinstatement of capital punishment in 1976, and there can be little doubt that innocent persons remain candidates to be "dead men walking" (Jeter 1999; Prejean, 1993).

Ambiguity and confusion seem to dominate consideration of the issue of capital punishment, with conflict between competing values and theories. Some advocate execution as a deterrent, some as "just desserts" (or related variations on the "revenge" theme), and some for "closure." Another position taken by advocates is that execution incapacitates—the executed person will not offend again. Presumably, most citizens who support capital punishment blend these considerations together into a psychological conglomerate of approval. Opponents, on the other hand,

note that there is no evidence that capital punishment deters, that it is more expensive than incarceration (due mainly to the lengthy legal process involved), and that it is applied unfairly and is prone to irreversible error. Another line of argument in opposition is that if killing is wrong, then the state should not kill, even in the name of justice.

In addition to remarkable state-to-state variations in the existence and application of the death penalty within the United States (Figure 8-36), international variation is also a hallmark of capital punishment. Indeed, the U.S. picture with respect to state-to-state variation mirrors the international scene in that some countries have capital punishment and some do not; some apply it ferociously, and some do not, much like American states. In the European Community, for example, capital punishment is regarded as a violation of human rights. Canada abolished the death penalty in 1976. Amnesty International estimates that about half the world's nations have abolished capital punishment either formally or *de facto* (Figure 8-37).

The U.S. is out of step with the rest of the developed world in that industrialized countries have distanced themselves from capital punishment while the U.S. has embraced it with increasing fervor in recent decades. U.S. execution totals now approach those of such repressive regimes as China, Iran, and Nigeria. However, U.S. murder rates are relatively high and public approval of capital punishment is basically a reflection of that fact. In the 1990s, the approval rating for the execution of convicted murderers reached about 90 percent, making opposition to capital punishment an unlikely platform plank, even for liberal politicians.

Historical Perspective

Figures 8-38 through 8-42 and Figures 8-43 through 8-46 illustrate an historical-geographic perspective on capital punishment, based on a remarkable data set compiled by M. Watt Espy of Headland, Alabama. Beginning in 1970, he worked out of his home to assemble information on some 15,000 executions carried out in the U.S. between 1608 and 1991. These data, available through the archives of the Inter-University Consortium for Political and Social Research (ICPSR) at the University of Michigan, are tagged with county of conviction, and are thus amenable to mapping, either as points representing the centroids of the counties, or in the form of shaded county maps. Mapping is done by county of *conviction* rather than county of execution because the latter tend to be constant (typically the state penitentiary) over time and fail to provide insights relating to regional variation. V. Schneider and J.O. Smykla (1991)

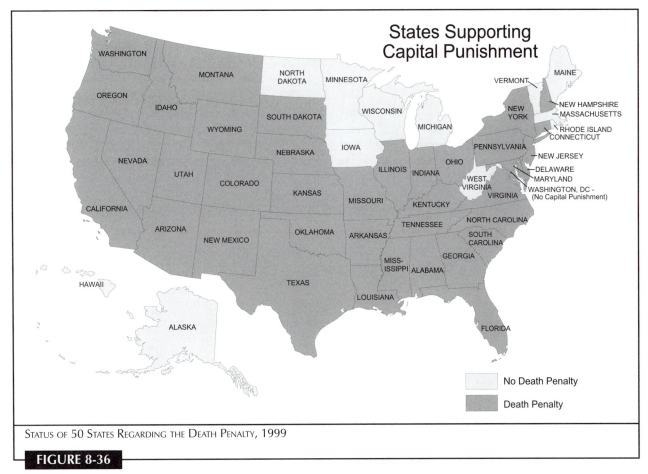

STATUS OF 50 STATES REGARDING THE DEATH PENALTY, 1999

FIGURE 8-36

Source: U.S. Department of Justice, Bureau of Justice Statistics.

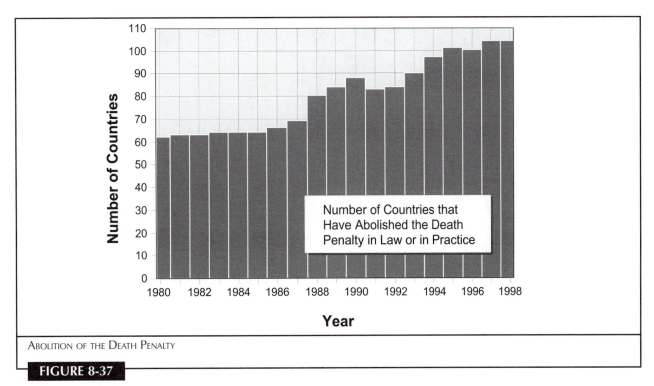

ABOLITION OF THE DEATH PENALTY

FIGURE 8-37

Source: Amnesty International, 1999.

have suggested that capital punishment history can be divided into four eras: growth (1608-1879), stability (1879-1929), peak (1929-1939), and decline (1940-1991).

This information is shown here in two different ways. In Figures 8-38 through 8-42, each dot represents four executions, with a summary map (Figure 8-38) showing the pattern for the period 1608 to 1991. Totals for each execution era are shown in Figures 8-39 through 8-42. The overall pattern could be seen as a rough reflection of population distribution, and is thus unremarkable in that it would be expected that, other things being equal, capital punishment would perfectly reflect population density for any given time frame. However, if one looks more carefully at Figure 8-38, one sees that the small scale of the map masks some important anomalies. Most obvious is the void in the upper Midwest, with blank areas in Michigan and Minnesota, which lack capital statutes. Also, while the colonial coast of the Northeast has a dense pattern, so also does the South, an observation that is anomalous owing to the relatively low population density of that region historically. These observations indicate significant regional variation.

Executions
1608 to 1991

Each dot represents four executions

Note: Dots have been placed in the county of conviction.

EXECUTIONS FROM 1608 TO 1991

FIGURE 8-38

Source: M. Watt Espy and John Ortiz Smykla, *Executions in the United States, 1608-1991: The ESPY File.* ICPSR Study Number 8451.

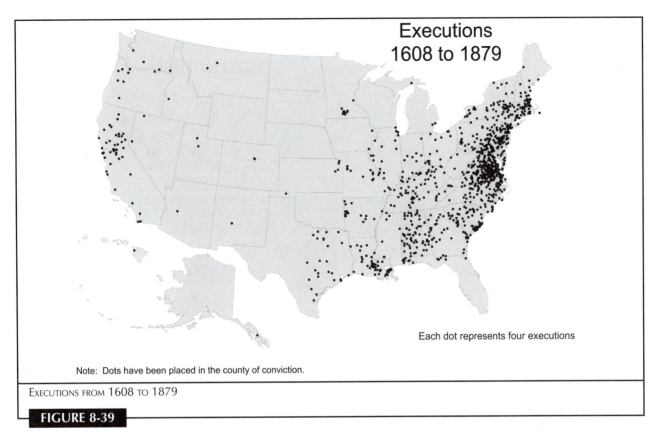

Executions
1608 to 1879

Each dot represents four executions

Note: Dots have been placed in the county of conviction.

EXECUTIONS FROM 1608 TO 1879

FIGURE 8-39

Source: M. Watt Espy and John Ortiz Smykla, *Executions in the United States, 1608-1991: The ESPY File.* ICPSR Study Number 8451.

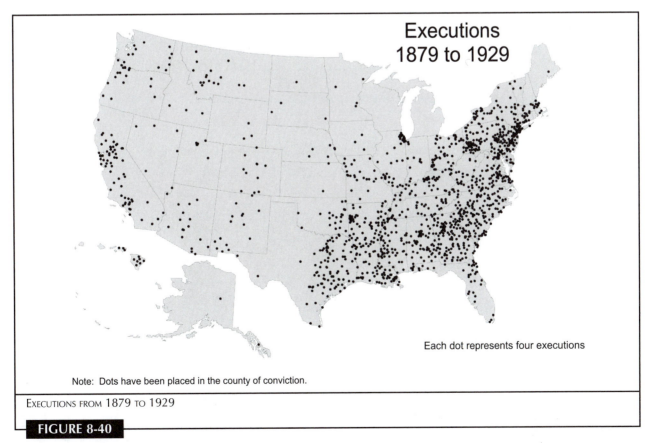

Executions
1879 to 1929

Each dot represents four executions

Note: Dots have been placed in the county of conviction.

EXECUTIONS FROM 1879 TO 1929

FIGURE 8-40

Source: M. Watt Espy and John Ortiz Smykla, *Executions in the United States, 1608-1991: The ESPY File.* ICPSR Study Number 8451.

Note: Dots have been placed in the county of conviction.

EXECUTIONS FROM 1929 TO 1939

FIGURE 8-41

Source: M. Watt Espy and John Ortiz Smykla, *Executions in the United States, 1608-1991: The ESPY File.* ICPSR Study Number 8451.

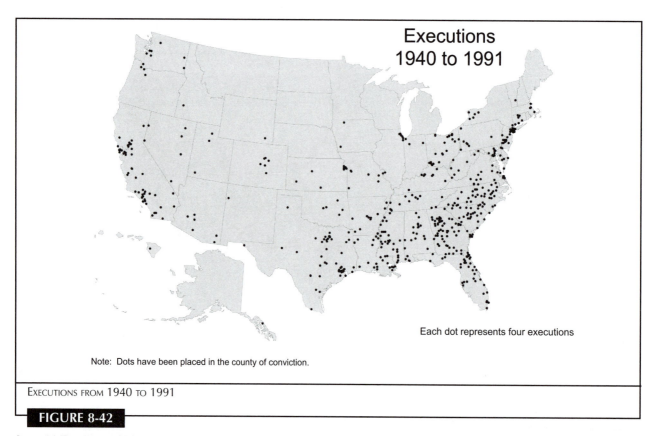

Note: Dots have been placed in the county of conviction.

EXECUTIONS FROM 1940 TO 1991

FIGURE 8-42

Source: M. Watt Espy and John Ortiz Smykla, *Executions in the United States, 1608-1991: The ESPY File.* ICPSR Study Number 8451.

Regional bias is most apparent in Figures 8-41 and 8-42, roughly coinciding with the Peak and Decline eras (1929-1991). The South appears to have many more executions than its population would warrant, based on visual comparison with the Northeast and Midwest. Interpretations attribute this regional variation to conservative, fundamentalist, and rural values, emphasizing "an eye for an eye, a tooth for a tooth," in combination with a legacy of racism from the slavery era, which tends to place a lesser value on the lives of African Americans in the criminal justice system. The disparity in the execution of black offenders with white victims, compared to the execution of white offenders with white victims, is noted throughout the literature. Analysis based on recent data noted that African Americans were more likely to receive capital sentences for crimes less than murder, such as rape (Harries and Cheatwood 1997).

Figures 8-43 through 8-46 represent the data somewhat differently. While maintaining the breakdown by eras, each map shows the percentage of all the executions of that era occurring in each county. Readers who are reasonably familiar with their local areas should be able to pick out their counties of residence. Large population counties, such as Los Angeles or Cook (Chicago), would be expected to account for higher percentages, since the percentages are not adjusted for population. (Population adjustment is problematical when long time periods are involved because population may have changed substantially over the period and one arbitrary population total may be hopelessly unrepresentative.) While Figures 8-39 through 8-41 show the raw distribution of executions, Figures 8-43 through 8-46 depict county concentration for each era. The darker shaded counties in Figures 8-43 through 8-46 can be regarded as major "hot spots" of capital punishment, relative to the era.

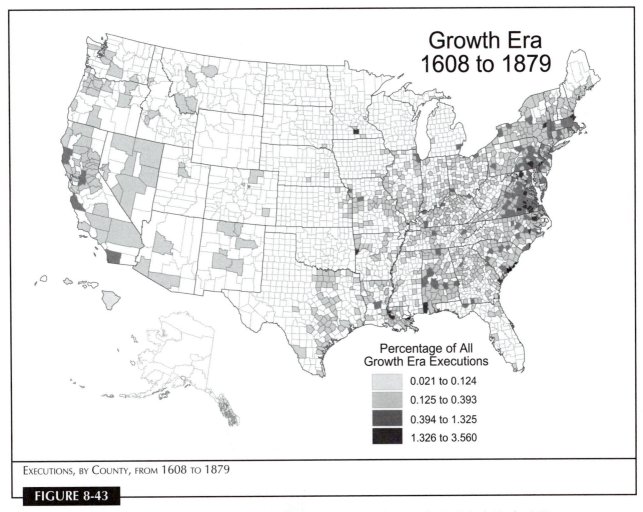

**Growth Era
1608 to 1879**

Percentage of All
Growth Era Executions

	0.021 to 0.124
	0.125 to 0.393
	0.394 to 1.325
	1.326 to 3.560

EXECUTIONS, BY COUNTY, FROM 1608 TO 1879

FIGURE 8-43

Source: M. Watt Espy and John Ortiz Smykla, *Executions in the United States, 1608-1991: The ESPY File.* ICPSR Study Number 8451.

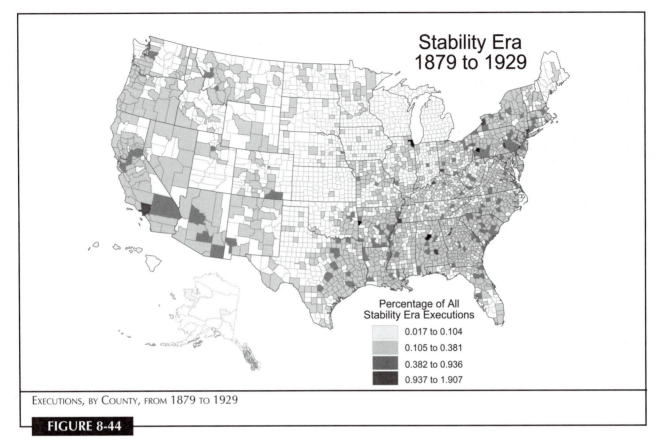

EXECUTIONS, BY COUNTY, FROM 1879 TO 1929

FIGURE 8-44

Source: M. Watt Espy and John Ortiz Smykla, *Executions in the United States, 1608-1991: The ESPY File.* ICPSR Study Number 8451.

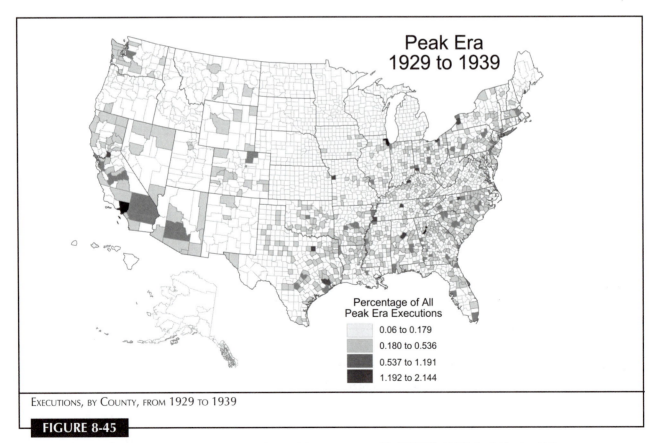

EXECUTIONS, BY COUNTY, FROM 1929 TO 1939

FIGURE 8-45

Source: M. Watt Espy and John Ortiz Smykla, *Executions in the United States, 1608-1991: The ESPY File.* ICPSR Study Number 8451.

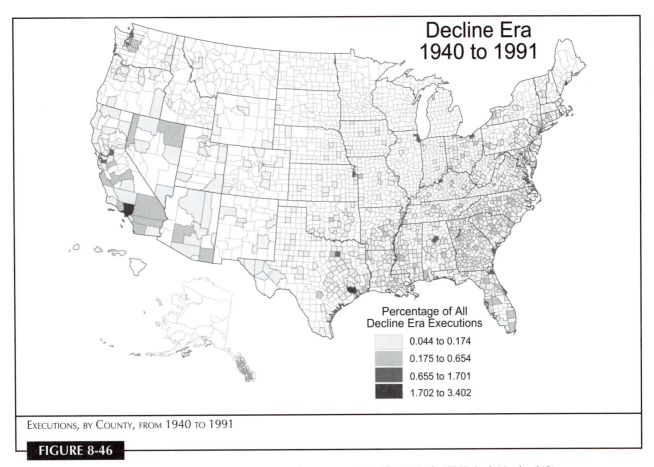

EXECUTIONS, BY COUNTY, FROM 1940 TO 1991

FIGURE 8-46

Source: M. Watt Espy and John Ortiz Smykla, *Executions in the United States, 1608-1991: The ESPY File.* ICPSR Study Number 8451.

Issues of Race and Gender

The fundamental facts concerning race and gender are that minorities and men are executed more frequently than their population fractions would suggest, although when the demographics of homicide (the most likely offence to attract the death penalty) are considered, the imbalance diminishes. Males constitute about 90 percent of those arrested for homicide, African Americans about 50 percent (Maguire and Pastore 1996), proportions roughly reflected in the long-term historical record of execution proportions, although not necessarily reflected in the short term. Various studies have pointed to racial disparity in the application of the death penalty, most recently in an analysis of capital murder cases in Philadelphia that found that blacks were about four times more likely to receive the death penalty compared to other defendants committing similar crimes (Fletcher 1998; see also Dieter 1998; Kroll 1991).

Note that the relationship between abolitionist jurisdictions and the geography of homicide will affect the demographics of capital punishment. For example, Washing-

ton, D.C., and Baltimore, both majority African-American cities, have been hot spots of homicide in recent decades. However, Washington, D.C., has no capital statute and Maryland has shown de facto reluctance to execute, thus depressing the statistics for executions of blacks compared to the situation that would arise had those homicides been displaced to, say, Texas or Virginia, where capital punishment is more frequent. Thus, if the proportion of blacks arrested for homicide is greater that the proportion executed in a given year or decade, it may be tempting to conclude that African Americans are receiving favored treatment in the courts. Clearly, however, this may have more to do with the "supply" of capital punishment than with the actions of prosecutors and courts.

Few women (less than 400) have been executed in the course of American history. In effect, a glass ceiling exists, reflecting reluctance, apparently embedded in American culture, to execute women. The execution of Karla Faye Tucker in Texas in 1998, for example, was the first execution of a woman in Texas since the Civil War (The Execution in Texas 1998).

Geography and Methods of Execution

Methods of execution have a distinctive geography in terms of their origins and patterns of diffusion. Electrocution began in Erie County, New York, in 1890 and was widely adopted in the East and South, with more than half the capital punishment states adopting it by 1930. The gas chamber was first adopted in Nevada in 1924, and then spread to Arizona and Colorado, followed by North Carolina, Wyoming, Missouri, Oregon, and California. Lethal injection originated in Oklahoma, followed by Texas and 26 other states. This method is now prevalent among the capital punishment states (Harries and Cheatwood 1997). Discussion of methods prompts mention of the geography of "botched" executions—those that went awry for some technical reason, such as the inability of the technicians to find a vein for lethal injection. Of 24 instances between 1983 and 1998, all but three were in the South (Radelet and DPIC 1999).

Underlying Geography

Federal, state, and military authorities operate under statutes permitting the application of capital punishment. Some 60 federal laws provided for the death penalty in 1997, including those against espionage, murder during a kidnaping, treason, and death resulting from an aircraft hijacking. Also included was the notorious Oklahoma City-type bombing crime: "death resulting from offenses involving transportation of explosives, destruction of government property, or destruction of property related to foreign or interstate commerce" (Snell 1998; DPIC 1999). However, federal capital crimes are relatively uninteresting from a geographic perspective. First, the statutes apply to all states, thus removing geographic effects, at least nominally, and, second, federal executions are so rare as to be of no consequence from a public policy perspective. No federal executions have taken place since Victor Feguer was hanged for kidnapping in 1963 (DPIC 1999).

Similar considerations apply to military capital punishment, where no one has been executed since the 1960s, and only eight persons were on death row as of mid-1999. One quirk that gives federal capital punishment a geographic component is that the method of execution to be used is that of the state where the death sentence is handed down. If the state has no capital statute, the judge can choose another state. Even this is moot, however, if in practice no executions are occurring.

The "real" geography, then, is at the state level, where 38 states had capital statutes as of the end of 1997 (Figure 8-36). Analysis of state-level data reveals two major dichoto-

mies. First, a distinction exists between states that have capital punishment and those that do not. Second, a contrast exists between death penalty states that apply it with energy and those that do not.

Current Geography of the Death Penalty

Executions since 1976, when capital punishment was reconstituted following the landmark *Furman v. Georgia* case (1972), have concentrated heavily in the South, particularly in Texas (Figure 8-47), where 33 percent of all executions (173 of 530, as of March 30, 1999) had taken place. Other major contributors were Virginia (63), Florida (43), Missouri (35), and Louisiana (25). In all, 11 of the 13 states accounting for at least 12 executions since 1976 were in the South. Virginia and Texas are remarkably efficient in terms of their "production" of executions. An article in the *Washington Post* assessing Virginia's experience (Fehr 1999) noted that Virginia's rate of executions, adjusted for population, was highest among larger population states, exceeding even that of Texas. Appeals have been limited, with the average nine-year process cut to five years. Observers have also noted that the Virginia public defender system is inferior, thus providing persons accused of capital crimes with less effective counsel. In contrast, neighboring Maryland has a better public defender system and the process is more deliberate. Compared to Virginia's 63 executions (10 per million inhabitants), Maryland has executed only three persons since 1976 (0.6 per million).

Conclusion

Capital punishment in the U.S. exhibits marked geographic variations in its state-to-state presence and application. Disparities are clear enough that some prominent institutions, including the American Bar Association and the Roman Catholic Church, have called for the abolition of capital punishment. The disproportionate application of capital punishment in the South suggests the ineffectiveness of execution as a general deterrent to violence in that relatively high rates of both homicide and capital punishment have been present in the South for at least the last century. If capital punishment were a deterrent, a decline in southern violence would have been expected, but none has occurred on a long-term basis. Popular support for capital punishment remains strong, and substantial changes in capital statutes seem unlikely at this time. (For a more detailed analysis of the geography of capital punishment, see Harries and Cheatwood 1997.)

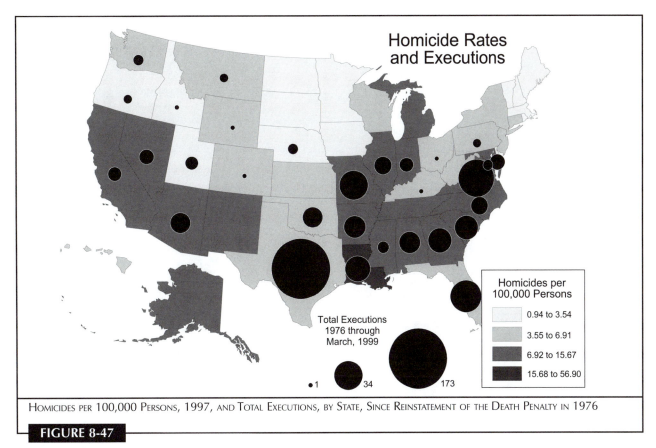

Homicide Rates and Executions

Total Executions
1976 through
March, 1999

Homicides per
100,000 Persons

	0.94 to 3.54
	3.55 to 6.91
	6.92 to 15.67
	15.68 to 56.90

•1   34   173

HOMICIDES PER 100,000 PERSONS, 1997, AND TOTAL EXECUTIONS, BY STATE, SINCE REINSTATEMENT OF THE DEATH PENALTY IN 1976

FIGURE 8-47

Sources: FBI *Uniform Crime Reports*, 1997.

References

Dieter, R.C. 1998. The Death Penalty in Black and White: Who Lives, Who Dies, Who Decides. <http://www.essential.org/dpic/racerpt.html>.

DPIC [Death Penalty Information Center]. 1999. *Federal Death Penalty*. <http://www.essential.org/dpic/feddp.html>.

Espy, M. Watt, and John Ortiz Smykla. *Executions in the United States, 1608-1991: The ESPY File*. ICPSR Study Number 8451. Available through the Inter-university Consortium for Political and Social Research at <http://www.icpsr.umich.edu/index.html>.

The Execution in Texas. 1998. *Washington Post*, February 5, p. A16.

Federal Bureau of Investigation (FBI). 1997. *Uniform Crime Reports*. Preliminary Annual Release and Death Penalty Information Center. <http://www.essential.org/orgs/dpic/dpic.html>.

Fehr, S.C. 1999. Virginia's Efficient System of Death: Rate of Executing Murderers Has Surpassed That of Other Large States. *Washington Post*, April 4, pp. C1, C8.

Fletcher, M.A. 1998. Study Finds Wide Racial Disparity in Death Penalty. *Washington Post*, June 5, p. A24.

Harries, K. 1995. The Last Walk: A Geography of Execution in the United States, 1786-1985. *Political Geography* 14: 473-95.

Harries, K., and D. Cheatwood 1997. *The Geography of Execution: The Capital Punishment Quagmire in America*. Lanham, MD: Rowman and Littlefield.

Jeter, J. 1999. A New Ending to an Old Story. *Washington Post*, February 17, pp. C1, C8.

Kroll, M. 1991. Chattahoochee Judicial District: Buckle of the Death Belt. The Death Penalty in Microcosm. <http://www.essential.org/dpic/dpic.r11.html>.

Maguire, K., and A.L. Pastore. 1996. *Sourcebook of Criminal Justice Statistics, 1995*. Washington DC: U.S. Department of Justice, Bureau of Justice Statistics. Table 3.136, p. 361.

Prejean, H. 1993. *Dead Man Walking*. New York: Vintage Books.

Radelet, M.J., and DPIC [Death Penalty Information Center]. 1999. Post-Furman Botched Executions. <http://www.essential.org/dpic/botched.html>.

Schneider, V., and J.O. Smykla. 1991. A Summary Analysis of Executions in the United States, 1608-1987: The Espy File. In R.M. Bohm, ed. *The Death Penalty in America: Current Research*. Cincinnati: Anderson Publishing, pp. 1-19.

Snell, T.L. 1998. *Capital Punishment, 1997*. U.S. Department of Justice, Office of Justice Programs, Bureau of Justice Statistics. <http://www.ojp.usdoj.gov/bjs/abstract/cp97.htm>.

Who Gets Executed? 1999. *Washington Post*, March 20, p. A18.

INDEX

Note: Page numbers in **bold** refer to an illustration, graph, data, map, figure, or table.

Index

Index

Index

Index